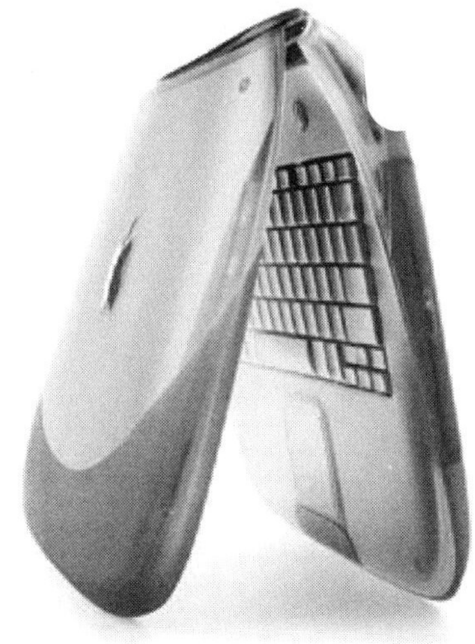

The *Ultimate* iBook Book

Dan Parks Sydow

MacCentral
Press

MacCentral
Press

MacCentral Press
A Division of MacCentral, Inc.
http://www.maccentral.com
email@maccentral.com

ISBN: 0-9667026-1-1

10 9 8 7 6 5 4 3 2

Printed in the United States of America

For sales inquiries and special prices for bulk quantities, please contact The Mac Book Source by sending e-mail to sales@macbooksource.com.

Limits of Liability and Disclaimer of Warranty

The Author and Publisher make no warranty of any kind, expressed or implied, with regard to the accuracy or completeness of the contents of this book and specifically disclaim any implied warranties of merchantability or fitness for a particular purpose. There are no warranties that extend beyond the descriptions contained within this paragraph. Neither the Author nor the Publisher shall be liable for any loss of profit or any other commercial damages, including but not limited to special, incidental, consequential, or other damages.

Managing Editor: *William Peterson*
Production Editor: *Anne Aramano*
Copy Editor: *Jennifer Trundel*
Technical Editor: *Kevin Collins*
Print Coordination: *Wunderlich, Pearson, & Tetzlaff, Inc.*

To Nadine

— Dan

Acknowledgments

I'd like to extend a thanks to a few of the many people and organizations that made this book happen...

Stan Flack and Dave Moser of the online Macintosh news source MacCentral, Inc., <http://www.maccentral.com>, for book concept, ideas, and support.

MacToday online <http://www.mactoday.com> and MacToday magazine for their past and continuous support of MacCentral.

Bill Tetzlaff of Wunderlich, Pearson, & Tetzlaff, Inc., for turning electronic bits and bytes into printed words.

Larry Magid, syndicated columnist for the Los Angeles Times, Editor-at-Large for CMP Media's PC Group, columnist for HomePC and Computer Currents, and much more, for his presence on the Internet. I've never met Larry, but I can't seem to avoid him—I keep stumbling across useful Web pages of his! His home page at <http://www.larrysworld.com/> includes links to a variety of useful articles and resources.

David Murphy of Verio, for Web page hosting and e-mail support. Verio, at <http://www.verio.com>, hosts over a quarter of a million Web sites—including my own at <http://www.sydow.com>.

Contents at a Glance

Table of Contents

Part I: Getting Started

Chapter 9: Where to Go on the Web 199

Part III: Adding to the iBook

Chapter 10: Peripherals 233

Part IV: Work and Play

1

Introducing the iBook

If you just bought your iBook, you'll certainly want to read this chapter. If you've had an iBook for a while, then you might be tempted to skip this chapter. You've looked at your iBook, and you've used your iBook. But that doesn't tell you about what's *inside* your iBook. So whether your iBook is just out of the box or has some scuff marks on its shell, you'll want to read on.

Do you know what makes your iBook tick, and what gives it such bang for the buck? If you're asked why the iBook is supposedly better than other notebook computers, can you give some convincing reasons? Do you know about the iBook's *ports*—the interface between the inside and outside of the iBook? This chapter clues you in to these computer *hardware* issues. Finally, if you haven't explored all of the software that comes preinstalled on your iBook and on the set of CD-ROMs that came packaged with your computer, you can get an overview of those programs here.

Apple claims that the pairing of its new computer with the Macintosh operating system gives the iBook a great combination of price and performance and makes the iBook the best valued (not to mention the coolest looking) consumer portable computer on the market. This chapter will convince you that these claims aren't simply Apple hype!

Hardware

You may have bought the iBook for its looks, but there's a lot more to the iBook than meets the eye. Looks alone aren't enough to make a computer a great buy. The excitement the iBook generates is based only in part on the computer's looks. The iBook is loaded with impressive, state-of-the-art components, too. In this section you'll take a look at those components, which include:

- 300 MHz PowerPC G3 processor
- 512K of backside Level 2 cache
- Built-in 12.1-inch TFT SVGA active-matrix display with 640x480 and 800x600 resolution with millions of colors
- 32 MB main memory (expandable to 160MB)
- 4 MB video memory
- ATI RAGE Mobility graphics controller for built-in 2D/3D graphics acceleration
- 3.2 GB IDE Hard disk drive
- 24x CD-ROM drive
- Built-in 10/100Base-T Ethernet
- *Optional* AirPort wireless networking card
- Built-in full size keyboard
- Built-in solid-state Apple trackpad
- Built-in 56K (V.90) hardware-based modem
- Lithium-ion battery offering up to 6 hours of battery life
- One 12 Mbps Universal Serial Bus (USB) ports
- Built-in mono speaker
- 66 MHz system bus
- Mac OS 8.6 or Mac OS 9 operating system

If you aren't familiar with some, or much, of the terminology appearing in this list, don't worry. Explaining these concepts is a key part of this chapter's goal.

Note
Some features, such as processor speed and operating system version, will change as new revisions of the iBook are released.

Tip
If you want to know all the *really* technical details about the iBook, visit `<http://www.apple.com/ibook/specs.html>`. There you'll find out details such as the recommended environmental storage temperature (–13° F to 140° F or, for you readers outside of the United States, –25° C to 60° C) and the fact that the iBook should not be used in an environment with a relative humidity outside the range of 20% to 80% noncondensing. This Web page also offers the iBook Data Sheet in Adobe Acrobat (PDF) format for downloading.

Internal Components

The iBook has quite a unique look. But looks alone don't distinguish this notebook from all the others on the market. It's also what's inside this machine that count. You may be impressed with how the iBook looks, but you can bet that when people ask you about your computer they'll inquire as to what it has *inside*.

Microprocessor

A computer's *microprocessor* (or *central processing unit*, or *CPU*) is often described as the "brain" of a computer. In terms of physical size, a microprocessor seems pretty benign—it's a microchip that is only about the size of a fingernail. But in terms of computational power, a microprocessor is an incredible little piece of circuitry. Raw data flows into the microprocessor, is manipulated, and emerges as something meaningful. My former physics and computer engineering professors would be pulling their hair out if they read that very figurative explanation, but you get the point. The microprocessor makes things happen. And the faster a microprocessor works, the faster things happen. Often, how fast a computer works is important to the user—that's why computer manufacturers and computer salespeople tout processor speed so much, and why computer users argue incessantly about just exactly how much better one processor might be over another because of its slight edge in speed.

Microprocessor speed is stated in *megahertz* (MHz). The first iBook shipped with a 300 MHz PowerPC G3 microprocessor. Like the iMac, which initially came equipped with a 233 MHz processor and as of this writing now comes with up to a 400 MHz processor, the iBook will see processor speed bumps (increases) as new models come out. A 300 MHz processor is fast—it's a pretty impressive speed for an inexpensive computer. If you see an advertisement for a PC notebook with a higher MHz processor, it most likely is a more expensive notebook than the iBook. And there's one other factor that makes the iBook's microprocessor special. Apple claims, and independent testing bears out, that a PowerPC chip is faster than an Intel chip of the same MHz rating. Due to differences in the internal architecture of these competing chips (the technology defining just how a microprocessor works), megahertz-to-megahertz, the PowerPC chip works faster than the Intel chip used in PCs.

Cache

You just read that the faster a microprocessor, the better. But a microprocessor doesn't work in isolation: it works in conjunction with other components inside a computer. Regardless of how fast a microprocessor is, some of the other components can prohibit the microprocessor from utilizing its own speed. The relevant term here is bottleneck. Just as the small neck of a bottle slows down the rate at which fluid pours out (regardless of how big the rest of the bottle is), slow components in a computer can slow down the rate at which the microprocessor works (regardless of how fast the microprocessor is *capable* of working).

One important means of reducing bottlenecks is *cache* memory (pronounced *cash* memory). A microprocessor gets data from (and sends data to) computer memory by means of a *bus*. A bus is simply an electrical pathway. How fast data travels along a bus is important to how quickly a microprocessor can operate. Most modern computers make use of a small amount of high-speed memory to speed up the rate of transfer of data between the main memory store and the microprocessor. This cache memory holds frequently or recently accessed data that the computer suspects may be accessed again soon. The iMac comes equipped with 512 K (one-half of one megabyte) of backside Level 2 (Type L2) cache memory. You don't need to know the specifics of just what that type of cache is or how it works. What is good to know is that this memory helps to speed up the performance of the iMac.

Main Memory

RAM (for *Random Access Memory*) is a computer's main memory. When you run a program, what actually takes place is that the computer loads the program's code into RAM. Any program consists of code, and in order for a computer to start interacting with a program, the computer needs to place that code into RAM. Because a computer can run more than one program at one time, the amount of RAM a computer has is important—the more RAM a computer has, the more programs it can run simultaneously.

Like a microprocessor, RAM is a type of computer chip. If you buy additional RAM for a computer, you'll be buying one or more chips. For a particular computer, not just any RAM will do—different computers use different types of RAM chips. The iBook uses 1.25 inch 144-pin 15 ns *SDRAM SO-DIMM* memory chips. That's quite an eyeful, so it's fortunate that when ordering RAM you can simply say to the salesperson or technician: "I need more RAM for my iBook". If you're the inquisitive type, though, just ahead I've included a technical note that defines what all those memory chip letters mean.

The iBook comes with one RAM slot that accepts a single SDRAM SO-DIMM chip. Memory chips come in different capacities, with 32 MB, 64 MB, and 128 MB chips being common. Because an iBook comes with a fixed 32 MB of RAM (a chip soldered to the motherboard, or main board of chips in the iBook), the total amount of RAM an iBook can have is 160 MB (the pre-installed 32 MB that isn't held in the one slot, plus a single 128 MB chip in the one RAM slot). If single RAM chips in sizes larger than 128 MB become available for the iBook, than an iBook will of course be able to have a larger RAM capacity.

To increase the amount of RAM in your iBook you purchase and add a RAM chip in the one empty RAM slot. Installing the largest capacity (128 MB as of this writing) chip in the empty slot gives your computer a total of 160 MB of RAM.

Note

Some local Apple dealers and some Macintosh mail order companies entice people to buy an Book by offering a free RAM upgrade. So, though an iBook that ships from the factory is configured with a single 32 MB memory chip, your iBook may have a different configuration (typically a second 32 MB chip installed by the place where you bought your iBook).

If you want to increase the amount of memory in your iBook, you can drop your computer off at your local authorized Apple dealer and let that store's Macintosh technician do the job. Alternatively, you can order a memory chip and then tackle the task yourself. If you go the solo route, refer to Chapter 12 for some tips.

Technical

Warning: A bunch of seemingly meaningless letters, words, and phrases follow. Read this definition of a 15 *ns SDRAM SO-DIMM* memory chip at your own risk!

The 1.25-inch and 144-pin parts of the memory chip name refer to physical traits of the memory chip itself. The 1.25-inch is one of the physical dimensions of the chip. The 144-pin part means just that—the chip has 144 pins that get inserted into the RAM slot in the iBook.

Memory is rated at different speeds, with speed being referred to in *nanoseconds*, or ns. So a computer that requires 15 ns memory needs a memory chip rated at a speed of 15 nanoseconds.

The *SDRAM* part of the memory chip name stands for *Synchronous Dynamic Random Access Memory*. There are other types of RAM chips, such as Extended Data Output (EDO) chip or a Fast Paged RAM chip—but those types aren't for the iBook.

The *SO-DIMM* part of the memory chip name stands for *Small Outline Dual Inline Memory Module*, and refers to the physical size and layout of the chip. There are "plain" DIMM chips, but the iBook requires the smaller sized (Small Outline, or SO) DIMM chips.

Video Memory

It wasn't too long ago that when you went to buy a personal computer, you only inquired about one type of memory: the main, or RAM, memory described above. Lately, though, computer buyers have had to become aware of a second type of memory: video memory (or video RAM, or VRAM).

Increasingly, personal computers have moved from simple boxes that displayed mostly text, to workstation-like machines that produce graphics, animation, and movies. The graphic-intense programs that display these visual images require a lot of memory. Unlike the memory used to hold data for use by the microprocessor, much of the extra memory a graphics-intense program requires is dedicated to keeping track of images displayed on a monitor. A computer monitor is made up of hundreds of thousands of tiny dots, or pixels, each of them capable of displaying one of thousands or even *millions* of colors at any given time. To keep track of the current color of each pixel requires a lot of memory. Computer manufacturers have found it efficient to add extra memory dedicated specifically to the job of displaying graphics. Inclusion of this *video memory* speeds up the ever-changing display of images that are the hallmark of recent 3D computer games and full-motion video programs. In fact, some recent programs won't even run on a computer that doesn't have video memory.

The original iBook shipped with the ATI RAGE Mobility graphics integrated controller that includes 4 MB of video memory (like the processor, the video memory may be upgraded with subsequent iBook models). That's a bit to remember, so if anyone asks about iBook video memory, you can just say that the iBook has 4 MB of VRAM. Besides helping out in the display of 2D and 3D graphics, the RAGE IC enables the iBook to display either an 800-by-600 or 640-by-480 pixel image. That is, the size of objects on the iBook screen can be set to appear in either of two sizes. More about screen size, or resolution, later in this chapter.

Note

The VRAM in the iBook can not be upgraded—the memory is embedded in the ATI RAGE Mobility chip. That's okay, though, because the 4 MB of VRAM on the RAGE chip supports a pair of resolutions and millions of colors on the internal iBook display (see just ahead for more on the monitor display).

External Features

You can give your iBook a good once-over and you'll be able to have a pretty good idea of what the computer includes, as far as external features go. But if you want the *details* of these features, read this section—and refer to Figure 1-1.

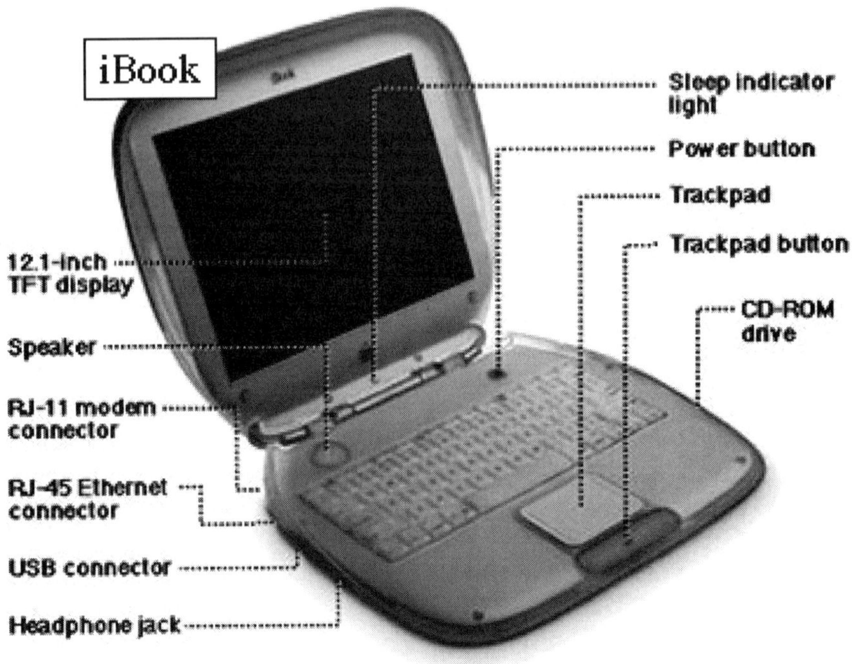

Figure 1-1 Features of the iBook.

Display

The iBook includes a built-in 12.1-inch high-quality, TFT SVGA active-matrix LCD screen. If that sounds like it might be a shopping list for a good monitor, it is.

Unlike a standard Cathode Ray Tube (CRT) monitor, a Liquid Crystal Display (LCD) is a screen that doesn't emit light. Instead, an LCD reflects and blocks light. An LCD works using some combination of a backlight, sidelight, reflector, a layer of liquid crystals, polarizers, and in some cases a bulb. There's no need to get into the physics of just what's going on in an LCD, but it is important to note that there are two main categories of LCDs: passive matrix and active matrix. An active matrix, or Thin-Film Transistor (TFT) LCD is of higher quality and more expensive than a passive matrix, or Film SuperTwist Nematic (FSTN) LCD. With an active matrix display, your viewing angle is greatly increased. That is, you can sit towards the side of an active matrix display and still see the screen. A passive matrix display, on the other hand, is best viewed straight on. As mentioned, the iBook has the more expensive, higher quality TFT active matrix screen.

The built-in monitor, along with the just-mentioned ATI RAGE graphics integrated controller, supports a pair of resolutions. The *resolution* of a monitor is the number of tiny dots, or pixels, the monitor displays. Changing the resolution doesn't change the overall display area of the iBook's monitor, but it changes the size of everything displayed. Take a look at Figure 1-2 to see how this works.

If you look closely at the two faces shown in Figure 1-2, you should be able to determine that both faces are comprised of the same arrangement, and same number, of dots. The two faces differ only in the size of the dots used in their creation. Each dot used to make up the face on the left is larger than each dot used to make up the face on the right. The face on the right is drawn with smaller, more compactly spaced dots than is the face on the left. Because of this, the face on the right is said to be drawn at a higher resolution then the face on the left.

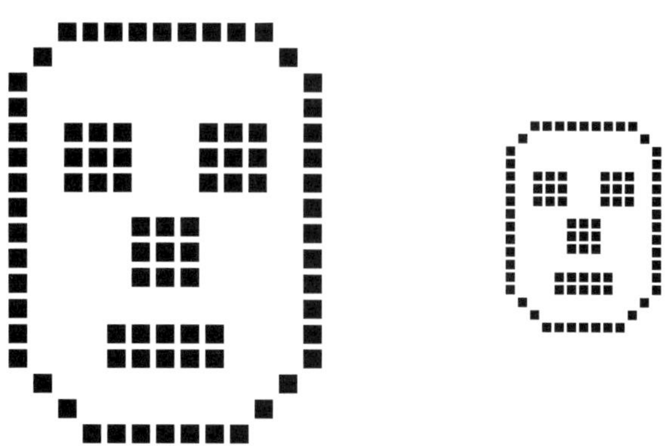

Figure 1-2 An image displayed at two resolutions.

As you can see from the figure, a higher-resolution image is capable of displaying more information in a given area; consequently, the size of the image is reduced. Which resolution is better? That's a subjective question, and one that's answered by raising still another question. Do you want to see less of a bigger image or more of a smaller image? If you like to see as much information on your screen as possible, go with a higher resolution. If you find yourself straining to read file names or other text on your screen, you'll want a lower resolution.

The iBook supports the two resolutions listed below. The first value in each resolution represents the number of pixels displayed horizontally across the iBook's screen, while the second value represents the number of pixels displayed vertically up and down the screen.

- 640 x 480 pixels
- 800 x 600 pixels

Use the monitor resolution icon on the Control Strip (the row of icons housed together in a small strip along the bottom of your iBook and discussed in Chapter 3) to adjust your iBook's resolution. Each of the two resolutions produces very different views, so try both of them to determine your preference.

Note
The iBook doesn't come equipped with a video output port—but you can circumvent that problem. Chapter 10 describes AVerMedia Microsystems' USBPresenter. This adapter plugs into the iBook's USB port and allows you to then connect a video device (larger monitor, TV, etc) to the iBook.

Keyboard

The keyboard that is built into the iBook is a compact, low profile design that includes a row of function keys and an inverted-T cursor arrow keys. Figure 1-3 shows the layout of this keyboard.

Note
The keyboard is removable to allow access to the iBook internals. You'll remove the keyboard if you add an AirPort card or memory upgrade. Removing the keyboard (and adding the just-mentioned components), is discussed in Chapter 12.

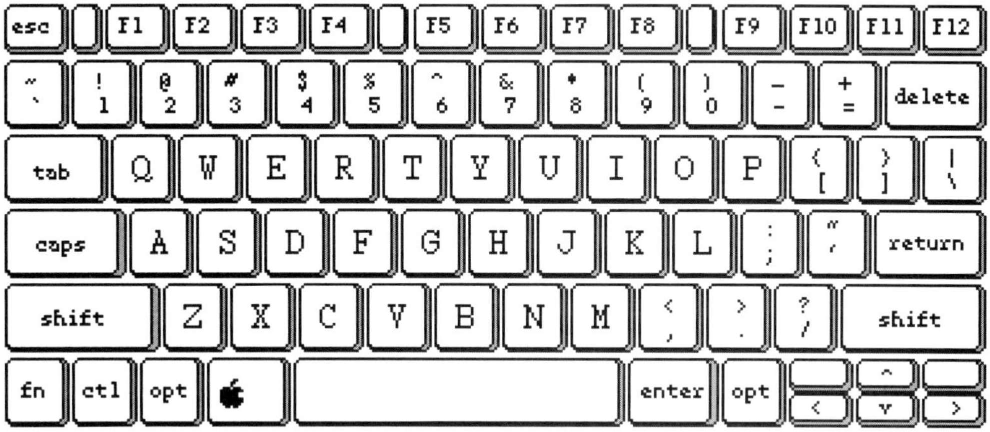

Figure 1-3 The keyboard layout.

The twelve function keys (F1-F12) are located along the top of the keyboard. The iBook uses a clever trick to give these keys extra power. When you press the fn key (located at the lower left of the keyboard—see Figure 1-4), each of these twelve keys acts as a function key. In that case the program that is currently active determines the exact use of each of these keys. That is, when you're working in a program, it is that program that sets the usage of the function keys. Some (in fact, many) programs don't assign any functionality to these keys. When working on the desktop (in the Finder), the F2-F4 keys can be used for editing selected text. For instance, if you select the name of a folder and then press the fn and F2 key, the name will be cut. Pressing the fn and F3 key has the same effect as choosing **Copy** from the **File** menu, and pressing the fn key and the F4 has the same effect as choosing **Paste** from the **File** menu.

So, why do need to press the fn key and a function key in order for the function key to behave as expected? Because Apple allows each function key to take on a second role. If you don't hold down the fn key at the time you press a function key, that key acts as a *hot key* (as Apple calls it). Function keys F1 through F6 are assigned unchangeable roles by Apple. For instance, pressing the F1 key (without pressing the fn key), decreases the brightness of the monitor. The following table shows the purpose of each of these six function keys. Figure 1-4 highlights the fn key and the six Apple-defined hot keys.

Function Key	Purpose When fn Key Not Pressed
F1	Decreases display brightness
F2	Increases display brightness
F3	Decreases speaker volume
F4	Increases speaker volume
F5	Toggles the Num Lock
F6	Turns off (mutes) the speaker

Figure 1-4 Apple-defined function key/control buttons.

The other function keys—keys F7 through F12—also act as hot keys. But that affect can't be placed in a table as is possible for the F1 through F6 keys. That's because the behavior of the F7-F12 keys is user-definable. To define the use of one of these function keys (to have a press of the F7 key run Microsoft Word, for instance), use the Keyboard control panel (which is discussed in Chapter 3).

Note
As described above, when the fn key *is* pressed, the function keys act as function keys. And when the fn key is *not* pressed, the function keys act as hot keys. This situation can easily be reversed (and may in fact already be reversed if you, or someone else, has dabbled with the settings). Open the Keyboard control panel from under the Apple menu and the click the **Function Keys** button. At the bottom of the window that appears you'll see a **Function Key Settings** checkbox. When unchecked, you need to press the fn key in order to have a function key act as a function key. If you check this box, then you won't need to hold the fn key down.

If you frequently use a numeric keypad, then you'll be glad to know that Apple has embedded one right into the iBook's built-in keyboard. Embedded means that you can set a portion of the keyboard to act as a numeric keypad. To do that, press the function (fn) key. When you do that, a number of keys on the right side of the keyboard act as the numeric keypad (see Figure 1-5). Here are the keys that change function to become the numeric keypad:

Key	Numeric Keypad Function (fn pressed)
6	Clear
7	7
8	8
9	9
0	/ (divide)
-	= (equals)
U	4
I	5
O	6
P	* (multiply)
J	1
K	2
L	3
;	- (subtract)
M	0
,	(nothing)
.	. (decimal)
/	+ (add)

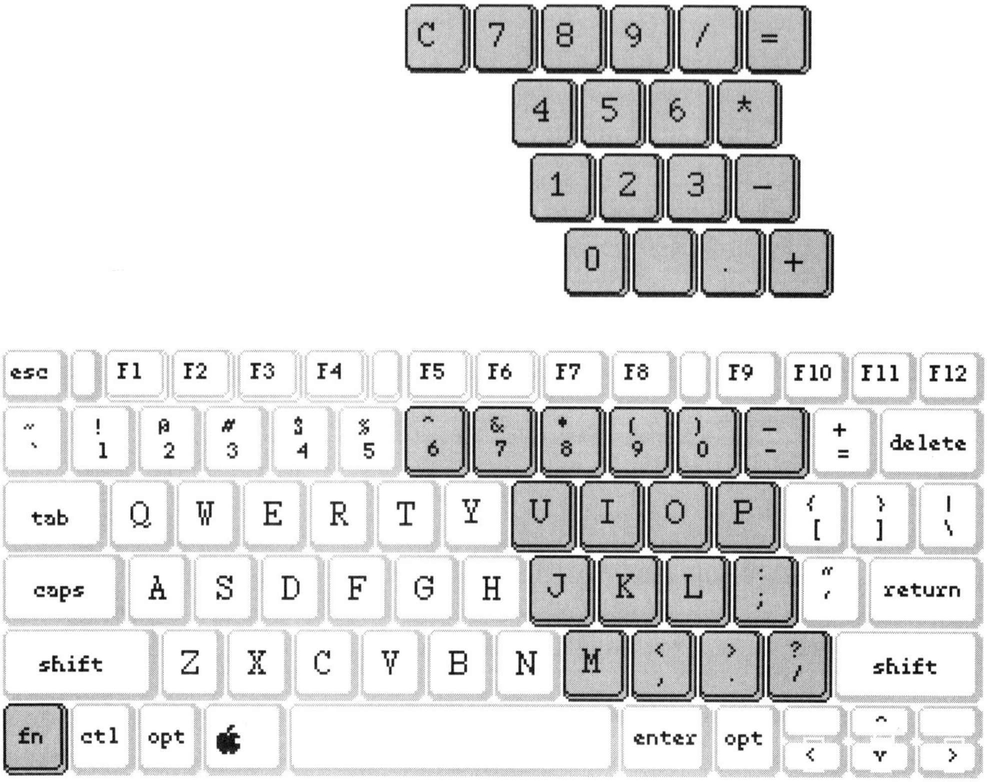

Figure 1-5 The embedded numeric keypad.

Trackpad

Like other Apple notebook computers, the iBook has no mouse. Instead, the iBook's pointing device is a built-in trackpad. The trackpad is a digital device that acts like a mouse by sensing the motion of your finger over its surface. As you touch, then slide, your finger over the trackpad surface, the trackpad translates the motions into digital signals. Just as a desktop Mac knows how to interpret the dragging of a mouse, so too does the iBook know how to interpret the motion of your finger as it moves across the trackpad.

Below the trackpad is a single, large button (see Figure 1-6). Use this button as you would the button on a mouse. Alternatively, you can tap on the trackpad itself to act as a button click. To double-click, you can tap two times in succession on the trackpad. To simulate a click and drag, tap once on the trackpad and then drag your finger along the trackpad.

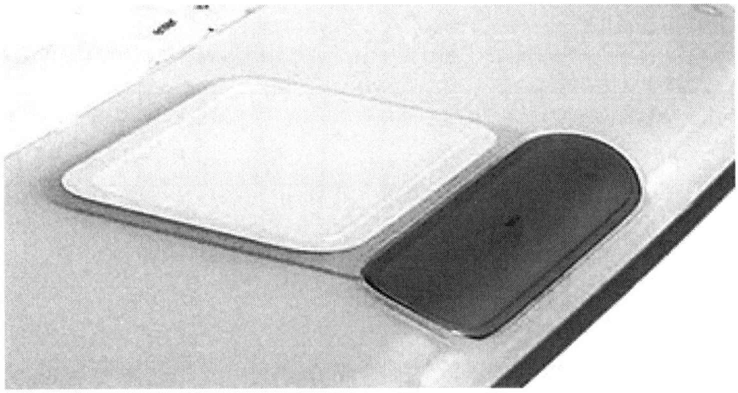

Figure 1-6 The trackpad and trackpad button.

You can adjust how the trackpad and button respond to your actions by changing the settings in the Trackpad control panel (discussed in Chapter 3). As shown in Figure 1-7, the Trackpad control panel lets you vary the speed of the cursor in relation to the speed at which you drag your finger.

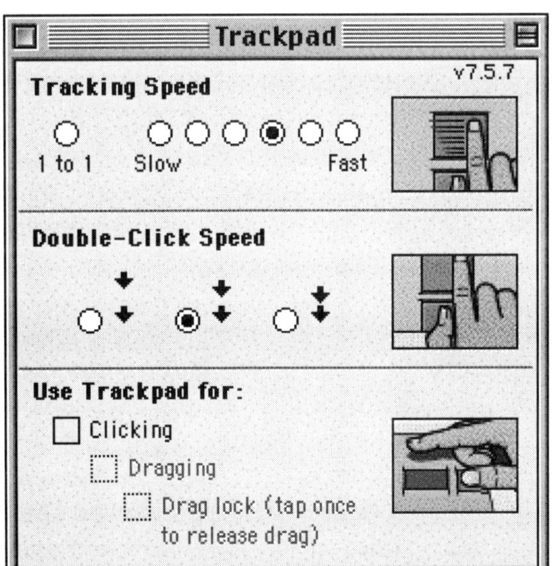

Figure 1-7 The Trackpad control panel.

Sound System

The iBook includes 16-bit stereo audio circuitry. But, because the iBook has only one speaker (located on the left side of the iBook, between the keyboard and the display), you'll hear only mono sound. If you're insistent on hearing stereo sound, though, you're in luck. The iBook has a headphone jack (located on the left side of the iBook by the left palm rest) which does output stereo sound You can listen to stereo sound through a set of headphones plugged into this jack, or you can plug a pair of externally powered stereo speakers into this same jack.

Note
The iBook doesn't come equipped with a microphone or sound input jack—but solutions exist. In Chapter 10 you can read about Griffin Technology's iMic Audio adapter. This inexpensive adapter (about $25) plugs into the iBook's USB port, and allows you to make use of just about any inexpensive or expensive microphone.

CD-ROM Drive

On the right side of the iBook is the 24x (twenty-four speed) CD-ROM drive. Some Macs have CD-ROM trays that slide all the way out at a press of a button, but the iBook uses a model that only slides out a short way when the CD-ROM button is pressed. After pressing the button, gently pull the exposed tray open until it "clicks" into place. After inserting or removing a CD-ROM disc, close the tray by pushing it back into its slot. The tray will be flush with the side of the iBook and lock into place when it is completely closed.

Power On Button

To turn the iBook on, press the power on button located on the right side of the iBook, between the keyboard and the display. Once your iBook is on and started up, closing the iBook lid places the computer in sleep mode. When at sleep, the iBook seems like it's turned off. And it is—almost. While asleep the screen is dark and the computer uses very little power. But it does use a little power—enough to quickly wake up when the lid again opened. In contrast to sleeping is shutting down (turning off). When you shut down (by choosing

Shut Down from the **Special** menu) the iBook, it's really off—it uses no power at all. To restart the computer you press the power button and wait awhile as the computer starts up.

When should you put your iBook in sleep mode, and when should you shut it down? If you're taking a break, but you'll soon be using the computer again, shut the lid to place the iBook in sleep mode. Lifting the lid quickly wakes the computer up and you're ready to resume your work. If you're taking an extended break, or are finished for the day, shut down the computer. It will take longer to start back up then it would from sleep, but it won't drain any battery life during the extended down time.

There's still more involved in powering your iBook. The Energy Saver control panel (see Chapter 3 for more on control panels) lets you specify a period of inactivity that signals the iBook to go to sleep on its own—even if you don't close the lid. If you walk away from your computer "for just a minute," and that "minute" turns out to be a lot longer, the iBook can place itself into sleep mode to start conserving its battery. In the Energy Saver control panel you control what this period of inactivity is before automatic sleeping takes place. There's another nifty feature in the Energy Saver control panel. Here you can specify that the contents of RAM (what's stored in memory) be saved to a special file on the computer's hard drive when the iBook goes to sleep or when it's shut down. Saving the contents of RAM to disk doesn't have a discernable difference when the iBook sleeps and wakes up, but it does make a big difference when the iBook is shut down and then restarted. When an iBook that had its RAM saved at shut down restarts, it doesn't need to go through the fairly lengthy startup process—it just very quickly restores the iBook to the state it was in when last shut down.

Here's a summary of the different degrees of "turning off" your iBook:

Sleep Now This tells the iBook to go to sleep. The computer appears to be off, but it is in fact continuously drawing a little bit of power so that it can be quickly awoken.

Save and Sleep Now This is the same as Sleep Now, but the contents of memory are saved to a file. Waking from sleep mode is normally quick, so this option doesn't offer much of an advantage.

Save & Power Off Now Here again the contents of RAM are saved to a file and used to restore, or return, the iBook to the state (it's same condition) it was in when shut down. This option does reap benefits—the time to restart the iBook is reduced by minutes.

Power Off This is a "normal" shut down that doesn't save the current RAM contents to a disk file. After pressing the power on button, expect a wait of a few minutes as the iBook starts up.

Handle

The iBook sports an integrated carrying handle that, when not in use, becomes flush with the computer by folding down onto the area between the display and the keyboard. The number one means of damaging a notebook computer? Dropping it. Use the carrying handle!

Storage

The original version of the iBook contains an internal 3.2 GB hard disk. That's a fair amount of storage for a notebook, but if you need more you'll be able to add an external hard drive or a removable media drive. Refer to Chapter 10 for more information on adding peripherals to your iBook.

Now, about that lack of a floppy drive. When the first iMac computers came out a while back you certainly heard the controversy surrounding that "floppy driveless" computer. Like the iMac, the iBook is without floppy. Expect Apple to make the transition to a product line that consists of nothing but machines lacking floppy drives. Apple's philosophy is that floppy drives are a dying technology and that the use of floppy disks to store or transfer information is inefficient. Consider the following:

- It takes well over two thousand floppy disks to back up the contents of the iBook's 3.2 GB hard drive
- Transferring a file via a floppy disk requires the physical transfer of the disk from one computer to another

Using a much larger-capacity removable media storage medium, such as an Iomega 100 MB or 250 MB USB Zip drive, or an Imation SuperDisk 120 MB USB drive, is best for backing up files. These and other iBook-compatible drives are discussed in Chapter 10 . A second option for backing up files is Internet backup. If you use your iBook to connect to the Internet (of course you do!), then you can use one of a few different Internet backup services to frequently upload to the Internet copies of files. If you need any of these uploaded files (for instance, if you accidentally delete a file), you simply download it from it's safe home on the Internet. Chapter 9 describes this type of service.

As for transferring files from one Mac to another, networking can be a more efficient solution than floppy disks. If you want to transfer a file to someone (even yourself) at school, for instance, just e-mail the file to that person and have them download the mailed file from the machine the file is destined for. For more information on e-mailing files, read Chapter 7 if you're an ISP user, or Chapter 5 if you're an America Online user. If the computer the file is to go to is another one of your own Macs (whether another iBook, an iMac, or any other type of Macintosh), then consider networking the two Macs. Connecting two or more of your Macs is cheap and easy—refer to Chapter 11 if you're skeptical.

Ports

An iBook is loaded with a lot of circuitry and software that enable the computer to effectively communicate with all sorts of *peripherals*, or *devices*, such as a printer, a microphone, speakers, even other Macs. All these peripherals, of course, need some means of accessing the iBook's internal electronics and software. Ports do just that. The iBook's modem, Ethernet, USB, and headphone ports are conveniently located on the left side of the computer—as shown back in Figure 1-1. In this section you'll get an overview of these ports. More port details are revealed throughout the book as different peripherals, and their connections to the iBook, are discussed.

Headphone Jack (Sound Output)

An iBook emits sound through a single speaker built into the computer, just above the keyboard. But Apple doesn't force you to use this speaker. The sound signals are also available through a headphone jack located on the left side of the iBook (refer to Figure 1-1). The built-in speaker provides adequate sound, but if you want stereo sound, you'll want to either plug in a set of headphones or a pair of speakers to the 16-bit stereo sound output headphone minijack. Stereo speakers, such as those sold by CoZo, are described in Chapter 10.

Note
Plugging headphones or speakers into the sound output jack automatically cuts off sound from the built-in speaker.

Modem

The iBook computer ships with a built-in 56 Kbps (supporting K56flex and V.90 modem standards) modem that also supports a fax modem bit rate of up to 14.4 Kbps.. The modem port is an RJ-11 modem connector, which simply means that to make use of the internal iBook modem you plug a standard, active phone line into the modem port. As shown back in Figure 1-1, the modem port is located near the left rear corner of the computer.

10/100Base-T Ethernet

For quite some time, most Mac models shipped with built-in Ethernet networking capabilities. In particular, you'll find a 10Base-T Ethernet port on the back of just about any recent Macintosh. The *10* in *10Base-T* refers to the capacity of the network connection. That is, a Mac connected to a network by way of a 10Base-T port can carry 10 megabits of data, or information, per second. That's a large capacity that allows information to be quickly transferred to and from the Mac. However, a 100Base-T connection is better. The iMac was the first Macintosh to come equipped with the built-in capability to connect to a network at either 10Base-T or 100Base-T. Other Macs, including the iBook, are similarly equipped. A single Ethernet port, a 10/100Base-T port allows you to quickly connect your iBook to an existing Ethernet network. When you do that, the iBook automatically detects the speed of the network to which it's connected, and adjusts itself accordingly.

Note
Networking is described in Chapter 11. If you have an iBook and a second (or more) Mac, consider networking them together to make it easy to transfer files and share applications. Even if you know *nothing* about networking, look over Chapter 11. Networking a couple or a few Macs is truly a simple and inexpensive task. Really!

Universal Serial Bus (USB)

SCSI (Small Computer Serial Interface) is a technology used for connecting peripherals (such as hard drives) to a computer. The very first Macintosh computer, released in 1984, didn't include a SCSI port, but since then all other Macs have. Until the iMac. Other recent Mac models, including the iBook, forego SCSI. In its place you'll find *USB (Universal Serial Bus)*. USB is a "plug and play" interface that makes it easy to connect any USB peripheral (such as a many types of printers, scanners, digital cameras, and so forth) to a USB-ready computer. If you also own an older Mac (older here meaning more than a year or so old), you'll notice that the serial (printer and modem) ports and the ADB (Apple Desktop Bus) port, as well as the SCSI port, are missing from the iBook. USB replaces all of this assortment of peripheral interfaces.

Some PCs have USB ports, but it was Apple's iMac that turned out to be the machine that jump-started this technology. Apple intends to use USB in place of SCSI in all future Mac computers. Third party (non-Apple) manufacturers of peripherals are aware of this, and have a variety of USB peripherals available now, with more in the works. In Chapter 10 you'll read much more about USB technology, as well as about USB printers, hard drives, removable media drives (such as the Zip drive), and other types of peripherals that are already available and waiting to be connected to your iBook.

Sound In

Unlike the iMac, the iBook does *not* come equipped with a built-in microphone or sound input jack. I mention sound input here because many people will be expecting such a port—it's one common to most notebook computers, such as Apple PowerBooks. If you want, or need, to input sound, though, don't despair—there are workarounds. For instance, Griffin Technology offers a USB microphone/line input called the iMic audio adapter that can be used with the iBook's USB port. Plug the iMic into the iBook's USB port and you're all set to then plug in just about any microphone into the iMic adapter. Read more about the iMic in Chapter 10.

Video Out

Like the non-existent Sound In port just mentioned, a video out port won't be found on your iBook. Again, I mention this type of port because many people will be interested in such a port—it's found on many PowerBook models. Such a port is used to connect an external video display or recording device (such as a VCR) to a computer in order to either "mirror" what's on the computer screen (as in the case of giving a presentation using a television) or to record what's on the computer screen (as in the case of recording a videocassette of something occurring on the screen).

Again like sound input, there are "portless" solutions to video output. One such solution is USBPresenter by AVerMedia Microsystems. Plug the USBPresenter into the iBook's USB port, then connect the USBPresenter to the video input port of a TV, VCR, or projector. For more information on the USBPresenter, refer to Chapter 10.

Note
The iBook has a single USB port, but that doesn't mean you can add just a single USB device (such as the iMic, or a printer, and so forth) to the iBook. You can easily and inexpensively plug a USB hub into the iBook's USB port and then plug a number of peripherals into that hub. For more on hubs, refer to Chapter 10.

Reset Button

Okay, so it's a button, not a port. The Reset button is located directly above the power button on the keyboard—it's tucked away between two of the narrow air vents. If your iBook crashes (freezes or hangs), you should first try simultaneously pressing the Control, Command, and Power keys to restart it. If that doesn't work, resort to pressing the Reset button. To do that you'll need to insert the end of an unbent paper clip into the small reset hole. You'll feel the button depress—when you do, remove the paper clip.

Note
Pressing the reset button results in the loss of unsaved data. Consider, for instance, that you're busy typing a letter when the iBook inexplicably freezes, You press the reset button and your iBook turns off, then restarts. When you open the document you'd been working on before the restart, you see that anything you typed into that document from the time of the last saving of it to the time of the freeze is gone.

Software

System software is the code that makes your iBook display things and do things. Without the system software, powering up your iBook wouldn't do much—there'd be no *desktop*, or *Finder* (interchangeable names given to the "work area" displayed on your iBook after it starts up), and you wouldn't be able to work with files, folders, and programs. The other type of software is *application software*, or what are more commonly referred to as *programs*. The iBook comes with system software and some programs installed. A back-up of the system software (a copy that exists so that you can restore the computer to its original state in the event of a disaster) and some additional programs are bundled with the iBook on a number of CD-ROM discs.

Macintosh System Software

Any computer requires some type of system software in order to run. Right out of the box, an iBook is ready to go because it comes with the Macintosh operating system installed.

What the System Software Is

The first iBooks came with Mac OS 8.6, while the iBooks making up the second "wave" of machines are each equipped with Mac OS 9. Because enhancing the operating system software is an ongoing effort at Apple, future iBooks will naturally have a still-later version of the OS.

Most of what the operating system software does takes place "behind the scenes." For example, when you specify that a copy of a file should be made, the operating system handles the details of creating the duplicate file. The iBook (and every other Mac) provides a *graphical user interface* (*GUI*) that enables a user to easily communicate with the operating system. The Macintosh GUI is composed of menus, windows, and icons—all of which are discussed in Chapter 2.

Correcting Problems With the System Software

Each time your iBook starts up, it should do so without any problems. But there *could* come a time when such is not the case. Software, including system software, is not infallible. While not common, system software is subject to becoming *corrupt*, or damaged. If that happens, you'll need to restore the system software on your iBook's hard drive. Apple bundles two CDs with the iBook for just such an emergency. The following is a brief summary of the purpose of each of these discs—refer to Chapter 12 for more information on repairing a damaged system, and on the use of the following two CDs.)

iBook Software Install CD This CD holds a Mac OS software installer program named Mac OS Install, as well as copies of the applications (such as Bugdom and AppleWorks) that came preinstalled on your iBook's hard drive. Use this CD to reinstall the system software, or to reinstall just one or some of the bundled programs. If your computer frequently crashes in a variety of circumstances, you'll need to reinstall the system software. If instead your iBook seems to be working fine except when one particular program is running, you'll want to reinstall just the one troublesome program.

iBook Restore CD This CD holds a "picture" of just what your iBook's hard drive looked like when it left the Apple factory. If you can't, for the life of you, figure out why your computer seems to be crashing, you can use this CD to restore your iBook's hard drive to its original state. In other words, a lot of software on your hard drive will be erased, and new, pristine versions of it all will be copied from the Restore CD to the hard drive. Before taking this bold step, the CD's installer program gives you the opportunity to specify that the restore operation should not remove any of your own personal files. That is, you can tell the installer to replace all of the Apple-supplied files while leaving untouched any of the files you've created.

Included Programs

The iBook includes several *bundled* (included at no additional charge) *third-party* (non-Apple) software programs. You may not be familiar with all of the included software. If that's the case, read over the summaries below. Most of the programs come preinstalled on the iBook hard drive, while a few are on the bundled CD-ROM discs. If a program is preinstalled, you'll find it in either the Applications folder or the Internet folder on the hard drive of your iBook. If a program isn't preinstalled, you'll need to get a copy of it on to your hard drive. Typically, all that's necessary to do that is to place the CD that holds the program of interest in the iBook CD-ROM drive and start up the installer program that's on that CD.

Note

In general, once a program is installed on a computer's hard drive, the CD that contains the original program doesn't have to be placed in the computer's CD-ROM drive in order for the program to work. Exceptions exist, though. If a program requires the CD-ROM disc to be present, you'll be told of that fact when you start up the program from the iBook hard drive.

AppleWorks

AppleWorks appears to be a single program—but it's actually a number of programs rolled into one. Among other things, this software is a word processor, drawing program, painting tool, spreadsheet, Web site design utility, and database management program. That's a lot of bang for the buck. In the case of the iBook, it's really a lot of bang for the buck—the complete AppleWorks suite is included on your iBook.

When you start up AppleWorks you'll see an introductory window like the one shown in Figure 1-8. Here you select the type of document, or file, you'd like to create. To do that, double-click on the document type.

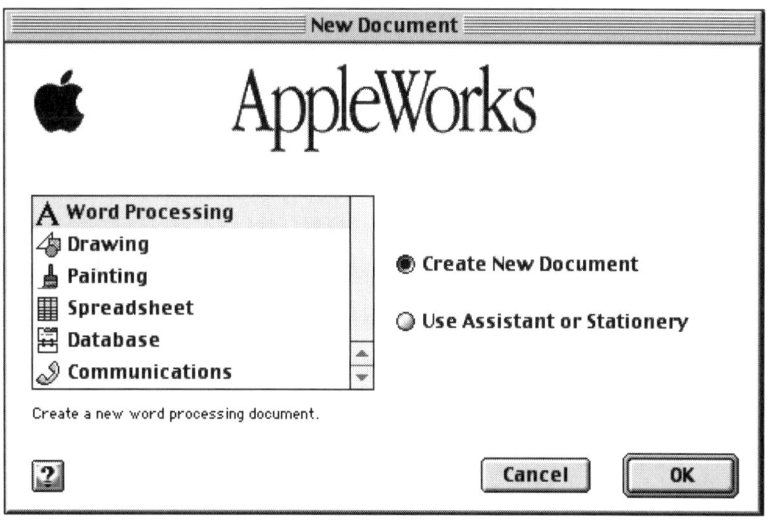

Figure 1-8 Creating a new AppleWorks document.

For instance, if you'd like to write something (such as a letter, memo, or report), create a Word Processing document. Doing that brings up the appropriate set of menus in the menu bar, displays a text-editing toolbar, and opens a new, empty document window in which you can type. In Figure 1-9 I've started typing in such a new document.

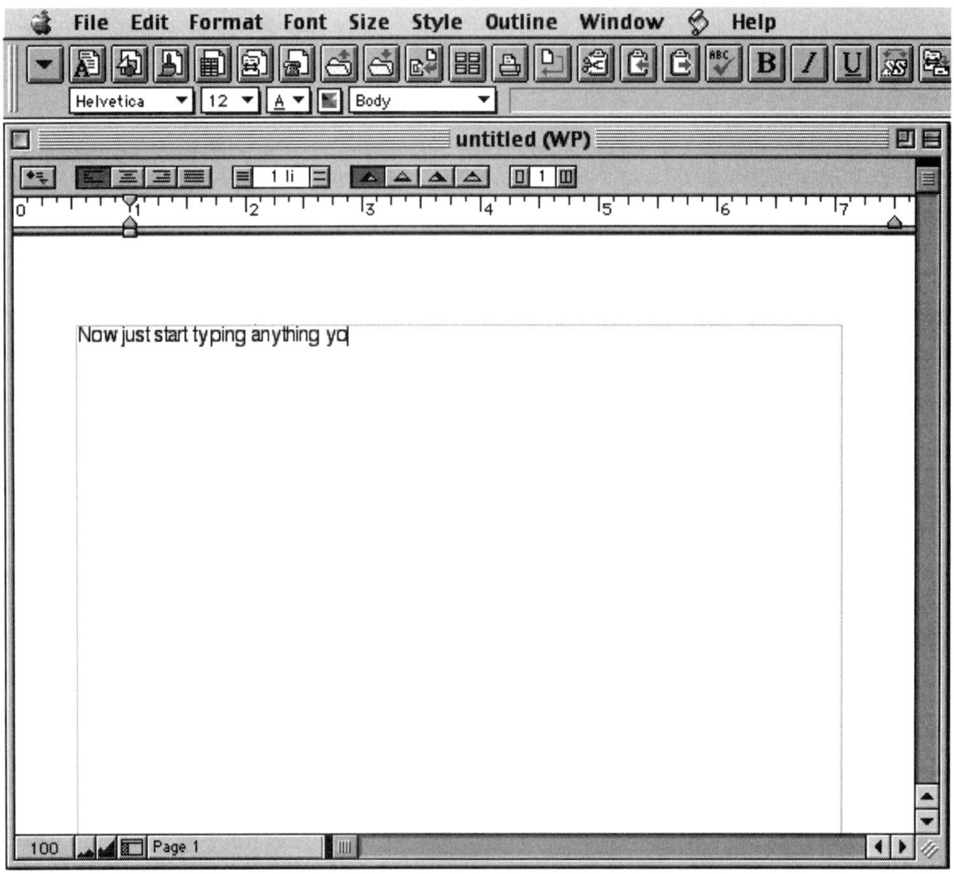

Figure 1-9 A new Word Processing document.

If AppleWorks is new to you, then make sure to look under the **Help** menu in the menu bar of the AppleWorks program. There you'll find a lot ways to get assistance in working with AppleWorks. Choose **AppleWorks Help Index** from this menu to see a list of all the available help topics.

FAXstf

FAXstf, by STF Technologies, is fax communication software that allows your iBook to mimic a fax machine. With your iBook, a modem, and FAXstf software, you can fax electronic documents: word processor files, graphic images, spreadsheetsæanything that's displayable on your computer screen. FAXstf also allows you to receive any fax, regardless of its source. Instead of being received as printed hardcopy on a fax machine, you'll receive faxed information as electronic documents that you can view on screen, save to disk, and print on a printer connected to your iBook.

Nanosaur

Nanosaur, by Pangea Software, is a high-quality 3D action game. Even if you aren't a game player, you'll want to give Nanosaur a look: it's designed for the average Mac user. In the game, you are a futuristic dinosaur sent back in time. Of course, you're no ordinary dinosaur (as if there was such a thing). Instead, you're a dinosaur that can run, jump, and swim, and you're equipped with weapons, a jet pack, and more.

Bugdom

The clan of the Fire Ants has overthrown the once-peaceful Bugdom. It's up to you, a Rollie Pollie bug named Rollie McFly, to defeat the Fire Ants and save the Lady Bugs. Bugdom is a game that shows off the power of the iBook. Smooth, 3D action demands a lot of processor power—and the iBook delivers. And Bugdom is a game that's only offered on the Mac. If the sight of this game running on your iBook doesn't get your Windows friends and coworkers a little envious, nothing will!

EdView Internet Safety Kit Family Edition

Concerned about what your children or students are "discovering" online? If so, you want Internet filtering software on your (or your school's) iBook computer or computers. One such filter comes free with every iBook—the EdView Internet Safety Kit Family Edition. With the EdView software installed on an iBook, a teacher, parent, or guardian can greatly limit the sites that a user is allowed to access. EdView, and other Internet precautionary aids, are described in Chapter 9.

World Book Encyclopedia

The 22-volume World Book Encyclopedia is the world's best-selling encyclopedia. In conjunction with IBM, World Book has placed every article from the print edition—along with multimedia presentations—onto a Macintosh CD-ROM disc. And Apple has bundled this CD-ROM disc with your iBook. Here you'll find plenty of text, of course—but you'll also get pictures, sound clips, maps, and video animations.

Palm Desktop Organizer

If you have a Palm handheld organizer, then the Palm Desktop Organizer software that comes with your iBook should be of interest. The Palm Desktop Organizer enables you to back up and exchange data between your Palm organizer and your iBook.

SimpleText

A *text editor* and a *word processor* are both programs that allow you to type, edit, and save text in a file. A word processor offers a multitude of ways to *format* text. That is, a word processor gives you near-complete control over the look of text (such as including bold or italicized words), the positioning of paragraphs (such as allowing you to double-space lines of text), and the way your words appear on a printed page (by allowing you to specify page margins). A text editor *doesn't* provide you with this word-management power. A text editor *might* let you adjust a few features, such as changing the text font (the typeface that the words appear in), but that's about it. A word processor is thus much more powerful than a text editor is. However, a text editor does serve a very important purpose—it allows you to create a file that can be transferred to any type of computer. Because it saves your work as plain text, a text editor creates a file that can be transferred—and opened and read—on just about any type of computer (including a computer running any version of Windows). If you have a text editor, you can create files that can be read by anyone, regardless of the type of computer that person has. And equally as important, you can read a text file created on a computer other than a Mac.

And the reason for that lengthy distinction between a word processor and a text editor? Because without it, you might not realize how important it is to have a text editor as one of the programs on your computer. Apple knows it, and now you know it. SimpleText is a text editor developed by, and widely and freely distributed by, Apple. When you run SimpleText, you can open and read any text file.

EarthLink's TotalAccess

Before you can connect to the Internet and World Wide Web, you need to have Internet access. That is, you need the phone number of an Internet host so your iBook can connect to the Internet via your iBook modem. EarthLink is such a host company. EarthLink, like any Internet service provider (ISP), has thousands of modems all ready to accept connections from people like you. You pay a monthly fee, and EarthLink gives you an access phone number (local to your area so you don't incur long distance fees) and a password. You then use your iBook to connect to the provided number.

EarthLink's name for their Internet connection package is TotalAccess. The package consists of unlimited Internet access, technical support, server space for your own Web site, Internet software (including Web browsers, email programs, and multimedia plug-ins such as Shockwave). As of this writing, TotalAccess is available for $19.95 per month, which is a price competitive with other Internet service providers.

Note

Apple has selected EarthLink as the ISP-of-choice for iBook users. But be aware that there are numerous ISPs from which you can get Internet service.

Tip

Read Chapter 6 for information on connecting to the Internet using an Internet Service Provider. Chapter 7 describes the use of e-mail. Read Chapter 8 to learn about Web browsers and plug-ins.

America Online

The America Online software allows you to connect to America Online's own online service. After you do, you'll need to choose one of America Online's monthly payment plans. If you want to access the Internet as well as America

Online's own online service, choose the $21.95 per month service for unlimited Internet access.

Netscape Navigator and Internet Explorer

To connect to the Internet and surf the Web, you need service from an Internet Service Provider, or ISP (see EarthLink's TotalAccess above) and a Web browser. For Web browsing software, your primary choices are Netscape Navigator and Microsoft Internet Explorer. Apple has supplied you with both these browsers, so once you're connected you can try out both.

Outlook Express

If you choose Microsoft Internet Explorer as your Web browser, you'll want to consider using Microsoft Outlook Express as your e-mail software. And if you use the Netscape Web browser, you too might be interested in giving Outlook Express a try—even though Netscape Communicator includes e-mail tools. Outlook Express provides easy set-up and offers a host of features to make creating, sending, and reading e-mail simple and efficient. Outlook Express is covered in-depth in Chapter 7.

2

Introducing the Mac OS

When a person says he or she is "using a computer," what that person is in fact using is the computer's *operating system*, or OS (just say the letters to properly pronounce it: *oh-ehs*) Different types of computers have different types of operating systems. A PC user (a PC being just about any computer other than a Macintosh) typically uses a version of Microsoft Windows, such as Windows 95, Windows 98, or Windows NT. A Mac user typically uses a version of Apple's Mac OS, such as Mac OS 8.1, Mac OS 8.6, or Mac OS 9. The first iBook computers shipped with Mac OS 8.6.

An operating system is computer code written by a *lot* of programmers—so you can guess that an OS is complex. Fortunately, modern operating systems include a *layer* of software the sole purpose of which is to make easier the accessing of the operating system's services. For us Macintosh users, more fortunate still is the fact that this OS-accessing software is the user-friendliest of any of the popular operating systems. On a Mac, this software is called the *Finder*. When you know how to work with the Finder, you know how to work with the iBook—or any other Macintosh computer. The focus of this chapter is on getting familiar with the Finder. If you're a first time Mac user, don't skip this chapter—read it, then make sure to carry on in your quest to master the Mac OS by reading the next chapter. If you've used a Mac before, but aren't entirely comfortable with how things are done on a Macintosh, you can skim this chapter and move quickly on to the next chapter.

Mac OS: the Very Basics

If you've never used a Macintosh, then you need to know a few very basic techniques before you can do anything at all with your iBook. First time Mac users—read this section!

The Desktop

When your iBook is turned off, you see a blank screen. When your iBook is turned on, you see the Macintosh desktop. Why did Apple name the look of the screen the *desktop*? The analogy here is that the screen serves as a sort of desk, with your work scattered about the desktop. In Figure 2-1 you see some folders and files on the desktop. Like a real world folder, a Mac folder holds papers, or files. It's convenient to keep files in a folder, but, again like the real-world, on a Mac a file can be kept outside of a folder—it can be left laying on the desktop. Figure 2-1 shows a desktop with three folders and one file. Of course by looking at this figure you can't tell how many files are actually on this iBook, since numerous files can be (and most likely are) found within the folders. In fact, the figure does show that at least one of the folders holds files. The *window* in Figure 2-1 displays the contents of the folder named Really Important Stuff. In the figure you see that this folder contains two files: one named *ListOfLateProjects*, the other named *ListOfVeryLateProjects*.

In Figure 2-1 you see that the folder named *Really Important Stuff* is highlighted—it, and its name, appear darker than the other items on the desktop. When an item is highlighted it means that item has been *selected*. To select an item you move the arrow cursor (which is discussed just ahead) over the item and then click the trackpad. Once an item is selected you can perform some action on that item. The action that's to be performed on an item depends on what type of item is selected. In the case of a folder, you'll most likely want to open the item. To open a folder means to display the folder's contents in its own window. That's exactly what I've done for the *Really Important Stuff* folder in Figure 2-1.

Note
What's displayed on the desktop is very variable—so don't expect the desktop of your iBook to look just like the one shown in Figure 2-1!

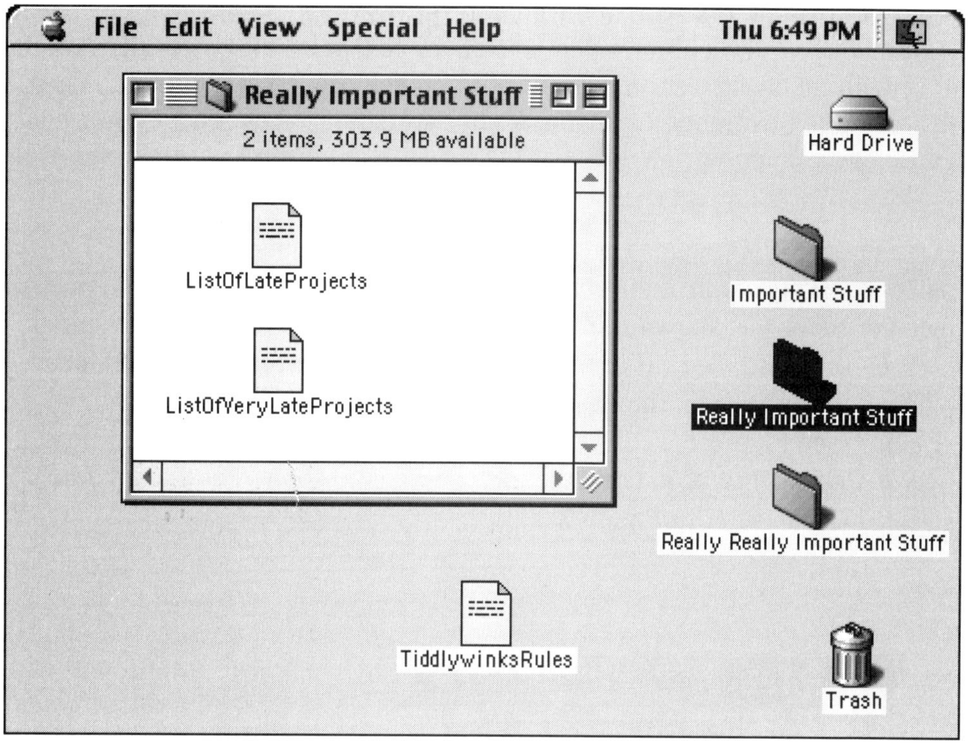

Figure 2-1 The Macintosh desktop.

Note

No analogy is perfect. You've probably determined that this is the case for the Macintosh desktop. For instance, if the screen represents a desktop, then what the heck is a trash can doing there—shouldn't it be on the floor somewhere?

The Cursor

We all get frustrated that at times a computer doesn't do exactly what we want it to do—so you will very quickly learn to curse at your iBook! But the word cursor has nothing to do with foul-language. Instead, it has to do with that little arrow that appears somewhere on your iBook monitor. When you find it, touch your iBook trackpad and watch the arrow move on the monitor. The little arrow serves as a pointer that is used to, yes, point to something. Pointing at something doesn't do much—until you click the trackpad button. Then, if the arrow is positioned over something, an action takes place. *What* action takes place is appropriate to what the arrow is pointing to at the time of the click.

If at the time of a trackpad button click the arrow is positioned over a *menu* name in the *menu bar* that runs horizontally along the top of the monitor, a menu appears—as shown in the left of Figure 2-2 (notice the arrow cursor right by the word *File*). If at the time of the click the arrow is positioned over a hard drive *icon*, the icon darkens to indicate that the hard drive is *selected* (see Figure 2-2). If at the time of the click the arrow is positioned over a *document*, or *file*, icon, the icon darkens to show that the document is selected (again refer to Figure 2-2).

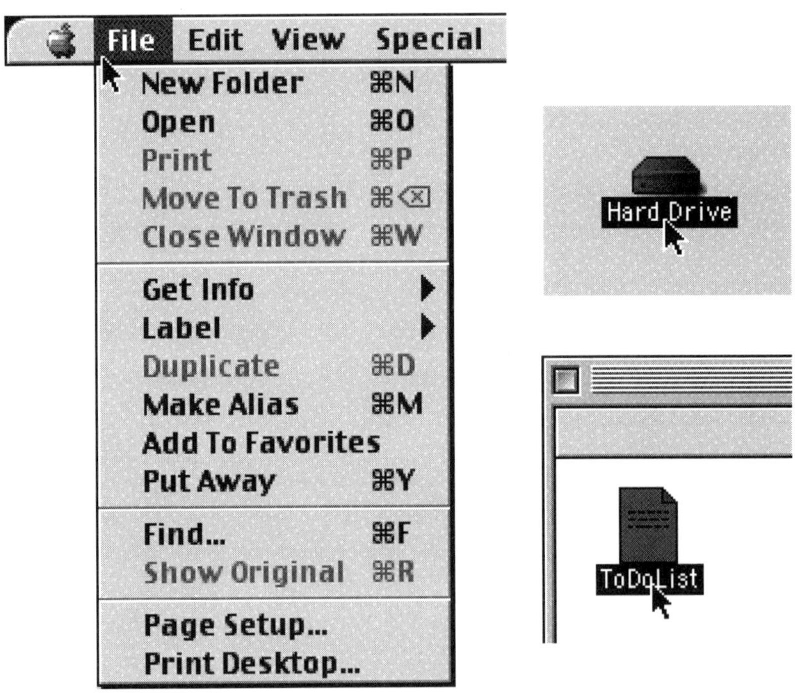

Figure 2-2 The arrow cursor pointing at a few different things.

The cursor looks like a little arrow—so why isn't the *cursor* instead called the *arrow*? Because the cursor *doesn't always* look like an arrow. The cursor takes on the appearance of an arrow when its purpose is to point to something, which is often the case. But it takes on other shapes too. If you're using a program that allows you to type text (such as a word processor program that's used to write letters, memos, and reports) into a window, then you'll notice that the cursor often takes on a shape like the cursor positioned Beneath the word "end" in Figure 2-3. This *I-beam* look is used to help you position the cursor between words so that you can edit (add, take away, or change) text at a particular point in your writing.

Figure 2-3 The cursor taking on the look of an I-beam.

Basic Terminology

The preceding sections introduced a handful of new Mac-related terms—terms that are covered in this and the next chapter. Be aware that the following is a quick overview of those terms—you'll get more thorough explanations of each as you read this and the next chapter.

The following terms are listed in alphabetical order, You'll want to read about each term because there's a bit of a "circular definition" taking place here. That is, the definition of one term might make reference to still another term. For example, the definition of a *window* mentions a *file*, and the definition of a *file* mentions a *window*!

dragging To move an item on the desktop you drag it. To drag an item first place a finger on the trackpad and move your finger. As you do, the cursor on the screen follows the direction of your finger's movement. Use the trackpad in this manner to move the arrow cursor until the cursor is positioned over the item to drag. Then use your thumb to click—and hold down—the trackpad button. With the button held down, place a finger on the trackpad and slide your finger in the direction you want the clicked-on item to move. As you move your finger, the selected item follows. Once you reach the desired destination (for instance, once you've dragged a selected file until it's icon appears over the icon of a folder you wish the file to end up in), lift your thumb off the trackpad button. Once you release the trackpad button, the dragged item moves to the location of the cursor..

file When you do some work in a program—any program—you'll typically want to save the results of your efforts. For instance, if you use a word processor program to write a letter, then you'll want to save that letter so that at any time you can print it out or edit it (reopen it in a *window* and make changes to it). You accomplish this saving of your work by storing your information (whether a letter, memo, drawing, or household budget) into a file. The file remains on your iBook hard drive, where it's always accessible. A *file* is sometimes also referred to as a *document*. A file is represented on the desktop by an icon that looks like a small piece of paper.

folder You could have one, ten, or a thousand files spread out all over your desktop—but then your iBook desktop would look a lot like my real desktop. And no one wants that. Instead, you'll want to organize your files in folders. A folder is represented on the desktop by an icon that looks very much indeed like a folder. You can move a file in or out of a folder by *selecting*, and then *dragging*, the file.

icon The computer needs some way of visually representing things so that you know how to find them, view their contents, and work with them. An icon—a little picture, or symbol—is the chief way the Macintosh conveys this information to you. Your iBook hard drive is built in to your iBook. So how do go about finding out what information is stored in it? Find the little icon that looks like a hard drive (like a hard drive that would hook up to the outside of a computer, anyway). Double-click (click the trackpad button twice, without a pause between clicks) on the hard drive icon and a window appears. The window displays information—such as the names of the files. The upper-right of Figure 2-2 shows a hard drive icon. Each icon has a name. In Figure 2-2 the hard drive icon has the name of *Hard Drive*. I gave the icon that name (okay, so my icon-naming reveals that I can't claim to be incredibly clever). You can change the name of an icon by first clicking on the name, then typing a new name. Go ahead and try that with your own iBook hard drive icon.

menu A single menu appears when a menu name in the menu bar is clicked. A menu holds a number of *items*. Each item can be chosen and, when chosen, acts as a command that carries out some action. In Figure 2-2 you see the **File** menu. Its items are too numerous to mention here, but, starting from the top, they include **New Folder** and **Open**.

menu bar Running along the top of the monitor is a bar that holds a few, or several names. Each name represents one menu. Clicking on any name in the menu bar reveals a menu. In Figure 2-2 the menu bar shows five menus: the Apple symbol, **File**, **Edit**, **View**, and **Special**.

Note
While the Apple menu looks different from other menus in the menu bar, it behaves in the same manner—move the cursor over the menu name, click the trackpad button, and down drops a menu. The Apple menu holds some folders as well as a number of small programs. Dragging the cursor over a folder name reveals a submenu (a second menu) that lists the contents of the folder. Dragging the cursor over a program name and releasing the trackpad button starts up that program.

selecting When you move the arrow cursor over something and then click the trackpad button, you've selected that *something*. Selecting an object usually highlightens that object (usually by darkening the object). That shows you that the object is selected. Selecting something is often a prerequisite to performing some action on that object. For instance, to make a copy of a file you can click on it to select it, and then choose **Duplicate** from the **File** menu. Only the selected file will be duplicated (you'll see a copy of the selected file right beside the original file).

window A window displays the contents of something. That *something* could be a hard drive (where the window lists all of the *files* and *folders* stored on that drive), a folder (where the window lists the files and, perhaps, other folders, in that folder), or a file (where the window would display whatever information is stored in that file, such as the text of a letter, or the graphics that make up a picture you drew). The lower-right of Figure 2-2 shows a part of a window that's displaying the contents of a hard drive (you see only one file named *ToDoList*). Figure 2-3 shows a window that's displaying some text from a word processor file.

Windows (and Things Like Windows)

A window is used to display something. In a word processor program, a window displays the words you've typed. In a paint program, a window displays a picture you've created. On the desktop, a window displays the contents of a disk or a folder.

Opening a Window

To view the contents of a folder or a disk (such as a hard drive, which is also called a hard disk), double-click on that item's icon. Figure 2-4 shows the windows I encounter when I double-click on a couple of folder icons. When you try this on your own hard drive icon or folder icons, you will, of course, see something different (unless, that is, you too happen to be writing a book…).

The larger window in Figure 2-4 is the result of double-clicking on the icon of a folder named *My Book*. You know this to be the case because the window's title names the folder (or hard drive) that is being displayed in the window. The smaller window appears when I double-click on the folder named *Figures*—a folder which is *nested* (located within) the *My Book* folder.

Note

Here I'm discussing desktop windows—windows that display the contents of your iBook hard drive. With a program running (whether a word processor, drawing program, or just about any other type of program), a window is usually opened by choosing **New** from the program's **File** menu. Such a window often opens empty, ready for you to type or draw in it. As you'll see in the *Opening a Window* and *Changing the View of a Window* sections, this differs from how the desktop works with windows.

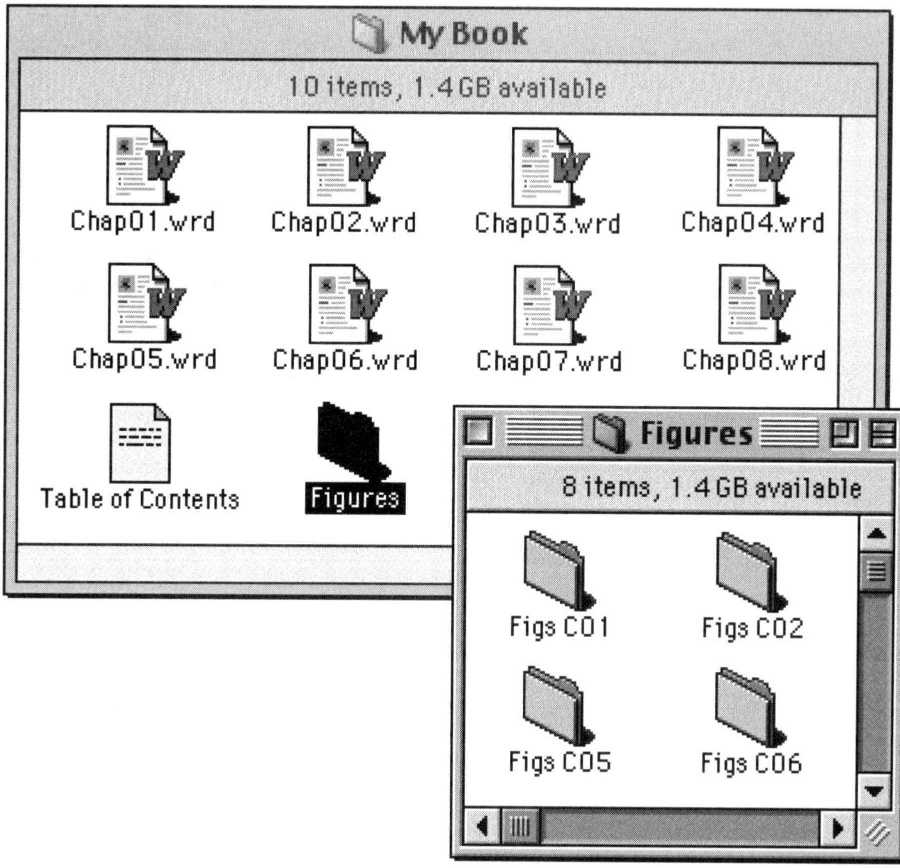

Figure 2-4 The contents of two folders, each displayed in a window.

Changing the View of a Window

How the contents of a hard drive or folder are displayed in a window is something you can control. One type of view is shown in Figure 2-4. This view is simply referred to as the Icon view. If you prefer to see the contents of a window in the form of a list, click on the window whose view you want changed and then choose **as List** from the Finder's **View** menu. Figure 2-5 illustrates how the contents of the *Figures* window shown in Figure 2-4 get rearranged when the window is displayed in List form rather than Icon form.

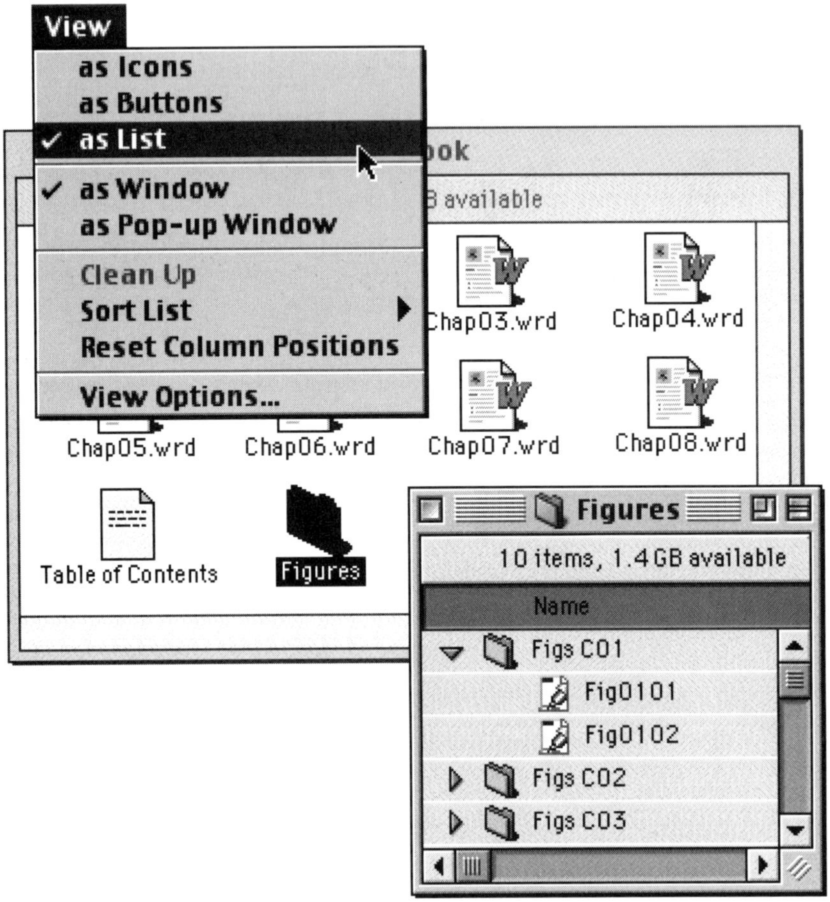

Figure 2-5 Changing the view of one folder.

In List form, each item, or object, (such as a folder, file, or program) appears on its own line. If there is a folder nested within the window, you can see its contents by clicking on the small arrow icon to the left of the folder. Figure 2-5 reveals that the folder named *Figs C01* holds two files (named *Fig0101* and *Fig0102*).

I've just described the two principle ways of viewing the contents of a hard drive or folder, but the Finder's **View** menu offers you a variety of view formats. You'll want to open a folder and then try out the different options to get a feel for the display choice you like best.

Note
Here again I'm discussing desktop windows—windows that display the contents of your iBook hard drive. When you run a program, that program will display very different information in its window or windows. For instance, a word processor window usually starts out empty, and then displays the text you type into it. The next chapter offers more information on working with windows from within a running program.

Working With a Window

Once a window is opened (whether in the Finder or in just about any program), you don't have to leave it stuck to that spot on the screen. Instead, you can move it around, change its size, close it, and more. Performing any of these acts is quite simple, as you're about to see.

Activating a window

Before working with a window, it must be the *active*, or *frontmost*, window. You can tell when a window is active by looking at the top of the window at the *title bar*, or *drag bar*: that's the thin, horizontal strip running the length of the window. If the window is active, its title bar will appear highlighted: its features (such as the little boxes at either end) will be present, and the window's title will change from light gray to black dark. If the window is inactive, its title bar will be dimmed: its features will be missing, and the window's title will appear faint. Clicking anywhere on a window is all that's necessary to activate it.

Changing a window's size

A window will usually have a grow box in the lower-right corner. To resize the window, move the cursor over the box, click and hold the trackpad button down, and slide a finger along the trackpad.. As you slide your finger, an outline of the window moves as well. This outline reflects how the trackpad movements will affect the window's size. When you release the trackpad button, the window will become the size of the outline.

Closing an open window

A window's *close box* is the small square at the top-left of the window. To close the frontmost, or active, window, click its close box. To close a window that's partially obscured by another window, first click anywhere on the hidden window to make it active. Then click that window's close box.

Moving a window

You can move a window by clicking on the window's title bar and then, with the trackpad button held down, dragging your finger on the trackpad. As you move your finger on the trackpad, an outline of the window follows your finger's movement. When you release the trackpad button, the window moves to its new location. Alternatively, you can click on any one of the four edges of the window and then drag. If you use this technique, make sure the cursor is positioned over the very edge of the window.

Collapsing a window

If your iBook's desktop is cluttered with windows, but you don't want to close any of them, you can *collapse* one or more of them. Collapsing a window temporarily hides the entire content of the window. That is, only the window's title bar remains visible. To collapse a window, click on the window's *collapse control*—the small box at the far right end of the window's title bar. To again view the entire window, click again on the collapse control.

Dialog Boxes

A dialog box looks much like a window—it just has a little bit more going on inside it. A dialog box appears on screen when your iBook needs information from you. For instance, if you choose **View Options...** from the **View** menu (see Figure 2-6), you'll see a dialog box like the one pictured in Figure 2-7. How do you know which menu item will result in the display of a dialog box? If a menu item name is followed by an ellipsis (the three dots like those following **View Options...**), then choosing that menu item brings on a dialog box.

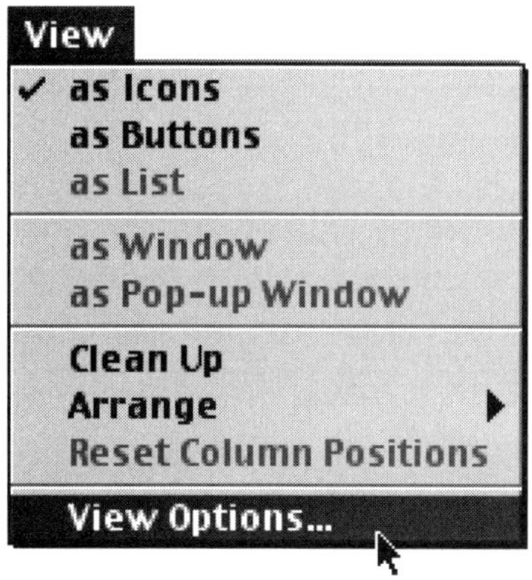

Figure 2-6 Choosing the View Options menu item.

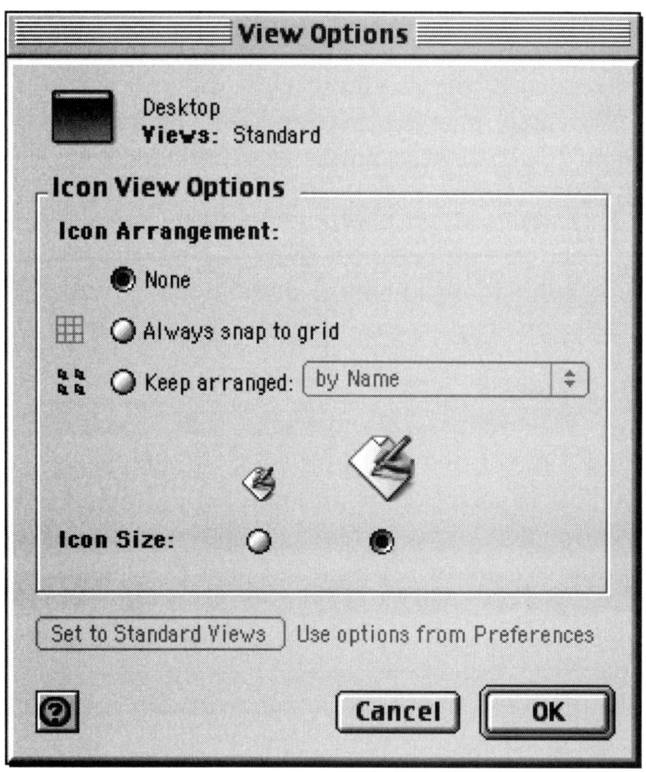

Figure 2-7 An example of a dialog box.

Note
In the preceding paragraph you see that the **View Options...** menu item name includes an ellipsis. In most Mac books and manuals menu item names don't include those three dots—even if they are in fact a part of the menu item name. I included the ellipsis here because it directly pertains to the discussion of how a dialog box is typically opened. Throughout the rest of this book I go with the convention of not including the ellipsis.

Dialog boxes can have a variety of looks, but the one shown in Figure 2-7 is pretty typical. You can usually (but not always) drag a dialog box about the screen. A dialog box usually doesn't include so much information that a scroll bar is needed (though a dialog box might hold a list of items where the list itself has a scroll bar). A dialog box has a number of items, or controls, that allow you to supply information to the program _you are, in a sense, carrying on a *dialog* with the computer). The following are descriptions of the most common items.

Text box This rectangle allows you to type text in order to enter a name or number. Move the cursor over the text box, click the trackpad button, and then start typing. Figure 2-8. provides a look at a text box.

Push button This item (which is often simply referred to as a button) provides immediate action. For instance, move the cursor over a button labeled **OK** or **Done**, click the trackpad button, and the dialog box will close. On the left of Figure 2-9 you see two push buttons: one labeled **Cancel**, the other labeled **OK**.

Radio buttons This item travels in packs: there are always two or more together. Move the cursor over one of the little round circles, click the trackpad button, and you've selected one option from a group of options. The right of Figure 2-9 shows three radio buttons—the **None** radio button is considered on, while the other two are off.

Check box This is a "Yes" or "No" type of control that toggles between these two states. If the check box has a check in it, that means you're saying "Yes" to this particular option. If the check box appears empty, you're declining the option. To change the check box to its opposite state (to turn an off check box on, or to turn an on check box off), just move the cursor over the box and click the trackpad button. Figure 2-10 shows a check box that is unchecked.

Pop-up menu This item looks like an elongated button. Moving the cursor over the item and clicking the trackpad button reveals a menu—a menu that "pops up." Here you make a selection just as you would from a menu that is housed in the menu bar that is always present along the top of your iBook's screen. In Figure 2-11 you see a pop-up menu that displays six items.

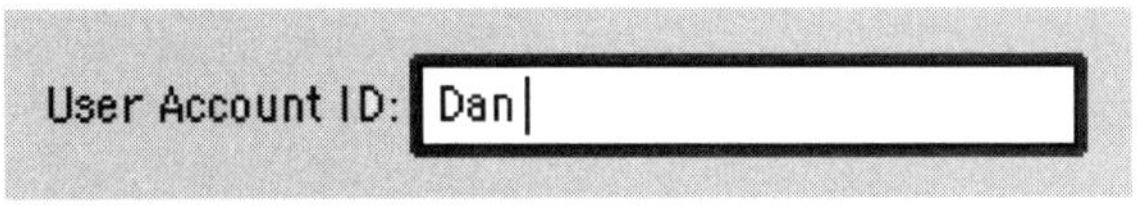

Figure 2-8 A text box.

Figure 2-9 Two push buttons (left) and three radio buttons (right).

Figure 2-10 A check box.

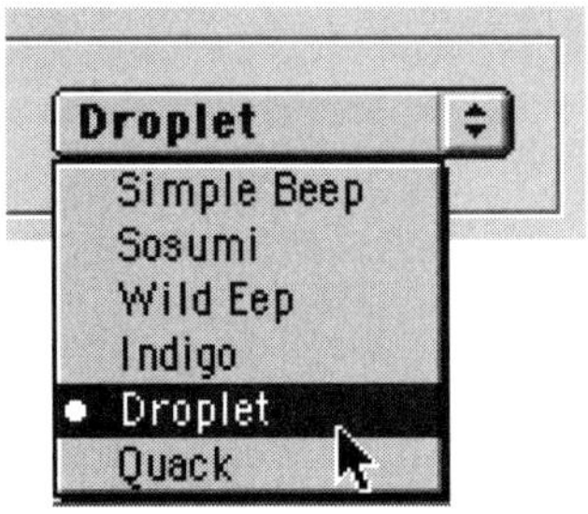

Figure 2-11 A pop-up menu.

As in the case of the View Options dialog box shown in Figure 2-7, a dialog box might not have a close box—you often need to press a button (such as the **OK** or **Cancel** button) to dismiss (close) the dialog box. Clicking the **OK** button indicates that you're satisfied with the choices that you've made in the dialog box. Clicking the **Cancel** button means that any changes you made to the items in the dialog box will not take effect—the result being the same as if you had never made the dialog box appear (so if you played around with a dialog box, and then wish you hadn't, click the **Cancel** button).

Alerts

An alert is a like a trimmed-down dialog box. An alert usually contains an icon, some informational text, and one or more push buttons—and that's it. The purpose of an alert is not to *get* information *from* you, but rather to *give* information *to* you. This information is usually a warning of some sort.

An alert may appear when you're trying to do something that might be detrimental to your work. An alert usually has only a couple or a few buttons. This keeps your choices—and thus your confusion, and possibility of making a mistake—to a minimum. Look at Figure 2-12 for an example of an alert.

If you're using a word processor or text editor and you click on the close box of a window before saving your work, the program will display an alert questioning if this is really the action you want to take. Figure 2-12 shows this type of alert when an unsaved window is about to be closed in the SimpleText text editor program. If I really did intend to close the window and lose my work, I'd click the **Don't Save** button. I could optionally click the **Cancel** button to cancel my attempt to close the window. That would, in effect, do nothing. More than likely, though, I hadn't realized that my work wasn't saved—so I'd click the **Save** button to let the program bring up a dialog box that let's me name and save my work.

Note

In Figure 2-12 the **Save** button is outlined. An alert (or a dialog box) has one (and only one) button with such a border. This is the *default* button. This button is the one the program anticipates is your safest choice. For instance, in Figure 2-12 it's a pretty safe bet that I forgot to save my work and that I do indeed want to save it before closing the window.

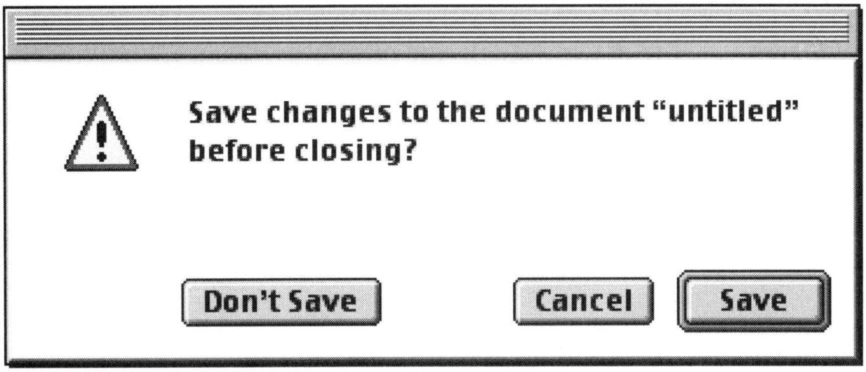

Figure 2-12 **A typical alert.**

The Finder and the Mac OS

A computer's operating system, is usually regarded in one of two ways: as complex software that's best ignored or left alone, or as a boring but necessary part of computing. Neither philosophy is altogether naive. A computer's OS is indeed large and intricate, and it's more than a bit intimidating. And the operating system is the software used to carry out tedious chores, such as copying a file from one place to another. Apple, however, has come up with the *Finder*—a means of making the Macintosh operating system simple to use and, yet anything but boring.

While you don't have to run the Finder as you do other software programs, the Finder is indeed a program. It just happens to be one that's always running (as long as your iBook is turned on, of course). You can confirm this by clicking on the **Application** menu—the menu that's always present on the far right of the menu bar running along the top of your iBook monitor. The menu lists, among other things, the names of all of the programs that are currently running (a program is also referred to as an *application*, thus the name of the menu). The items in your **Application** menu will no doubt vary from those shown in the menu pictured in Figure 2-13, but it will most certainly include the Finder.

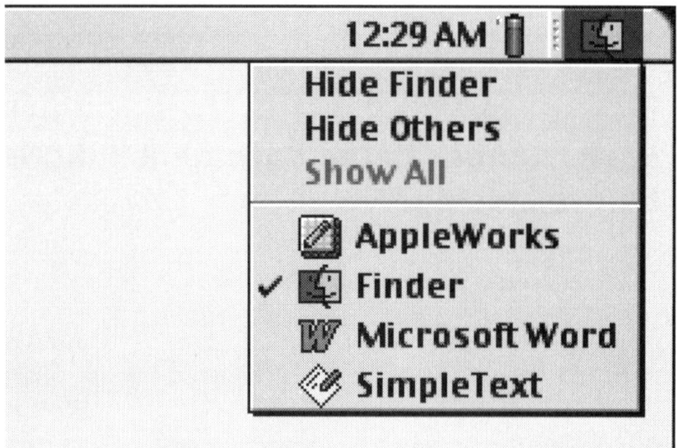

Figure 2-13 The Finder is always listed in the Application menu.

One of the chief responsibilities of the Finder is displaying the *desktop*. The desktop is the background that appears on your iBook monitor. The Finder also displays everything that appears on the desktop. The "things" on the desktop are *icons*—small pictures representing various items, or objects, such as a trash can, hard drive, folders, programs, and files. From the Finder, you perform the tasks that are basic in using a computer. Here you run programs, copy and erase files, organize files into folders, and display the contents of folders. This chapter is dedicated to getting you started with the basics of working with the desktop, and to exploiting a few of the more interesting aspects of the Finder.

Note

The Finder is so intertwined with the desktop that some people refer to the Finder itself as the desktop, or the Desktop. You can use these terms (Finder, desktop, Desktop) interchangeably and people skilled in the use of the Macintosh will understand what you're talking about.

Apple keeps improving upon the operating system and the Finder. When a new version is ready, it gets a new version number. The iBook initially shipped with Mac OS 8.6 installed. Shortly after its introduction iBook's shipped with Mac OS 9 installed. In the future (or perhaps as you read this), iBooks will have a newer version of the Macintosh operating system. Because this chapter deals primarily with the basics of working with the Mac OS, just about everything covered in this chapter applies to your iBook, whether it's running Mac OS 8.6 or a later version of the Mac OS.

Tip
To determine which version of the Mac OS you have on your iBook, choose the first item, **About This Computer**, from under the **Apple** menu (the menu on the far left of the menu bar). An About This Computer window appears. In this window you see the version of the operating system.

Working With Programs

Plain and simple: you bought your iBook to run programs. To connect to the Internet and surf the Web, you run a Web browser program such as Netscape Communicator or Microsoft Internet Explorer. To type a letter or report, you run a word processor program such as Microsoft Word. To play a game, you run a game program like Bugdom.

Running a Program

There are a few ways to run (or *start*, or *launch*) a program. Try each so you'll become familiar with the options, then settle on whichever way works best for you. The file-running descriptions use the Apple's SimpleText text editor as a point of reference (see Figure 2-14), but you can use these methods to run any program.

Double-clicking the Program's Icon

Find the icon of the program you want to run, move the arrow cursor until it is over the icon, and then click the trackpad button twice, with no pause or only a very short pause between the two clicks. That's called double-clicking, and that starts a program running. It's also the quickest way to run a program. In Figure 2-14, I'm all set to double-click on the SimpleText icon to run the SimpleText text editor program.

Using the Open Menu Item

Again, find the icon of the program you want to run, move the arrow cursor is over the icon, and then click once. The icon darkens to indicate that the icon is selected. Now, choose **Open** from the **File** menu. The program starts up. Most people forego this method and use double-clicking. Since you've gone through the work of finding the icon and clicking once on it, you might as well just click a second time. Figure 2-15 shows that I'm about to run SimpleText using the **Open** menu item.

Application file

Some programs let you save your work in a file on your hard disk. For instance, after typing a letter in a word processor program such as Microsoft Word, you'll no doubt save the letter to a file so that you can view it or edit it at a later date. To open and display the contents of a file, you can double-click on the icon of a file. If the program that created that file *is* already running, the clicked-on file opens right up. If the program that created the file is *not* already running, it will automatically start up and *then* the clicked-on file will open. In Figure 2-16, I'm again about to run SimpleText and open the SimpleText file named *ToDoList* by double-clicking on the *ToDoList* file that I had previously created and save in SimpleText.

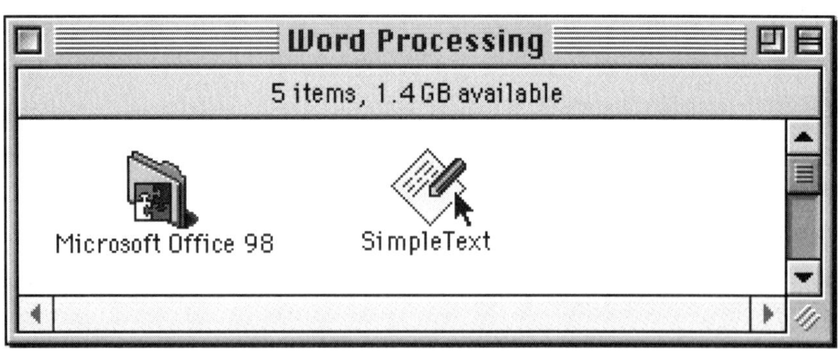

Figure 2-14 Double-clicking a program's icon to run the program.

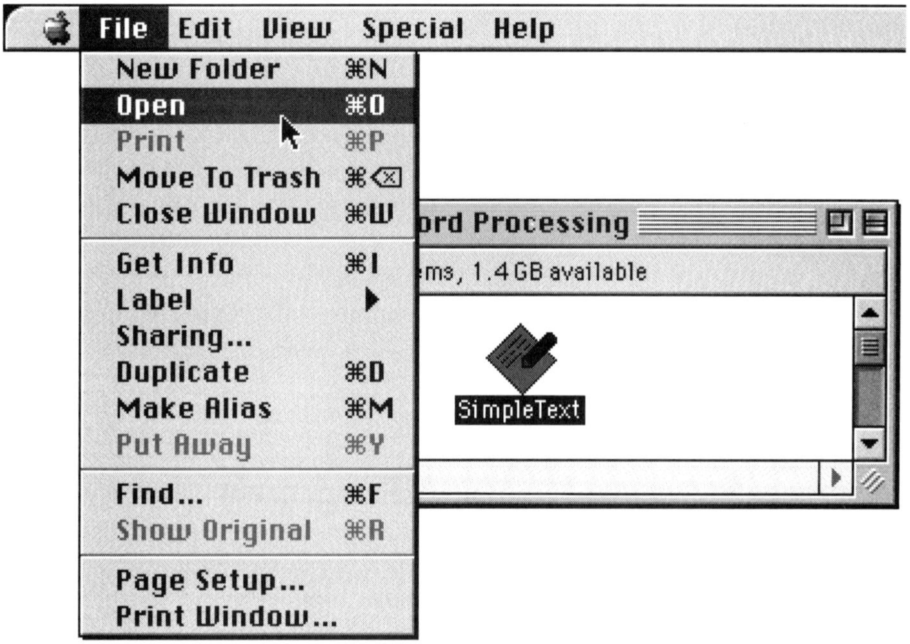

Figure 2-15 Starting a program by using the Open menu item.

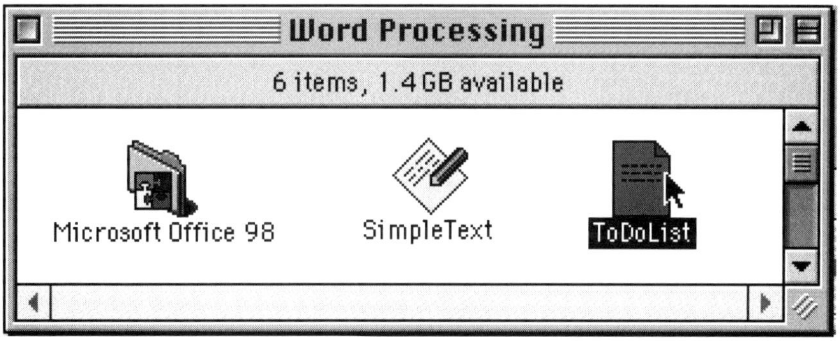

Figure 2-16 Double-clicking a file to start the corresponding program.

Using a Program

Once you've started a program, you can use it. Every program has a different purpose, so there's no one set of instructions that will cover using all programs. It's possible, however, to offer a variety of general tips that do apply to many programs. Once a program is running on your iBook, you're out of the realm of the Finder. Sure, you can probably still see a part of the desktop peeking out from behind any windows that the program's opened—but it is now the program that is in charge of your iBook. While getting a program running is done from the Finder, actually working within the program isn't Finder-related. With that in mind, program-running tips aren't appropriate for this section. For tips, look at the *Working With Software* section in the next chapter..

Switching Between Running Programs

The iBook's screen always has a menu bar running horizontally across the top. The names of the menus listed on the menu bar, however, will change depending on which program is *active*. Your actions on the computer affect only the active program. While a number of programs can run simultaneously, at any given time the iBook considers only one of the programs to be active. Other running programs are said to be running in the background.

Recall that the Finder is a program. If you move the cursor to a position anywhere over the desktop (as opposed to over a window that belongs to a different program that's running), and then click the mouse button, the Finder becomes the active program. Because it's active, the Finder's set of menus appears on the menu bar. Figure 2-17 shows the menus you'll see when the Finder is active.

When you click on a window belonging to a running program, that program becomes the active program, and as such, it takes over the menu bar and substitutes its own set of menus. For instance, Figure 2-18 shows what the menu bar looks like when a word processing document is open in Apple's own AppleWorks (a program included with the iBook) is running.

For comparison, Figure 2-19 shows what the menu bar looks like when the text editing program SimpleText (another program included with the iBook) is running.

Figure 2-17 The menu bar when the Finder is active.

Figure 2-18 The menu bar when a drawing is open in AppleWorks.

Figure 2-19 The menu bar when SimpleText is running.

When there's more than one program running, you'll have occasion to switch between them. That is, you'll want to work in one program (perhaps to, say, copy a picture from a graphics program), then another (to now paste the just-copied picture to, perhaps, a word processor window). To make any one program active you click on any open window that belongs to that program. To make the Finder active, move the cursor until it is anywhere over the Desktop and click the trackpad button.

An alternate means of making a running program active is to select it from the **Application** menu. As explained earlier, the **Application** menu lists by name all the currently running programs. Look back at Figure 2-13 to see this menu.

3

More Mac OS

If you're a first-time Mac user, then you've read the preceding chapter and are now ready to carry on with your quest to master the Macintosh operating system. If you've previously worked on a Mac, but only infrequently, then you too will want to work towards mastery of the operating system. In either case, you've come to the right place. In this chapter you move beyond the basics to discover how to work with files and folders. Here you also learn all about control panels—those marvelous little tools that reside under the Apple menu and allow you to customize many iBook features. Together the previous chapter and this chapter give you a solid foundation for getting the most out of the iBook. But at some point in working with your iBook you'll want to know more. This chapter closes by telling you where to go to learn still more about the Macintosh operating system.

Organizing Files and Folders

In the *Desktop Windows* section of the previous chapter you got a quick look at how the contents of a folder can be displayed in a window (refer back to Figures 2-4 and 2-5). But that section didn't discuss how to do anything with folders or with the files that are housed in them. That's what's covered here.

Many of the techniques discussed in the following pages can be carried out through the use of *contextual menus*. A contextual menu applies to a specific object; it appears and acts on only one object (which is the *context* of the menu). Because a contextual menu works with one specific object, you won't find the menu in the menu bar. Instead, it pops up right next to the object the menu is to act on. Just about every item on the desktop (and even the desktop itself) has a contextual menu associated with it. To see the menu, press and hold the Command key, move the cursor over the item, and then click and hold the trackpad button. On the left of Figure 3-1 you see the contextual menu for the desktop, while the right of the same figure shows the contextual menu for a folder.

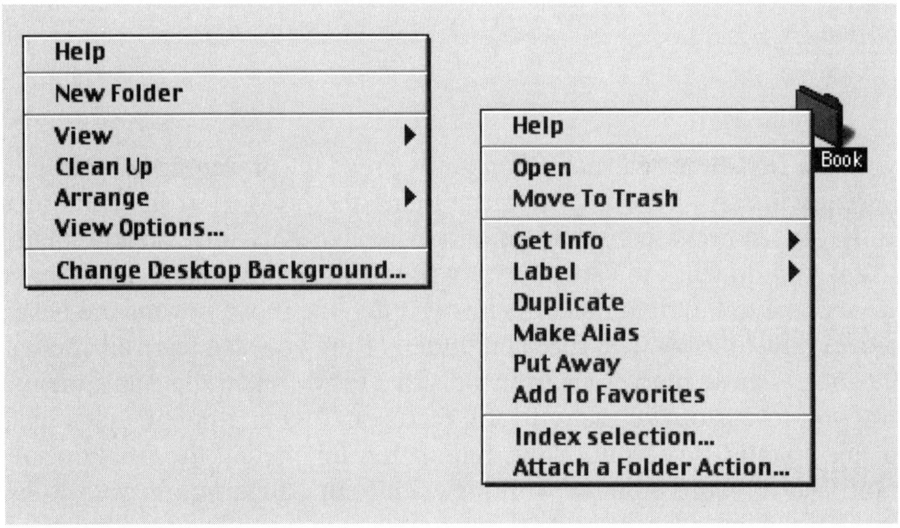

Figure 3-1 The contextual menus of the desktop and a folder.

Creating a New File or Folder

To create a new, empty folder, choose **New** from the Finder's **File** menu. If the desktop itself is active (if the desktop is the last thing you clicked on), that's where the new folder appears. If a window displaying the contents of a disk or folder is open and active, then the new folder appears in that window.

A new folder always appears with the name *untitled folder*. To change the folder's name, click once on the name, then type the new name.

Creating a new file isn't done on the desktop, it's done in the program appropriate to the type of file you're interested in. That is, if you want a new file that holds a letter to your mom, you'll need to run a word processor program and create the new file in that program. However, from the desktop you can create a *copy* of an existing file. To do that, see the *Copying a File or Folder* section below.

Moving a File or Folder

Moving a file or folder is simple—just drag it to where you want it to be. Specifically, you'll follow these steps:

1. Move the cursor over the icon of the file or folder you want to move.
2. Click the trackpad button and, with the button held down, drag the item to its destination—that is, to the icon of the folder or disk where you want the item to end up.
3. Release the trackpad button.

When you release the trackpad button, the item will appear wherever you've dragged it to.

Copying a File or Folder

Like moving a file or folder, copying a file or folder involves dragging the item—but with an added step. To make a copy, follow these steps:

1. Press and hold down the Option key.
2. Move the cursor over the icon of the file or folder you want to copy.
3. Click the trackpad button and, with the button held down, drag the file to its destination—to the icon of the folder or disk where you want the copy to end up.
4. Release the trackpad button.

When you release the trackpad button, the actual copying of the item begins. As the Finder performs the copy process, you will see a window in the center of the screen reporting its progress. That is, the window reports how long the process will take. Unless the item is very large (such as a folder filled with files), the Finder will copy the item in a matter of seconds.

Note
If you've added a second drive to your iBook (whether it is another hard drive or removable media such as a Zip drive), you can omit the first step when copying an item from one drive to another.

Deleting a File or Folder

You can *delete*, or *remove*, or *trash*, a file or folder (including the folder's contents) by placing the item in the Trash and then emptying the Trash. You move an item to the trash by dragging the item to the Trash can icon. To do that, click on the item's icon and, with the trackpad button held down, drag the item to the Trash can icon and release the button. Releasing the trackpad button moves the item into the Trash can.

As a precautionary measure, the Finder doesn't automatically delete an item that's been placed in the Trash can. Instead, you need to take the additional step of choosing **Empty Trash** from the Finder's **Special** menu. When you do that, a window appears that asks you to verify that you do indeed want to empty the Trash. If this sounds like a bit overcautious, it really isn't. Once an item is gone, it's gone forever, so the Mac just wants to make sure of your intent before it removes something permanently.

Tip
If you encounter the window that asks if you're sure you want the Trash emptied, and you can't remember just what it was that you put into the Trash (we've all done that at one time or another), press the **Cancel** button rather than the **OK** button. Then double-click on the Trash can icon to open a window displaying the contents of the Trash. If you've put an item in the Trash inadvertently, drag it out of the window now and place it on the desktop or in a folder.

Changing an Item's Icon on the Desktop

Every application displays a different icon. And files created by different programs have different-looking icons. Most folders—but not all—have similar-looking icons. You're probably content with the look of the icons on your desktop, but if you're not, you do have the freedom to change any of them. To do that, begin by clicking on the icon of a file or folder that has an icon you like. Then choose **Get Info** from the **File** menu. When you do that, you'll see a Get Info window similar to the one shown in Figure 3-2.

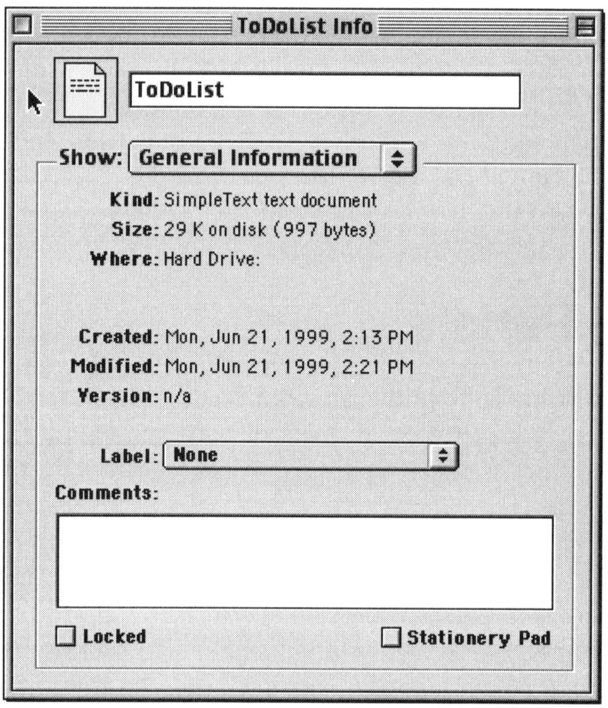

Figure 3-2 The Get Info window, with the icon selected.

This window provides you with a little information about the selected item. Just what information is revealed depends on the type of item it is. For a file, for instance, the Get Info window names the application that created it. That information wouldn't make sense for a folder or an application, so it's not given for an item of either of those types.

At the top of the Get Info window, you will see the item's icon. You can select this icon by clicking on it. Doing that places a thin frame around it, as shown with the icon of the *ToDoList* file in Figure 3-2. At this point, you can copy the icon to the clipboard by choosing **Copy** from the **Edit** menu. To transfer this copied icon to a different file or folder, repeat the above process: click on the file or folder of interest, choose **Get Info** from the **File** menu, and click on the item's icon in the Get Info window. Now, choose **Paste** from the **Edit** menu. When you close the Get Info window again, you'll see that the selected item now displays the new icon.

Important
Keep in mind that most files have a particular icon for a reason. Usually, it's so the user (that's you!) can quickly tell which program was used to create the file. With that in mind, you probably won't want to go about haphazardly changing the icons of all your files and folders simply because you know how to!

Control Panels

The biggest claim-to-fame of the Macintosh is that it is user-friendly. But with millions of users, who's to decide just what is user-friendly? Each and every one of those millions of users, that's who. True, by designing the Mac's graphical user interface—the system of menus, windows, and icons that make up the desktop and define how users interact with programs—Apple has made the biggest decisions on what's right for the user. But once the Macintosh operating system is in your hands (as it is now on your iBook), you have more than just a little control over how the desktop will look and behave. Back in the *Desktop Windows* section of Chapter 2 you saw an example of this when you read that the Finder's **View** menu allows you to customize the presentation of files and folders on the desktop. Here, you'll see that control panels offer even more flexibility in how the Finder looks and functions.

A *control panel* is a small software utility that acts as an interface between the Macintosh operating system and you, the user. Typically, a control panel has a specific, limited purpose. For instance, the Trackpad control panel defines how your trackpad responds. You use the Trackpad control panel to set how fast the cursor moves on screen in relation to how quickly you move a finger across the trackpad. You'll find a host of control panels in the Control Panels folder, which is easily accessible from the **Apple** menu located at the far left of the menu bar. To run a control panel, perform the following steps:

1. Move the cursor over the **Apple** menu and click and hold down the track pad button.
2. Use the trackpad to drag the cursor down to the **Control Panels** folder in the **Apple** menu.
3. Use the trackpad to drag the cursor over to the submenu (the secondary menu that appears off of the **Apple** menu).
4. Use the trackpad to drag the cursor over one of the control panel names and release the trackpad button to choose that control panel. I'm doing this in Figure 3-3 to run a control panel named Date & Time (which is discussed ahead).

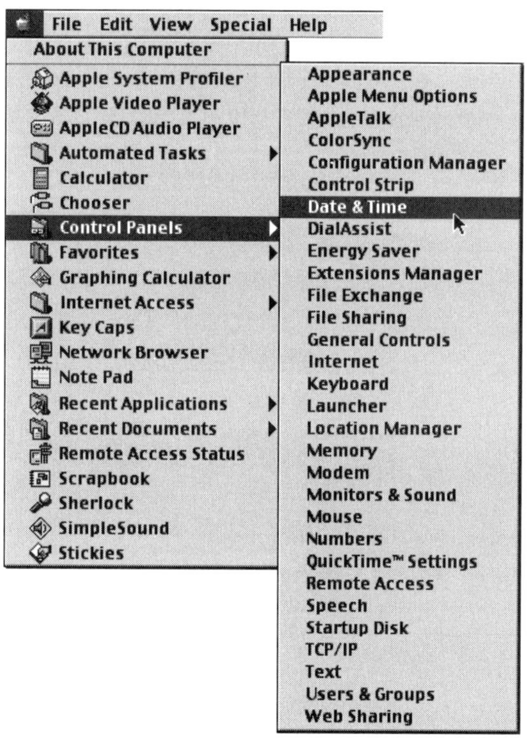

Figure 3-3 Choosing a control panel from the Apple menu.

Describing each of the dozens of control panels would take another couple of chapters, so I'll forego that task. Instead, I'll provide an overview of some of the more interesting panels, and leave the complete control panel exploration to you.

Appearance

Controls in the Appearance control panel affect the overall look of graphical elements, such as windows and menus. Using the Appearance control panel, you can define such things as the accent, or highlight, color used in the frames of windows, and the look of text used to display menu names in the menu bar.

Figure 3-4 shows the Appearance control panel. Note the tabs running along the top of the control panel. Clicking on any one tab changes the controls displayed in the content area of the control panel. That is, the various options in the control panel differ depending on which tab is currently selected. The Themes tab is perhaps the most interesting. Themes are a concept relatively new to the Mac OS. Clicking on a theme in the horizontally-scrolling list changes the overall look of your Mac's desktop. In the near future, you can expect that themes will give the user the ability to dramatically change the entire look of the desktop.

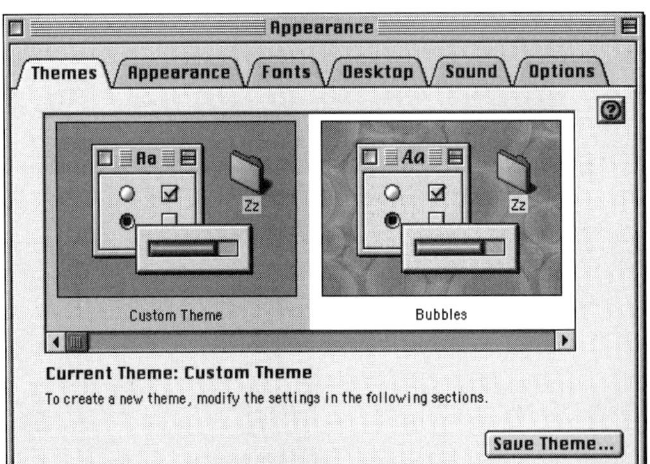

Figure 3-4 The Themes tab in the Appearance control panel.

Another tab of note in the Appearance control panel is the Desktop tab. You'll spend a lot of time gazing at the desktop, so it should have a look that is, at worst, neutral, and, at best, appealing. If your iBook's desktop doesn't fall into that range, use the Desktop tab to change it. Click the Desktop tab to see one of about fifty colors and patterns displayed in a miniature screen area in the control panel (see Figure 3-5). Use the horizontal scroll bar to view each and, when you encounter one you like, click the **Set Desktop** button to change the iBook's desktop to that color or pattern.

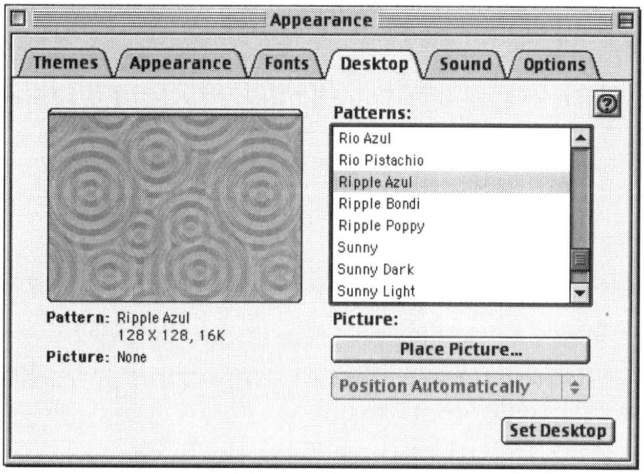

Figure 3-5 The Desktop tab in the Appearance control panel.

If you want something a little more exotic then a simple color or pattern, click on the **Place Picture** button (refer to Figure 3-5). That brings up a list of folders that hold available pictures to choose (see Figure 3-6). First click the **Show Preview** button to expand the window that holds the list. As shown in Figure 3-6, this additional area of the window displays a preview of the currently selected picture. Now click on the small arrow to the left of a folder to see the names of the pictures in that folder, then click on the name of a picture. When you've found a picture of interest, click the **Choose** button to dismiss the window and to return you to the Appearance control panel. The selected picture now is visible in the Appearance control panel preview area. Click the **Set Desktop** button to use the selected picture as the new desktop background. After choosing a picture, the control panel will appear similar to the one shown in Figure 3-6.

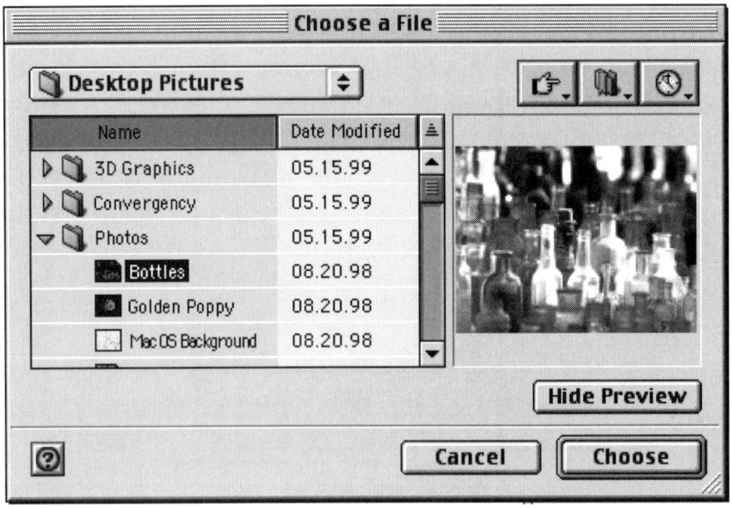

Figure 3-6 Choosing a picture to use as the desktop's background.

If you know how to use a graphics program or how to work with clip art, you can easily create your own patterns that will be recognized by the Appearance control panel. To add a color or pattern to the control panel, you must first get the desired item onto the clipboard. For instance, you can fill an area in a graphics program window with a pattern, use the program's selection rectangle tool to select part of the area, and then choose **Copy** from the **Edit** menu. Next, open the Appearance control panel. Now choose **Paste** from the **Edit** menu to paste the item into the control panel. That's it—the new pattern or color has been added to the dozens already stored in the control panel.

Adding a new picture to the ones recognized by the Appearance control panel is as easy as adding a new color or pattern. First, get the picture. This can be a graphic of your own creation, or an image from a CD-ROM collection, or a picture scanned into your computer. The Appearance control panel isn't too fussy about the *format* of the picture, either. For instance, you can use a PICT, GIF, or JPEG file and it will work fine (file formats are discussed in Chapters 4 and 14. Once you have a picture file, place it in the *Desktop Pictures* folder. As shown in Figure 3-7, you'll find this folder in the *Appearance* folder, which itself is in the *System Folder*. In Figure 3-7 I've added a picture named *My Own Picture!* to the *Desktop Pictures* folder. Now, when I click on the

Place Picture button in the Appearance control panel, my picture file will appear along with the names of the picture-holding folders that Apple has supplied.

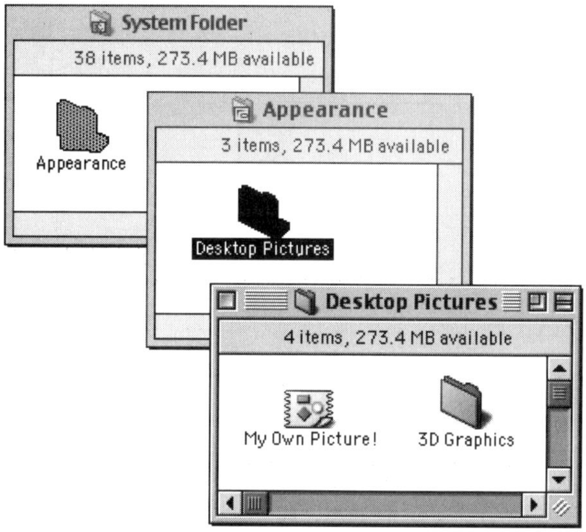

Figure 3-7 The folder that holds desktop pictures.

Control Strip

The Control Strip (see Figure 3-8) is a horizontal bar of icons. You'll find the Control Strip running along the bottom left of your iBook. If you see a small tab in the left lower corner of the screen, but no Control Strip, just click on the tab in order to cause the Control Strip to pop out. If there's not even a tab on the screen, open the Control Strip control panel (refer to Figure 3-9). In the Control Strip control panel you can choose to show or hide the Control Strip itself.

Figure 3-8 The Control Strip.

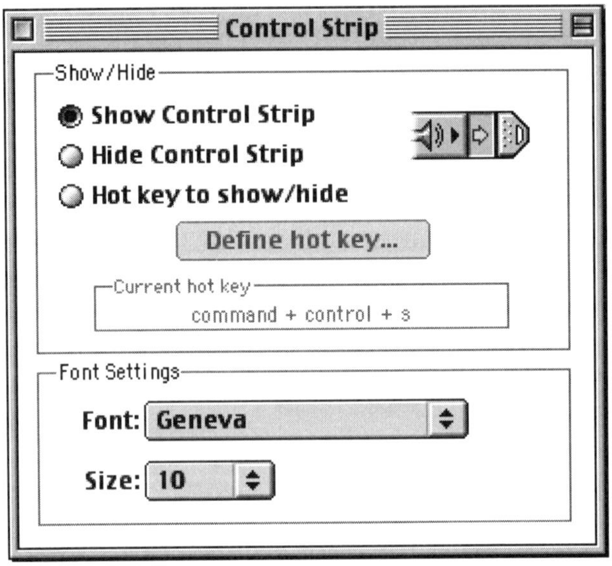

Figure 3-9 The Control Strip control panel.

Each icon on the Control Strip serves as a pop-up menu that provides you with access to setting some feature of the iBook—just click on an icon and hold the trackpad button down to view the icon's menu. In Figure 3-10 you see a few of the control strip menus. On the left is the energy menu—it lets you adjust various energy-saving settings. In the middle is the speaker volume menu, which is simply a slider that allows you to raise or lower the speaker volume. On the right is the monitor color depth menu—it lets you choose the number of colors your iBook's monitor is capable of displaying.

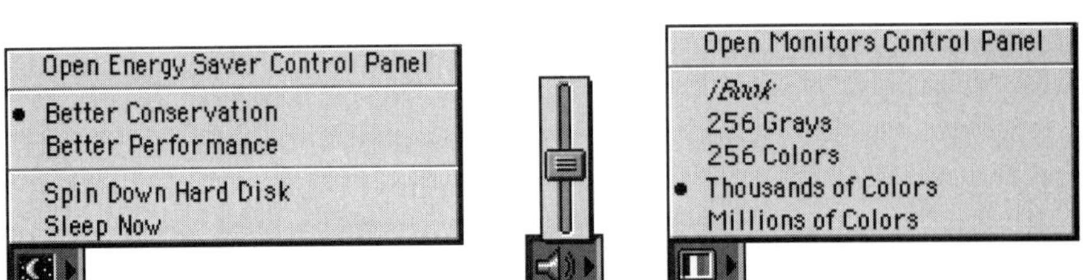

Figure 3-10 A few of the many control strip pop-up menus.

Note
The color depth refers to how many different colors can be displayed on the monitor at any given time. The more colors that can be displayed, the more realistic the appearance of detailed images such as digital photos. The drawback to setting the color depth high (to Millions of Colors) is that screen updating may slow down. The updating, or redrawing, or refreshing, of the screen occurs when the contents of the screen change (such as when a window is dragged to a new location). When the screen image changes, the iBook needs to redraw the image in its new location.

Date & Time

The iBook contains a battery that makes it possible for the computer to keep track of a few things, even when the iBook is turned off. The current date and time are two of the bits of information stored at all times. The Date & Time control panel allows you to change the time and date in case they are wrong, or in the event you move to a different time zone. You can also use this control panel to turn on or off the display of the current time and date near the right edge of the menu bar. When the display of the time and date is on, you can also use the Date & Time control panel to specify their format and appearance.

Keyboard

The Keyboard control panel lets you set a few key-related features, including the layout of the keyboard. Different countries have different keyboard layouts. That is, if you press one particular key on a computer set up for use in the United States, a different character may be displayed than would be when the same key was pressed on the keyboard of a computer set up for use in, say, France. If you check more than one country name in the Keyboard Layout section of the Keyboard control panel (see Figure 3-11), then a new menu will appear in the main menu bar after you close the Keyboard control panel. That menu will be just to the left of the Application menu that's always present at the far right in the main menu bar. Pick a different country from this menu and the keyboard layout will automatically change.

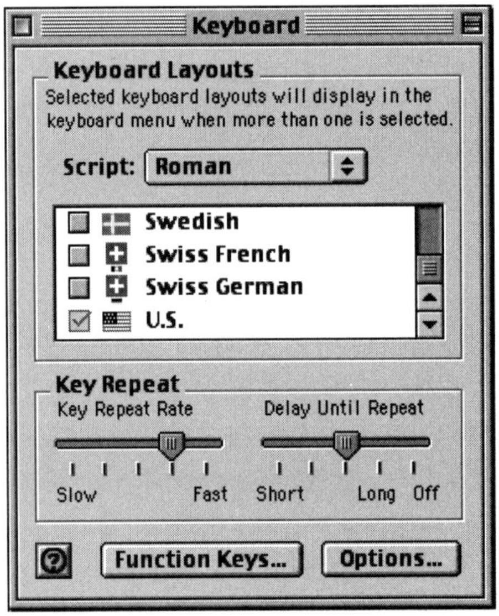

Figure 3-11 The Keyboard control panel.

The Keyboard control panel also lets you adjust the key repeat settings. The key repeat rate affects the speed at which characters are displayed should you hold down a key. The delay setting affects how short of a time must elapse before a holding down of a key is considered a signal to start repeating that one character on screen.

For iBook users the most interesting aspect of the Keyboard control panel is that it allows you to assign your own customized functions to some of the function keys. To do that, begin by clicking the Function Keys button (see Figure 3-11). Clicking this button brings up the Hot Function Keys window, as shown in Figure 3-12.

The F1 through F6 function keys are used to vary the monitor brightness, alter the speaker volume, and set a part of the keyboard to act as a numeric keypad (Chapter 1 offers more information on these function keys that have preassigned purposes). The F7 through F12 function keys are user-configurable. That is, you can set any or all of these function keys to act as shortcuts for opening servers, programs, folders, or documents. When you press one of these F7 through F12 keys in the Hot Function Keys window, a standard Open window appears. Here you select what it is you'll want started every time this one key is pressed. If you look at the box to the right of the F7 button in Figure 3-12, you'll see that nothing is assigned to this one function key. Now look at Figure 3-13 and you see that this function key now can be used to open the AppleWorks program. I set this one function key to do that by clicking on the F7 button (the button in the Hot Function Keys window, not the actual function key on the keyboard), navigating through the standard Open window that appeared until I came to the AppleWorks program, and then selecting that program. After closing the Keyboard control panel, anytime I want to run AppleWorks I simply press the F7 function key on my iBook keyboard.

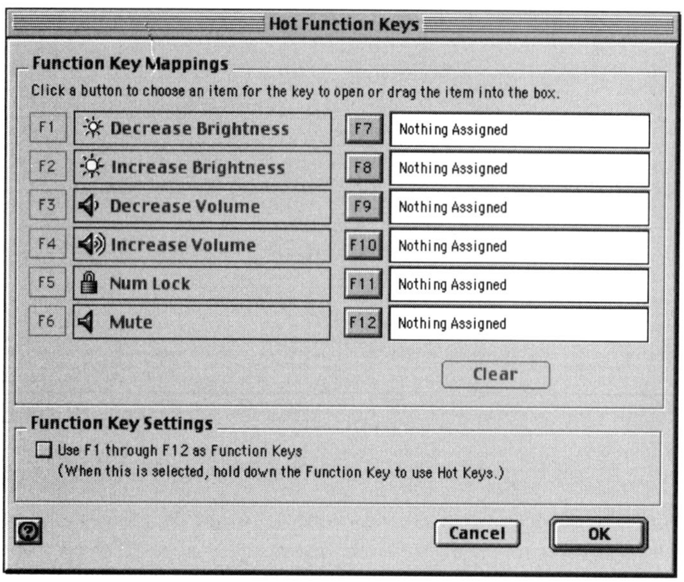

Figure 3-12 The Hot Function Keys window.

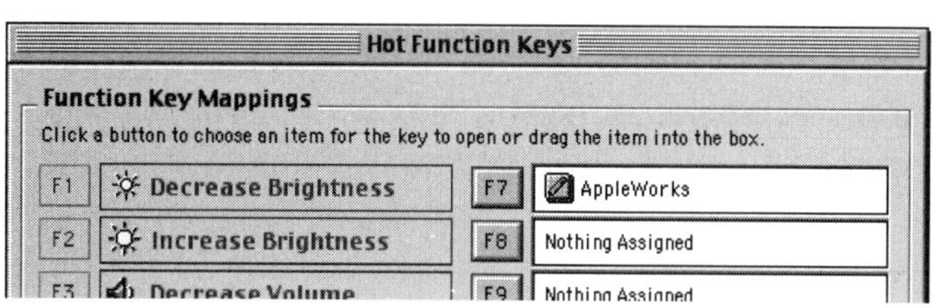

Figure 3-13 Setting up the Hot Function Keys keyboard.

Monitors

Use this control panel to specify information about the iBook's monitor. Clicking on either of the picture buttons at the top of the control panel window produces a different set of controls in the lower part of the window. Figure 3-14 shows the look of this control panel when the Monitor button is pressed. Here you set the number of colors (or shades of gray) that the monitor displays, as well as the monitor resolution.

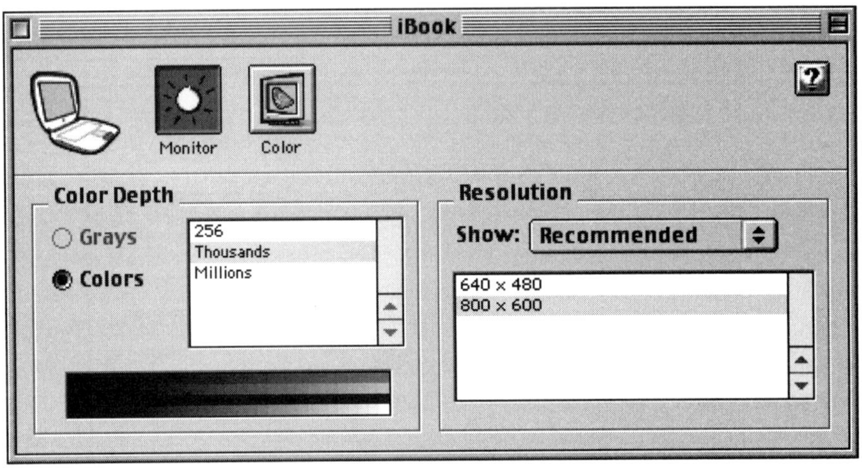

Figure 3-14 The Monitors control panel.

Clicking on the Color button in the Monitors control panel displays a list of ColorSync profiles. ColorSync is Apple's color management system that improves color consistency so that colors displayed on different devices match one another. If you aren't satisfied with how your iBook monitor is displaying colors, go ahead and experiment with this part of the control panel. Press the **Calibrate** button and you'll then walk through a series of windows that let you make immediate adjustments to the monitor. Don't worry about permanently affecting your iBook's display—when you reach the last window you have the option of canceling your choices to return to the original settings.

Sound

The Sound control panel—shown in Figure 3-15—lets you make a variety of sound-related adjustments to your iBook. Clicking on any one of the items in the list on the left of this control panel alters what's displayed in the rest of the panel.

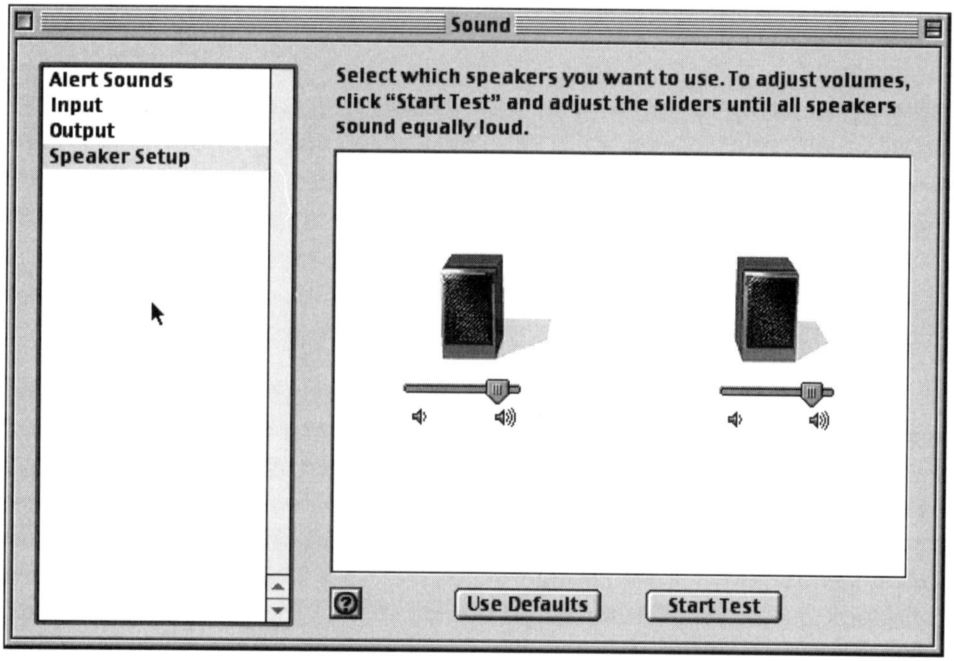

Figure 3-15 The Sound control panel.

Alert Sounds Click on Alert Sounds to display a list of sounds that can be used as the alert sound (the noise that gets played to alert you that some (usually) incorrect action just took place.

Input Here you choose a device for sound input. If you haven't added any input devices, then your iBook will be set up such that the sound input source is the CD drive. If you add an input device (such as the Griffen iMic as described in Chapter 10), then it will appear in the list of devices and you'll want to select it here.

Output Here you select a device for sound output. The iBook comes with a single built-in speaker, and that's the device that's selected initially. If you add externally powered speakers (refer to Chapter 10 for information), then you'll choose them here. Note that plugging in headphones in the iBook headphone jack doesn't require that you open the Sound control panel and alter the output device—your iBook automatically senses when headphones are plugged in, and switches the built-in speaker off to route sound output to the headphones.

Speaker Setup Use the speaker setup in the Sound control panel (Figure 3-15) to adjust the volume and balance of externally powered speakers. Even if you have only the single built-in iBook speaker, changes made here affect sound output. That's because the iBook has stereo sound capabilities, and the sound emitted from the one built-in speaker has both a "left" and "right" component.

Trackpad

If you've used a desktop Macintosh, then you may be familiar with the Mouse control panel—it lets you adjust mouse-related features such as the quickness at which you need to click the mouse button in order for two clicks to be considered a "double-click". The iBook has a Mouse control panel, but it won't see much use unless you buy and attach a mouse to your computer (you can do that with a USB mouse and the iBook's USB port—refer to Chapter 10). For iBook users, the Mouse control panel analogy is the Trackpad control panel shown in Figure 3-16.

In the Trackpad control panel you adjust how quickly the on-screen cursor reacts to your finger movement on the trackpad, how quickly you need to tap the trackpad button two times in order to have the clicks considered a double-click, and whether or not the trackpad itself (as well as the trackpad button) can be used as a button. The normal state of the trackpad is to have it be used to move the cursor. If you'd also like to be able to tap on the trackpad and have that tap recognized as a button click, then check the **Clicking** checkbox in the **Use Trackpad** for section of the Trackpad control panel.

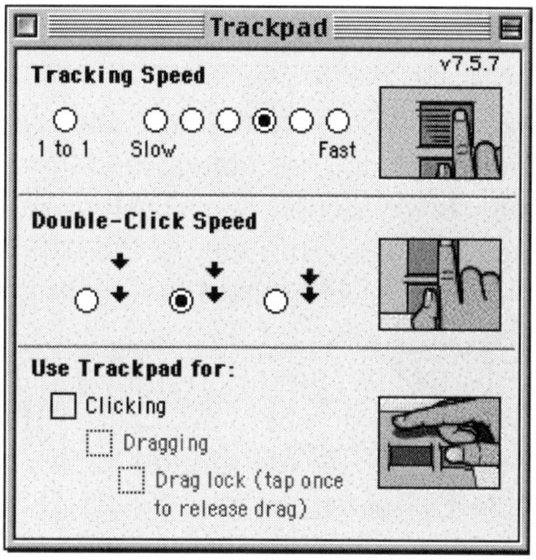

Figure 3-16 The Trackpad control panel.

Getting Additional Help

By now, you should be up to speed in working with the Macintosh operating system from the Finder (the desktop). But I won't claim to have covered every conceivable Finder topic in a single chapter. So, where to next? Apple offers a couple of online aids to help you learn more about working with your Mac. Both can be found in the **Help** menu, which is shown in Figure 3-17.

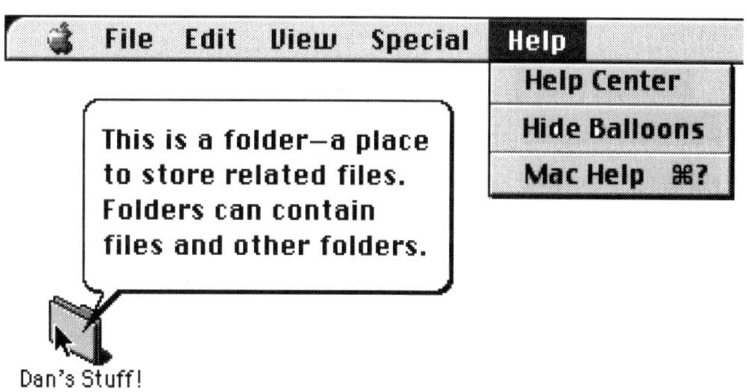

Figure 3-17 The Finder's Help menu and Balloon help.

Balloon Help

To get information about items located on the desktop, choose **Show Balloons** from the **Help** menu. This activates *Balloon help*. Now, as you move the arrow cursor slowly across the desktop, small cartoon-style balloons appear as the cursor crosses an item. In the balloon is a brief explanatory text that tells you what it is the cursor is hovering over. For instance, in Figure 3-17 I've got the cursor over a folder. You can see that Balloon help is letting me know what the icon represents (a folder) and what the icon is used for (storing things). To turn Balloon help off, choose **Hide Balloons** from the **Help** menu (after choosing the **Show Balloons** item, the words of the menu item toggle to read **Hide Balloons**).

Mac Help

The last item in the **Help** menu is the **Mac Help** item. Choosing this item opens the window shown in Figure 3-18. On the left of the Mac Help window is a list of main categories, such as *Disks* and *Memory*. Clicking on a category displays a list of subtopics on the right of the window. Clicking on a subtopic displays information about that subtopic. In Figure 3-18 you see that I've clicked the *Memory* category and am now about to click on the *Adjusting your memory usage* subtopic. After I do that, the contents of the window change to display information about the selected subtopic (see Figure 3-19).

Note

Choosing the first item in the **Help** menu, the **Help Center** item, brings up a window similar to the one shown in Figure 3-18. If you click on the Mac OS Help link in this window, you'll be right where you would be had you selected **Mac Help** from the **Help** menu. The Help Center window is used as the starting point for getting help on a few broad topics, such as the Macintosh operating system, QuickTime (the Macintosh movie-playing software) and Apple scripts (a means of automating some Mac tasks).

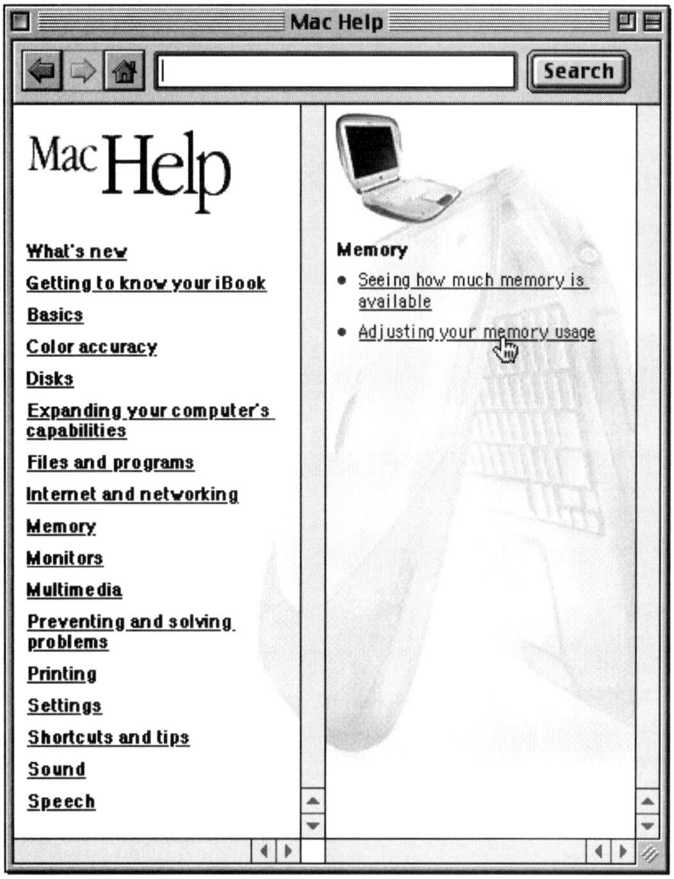

Figure 3-18 Categories of Mac help information.

Don't Forget to Get Help!

Balloon help is a good way to get a quick introduction to the major items on the desktop. After that, you may find it somewhat annoying to have balloons popping up all over the place! On the other hand, you should find Mac Help useful long after you've become familiar with the basics of working with the Finder. Mac Help includes information about a wealth of topics—some of which are a bit obscure. After using the iBook for a while, you may forget about Mac Help. If there's a task you want to attempt, and you can't figure out how to do it, don't forget about the **Help** menu!

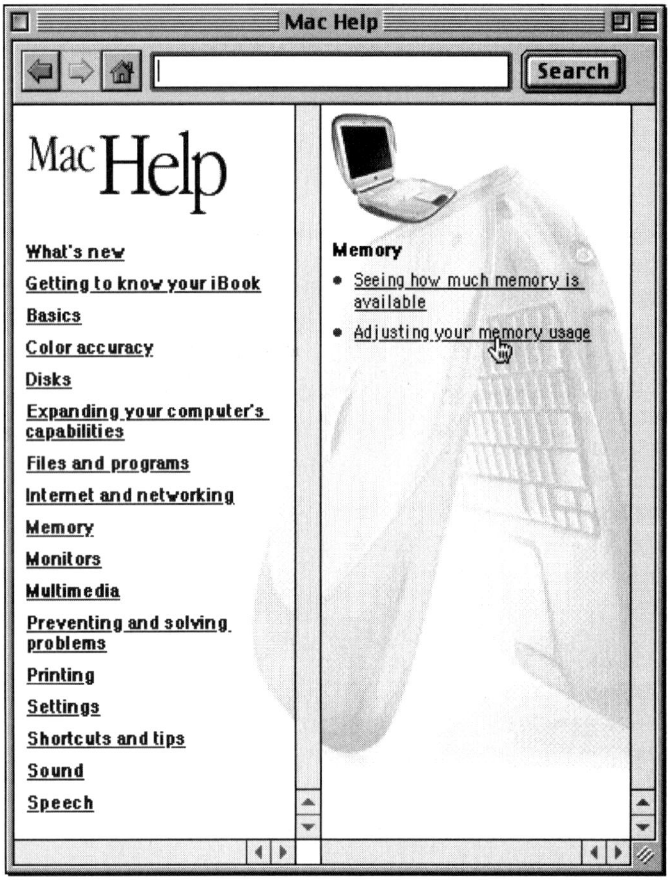

Figure 3-19 Help on one particular topic (memory).

4

Macintosh Software

In Chapter 2, you read that the Macintosh operating system is software that starts up automatically when you turn on, or *boot*, your iBook. But when people talk about software, they're usually referring to a particular software program. A Mac program has an icon on the desktop (or in a folder somewhere on the desktop) that you can double-click on in order to start that program running. A program also has a main purpose: a word processor is for creating letters and reports, a spreadsheet or database program is for organizing information, and a game is for, well, playing!

Where does software come from, what do you do with it once you have it, and how do you ensure that it doesn't "break" once you have it? In this section, you'll find several tips and pointers on finding, getting, and working with software.

Working with Software

Programs exist to serve different needs, and each requires that you have some different background information in order to take full advantage of the program's power. So it's *not* possible to describe how to use every Mac program in a few pages of this book! It is possible, though, to cover a few techniques that will work in a variety of programs. Your iBook comes with a number of programs already installed on its hard drive (and this chapter's *Getting Software* section tells you how to get more). Most of the techniques covered here apply to these programs, so go ahead, start one up and give it a try.

Using the File Menu

The **File** menu of most productivity programs such as word processors, drawing and painting programs, and spreadsheets have a number of menu items in common. In particular, you'll want to get acquainted with the **New**, **Open**, **Save**, **Print**, and **Quit** items. You can run the SimpleText program (included on your iBook) and click on the **File** menu (shown in Figure 4-1) to verify that it includes all these items.

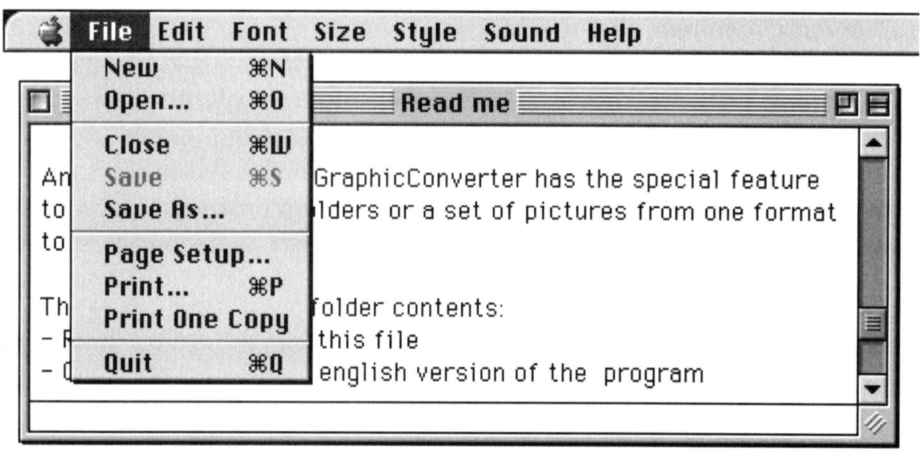

Figure 4-1 The File menu of the SimpleText text editor.

Here are some pointers to get you started with productivity programs. Note that these tips don't apply to games and some other types of "nonproductive" programs:

- **Creating a new work window** To create a new, empty window, choose **New** from the **File** menu. Then go ahead and create something. What you create depends on the type of program you're using, of course. In a word processor, you'll type in some words; in a drawing program, you'll draw something.
- **Saving your work to a file** After creating something, save your efforts by storing a window's contents in a file on your hard drive. Do that by choosing **Save** from the **File** menu.
- **Printing the contents of a window** Send a window's contents to your iBook's printer (if you have one, of course) by choosing **Print** from the **File** menu.
- **Opening an existing file** After creating a file, you can reopen that file at any time by choosing **Open** from the **File** menu.
- **Quitting the program** When you're all finished, quit, or exit, the pro gram by choosing **Quit** from the **File** menu.

Using a Program's Electronic Documentation

To get the most out of any program, you'll need to refer to the documentation that came with it. In the old days of personal computing (about two years ago!), each program typically came with one, two, or several printed instruction manuals. Now, most software vendors save money by placing the documentation in electronic files on the same CD-ROM that holds the program itself. Large, complicated programs often come with documentation in Adobe Acrobat *format*. On the left of Figure 4-2 is the icon of Acrobat Reader, Adobe's program that allows you to open and view Acrobat files. On the right, is the icon of a file created with the Acrobat program.

Tip

A file holds information. A file's *format* simply defines what particular program (such as Microsoft Word), or what type of program (such as any word processor), is capable of opening the file and displaying that file's contents in a window. No single program can open all types of files. The lowdown on file formats appears later in this chapter.

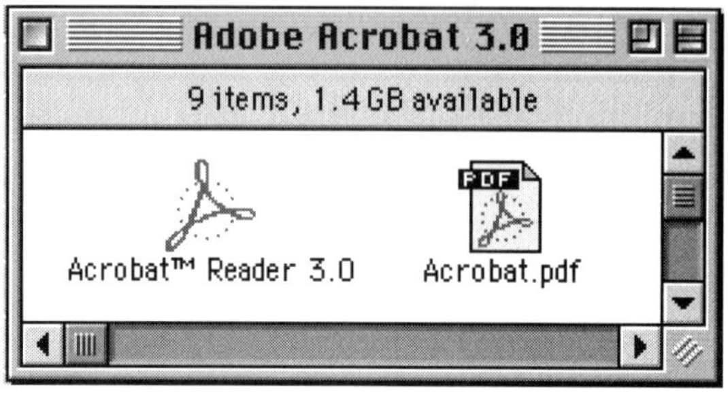

Figure 4-2 The Acrobat Reader program and an Acrobat file.

Simple programs usually include much less documentation, which is often in the format of a SimpleText file. Unlike the icon associated with the files of most other programs, SimpleText files have a variety of looks. The *About KeyWack* file shown in the bottom window in Figure 4-3 sports the "generic" icon you'll usually see on a SimpleText file. The *Solitaire Till Dawn User Guide* and the *Read Me* files in the upper window also are SimpleText files, even though their icons look quite different.

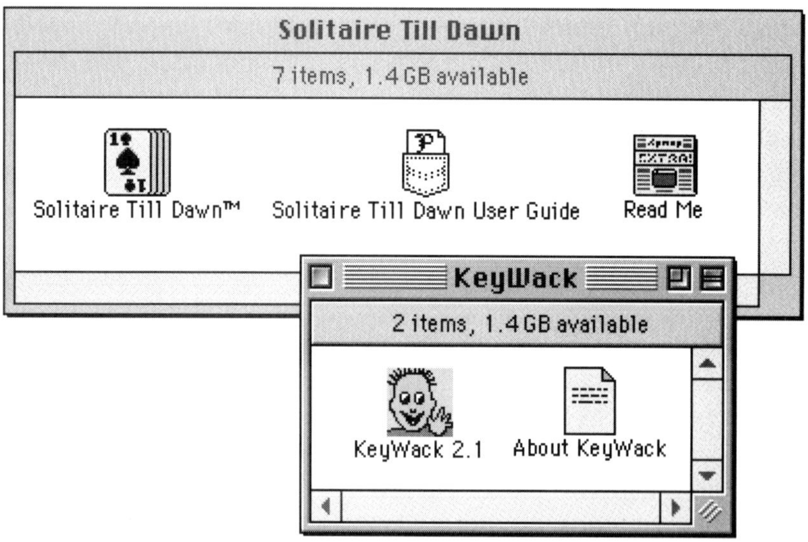

Figure 4-3 Documentation in a couple of different formats.

Note

Actually, SimpleText itself doesn't generate all these different icons for its files. The company that creates the documentation file customizes the look of the icon.

If you need to know all about a program, and that program is a sophisticated one, and it's included documentation is sparse, consider buying a third-party book. That is, a book distributed by a company other than the software supplier. You certainly can't be too averse to this idea, considering that you've followed this advice for hardware—you've purchased a third-party book rather than relying solely on the documentation supplied with your iBook!

Note

While I'm an author, this tip about buying books isn't a self-serving ploy! Though I've written close to twenty Mac-related books, only one of them (*Word 98 For Macs For Dummies*, co-written with Dan Gookin) is about a particular software package.

Using a Program's Online Documentation

The increase in online help included in programs coincides with the demise of printed documentation in software packages. Most programs now include one or more menu items that, when selected, offer you instructions or tips on using the program.

In the Chapter 3 *Getting Additional Help* section you read about the Finder's **Help** menu. This same menu appears not only in the Finder's menu bar, but also in the menu bar of any running program. Regardless of which program you're running, when you click on **Help** in the menu bar, you will notice that Balloon help is available. Choose **Show Balloons** to turn on Balloon help. Then move the cursor over an object onscreen (such as a button in a program window). A balloon holding text describing the item the cursor is over may appear. I say *may* because not all programs support Balloon help; Apple leaves it solely to the discretion of software developers whether or not

Balloon help is to be included in a product. To turn off Balloon help, again select the second item in the **Help** menu (which will have changed from **Show Balloons** to **Hide Balloons**).

If you look a little further down in the **Help** menu, you may find one or more menu items that offer assistance directly relating to the program you're working with. Like Balloon help, the inclusion of these additional helpful menu items is the software company's prerogative. As an example, in Figure 4-4 you can see that Netscape has elected to offer a wealth of information about using its Netscape Communicator browser software.

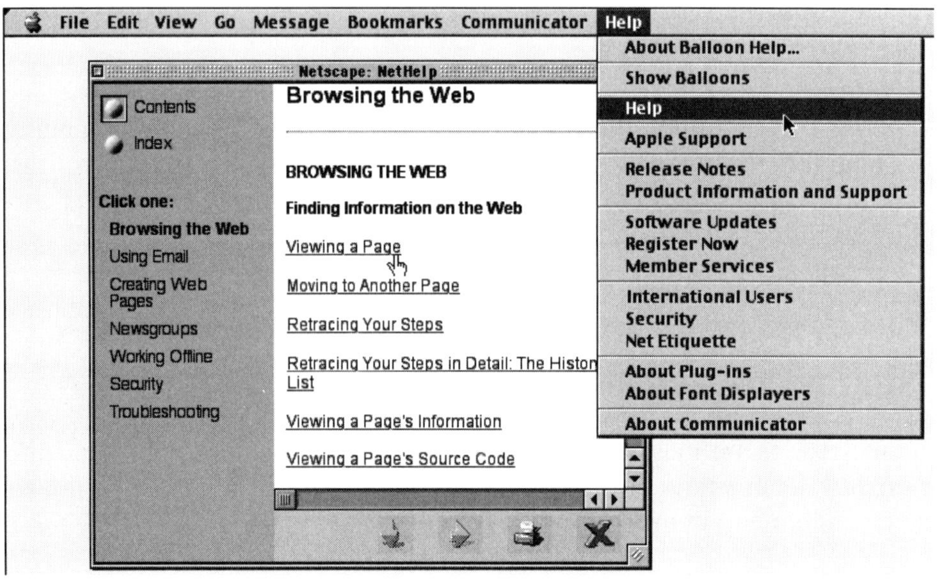

Figure 4-4 Some programs add help items to the Help menu.

What happens after you choose a program-specific item from the **Help** menu depends on how the software company implemented its help system. Here are a few common ways a program supplies you with online help in response to a selection from the **Help** menu.

- **Help Viewer** When you choose **Mac Help** from the **Help** menu of the Finder, you'll see the Mac Help window pictured near the end of Chapter 3 (see that chapter's Figure -18). This window is a Help Viewer window, which can be used to display more than just information on the Mac OS. Some programs opt to use the Help Viewer to supply users with program help. When they do, you'll see a window that looks and works just like the one shown in the previous chapter's Figure 3-18. Instead of information on how to use the Macintosh operating system, though, this window is now used to navigate to information on topics specific to the program being used.
- **On-disk files** Selecting a **Help** menu item in some programs opens a file that was placed on your hard drive during the installation of the program being used. In Figure 4-4 the content of the Navigator help window is dis playing information from disks.
- **Internet-based help** Some programs store help at the software vendor's Web site. If you choose such a menu item, and you're currently connect ed to the Internet, your Web browser will load the appropriate informa tion from the Web.

File Formats

Every file holds data, or information. Every file has a *format* that defines the organization of the file's data. If your iBook understands the format of a file, it associates the appropriate icon with that file. Figure 4-5 provides a few examples.

Figure 4-5 A folder with files of a few different types.

The file named *XMasList* bears the icon of a SimpleText file. SimpleText is a text editor program, so you know that the *XMasList* file holds nothing but text. Double-clicking on the *XMasList* file automatically opens the file. (If the SimpleText program isn't running at the time the file is double-clicked on, then that act automatically starts up the SimpleText program and then opens the file.) The file named *BanksToRobFor$XMasListItems* has the icon of a Microsoft Word word processor file, so you know that it can be opened by Microsoft Word. (By the way, if you are an FBI agent, or a representative of any other policing agency, please note that the file names in Figure 4-5 are a joke, okay? A joke, really!). The *generic* icon associated with the file named *ABC.xyz* doesn't provide a clue as to what program it's associated with. It isn't the mysterious file name that's stymied the iBook. Rather, the computer has been confused by its inability to determine the file's type.

Note

A file is often thought of as something that's opened by a program. That's true. But the program *itself* is a type of file, too. So when people talk about downloading a file, they could be referring to a file that you open with an application program (such as a Word document that you open with Microsoft Word), or a file that actually is a program (such as a shareware game).

Any one program recognizes only a limited number of file formats. If you run a program and choose **Open** from its **File** menu, you'll be able to see the type of files that that program can work with. Figure 4-6 shows the Open window for Microsoft Word.

In Figure 4-6, I've dropped down the **List Files of Type** pop-up menu to show all the types, or formats, of files that Microsoft Word is capable of opening. Besides being able to open files that it created itself (called Word Documents in the pop-up menu), Word is able to open plain text files, files created by some other Microsoft programs, and several other types of files.

Microsoft Word can open a variety of types of files. Some programs can open fewer types, some more. But no single program can open all types of files. While it would be nice if there was a single, monolithic, all-encompassing Mac program that *could* understand, open, and display *all* file types, such a beast just doesn't exist. And, of course, there's a good reason for this: it takes a lot of programming effort to support many different file formats. That's a point that may raise the question of why different formats exist in the first place.

A file format defines how data is organized in a file. Different types of files hold different types of data, so different organizational *schemes*, or plans, are needed. Chapter 14 describes creating your own Web page. If that's a topic that interests you, then in that chapter you'll see that the chief step in building a Web page is the creation of an HTML file. Figure 4-7 shows the contents of a very simple HTML file, as displayed in a window.

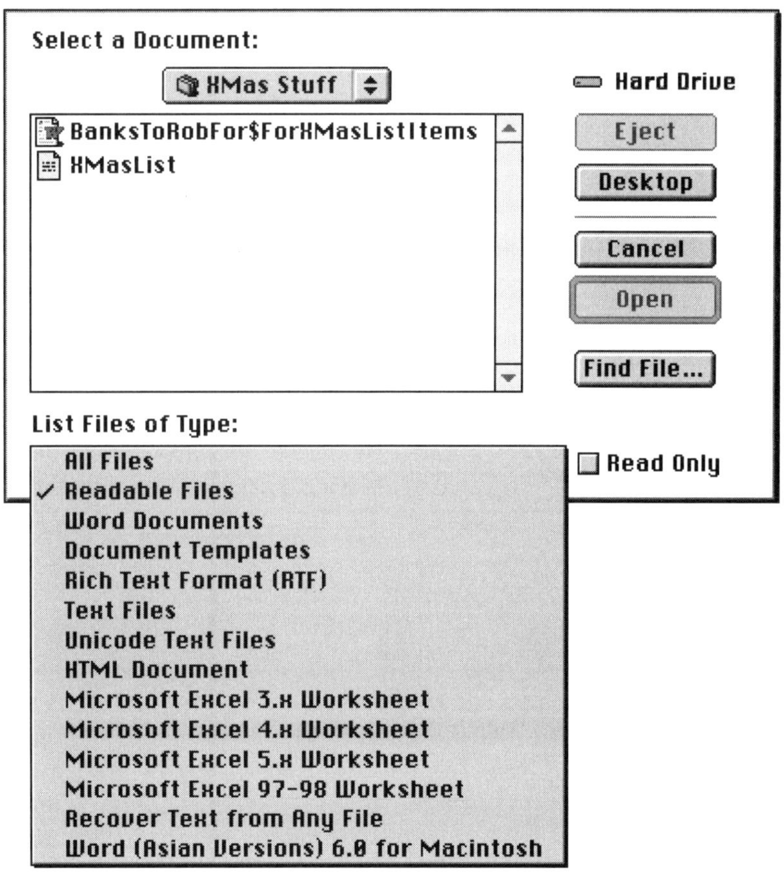

Figure 4-6 Microsoft Word can open different types of files.

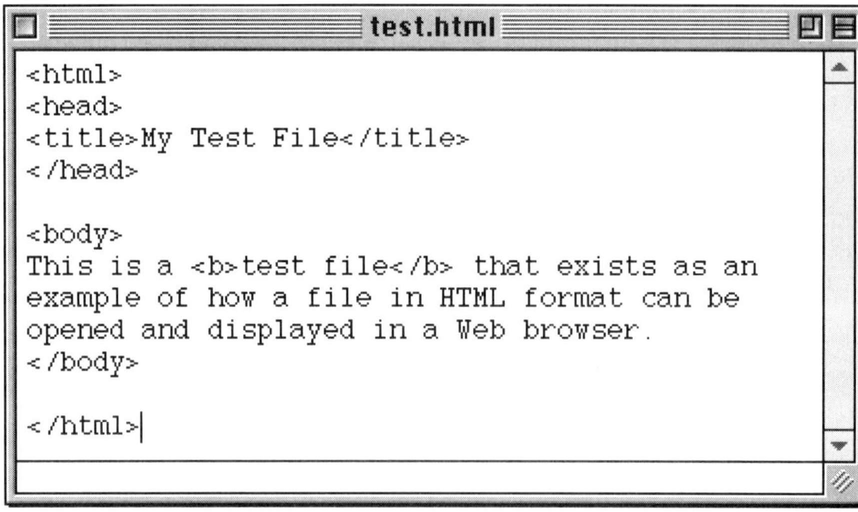

Figure 4-7 An HTML file opened in a text editor.

In Figure 4-7, the file named *test.html* was opened in the SimpleText text editor. When that same file is opened from a Web browser, its contents look different. Figure 4-8 shows how the same file looks when opened by Microsoft Internet Explorer.

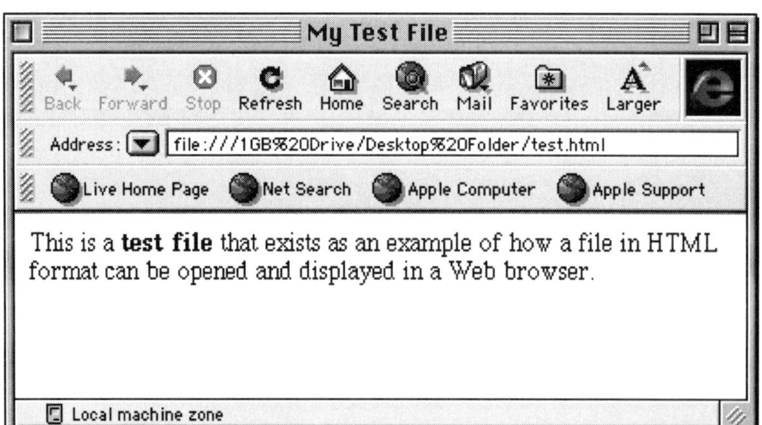

Figure 4-8 An HTML file opened in a Web browser.

In Figure 4-7, you can see that SimpleText displays a lot of information that isn't displayed by the browser. That's because SimpleText isn't equipped to treat an HTML file any differently than it treats a text file. SimpleText interprets the *test.html* file as one that simply holds text. Internet Explorer, on the other hand, was designed to recognize the HTML file type. When a file has a name that ends with *.html* or *.htm*, Internet Explorer knows its contents are in HTML format. When it opens such a file, it knows how to interpret the text between the angle brackets (< >). For instance, when Internet Explorer encounters words between the <b> and </b> "flags," it places those words in boldface type.

Note

There's nothing in particular you need to memorize or fully understand about the HTML example. It's simply presented here to reinforce the idea that different programs recognize different types of files, and that it would be a mighty task for one program to be able to recognize all types of files.

Finding and Getting Software

The iBook comes with a nice assortment of software—but it isn't enough! It won't be long before you will want to pick up a few more programs. Many computer and appliance stores sell Macintosh software, but no single store can possibly carry the *thousands* of Mac titles that exist. In this section, you'll read about the different categories of software available for the Mac, and where to get programs from each category.

Types of Software: Commercial, Shareware, and Beta

There are several ways to categorize software, one of which is by the way programs are distributed.

Commercial Software

When you walk into a CompUSA or Best Buy store and peruse its shelves of boxed software, you're looking at commercial software. A commercial program is one that is sold through what's thought of as "normal" distribution channels (such as stores and perhaps directly from the manufacturer). A commercial program is also one that's paid for in a "normal" way—you need to pay for the product before you can possess it.

A commercial program may be developed by a legion of programmers working for months or even years. The result of these efforts is mass-duplicated on CD-ROMs, boxed, distributed to retail stores, and often advertised in national computer catalogs and magazines. As you can imagine, it's an expensive process. So, while some commercial programs sell for $19.95 or $29.95, many sell for hundreds of dollars.

Shareware and Freeware

Creating and selling a commercial program takes a lot of labor and a lot of marketing. So it's expensive. But what if just one, two, or a few programmers can develop a program (often a *utility*—a small program that serves some very specific purpose)? How can an individual, or a few people, who perhaps wrote a program in their spare time, afford to package, distribute, and advertise their software? They can't. The best option for a small developer is to release a program as *shareware*. A shareware program is usually made available at a Web site, where you (or anyone else) can download it directly to your computer.

After trying out the program for a trial period (typically 30 days), you must decide whether to keep the program (if you find it useful) or to remove from your hard drive (if it didn't meet your expectations). Only if you keep the program do you buy it, by sending money to an address listed in the program's introductory screen. With shareware, you take possession of a program before you pay for it. So what prevents people from simply keeping a shareware program without paying for it? Low fees and honesty. A program distributed as shareware costs far less than a commercial program, so paying the $5 to $30 that most shareware programs cost isn't a big expense. And while some people find it possible to justify not paying a large, faceless company for its efforts, most people have trouble withholding a few dollars from a person they know has worked hard and then placed trust in the public to make those efforts pay off.

Freeware is similar to shareware in that it is generally developed by just one, or a couple, of programmers, and is then distributed on the Internet. As its name implies, however, the developer of a program described as freeware expects no compensation from anyone who downloads and keeps the program. Yes, some people enjoy programming *that* much!

Important
Support shareware! If you obtain a shareware program and, after a trial period, find it useful, *pay for it*! Shareware fees are usually low, so paying for a program *won't* be a great financial burden for you. Not paying for a shareware program that you use *will* be a great financial burden on the developer. For a shareware developer, paid shareware fees are the *only* means of compensation for hundreds or even thousands of hours of hard work. Someone who develops one good shareware program but doesn't reap any benefits from the effort won't be likely to develop a second program. And the whole Macintosh community suffers when that happens.

Beta

When a company decides to upgrade a program, it spends time determining what features should be added to the program. While a particular feature may sound good in theory, the only way to find out if users really want the supposed improvement is to add the feature and let users try out the program. A similar situation exists for bugs—errors in the program's code that manifest themselves by causing a program to do unexpected things, including crashing. A company may feel it has "squashed" the bugs in the new version of a program, but it can't be sure until the program is tested on a large variety of configurations (that is, a number of different Mac models, with different combinations of system software). How much would *you* pay for a program that may have poorly designed features and computer-crashing bugs? Right. A software company knows this, so what it may do is to *freely* distribute a beta, or pre-release, version of a program before marketing the final version.

Anyone who opts to obtain a beta version of a program (usually by downloading it from a company's Web site) is expected to report back to the company (typically by jotting off an e-mail) with a list of any discovered problems. The company then incorporates the feedback into the new version of the program. Shareware, too, can be released in beta form, but that's a less likely scenario.

Important
Use beta software at your own risk! There's a good reason that a program that may normally sell for hundreds of dollars is given away free: it very likely still has some undiscovered bugs.

Commercial Software: What and Where

When it comes to Mac software, "Where to buy?" isn't the only question you may have. With thousands of programs available, you'll probably also wonder "What to buy?" Apple, and a few other companies, can help you answer both questions.

Apple's Software Site

Apple's own Macintosh Products Guide Web site at macsoftware.apple.com provides help in determining both what to buy and where to buy it. When you visit the Macintosh Products Guide site, you first navigate to the area of the site that displays information in your language. After that you can choose to view software information by clicking on the large **Software** button (there are a few other buttons, too, including **Hardware** and **Search**). Doing that displays a list of topics—as shown in Figure 4-9.

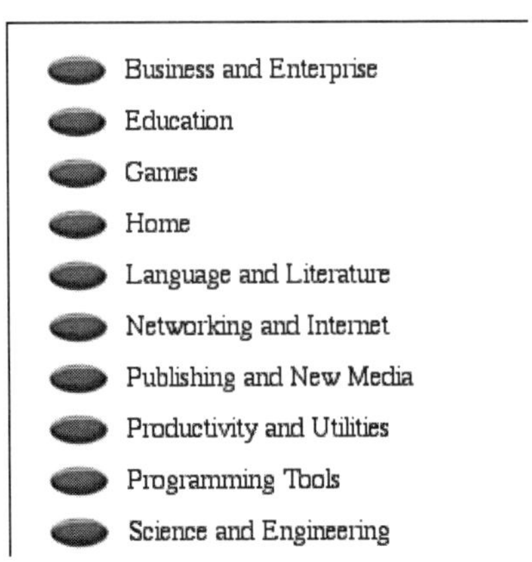

Figure 4-9 The software topics at the Macintosh Products Guide site.

Here, you only need to know the topic that appeals to you—you don't need to know the exact name of a program, or whether a program related to this topic even exists. Click on a topic in the list and you'll move to a page that displays a list of subcategories. For instance, if you select **Home**, you'll see a list that includes Early Learning (Ages 2 - 5), Astrology, Cookery, Health, Pets, and more. The leftmost window in Figure 4-10 shows a part of this list. Now click on a topic of interest and click the **Find** button to proceed to a list of programs that fall into the selected topic. The middle window in Figure 4-10 shows the list of programs that appeared when I selected Mythology. In college I didn't fare well in my Greek Mythology class, so back then I probably could have used a software-finding service like this! Click on the name of a particular program and you'll be whisked off to a page that describes it. The rightmost window in Figure 4-10 shows a part of that page for a program called Greek Mythology I.

Note
Okay, you caught me. I didn't do "not so well" in Greek Mythology, I "failed it". In my defense, I must say that if I had ever left the university's Computer Lab to attend the mythology lectures, I'm just *sure* I would have done fine in the course!

Figure 4-10 Locating information about a software program.

The program's description page includes a link to the program developer's Web site. If you think you may be interested in buying the program, you can visit that site to find out the price of the program and other ordering information.

Mail and Online Software Sales

There are a number of mail order companies that distribute Mac-only catalogs. If you don't know exactly what software you want, the simple act of paging through a catalog of Mac software may give you an idea of what programs are available and how much they will cost you. Macintosh mail order companies used to be just that—mail order. With the rise of Internet sales, though, most now offer online ordering, as well. These are some of the most popular mail order/online order Mac suppliers:

Mail Order Company	Online Address
ClubMac	`www.club-mac.com`
MacConnection	`www.macconnection.com`
MacMall	`www.macmall.com`
MacWarehouse	`www.md.warehouse.com`
The MacZone	`www.maczone.com`

Shareware and Freeware: What and Where

Macintosh shareware and freeware is everywhere. Everywhere on the Web, anyway. There are a variety of Web sites that exist solely to store such Mac programs. Some of the more popular such sites are listed here.

MacShare.com

A great site for downloading Macintosh programs and utilities is MacShare.com at `www.macshare.com`. From this page you click on a category name (such as Game'ware, Graphic'ware, Internet'ware, or the all-encompassing Other'ware) to move to a list of programs to download. Each listed program is accompanied by such information as the program's version number, size, and a brief but informative description. Click on a program name to download the program, or click on the Homepage link by the program of interest to visit the program creator's Web site.

Shareware.com

The Shareware.com site at `www.shareware.com` is another very useful site for finding shareware. This site doesn't play platform favorites, so before beginning a search for a program, you need to specify what *platform* (type of computer) the search should be limited to. Do that by choosing **Macintosh** from the **by platform** pop-up menu to limit the search to Macintosh-only files. Then enter a topic or program name in the **search for** box. Finally, click the **Search** button. Shareware.com returns a list of matching files and file descriptions; each file name serves as a link to download that file. The Shareware.com site searches a number of Macintosh shareware/freeware archives on the Web, so a search may return duplicate file names if the same file is stored at different Web archives.

AMUG Shareware Collection

AMUG (Arizona Macintosh Users Group) at `cdrom.amug.org` offers you a couple of ways to get hold of Macintosh shareware. You can buy their four CD-ROM set of shareware programs for $39, or you can freely download individual program from the AMUG site at `cdrom.amug.org/http/bbs/files.html`. Here you click on a topic (such as Games, Education, or Programming) in order to move to an area that holds programs of interest to you.

Info-Mac Archive

The Massachusetts Institute of Technology (MIT) maintains the Info-Mac archive—a large collection of Macintosh shareware and freeware. Don't let the location of this collection scare you into thinking that there's nothing here but programs for engineers. The programs here are gleaned from a variety of sources and fall into all sorts of categories. At the Info-Mac archive at `hyperarchive.lcs.mit.edu/HyperArchive/HyperArchive.html`, you can search for programs by keyword or look at a list of programs by category. Each entry in a list includes an Abstract link that provides a description of the program and a Download link that lets you download the program.

UMich Mac Archive

Are you getting the impression that college students like the Mac? Here's another university that maintains a Mac shareware/freeware site. Go to `www-personal.umich.edu/~sdamask/umich-mirrors/` (note that there is a hyphen between "www" and "personal", and another hyphen between "umich" and "mirrors") as the first step in reaching the University of Michigan's site for Macintosh shareware and freeware. Then scroll down the page a bit to the **University of Michigan Macintosh Archive Main Site** heading and click on the WWW box beneath it. Doing that takes you to a page of software categories. Clicking on a category takes you to a list of programs. A click on a program name downloads that program to your iBook.

The UMich Mac archive isn't big on file descriptions, so you'll either need to know the name of the program you're looking for or be able to surmise a program's purpose by its listed name. Better yet, visit a *search engine* (a Web site capable of searching either a different Web site or the entire World Wide Web) that's set up to search the UMich Mac archive and return descriptions of matching results.. One such engine is located at `www.nexor.com/mac-archive/mac-archive.html`.

Note
If you aren't familiar with *mirror* sites, the University of Michigan's Macintosh archive page may be a bit confusing to you. Some Web sites that provide programs for downloading have so much activity (many people attempting to visit the site at the same time) that the managers of the site mirror, or duplicate, the content of their site on other servers. That is, they find other Web sites willing to supply extra disk storage space for them. The University of Michigan's Macintosh archive is such a site, and one of the main purposes of its home page is simply to provide a list of links to the many other sites that serve as mirrors.

Beta Software: What and Where

By definition, a program's beta version is an unfinished version. A beta version is free, but there may still be a cost associated with the program. That cost is the aggravation you feel as you try to determine just why your iBook is crashing more often than usual. No, not all beta programs cause frequent crashes, but some do. And, infrequently, a beta version may even damage other files on your hard drive. The choice to download free beta software is, of course, your choice to make—but I won't encourage the practice here!

5

America Online: Internet Complete

When America Online began, its emphasis wasn't on the Internet. Instead, AOL came into existence to serve as a very user-friendly virtual community for computer users who were, by and large, not entirely comfortable with the technical side of computers. AOL created its own point-and-click software program that made it easy for even a computer novice to connect not to the Internet, but to America Online's own server computers. Once connected, this same software let AOL members send electronic mail to each other, download files, and gather news and information. As the Internet has surged in popularity, America Online has devoted significant resources to giving members an Internet experience that is also user-friendly.

If you're an America Online member, you can send and receive e-mail, transfer files across the Internet, visit newsgroups, and browse the World Wide Web. In this chapter you'll see how to do all that, and more. Once you're comfortable carrying out all these tasks, you'll be ready to move on to Chapters 8 and 9 to read more about Web browsers (you don't have to use the browser that's built into the America Online software) and what to do and where to go on the Web. If America Online is your means of connecting to the Internet, then you can safely skim or skip altogether Chapter 6, which discusses connecting to the Internet by way of an Internet service provider (though you may want to read that chapter's description of the Internet and World Wide Web). The same holds for Chapter 7, which talks about how those who connect with an Internet service provider can use e-mail and visit newsgroups.

Getting Started

If you've never accessed AOL from your iBook, and you want to now, you'll need to perform some basic setting up of the America Online software. This set up applies whether you're new to AOL or are an AOL member whose accessed America Online from a different Mac—so everyone should read the next section—*All Users: Setting Up*. After that, read one of the two sections that follow. If you don't have an AOL account, read the *New Users: Signing Up* section and skip the *Current Users: Using An Existing Account* section. If you already have an AOL account, just read the *Current Users: Using an Existing Account* section.

All Users: Setting Up

Your iBook has the America Online software in the *Internet* folder on its hard drive. Though the software is on your iBook, that software doesn't know anything about you or your iBook. To get set up, double-click on the America Online icon. When you do that you encounter the AOL Setup screen. As shown in Figure 5-1, here you'll click the **Begin automatic setup** radio button, then click the **Next** arrow.

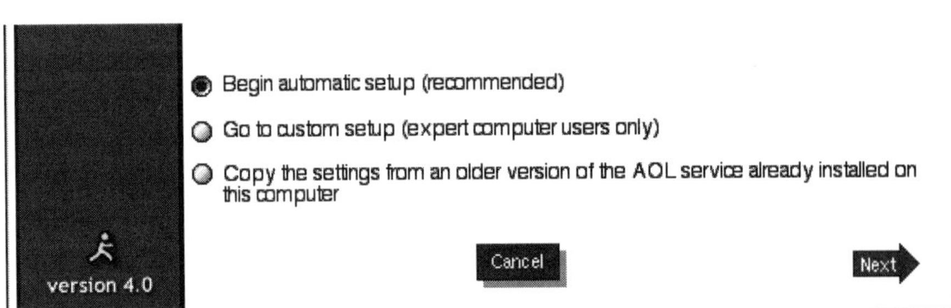

Figure 5-1 Starting AOL automatic setup.

Tip

There's also an America Online installer on your iBook Software Install CD should ever need to reinstall the program. That shouldn't be necessary. However...on rare occasions programs become corrupt (damaged), or accidentally deleted. In such a case you can use the installer to place a pristine copy on your iBook hard drive. To do that, insert the iBook Software Install CD into your iBook's CD drive, open the Internet folder and America Online folder, and double-click on the Install AOL 4.0 (PPC) program. A *path* is the folder route to take to find a file. In the above text the path to the America Online installer program is `iBook Software Install: Internet: America Online: Install AOL 4.0 (PPC)`. As new versions of the iBook come out, different software may be included, and the location of that software may vary from locations on previous iBooks. So, as you read this book—or any other computer book—don't immediately become alarmed if the path the author describes doesn't lead you to the file in question. Instead, use Sherlock (choose **Sherlock** from the **Apple** menu) to find the file you're looking for.

The AOL software now examines your iBook to determine the type of modem connected to the your computer. After a few moments it will report the result back to you in the Confirm Your Connection screen. Click the **Next** arrow.

The Confirm Your Dialing Options screen lets you set a few dialing options. Figure 5-2 shows the settings for many households. Most people have touch-tone service, so that check box gets checked (AOL automatically checks it for you). If your iBook is in an office, you may need to check the **outside line** check box and enter the number, followed by a comma, of the digit that needs to be pressed to gain access to numbers outside your company. If the phone service for the phone line you're using with your iBook includes call waiting, you may want to turn off that feature during the duration of each connection to America Online. If it's not turned off while you're connected, and someone tries to call you on that same line, your connection to AOL may get interrupted. Dialing *70 turns call-waiting off, so checking the call waiting check box is all you need to do here. Click the **Next** arrow when you're done.

In the Search for AOL Access Phone Numbers screen you'll choose the country you're dialing from. If your country includes an area code, type that in too.

Tip
Avoiding interruptions is another reason to get a dedicated line—a phone line that you use strictly for connecting to the AOL or the Internet (it's only a few bucks for the minimal service). I've got such a line, and to keep the cost down I don't have any extra features such as call waiting (that's why I don't have **call waiting** check box checked in Figure 5-2—there's nothing to turn off).

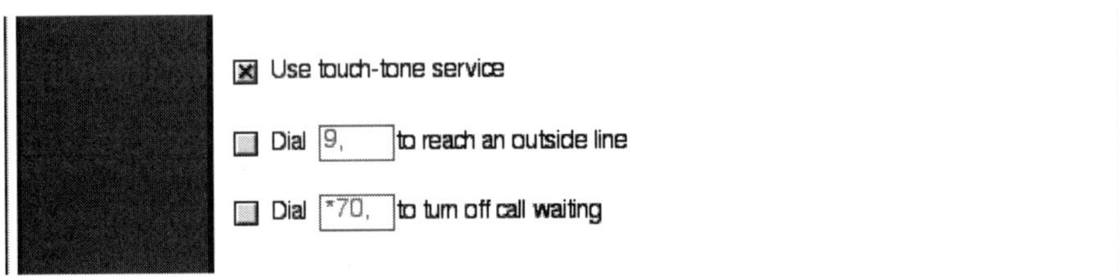

Figure 5-2 Setting dialing options.

Note
A comma (like the one after the 9 in the box in the **outside line** area shown in Figure 5-2) tells America Online to signal your iBook modem to pause before continuing. The modem's a quick dialer, so that pause may be necessary to ensure that an instruction like dialing a 9 to reach an outside line works properly.

The AOL software now moves to the Get AOL Access Phone Numbers screen and automatically dials up a toll-free number and logs into a special area of America Online where a database of AOL access numbers resides. Based on the country and (possibly) the area code you specified, AOL finds one or more numbers that are local to your area. These numbers are displayed in the Search for AOL Access Phone Numbers screen—as shown in Figure 5-3.

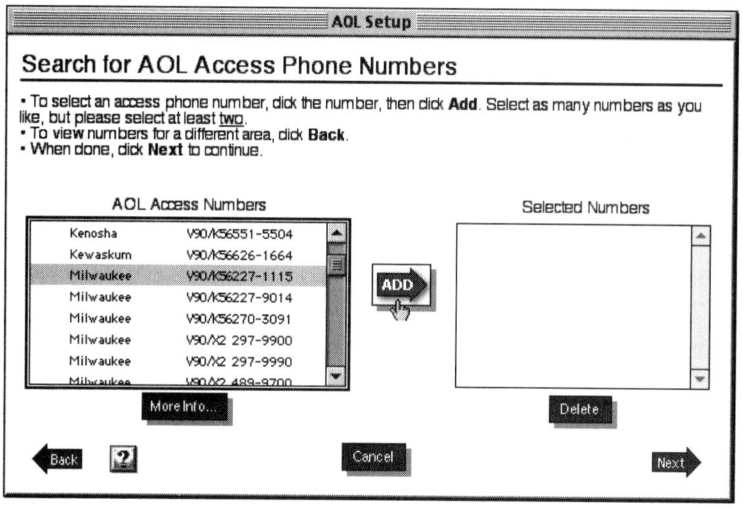

Figure 5-3 A list of AOL access numbers.

Click on a number in the list on the left side of the screen, click the **ADD** button, and the number moves to the (initially empty) list on the right side of the screen. You'll see a screen that describes the settings for the selected number—as shown in Figure 5-4. Here AOL simply uses the settings you specified earlier, so everything should appear as expected. Click the **OK** button.

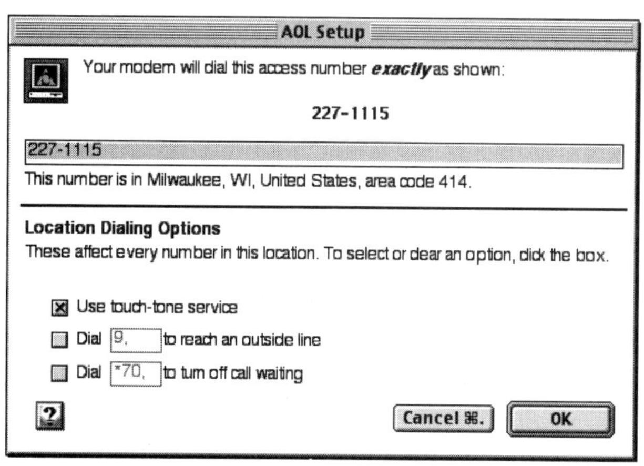

Figure 5-4 Setup specifications for one access number.

Now, about the number to select. The America Online center is located in Virginia, and that's where all access to America Online takes place. But unless you happen to live in Virginia, just down the street from the AOL world headquarters, you don't want to dial their number directly—it would be a long distance call the entire time you were connected. Not to mention that with 15 million subscribers their Virginia number might just possibly be busy. So America Online has established *thousands* of numbers throughout the country that allow members to make a local call which in turn gets routed to Virginia. Unless you live in a remote area of the world, or in a small city well outside a metropolitan area, there's a very good chance that America Online has established a phone number that's local to where you are. I have the good fortune of living in the fairly large city of Milwaukee, Wisconsin, which means that (besides tolerating miserable weather and subsisting on a diet almost exclusively made up of beer and cheese) I have a few local phone numbers to choose from. Figure 5-3 shows this.

Tip

AOL has different phone numbers for different modem speeds. You *can* use a number that's rated at a lower speed than your modem, but if you do you'll be accessing AOL *at a slower than ideal speed*. Your iBook's internal modem is a V90 one, which operates at 56K. That means you'll have the best access speed if you use any V90 connection number. In Figure 5-3 you see that I have a few such numbers local to my area (Milwaukee) to choose from. If there wasn't one available local to me, I'd choose a local slower speed connection number, such as one that included 33.6K or 28.8K in its name.

After selecting a number, you can click the **Next** arrow to move on. If you've only selected one number, though, the AOL software will respond by displaying the alert shown in Figure 5-5. America Online makes a good point here—it's best to select more than one number. That way, if your first choice number is ever temporarily down, or is constantly busy, you can opt to try connecting via a second choice. Go ahead and select a second number from the list shown back in Figure 5-3 and then again carry on by clicking the **Next** arrow.

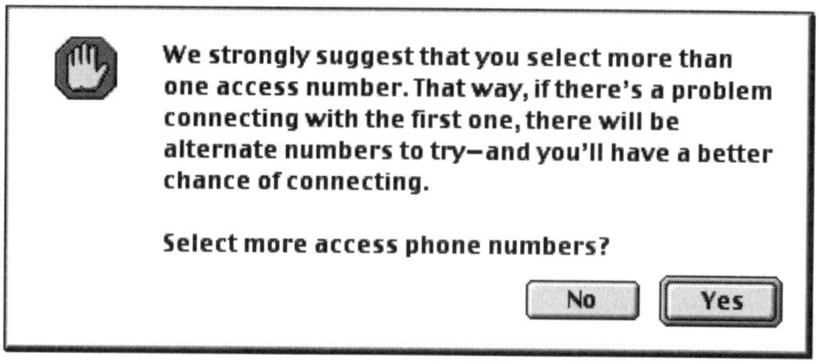

Figure 5-5 AOL reminds you to choose alternate access numbers.

You're all set to connect. And AOL does so—automatically. The America Online software now dials the first number you selected as an access number. After the connection is made, you'll either sign up as a new member (read the next section, *New Users: Signing Up,* if that's you) or you'll specify that America Online should use an existing account (skip the next section and move to the *Current Users: Using an Existing Account* section if that's you).

New Users: Signing Up

After the America Online software auto-dials into the America Online network, you're faced with the Create Your America Online screen (see Figure 5-6). If you don't have an AOL account, read on. If you do have an account, skip the following information and move on to the following section.

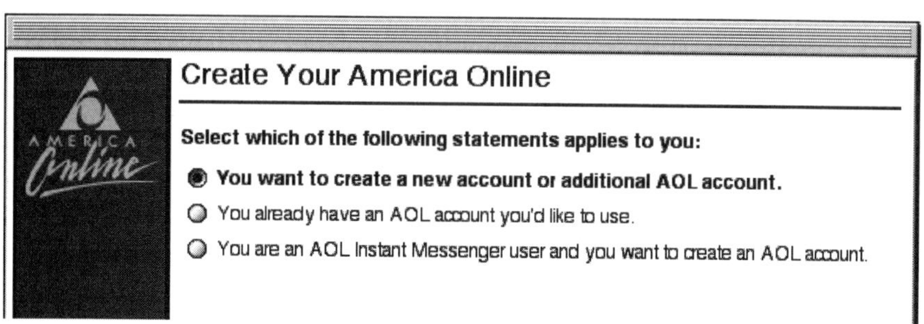

Figure 5-6 Creating a new account.

If the **You want to create a new account or additional AOL account** button isn't selected, click on it now. Then click on the **Next** arrow.

At the Member Information screen you'll be requested to enter information about yourself. Do that, then click the Next arrow. America Online responds by providing you with some information about what being an AOL member entails. Skim…er…read this thoroughly, then click the **Next** arrow.

Now, on the next screen or two, enter your credit card information (sorry, ya' gotta pay to play). After all the information has been entered, and you've clicked the **Next** arrow, read the membership acceptance agreement (click the **Read Now** button and **Next** arrow to view it). Click the **I Do** button, then the **Next** arrow to agree and to move on.

Now you're in—you're a member of AOL. You'll now need to choose a screen name—a name that's unique to your account. This name will become your America Online e-mail address, the format of which is `screen-name@aol.com`. So, for instance, if your AOL screen name is macbookman, then you're e-mail address would be `macbookman@aol.com`.

Because there are so many AOL members (15 million and counting), there's a more than fair chance that whatever name you pick, that name will already be taken by another member. Your screen name must be unique, so if that's the case, you'll need to try an alternative name. The AOL software will offer up a suggestion (which will be similar to your already-taken name with some number appended to it). You can accept AOL's suggested name, or you can type in a different name and see if *that* name too is spoken for. Don't worry—eventually you'll enter a name that no one else is using! When that happens, click on the **Continue** button or the **Next** arrow.

You'll use your screen name each time you log onto America Online. Because your screen name is visible to all AOL members, you'll also need a password. You'll need to enter it twice so that America Online is certain that you've typed the password correctly. Having a password ensures that you—and only you—will be logging onto America Online with access to your own account. Most importantly, this ensures that only you can read e-mail that others have sent to you.

After setting a password, you may encounter a Parental Control screen like the one shown in Figure 5-7. If you do, then you have the opportunity to choose the setting that best suits you situation. Here you can limit which areas of America Online can be accessed. If you're the only one accessing AOL from your account, then obviously you'll select the General Access setting in order to have the freedom to visit any area of America Online that you wish. If you have children who can log on to AOL using your account, then you'll need to use your own judgement and discretion in choosing an access setting.

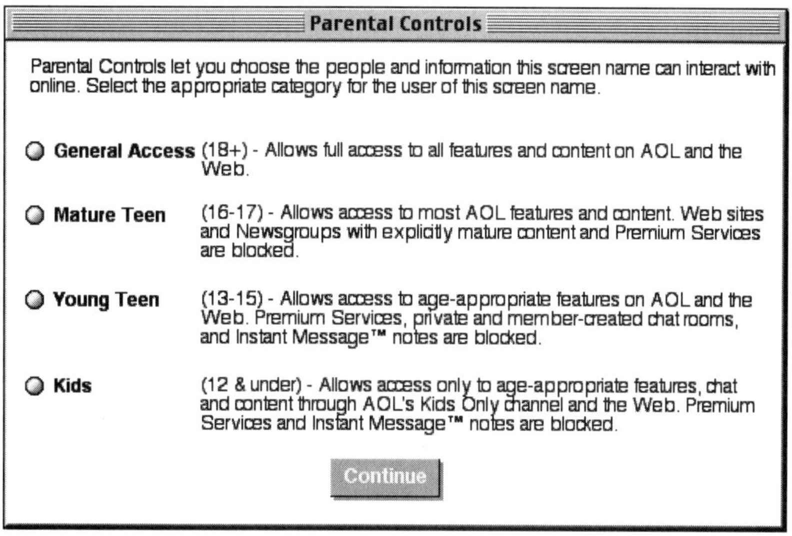

Figure 5-7 Choosing an AOL access level.

With a screen name and a password entered and accepted by AOL, you're all set to enjoy the pleasures of America Online and the Internet!

Current Users: Using an Existing Account

If you already have an America Online account, and you want to set up your iBook so that you can access that account from your iBook, then you're reading the right page!

After choosing your access number or numbers, the AOL software auto-dials America Online and gets you connected. Once connected, you face the Create Your America Online screen (shown in 5-8). If you already have an AOL account, click the **You already have an AOL account you'd like to use** button. Doing that causes two text boxes to appear—as shown in Figure 5-8. Type in your screen name and password. In Figure 5-8 you see that my screen name is DanSydow and my password is…ha—nice try! The AOL software hides your password as it's typed so that no one in the vicinity of your iBook monitor can see (unless someone is peering over your shoulder watching what you type on the keyboard, of course). With your screen name and password entered, click the **Next** arrow.

America Online studies the screen name and password you entered and, if they match what AOL has on record, then your done—your iBook is all set up for America Online access.

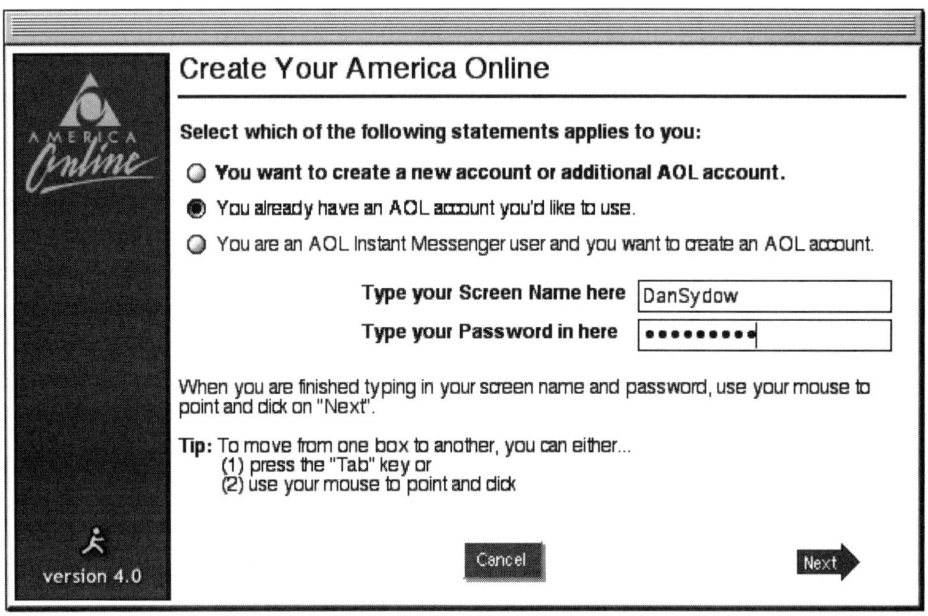

Figure 5-8 Entering an existing screen name and password.

Internet Service Provider Users

Some people pay a monthly fee to America Online to be a member of AOL, and a monthly fee to an Internet Service Provider to get Internet accesses via that ISP. If you fall into this category, read this section. If your iBook is set up to access the Internet only by way of AOL, go ahead and skip this section.

Note
Why have two means of accessing the Internet? In my case, I've been a member of AOL for over a decade—s o a large number of people know how to contact me by one of my AOL e-mail addresses. When I wanted to gain the ability to stay logged on to the Internet 24 hours a day, and have the ability to set up a Web site that was more flexible than the AOL-way of hosting a site, I signed up with an ISP. Making sure that people can stay in touch with me by my AOL e-mail addresses are one reason I retained my AOL account.

AOL Link

If you have an account with an Internet Service Provider (ISP) *and* an account with America Online, then you may encounter the alert shown in Figure 5-9 when you try to log on to AOL.

AOL Link is a small software program that's in the *Extensions* folder of your *System Folder*. It got there when the America Online software was installed on your iBook. AOL Link is the software that allows the AOL built-in Web browser to connect to the Web. Equally importantly, AOL Link makes it possible for you to optionally use Internet programs such as Netscape Navigator and Microsoft Internet Explorer while connected to America Online.

The AOL Link software makes some modifications to the settings in your iBook's TCP/IP software. If you only use America Online to access the Internet, these modifications are a one-time occurrence. If, however, your iBook is set up such that it can connect to America Online and connect to the Internet via an Internet Service Provider, you'll need to toggle the TCP/IP settings each time you switch your connection type.

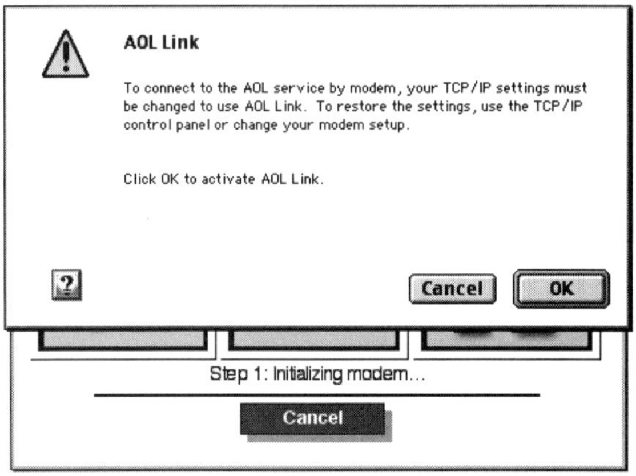

Figure 5-9 Making use of AOL Link.

Note
TCP/IP is short for *Transfer Control Protocol/Internet Protocol*, and is the language that allows computers to communicate with one another via the Internet. You don't need to know the details of TCP/IP. You only need to know that the TCP/IP control panel is used to set up your iBook so that it's TCP/IP settings match those required by your Internet Service Provider or by America Online.

If you've connected to the Internet using your ISP, and then try to connect to AOL, you see the alert shown in Figure 5-9. Just click the **OK** button to let AOL handle the modifying of your TCP/IP settings. Next time you try to connect to the Internet using your ISP, though, you'll need to change the TCP/IP settings again—if you don't you'll see an alert like the one in Figure 5-10.

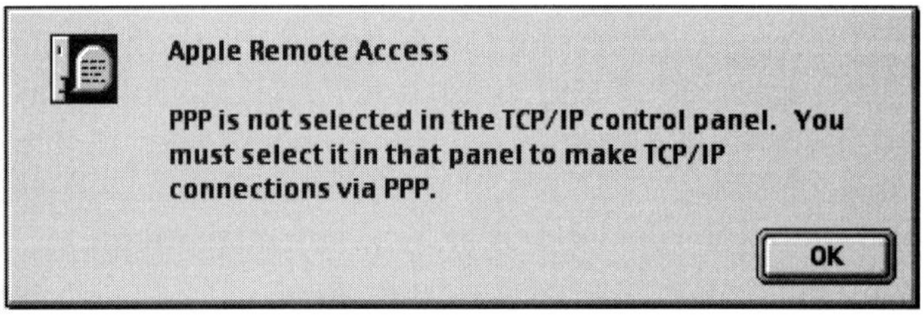

Figure 5-10 A reminder that you need to adjust your TCP/IP settings.

Toggling the TCP/IP settings back to the ones your Internet Service Provider prefers is easy enough to do from the TCP/IP control panel. Open the control panel by choosing **TCP/IP** from the **Control Panels** item under the Apple menu, then choose **Configurations** from the **File** menu (see Figure 5-11). Click on the configuration set name that is associated with your ISP (refer to Chapter 6 if you're confused here). Now click the **Make Active** button, then choose **Quit** from the **File** menu. Now you can use your ISP to connect to the Internet.

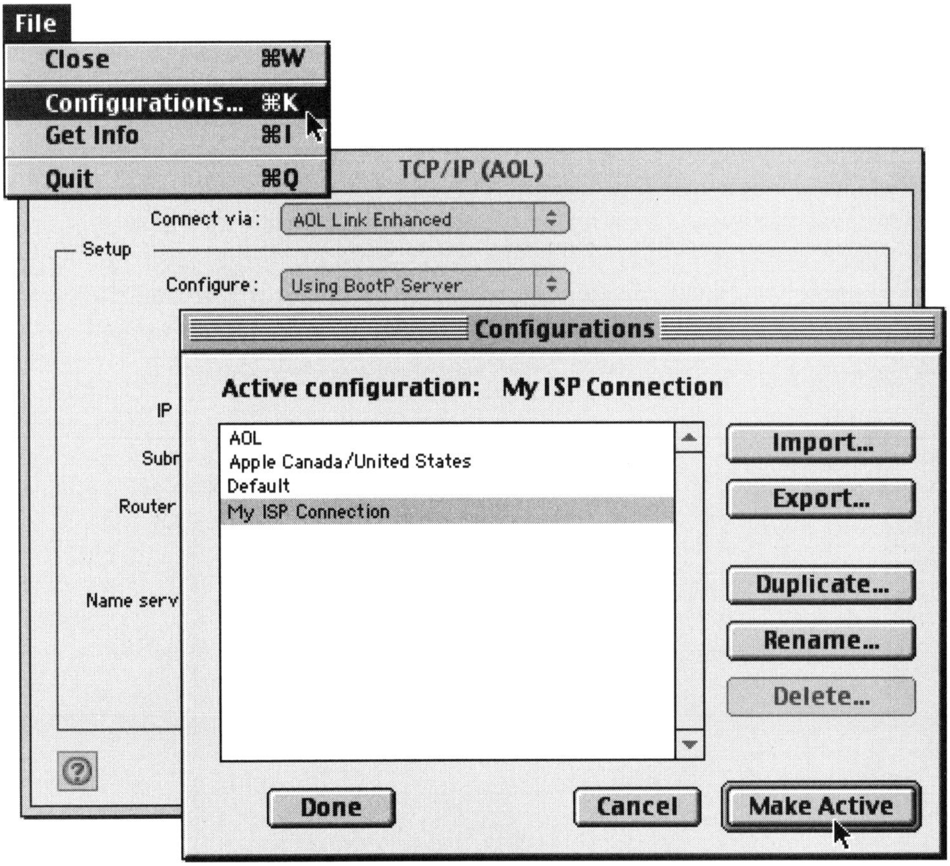

Figure 5-11 Changing TCP/IP settings.

Reminder

This business of switching between different sets of TCP/IP settings doesn't have to be done every time you connect to the Internet. It only needs to be done when you're switching *methods* of connecting. If, for instance, you connect via your ISP ten times in a row, you won't need to open the TCP/IP control panel each time. You may need to open it the first time, but only if your previous connection was via America Online. It's the changing of connection method, not the simple act of connecting, that requires the change in TCP/IP settings.

Using Your ISP to Connect to AOL

If you regularly connect to the Internet using your Internet Service Provider, then you can save the effort of toggling settings by first connecting using your ISP, and then log on to AOL. That's right—if you connect using an ISP, you don't need to dial up the AOL access number in order to log on to AOL. Once connected via your ISP, you'll launch the America Online software. From the Welcome screen you'll then use the **Select Location** pop-up menu to connect from your ISP—as shown in Figure 5-12. Now click the **Sign On** button. You're already connected to the Internet, so the AOL software doesn't attempt to dial a number—it just connects to the America Online area and the Internet. Now go ahead and make use of AOL as you normally do.

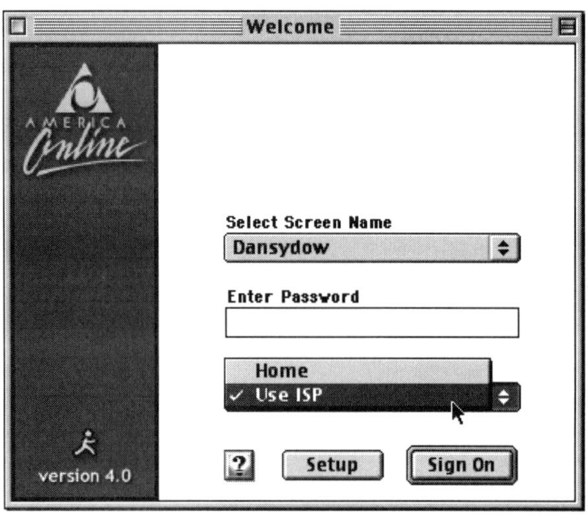

Figure 5-12 Accessing AOL while connected to the Internet.

If your AOL Welcome screen's **Select Location** pop-up menu doesn't include an option like the one shown in Figure 5-12, create one. To do that, click the **Setup** button on the Welcome screen (refer to Figure 5-12). At the AOL Setup window that appears, click the option button that lets you sign on from a new location—as shown in Figure 5-13. Now click the **Next** arrow. Near the top of the window you'll now enter a name for the new setup (see Figure 5-14). Any name will do, but it makes sense to include something about "ISP" in the name so you'll always remember just what this connection setup is for.

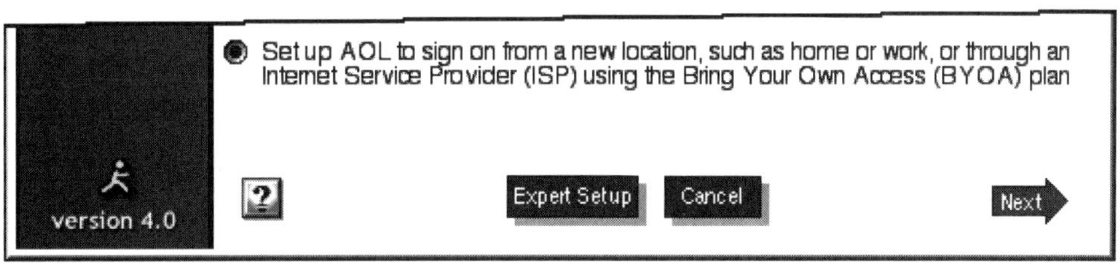

Figure 5-13 Specifying a new location.

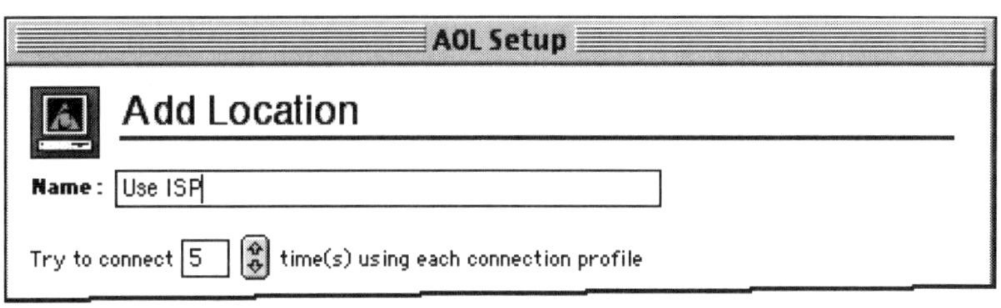

Figure 5-14 Naming the new location.

Click the **Next** arrow and then choose the **Add a TCP connection** option, as shown in Figure 5-15. Click the **Next** arrow and you'll see an alert window that tells you the new TCP connection setup has been added to your AOL software.

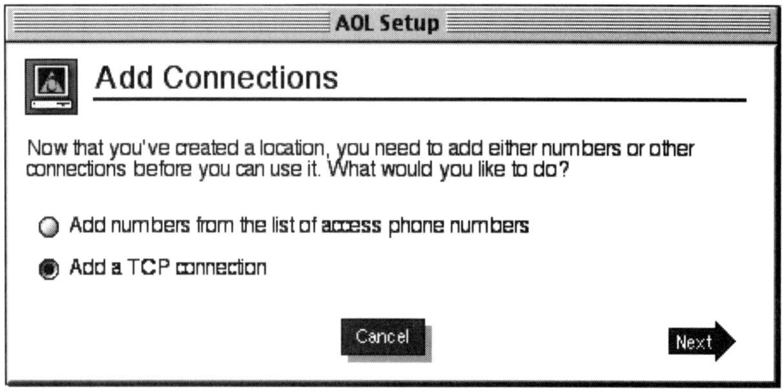

Figure 5-15 Adding the new location.

Click the **OK** button and you'll be back at the Welcome screen. Click on the **Select Location** pop-up menu to see that both your original setup (probably named **Home**) and your new ISP setup appear listed in the menu (refer back to Figure 5-12). Now, whenever you're connected to the Internet by way of your ISP, you can start the AOL software, choose your ISP item from the **Select Location** menu, and click the **Sign On** button to connect without disconnecting from your ISP. If you ever want to connect to America Online without first connecting to the Internet via your ISP, instead just choose the original (**Home**) location from the **Select Location** menu and then click the **Sign On** button.

All About E-Mail

Everyone loves mail, so the first thing you'll want to do on America Online is learn how to read and send e-mail.

Reading E-mail

AOL lets you know when you have new e-mail—your iBooks speaker will emit the words "You've got mail" when you log onto AOL and you'll see a small flashing mailbox icon on the far left side of the menu bar. If you're already logged onto AOL and new e-mail arrives, you won't hear the verbal notice, but you will see the flashing mailbox icon (though the icon might now appear on the right side of the menu bar, depending on whether the America Online software is the active program at the time). To view information about your mail, click the mail box icon that's always present on the left side of the AOL toolbar. The toolbar, shown in Figure 5-16, is the horizontal strip of icons that runs under the Mac menu bar. Clicking on this mailbox icon brings up a window like the one shown in Figure 5-17.

Figure 5-16 The AOL toolbar (mailbox icon on the far left).

Figure 5-17 The AOL Mailbox window.

The AOL Mailbox window shown in Figure 5-17 is where you'll select which e-mail message or messages to read. To read any message, double-click anywhere on the message in the Mailbox window—or click once on the message to highlighten it, and then click the **Read** button. In Figure 5-17 I've clicked once on the message that has the subject "*Question for you.*" Clicking on the **Read** button results in the opening of a new window—a window such as the one shown in Figure 5-18.

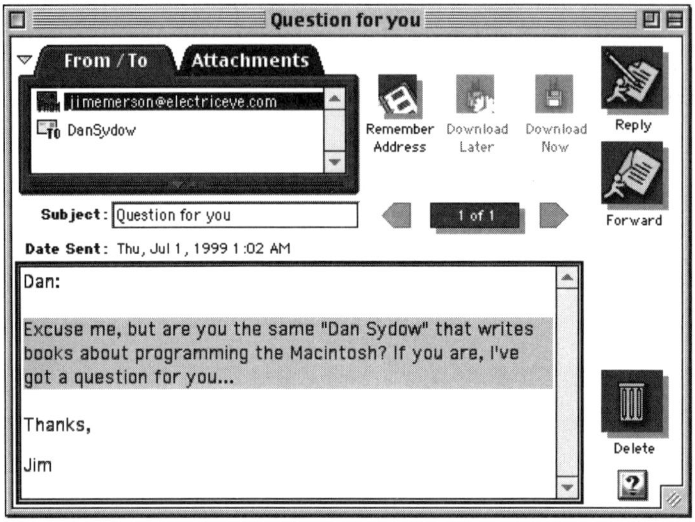

Figure 5-18 Reading an e-mail message.

When someone sends you e-mail, that person can optionally choose to attach one or more files to the message. While e-mail often is used to send a short message, sometimes it's used to transfer entire files (read this chapter's *Sending and Replying to E-mail* section to see how to *send* a message that includes attachments). If I message includes attachments you can see the names of the attached files by clicking the **Attachments** tab located at the top of the message window—it's the tab just to the right of the **Send To** tab. In Figure 5-19 I've clicked on that tab to reveal that a file named *1999.Annual.Report* is attached to the message I'm reading.

If a message includes an attached file, you'll see the **Download Files** icon highlighted near the right of the message. In Figure 5-19 I'm clicking that icon to download an attached file to my hard drive. After clicking the **Download Files** icon, the standard Save window appears to give you the opportunity to specify the destination folder for the about-to-be-downloaded file. After clicking the **Save** button AOL downloads the file. As the file's downloaded, the window shown in Figure 5-20 displays the time remaining to complete the transfer of the file from an AOL server computer to your hard drive.

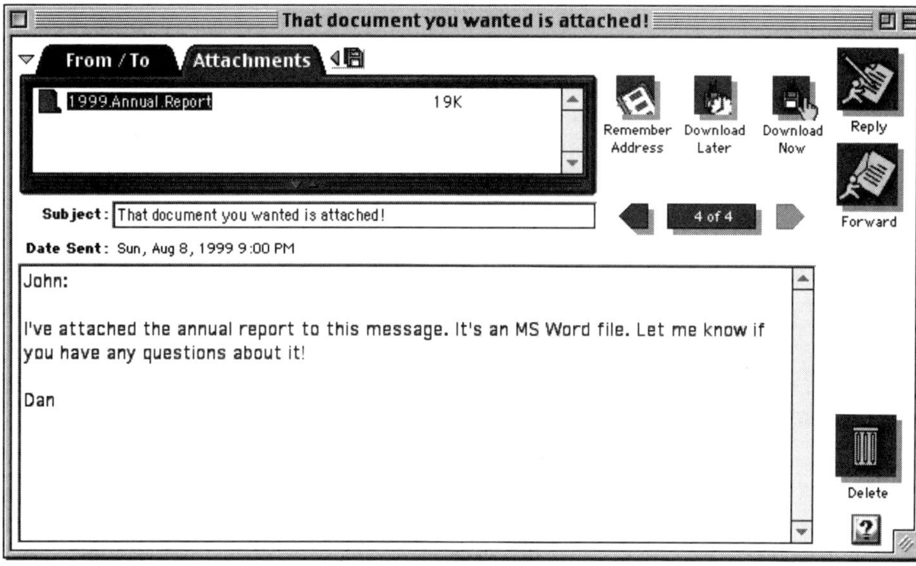

Figure 5-19 A message with an attachment.

Note

To reduce the size of a file, and/or to combine several files into a single file, a person may *compress* the file. Such a compressed, or *stuffed*, file may come attached to a message you receive. To read about how America Online deals with such files, read this chapter's *Sending and Replying to E-mail* section.

After you've read a message, click the message window's close box to close the message-holding window. If you need to re-read the message at a later time, or if you want to download the message's attached file (if it has one), you'll be able to. After reading a message, the AOL software moves it from the category of New Mail to the category of Old Mail. To again read a previously read message, first click on the **Old Mail** tab in the Mailbox window (the window shown in Figure 5-17—the one that appears when you click on the mailbox icon in the AOL tool bar). Now find the message in the list of messages, and double-click on it to again display the message contents in a window.

Note
Similarly, if you forget what you wrote to someone, click on the **Sent Mail** tab to bring up a list of all the messages you've sent.

Warning
America Online doesn't keep your mail indefinitely. Your mail occupies disk space on one of America Online's many servers (which are each basically a computer with a very large disk drive). Your own mail may not occupy much disk space, but when you consider that you are just one of over 15 million AOL members, every little bit of disk space counts (to AOL, anyway). After a certain amount of time, your already-read e-mail will be permanently removed from AOL's server. How quickly this happens depends on how much mail you receive—the more mail you get (and read), the quicker it's removed. If you want to retain the information in a message, save that message. To do that just display the message in a window and then choose **Save** from the **File** menu. You'll see a standard Save window that lets you choose where you want the message saved to.

Tip
If you also have access to the Internet via a means other than AOL (such as through an Internet Service Provider), you might be interested to know that you can check your AOL e-mail without logging onto AOL. So if you're working from your iBook and you're connected to the Internet, you can check your mail from your Web browser without disconnecting from your ISP and then connecting to AOL. Instead, go to `netmail.web.aol.com`. As shown in Figure 5-21, here you just enter your screen name and password. After doing that, you'll see a list of all your new AOL e-mail!

Sending and Replying to E-mail

Getting e-mail is fun, but you'll of course want to send your own messages to others too. America Online makes it easy to create and send e-mail. The AOL program also makes it easy to add attachments to a message in order to send someone not only a text message, but entire files as well.

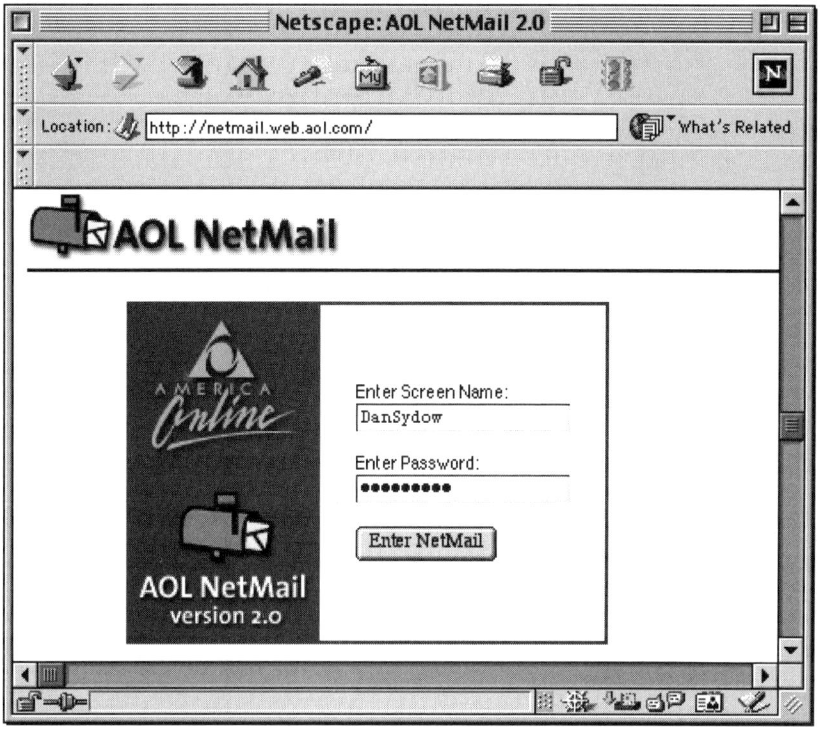

Figure 5-21 Checking AOL mail from the Internet.

Sending a Reply

An e-mail message may not include a question, but it quite often does (as in, *"Can we meet at 3:00 pm this Tuesday?"*, or *"I think you made a mistake on page 127 of this book and for that you should be, at the minimum, shot—what do you think about that?"*). So after reading the text of a message you've received, you may very well want to reply to it. That is, you may want to issue a reply statement to the sender (as in, *"Sure, 3:00 pm on Tuesday sounds fine!"*, or *"Couldn't we just agree on a mild flogging instead?"*). To reply to a message, first give it a read—as described in the previous section. Then, click the **Reply** button in the message window (refer back to Figure 5-18). Doing that brings up a new message window like the one in Figure 5-22.

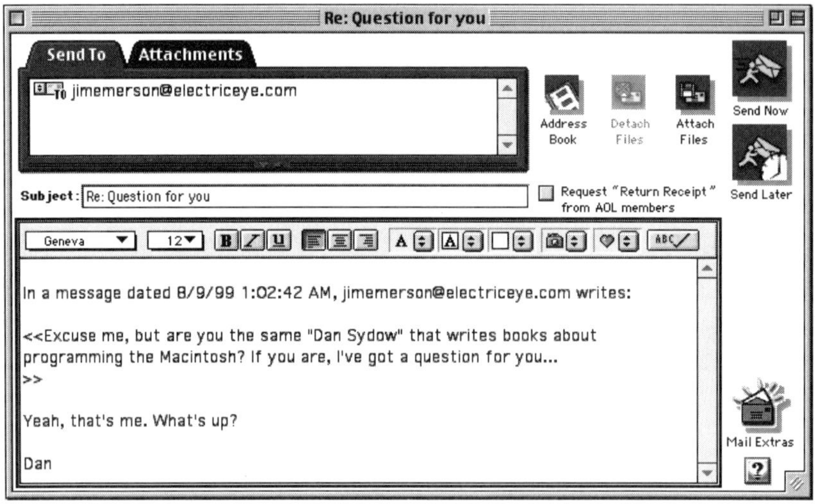

Figure 5-22 Replying to an e-mail message.

Figure 5-22 points out a couple of features of a reply message. Here you see that AOL has automatically filled in the Send To field near the top of the message—there's no need to type in who the message is going to. Because you said you're replying to a message, AOL knows who your message is going to. Also notice in Figure 5-22 that some of the text of the *original message* (the message to which I'm replying) appears in my reply. And notice that it appears listed between the "<<" and ">>" characters. If you select (choose) some of the text in the original message (the one that was sent to you) before clicking the **Reply** button, AOL will place that selected text between the just-mentioned characters and include this quote in your reply (compare the highlighted text in Figure 5-18 with the quoted text in Figure 5-22). Quoting some or the entire original message is a good way to remind the sender of the original message just what it is you're replying to.

Tip

Keep in mind that the sender of a message may have sent out any number of messages to any number of people. Someone who sends you e-mail may also have sent e-mail to two, three, or thirty other people on that same day. So a reminder of what initiated the conversation may be in order!

After typing in your reply text, click the **Send Now** button to send off your reply. Very shortly (generally minutes, or even seconds, later) the **Send To** recipient will receive your e-mail reply.

Sending a New Message

Many of the e-mail messages you send will be replies to messages you received from others. Many others will be ones you create "from scratch." That is, you'll be starting a topic rather than replying to, or carrying on with, a subject initiated by someone else. In such a case you begin by clicking on the **Write** icon in the AOL toolbar (the icon located just to the right of the **Read** icon—as shown back in Figure 5-16). Doing that brings up a fresh, clean, empty message window. In this window you'll type the e-mail address of the intended recipient—you do that in the **To** field near the top of the window. In Figure 5-23 I'm writing an e-mail message to an sjobs at Apple Computer, Inc.

You'll also want to include a descriptive subject for the message—one that gives the recipient a hint as to what the message is about. Then it's on to the body of the message itself.

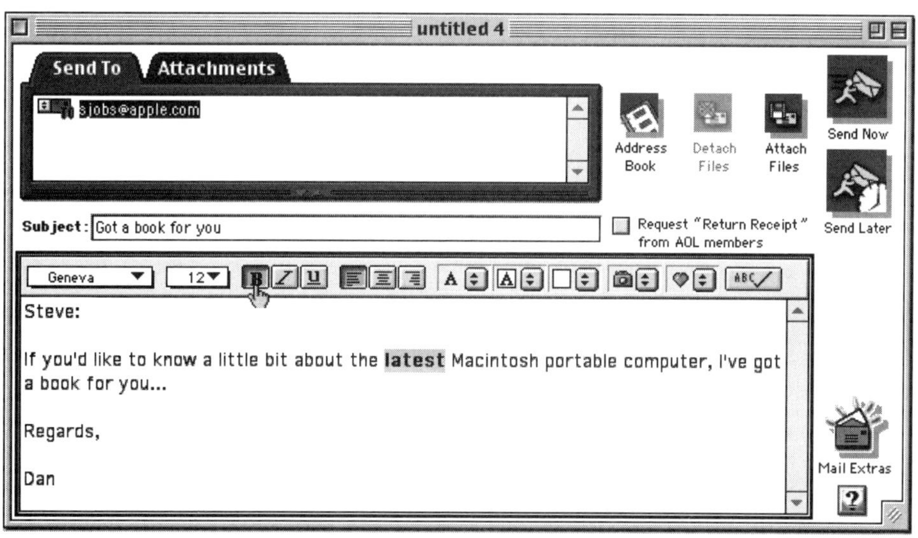

Figure 5-23 Creating an e-mail message.

Tip

To keep track of e-mail addresses, store them in the AOL Address Book. To access the Address Book, click on the **Address Book** icon located near the top of an e-mail message window (see Figure 5-23). You can click on the **New Person** icon at the bottom of the Address Book window to add an address to the book. To select an existing address for use in a message you're about to send, first click on the appropriate name—as shown in Figure 5-24. Now click the **Send To** icon. Doing that places the person's e-mail address in the To field of the e-mail message window. Click the close box in the Address Book window to close the Address Book.

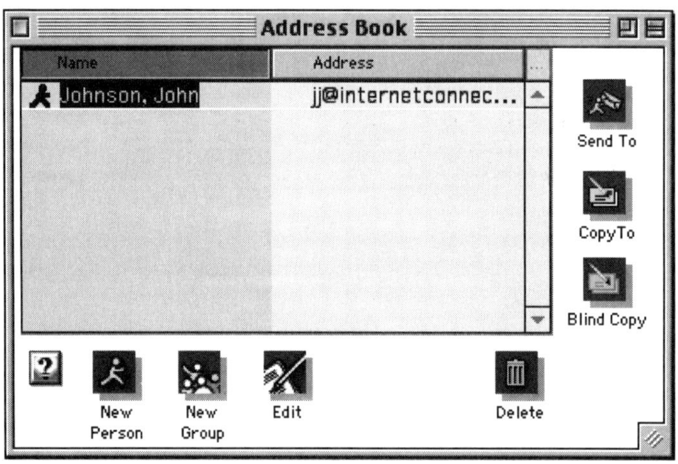

Figure 5-24 Using the AOL Address Book.

Write your message by first clicking in the large body text box and then typing away. AOL makes it easy to format some or all of the text of a message. That is, you can change the look of the text just as you might do in a document you create in a word processor. In fact, formatting text in an e-mail message is done in a manner very similar to formatting text in a word processor document: select the text to format, then click on the appropriate formatting button. In Figure 5-23 you see that I'm placing the word "latest" in boldface. To do that I selected the word and then clicked on the **B** button in the formatting toolbar that is a part of the e-mail message window.

When you're satisfied that your message is complete, click the **Send Now** icon. When you do that, off goes the message. The recipient will receive the message shortly—often in a matter of seconds.

Attaching a File to an E-mail Message

When you send an e-mail message, you add the text of the message—the words you want the recipient to see—by simply typing the text in the large body of the message. This holds true whether you're replying to a message you received or are sending a new message. A few words may be all you want to send—but be aware that you can also use e-mail to easily send entire files to someone. To do that, begin outlined above in the *Sending a Reply* or *Sending a New Message* sections. Before sending the message, though, you'll click the **Attach Files** icon located near the right side of the message window. Doing that brings up a standard Open window that lets you select a file to attach. After locating the file to send, click on the file's name and then click the **Attach** button. As shown in Figure 5-25, I'm attaching a Microsoft Word file named *1999.Annual.Report* to a message.

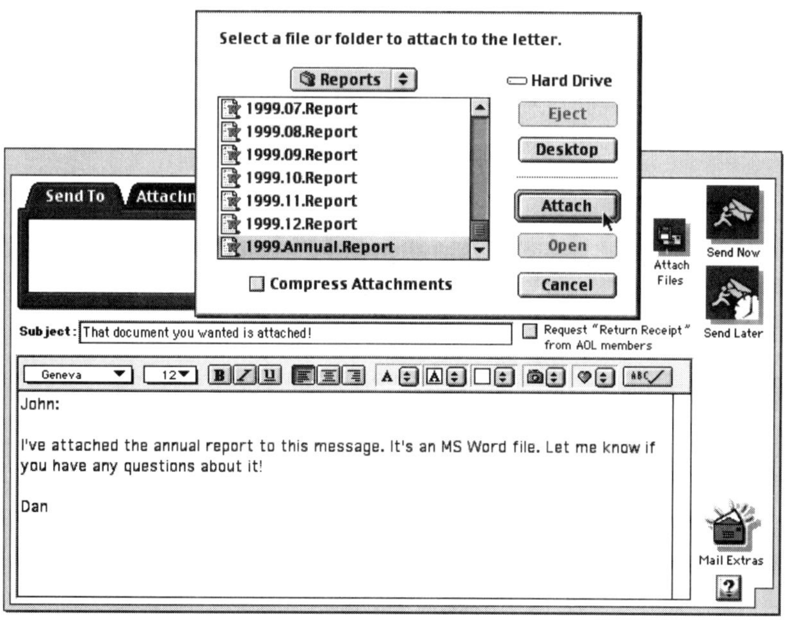

Figure 5-25 Attaching a file to an e-mail message.

If you'd like to attach more than one file to a message, for each file to attach you'll repeat the above steps of clicking the **Attach Files** icon in the message window, selecting a file, and clicking the **Attach** button.

After clicking the **Attach** button you can verify that the file is attached to your message by clicking the **Attachments** tab located at the top of the message window—it's the tab just to the right of the **Send To** tab. Figure 5-26 shows the one file I've attached to my message. Once the desired file is attached, click the **Send Now** icon to send the message, along with the file, to the recipient.

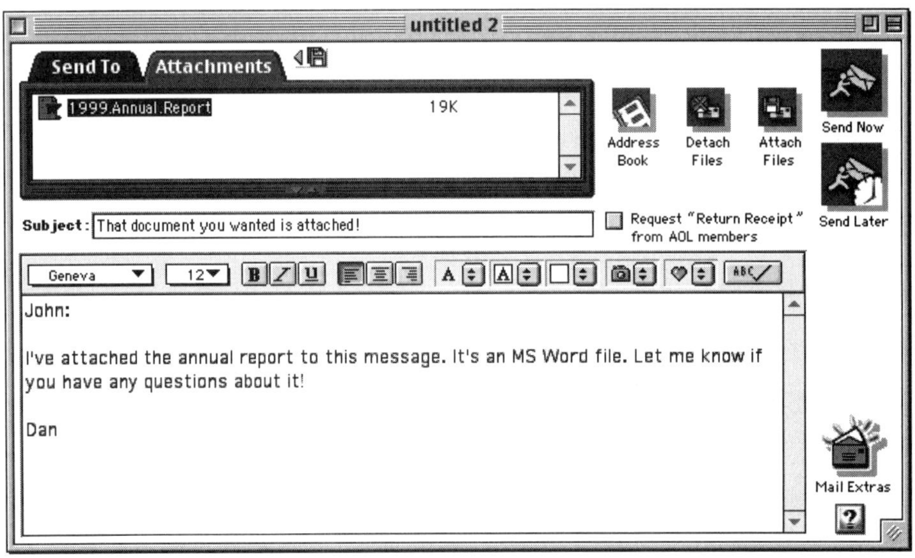

Figure 5-26 Viewing a message's attachments.

If you attach more than one file to a message, AOL will automatically *compress* all of the attached files and turn them into a single file. File compression is a technology that decreases the size of a file or files. Smaller files means a shorter transmission time when AOL e-mails the message and files to the recipient. America Online uses built-in Aladdin StuffIt software to compress files. When the recipient of your message receives the message with the compressed attachment, he or she will need to decompress, or unstuff, the file. If the recipient is also an AOL user, then that's no problem. When an AOL user receives a message that includes a compressed file, the AOL software automatically decompresses the file when the user signs off of AOL. Aladdin's StuffIt compression software is very popular, and works on both Macs and PCs running Windows. So even if the recipient of an AOL-sent message isn't using AOL (the recipient could be accessing the Internet by way of an Internet Service Provider), there's a very good chance that whatever software he or she is using also includes StuffIt.

Even if you send just a single file you can opt to compress that one file. When sending a small file (such as a 30 K text file), compression doesn't speed things up much. But if you're sending a big file (such as a 1 MB document that includes lots of graphics), compressing the file will allow AOL to send the file noticeably faster (perhaps reducing the sending time by several minutes). Before clicking the **Attach** button in the standard Open window, check the **Compress Attachments** check box (see the bottom of Figure 5-25 for a look at that check box). Compressing a file makes the file smaller in size—so when it comes time to send your e-mail message it will take AOL a shorter time to send the message. It will also take a shorter time for the recipient to download the attached file to his or her hard drive.

Newsgroups

If you want to find information about a topic—any topic—you *can* search the Web for existing material on the topic of interest (Chapter 9 covers that subject). If the question you need answered is very specific, though, you may not find the information you need. In such an instance, you'd be wise to seek your answer in a newsgroup.

Like the World Wide Web and e-mail, newsgroups (formally referred to as *Usenet*) is one of several services on the Internet. Each newsgroup is an area of discussion, with the conversation centered on one topic. For instance, there are newsgroups that deal with pets, hobbies, sports, travel, and so forth. There are tens of thousands of newsgroups, so there's a very good chance that a newsgroup dealing with your particular interest exists. Anyone can post a message to a newsgroup, and anyone can read any of the messages posted by others. America Online makes it easy to both post and read newsgroup messages.

Subscribing to a Newsgroup

To get to America Online's newsgroup area, type the keyword newsgroups in the **Address** box—as shown in Figure 5-27. Then press the Return or Enter key. Doing that brings up the Newsgroups window (again, as shown in Figure 5-27).

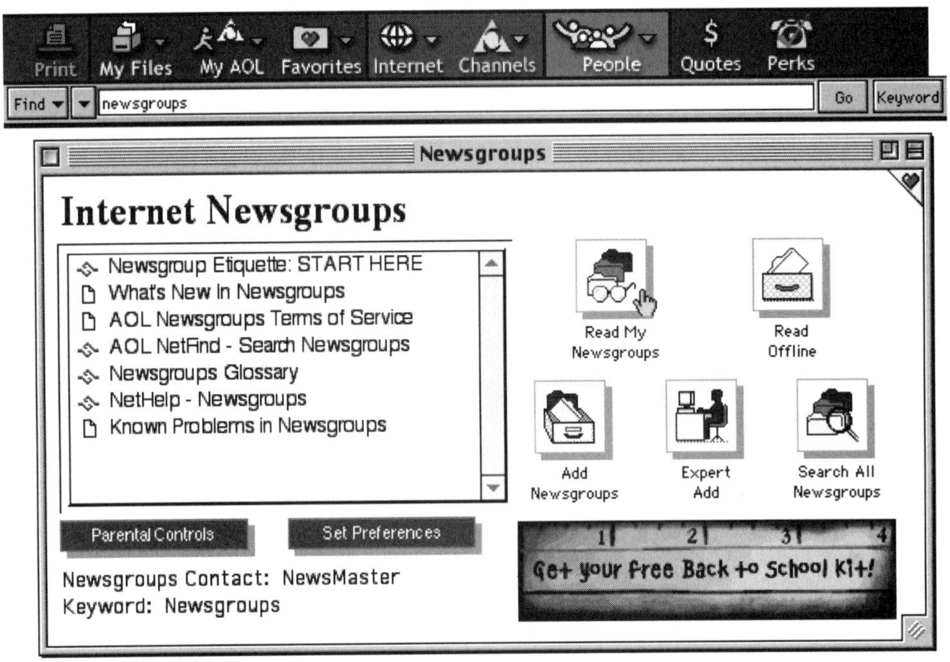

Figure 5-27 Moving to AOL's newsgroup area.

There are several thousand newsgroups, only a relative few of which hold messages of interest to you. So of course you won't attempt to read the messages in all of them. Instead, you'll *subscribe* to a few, or several, select newsgroups. Subscribing to a newsgroup simply means you want to be active in the group in that you want to be able to view the messages that get posted, and you want to optionally post your own messages to the group.

Newsgroup Naming

Newsgroups are organized into topics. Looking at a newsgroup name from left to right reveals the subject matter of the newsgroup from general to specific, with a period separating the words that make up the newsgroup name. The first word in a name is the hierarchy of the newsgroup. A *hierarchy* is a collection of things arranged in order of some kind of rank, or grade, or class. The following words in a newsgroup name define the category, or subcategories, in that hierarchy. A word in a newsgroup name may be a complete word or an abbreviation, but in all cases when looked at as a whole the newsgroup name should at least hint at what type of discussions are taking place within the group. For instance, the newsgroup `comp.sys.mac.games.adventure` is a newsgroup in the computer (`comp`) hierarchy. There are a number of computer-related newsgroups, dealing with a variety of computer systems. This newsgroup discusses systems (`sys`) running the Macintosh operating system (`mac`). This one newsgroup is for people interested in playing computer games (`games`). In particular, roll playing or adventure (`adventure`) games.

There are dozens of hierarchies of newsgroups, with a handful being the most popular and considered the more mainstream. The `comp`, for *computer*, hierarchy is popular, as is the `rec`, for *recreation*, newsgroup. The `misc` (*miscellaneous*), `news` (yes, *news*), `sci` (*science*), `soc` (*social* issues), and `talk` (*talk* about, or debate, topics) are the other commonly subscribed-to newsgroups. The most popular hierarchy of all is the `alt`, for *alternative*, newsgroup. Within the `alt` hierarchy you'll find an incredibly wide variety of categories, including the arts (`alt.arts`), books (`alt.books`), and medicine (`alt.med`).

Expert Adding

If you know the exact name of a newsgroup, you can click the **Expert Add** icon in the Newsgroup window (refer to Figure 5-27) to display a window that lets you type in the newsgroup name. If someone tells you just what newsgroup might be of interest to you (for instance, you now know about the `comp.sys.mac.games.adventure` newsgroup), then there's a chance you'll know exactly what to type. Otherwise, it's more likely that you'll search or browse through the newsgroup names to find a newsgroup to subscribe to. Read the very next two sections to see how to find a newsgroup to subscribe to.

Searching For a Newsgroup

If you have a topic in mind, but don't know the exact name of a relevant newsgroup, click the **Search All Newsgroups** icon (see Figure 5-27). Doing that displays the Search All Newsgroups window (see Figure 5-27). Click in the long text box and type in one or more words that apply to what you're searching for. To make sure the search doesn't overlook a newsgroup that's a potential match, it's best to generalize a bit as opposed to being too specific. For instance, type *mac* if you're looking for *Macintosh*, and type *game* if you're looking for *game* or *games*. After typing in a word or words, click the **List Articles** button to reveal a list of newsgroups containing your keyword or keywords. Figure 5-28 shows the result of searching for Macintosh game-related newsgroups

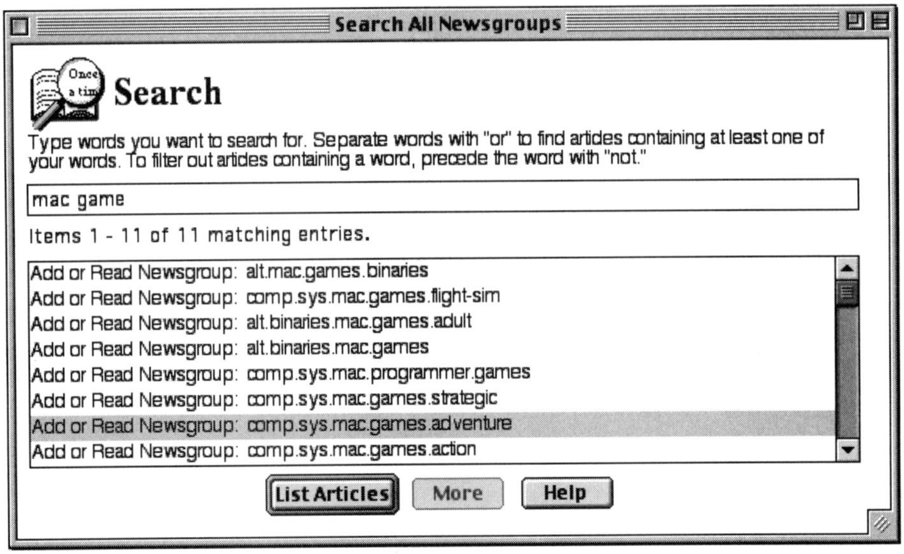

Figure 5-28 Searching for a newsgroup of interest.

To subscribe to a newsgroup, double-click on its name in the list. That brings up a window that provides a brief description of the newsgroup. This same window also lets you click on a **Subscribe** line of text. Doing that brings up still another window, and an alert box. Click the **OK** button in the alert box, then click the **Save** button in the window. You're now subscribed to the newsgroup. The next time you click on the **Read My Newsgroups** icon in the main Newsgroups window (see Figure 5-27), the name of the just-subscribed-to newsgroup will appear in your list of newsgroups.

Browsing For a Newsgroup

When you have a specific topic in mind, using the just-discussed newsgroup searching method is the best plan for finding and subscribing to newsgroups. If you're a little uncertain exactly what it is you're looking for (as in, "I think I'd like to get some information on recreation"), then you might want to browse through the names of the existing newsgroups to see what catches your eye. To do that, begin by clicking on the **Add Newgroup** icon in the main Newsgroup window (refer back to Figure 5-27). Doing that brings up a window that lists the newsgroup hierarchies. Double-clicking on a hierarchy opens another window—one that lists the major categories, and the number of newsgroups within each category, within that one hierarchy. Double-click on a category name and still another window appears—this one lists newsgroups within the selected category. In Figure 5-29 I double-clicked on the rec hierarchy, then double-clicked on the travel category. Now I'm about to subscribe to a newsgroup that holds discussions about traveling in Europe (`rec.travel.europe`).

Note
It would have been very possible to find this same `rec.travel.europe` newsgroup by using AOL's newsgroup search feature (by entering *travel*, or *europe*, or both, as keywords in the Search window). But I didn't have traveling in Europe in mind when I started browsing through the newsgroups!

Reading a Newsgroup's Messages

To read some of the messages in a newsgroup, you need to first go to America Online's newsgroup area. Type the keyword newsgroups in the **Address** box, then press the Return or Enter key (as shown back in Figure 5-27). That brings up the Newsgroups window. Click the **Read My Newsgroups** icon in the

Newsgroups window (again as shown back in Figure 5-27). Doing that brings up a Read My Newsgroups window like the one shown in Figure 5-30. Note that the names of the newsgroups you see differ from the names in the list of the window pictured in Figure 5-30. That's because I've subscribed to several Mac-related newsgroups (read the preceding section to see how to subscribe to newsgroups).

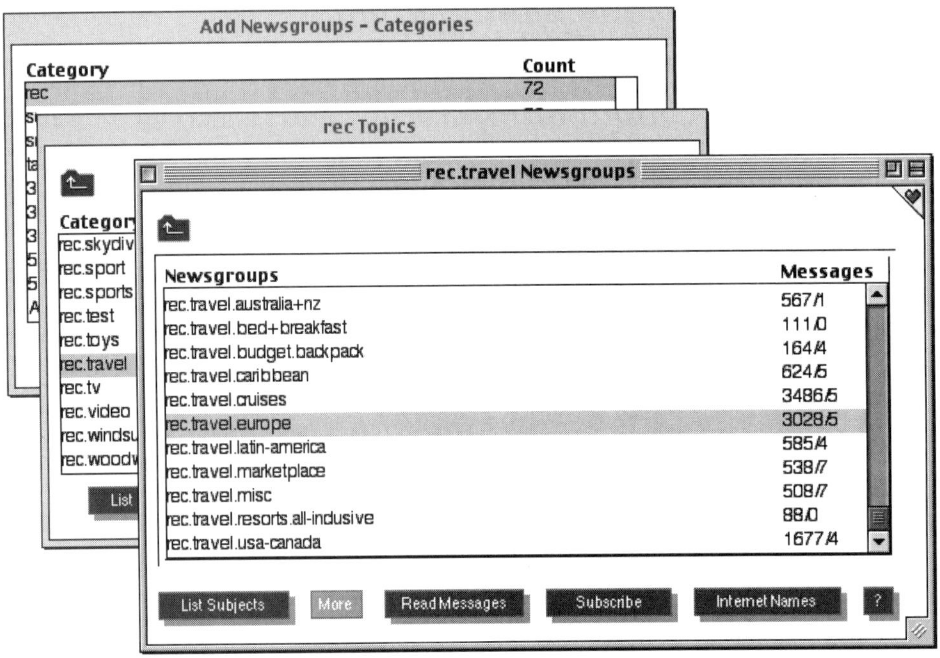

Figure 5-29 Browsing for a newsgroup of interest.

To read the messages in any one newsgroup, begin by clicking on the newsgroup name to highlighten it. Then click the **List Unread** button. In Figure 5-30 I'm about to view the messages that are currently posted in the `comp.sys.mac.portables newsgroup` (a newsgroup for people interested in the portable, or notebook, Macintosh computers). After clicking the **List Unread** button a window like the one shown in Figure 5-31 appears. On the left of this window are the names of the subjects—or *threads*—in this one newsgroup. On the right of the window are the number of messages currently in each subject. In Figure 5-31 I've clicked on a subject named *Book - why no expansion bay?* You can see that this subject holds six messages.

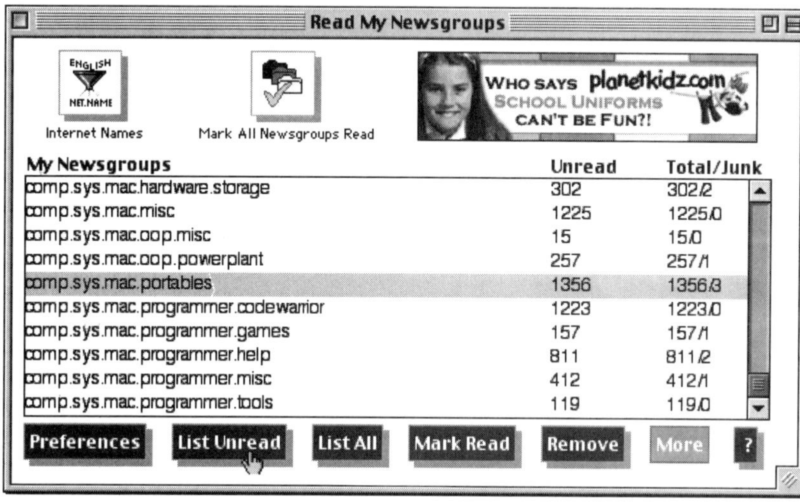

Figure 5-30 A list of newsgroups.

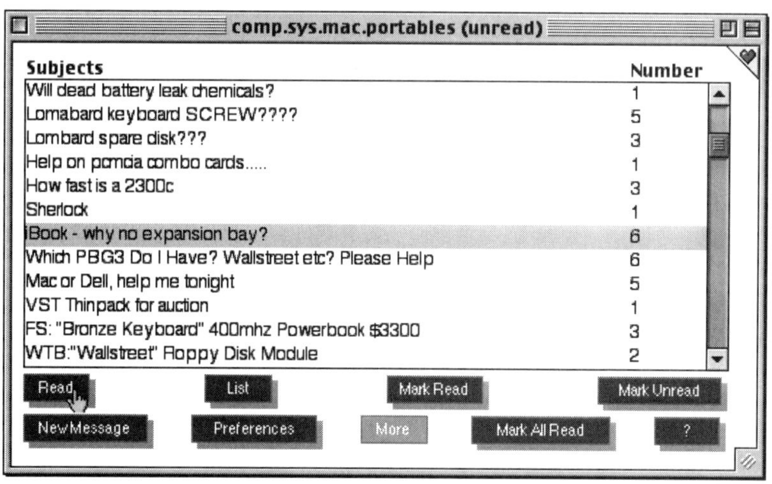

Figure 5-31 A list of subjects in a newsgroup.

To view the first message in a subject (thread), click on the subject to highlighten it, then click the **Read** button. Doing that brings up a new window holding the text of the message. Figure 5-32 shows the first message in the *Book - why no expansion bay?* thread.

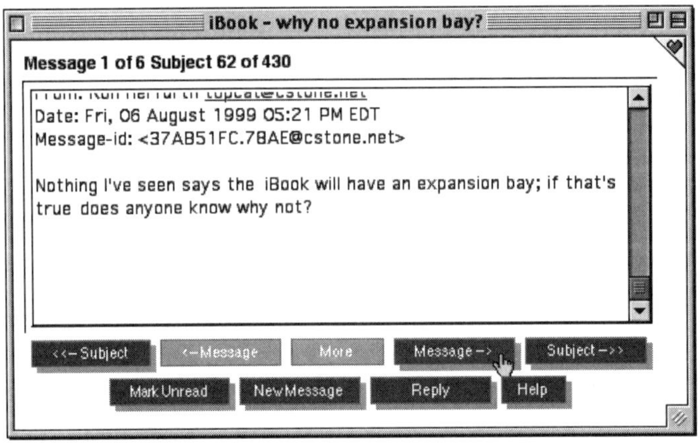

Figure 5-32 Reading a newsgroup message.

The first message in a thread is typically a question that someone has posted. The remaining messages in the same thread are typically answers to the question. The person posting a response could be someone very knowledgeable about the subject—or the person could know little or nothing at all about the subject! Keep in mind that *anyone with Internet access can post a message to a thread.* So it's up to you to determine if an answer is credible. To view the next message in a thread, click on the **Message->** button—as shown in Figure 5-32. You can read all the messages in any one thread, but you don't have to. Whenever you're finished with a subject, click the close box of the window that's displaying the message you're reading.

Posting a Message to a Newsgroup

If you have a question, you'll want to post a message to a newsgroup. If you come across someone else's question that you happen to know the answer to, you'll again want to post a message (the spirit of altruism makes the system of newsgroups work).

Replying to a Message

If you're reading the messages in a subject, and you'd like to supply your own input on the topic, click the **Reply** button (refer to Figure 5-32). Doing that brings up a window like the one shown in Figure 5-33. Click in the text box titled **Reply Window**, and type your message. When you're satisfied with your reply, click the **Send** button. Your message gets sent off to the newsgroup, where it will soon be posted alongside the other messages in this subject.

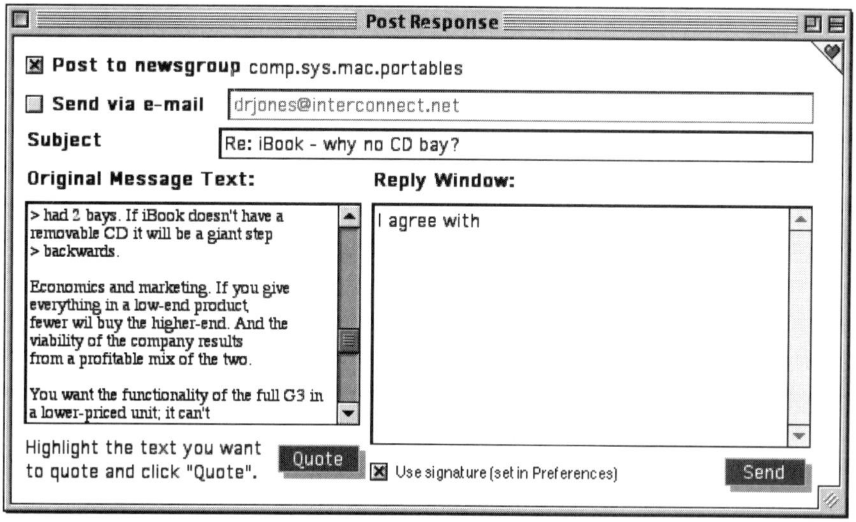

Figure 5-33 Writing a reply to an existing subject.

[Starting a New Subject

When you've found and subscribed to a newsgroup of interest, you may find a number of existing threads that are of interest. You may also find that a particular question you have isn't answered in any of the existing threads. In such a case, start your own thread. To do that, click on the **New Message** button (refer back to Figure 5-31). Doing that brings up a new window that lets you enter a subject and the text of your message. After doing that, click the **Send** button create a new subject and to have your message be the first (and, at this point, only) message in that subject. You'll want to log on to AOL and go to this same newsgroup occasionally (or often, depending on the urgency with which you're seeking an answer) to check for replies from others.

Browsing the Web

Your iBook came equipped with a version of America Online that includes a built-in Web browser. You can use this integrated software to easily get started surfing the Web. Or, you can use either of the two stand-alone commercial Web browsers (Netscape Navigator or Microsoft Internet Explorer) that came as part of the free iBook software bundle.

Using Navigator or Internet Explorer

If you're an AOL subscriber, you probably use the Web browser that's integrated into the America Online program. Be aware that while that browser is adequate, it isn't your only option.

Note
If you have no interest or intention in using a Web browser such as Navigator or Internet Explorer, feel free to skip this *Using Navigator or Internet Explorer* section. If you're content using the browser built into AOL, you don't need this information.

Using a Third-Party Web Browser

Once you're connected to AOL, you can optionally use a third-party Web browser. That is, you can use a browser other than the one that is a part of America Online's software. You can browse the Web with either Netscape Navigator or Microsoft Internet Explorer by simply double-clicking the preferred Web browser icon on the desktop. Launching a Web browser while connected to AOL sets that browser to work—it's able to access the Web without any extra work on your part.

So, if you've been using the built-in AOL browser, but would like to try out a different Web browser—go ahead! Then read the appropriate section in

Chapter 8 (either the *Microsoft Internet Explore*r section or the *Netscape Navigator* section) for some instructions and tips on using the browser.

For Users of AOL and an ISP

If you have an account with an Internet Service Provider (ISP) *and* an account with America Online, then you'll want to refer back to the *Getting Started* section that appears at the start of this chapter. In particular read the *Internet Service Provider Users* subsection to see how you can best use both your ISP and AOL. There you'll find information on TCP/IP, as well as a tip on how to simply use both your ISP and AOL and the same time.

Getting Started

America Online's Web browser is a part of the America Online program. When you log in to AOL, you're also connecting to the Internet. There are a number of ways in which you can display the AOL Web browser window. You can go to a preselected home page by clicking on the Home icon—that's the little icon that's near the top left of the screen and looks like, yes, a home (in this section's *Changing Your Home Page* subsection you'll see how to have a different Web site appear when you click this icon). Doing that brings a new window to the screen and delivers the contents of the home page to that new window. If you know the address of the Web page you want to visit you can instead click on the long address box that appears near the top of the screen, then type in the address of a Web page. In Figure 5-34 I've typed in the address of Apple's home page. Then click the **Go** button.

The main function of a Web browser is to make it easy to navigate the Web. If you know the Web address of a Web site of interest, just use the above method to get to that page. It's not always necessary, though, to know the address of a Web site in order to visit it. That's because one Web site may include mention of interesting information at some other Web site or at some other page of the site you're at. That first site will often include a *hypertext link* to the mentioned page. A hypertext link, or simply a *link*, is a highlighted word or picture (either by color, or underlining, or both) that acts as a shortcut to another page on the Web. To visit the mentioned site, place the cursor over the link and then click the mouse button. Doing that tells America Online to determine the address to visit, go there, and display the contents of that page in the browser window.

Figure 5-34 Entering a Web page address in America Online.

After going to a page, you may want to return to the point from which you started (the page that held the hypertext link). The small leftward-pointing arrow at the upper-left of the screen is the Previous arrow; click on it to return to the page you were previously at. After returning to the previous page, you can again jump ahead to the page you just came from by using the Next arrow located to the right of the Previous arrow.

Keeping Track of Where You've Been

As you surf the Web you'll soon find that you've lost track of where you've been. While you may recall the names of some of the sites you visited, it's unlikely that you'll remember the addresses of those sites. America Online provides you with a couple of ways to easily revisit a Web site of interest, and to do so without knowing that site's address.

Using the History Trail Menu

When you visit a Web page, AOL automatically creates a new menu item in a menu located just to the left of the **Address** box. Clicking on the arrow button reveals a menu that holds up to twenty-five items—the menu in Figure 5-35 has just four items in it. Every Web page that you visit has a title—you'll find it in the title bar of the browser window that displays the page's content. It's this title that AOL uses as the name of the new menu item. The contents of what AOL refers to as the *history trail* grows as you surf the Web. This menu reflects where you've been, thus providing a history of your travels about the Web. To return to any of the page's you've recently visited, just select the page's title from this menu.

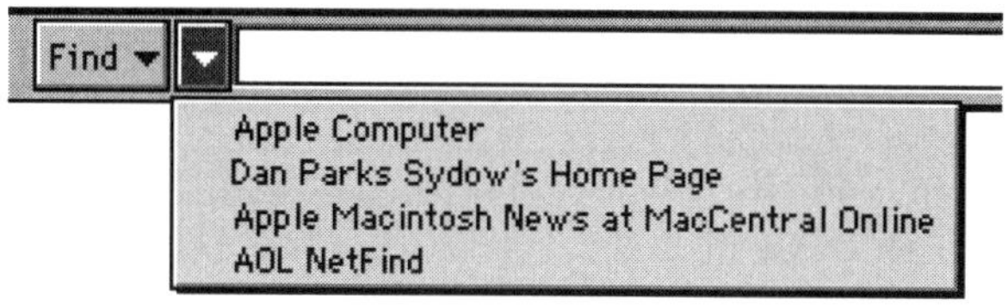

Figure 5-35 The AOL history trail menu.

Using the Favorites Menu

The **Favorites** menu is another means of keeping track of Web pages. Rather than having a page automatically added to the **Favorites** menu, though, you manually carry out this task. When you are at a Web page that you think you'd like to revisit in the near or distant future, click the small heart icon in the Web browser's upper right corner—as I'm doing in Figure 5-36. That brings up the alert box that's also shown in this figure. You can leave the **Add it to my Favorite Places** option selected and click the **OK** button.

Figure 5-36 Specifying that a Web page become a favorite.

Once you've followed the above steps, the Web page title appears in the **Favorites** menu. As shown in Figure 5-37, a favorite place appears below the Favorite menu folders and has a small heart to the left of it. To revisit a favorite page, simply select it from the **Favorites** menu.

Figure 5-37 A new favorite page appears in the Favorites menu.

Where to Go and What to Do

America Online provides you with a few pre-set "all-purpose" Web sites that you serve as a jump-off point to a variety of topics—visit one of these sites and you'll see a page that holds dozens of links to interesting pages from around the Web. Choose **AOL Netfind** from the **Internet** menu in the navigation bar (see Figure 5-38) to go to one such site. Figure 5-39 shows a part of the NetFind page that AOL displays in a browser window.

Figure 5-38 The Internet menu.

Note
Refer to the *Web Sites of Interest* section in Chapter 9 for a list of interesting sites to visit. Appendix A also holds plenty of Web sites addresses.

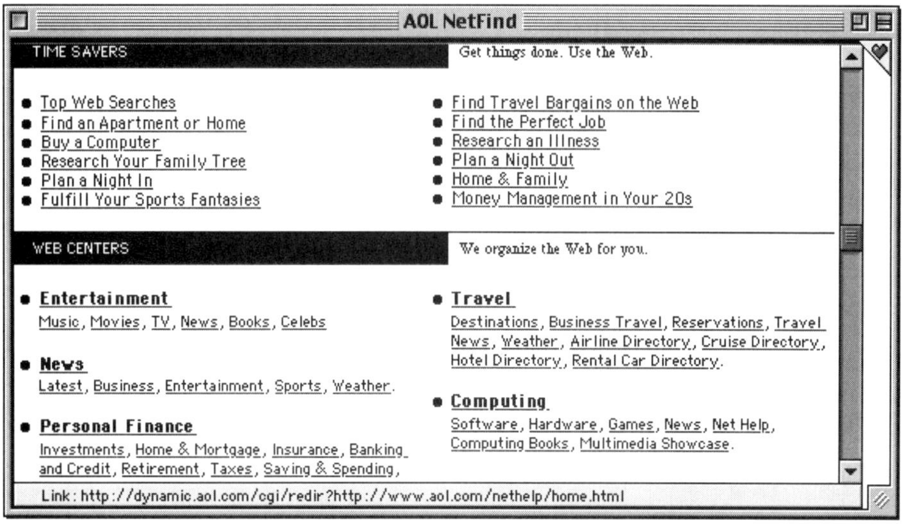

Figure 5-39 AOL's NetFind Web page.

Changing Your Home Page

When you log on to America Online, you're connected to the Internet. One way of opening a browser window is to click on the Home icon on the left of the navigation bar. When you do that a new browser window holding the contents of one of the pages from America Online's own Web site appears in that window. AOL calls this *default* page that the browser opens to the browser's home page. While America Online sets the AOL home page to one of their own pages, you aren't required to keep things in that state. Instead, you can select any Web page to be the browser's home page.

To change the home page, begin by choosing **Preferences** from the **My AOL** menu. Next, click on WWW icon in the scrollable list that appears on the left side of the Preferences window. Doing that displays Web Preferences options in the Preferences window. Here, in the Home Page box, you're given the opportunity to change the home page. In Figure 5-40 I changed the AOL home page to the MacCentral Web site so that whenever I click the America Online Home icon a Web browser window appears with updated news on Apple and the Mac.

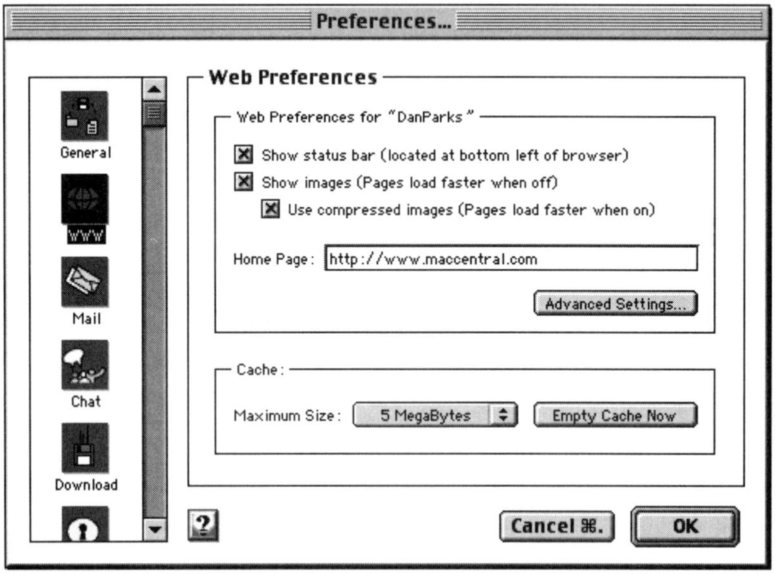

Figure 5-40 Changing the AOL home page.

6

Internet Service Providers

The *i* in iBook stands for *Internet*. So you no doubt have guessed that the iBook is a machine that can easily connect to the 'Net. Apple claims that an iBook owner can be online very soon after pulling the iBook out of its box. For many this is true. But if you've never been on the Internet, or you've never owned a Macintosh, then you might need just a *little* extra help. This chapter supplies you with that assistance.

About the Internet

The Internet is a worldwide *network* of computers. Each Internet computer is connected to another Internet computer. Collectively, all Internet computers are thus *indirectly* connected to one another. Because it's possible for communication to flow from one Internet computer *through* another and on to still a different Internet computer, *any one* Internet computer can communicate with *any other* Internet computer.

Internet-Connected Computers

The computers that make up the Internet exist in government agencies, universities, and businesses. Originally, one another shared information from these various centers. For example, a lawyer doing research at a law firm might have used the Internet to access data from a government agency. While scenarios like the above are more common now then ever before, now *any* individual—not just people associated with a group that has an Internet presence—can use the Internet to retrieve all sorts of information from others.

An Internet-connected computer is usually a powerful one, such as a mainframe computer, that houses all sorts of files. This Internet-connected computer typically has a *large* amount of disk drive space. To create an *Internet site*, a university, government, or business that's a part of the Internet opens up (allows) some part of it's Internet-connected computer's hard drive to be accessible by other Internet computers.

People with access to a different Internet-connected computer can access an Internet site. Any other computer user (such as a home computer user) can also access it provided the user has a means of connecting to an Internet-connected computer. Using your iBook, its built-in modem, and a standard phone line, you'll be able to access these Internet sites and browse through, or download, any number of files. While your iBook itself isn't actually a part of the Internet, it allows you to be a *user of*, or *visitor to*, the Internet.

Internet Users

In reading stories that include mention of the number of worldwide Internet users, you've probably come across huge numbers such as 60 million, 80 million, or even 150 million or more users. After reading the above paragraph, you now know that these numbers include people like yourself—people who *access* the Internet but might not provide any Internet *content*. As you'll read in Chapter 14, even though your iBook isn't a part of the Internet, you too can still provide Internet content via A Web page of your own creation. In Chapter 14 you'll see that this is a relatively easy and inexpensive thing to do, and something that anyone who becomes enthralled with the Internet should certainly attempt.

The World Wide Web (WWW)

The Internet is composed of different resources, or areas, or tools, that anyone with Internet access can make use of one. One such *subset* of the Internet is e-mail, the part of the Internet that allows electronic messages to be sent and retrieved by Internet users. Another popular subset of the Internet is the World Wide Web, or WWW, or, most commonly, simply *the Web*. To become a part of the Web, the webmaster (the person responsible for maintaining the information on an Internet-connected computer) creates one or more (most likely many) special files. Each file, or Web document, then becomes a Web page. Any Internet user who has *Web browsing software* (software that allows the information on Web pages to be properly transmitted to your computer) can visit just about any Web page. The exceptions are password-protected Web pages. Some businesses maintain some Web pages that a user must subscribe to (pay to visit). Most Web pages *aren't* password-protected.

The Web is what makes the Internet exciting. Much of the Internet used to be *text-based*—information displayed or transmitted existed as just text rather than text, graphics, video, and sound. When you visit a Web page, you'll view text—but you'll also encounter any combination of the just-mentioned multimedia elements. Another key feature of the Web is hypertext links. A *hypertext link* (or simply a *link*) is a highlighted word, phrase, or picture on a Web page that, when clicked on, transports you to a different Web page—a page that contains information related to the clicked-on link. The Web page that the link takes you to may on the same computer as the original Web page, or it may be on a computer in a different part of town or a different part of the world.

Hooking Up

To get connected to the Internet you need a computer, a modem, Internet access software, an Internet service provider, and an active telephone line. When you get an iBook, you get all but the last item. That exception is okay, though. If you were able to obtain a computer, it's pretty unlikely that you live in one of the remote places on Earth that doesn't have telephone service—so you're all set to get connected!

In short, to get connected to the Internet a computer user initially follows these steps:

1. Connect a modem to the computer
2. Connect an active phone line to the modem

3. Use Internet access software to tell the modem to dial up the phone number of a different modem—one that is located elsewhere and which is already connected to the Internet.

Once a connection is made, the user's computer is able to use Internet software (such as a Web browser) to access the features of the Internet (such as the Web). In this section we'll take a quick look at the physical connections that make Internet access a reality.

The iBook Modem

Modems are hardware devices used by computers to communicate with one another. For two computers to communicate via modems, each needs a modem connected to it. Then the two modems are connected to one another by way of a telephone line. The details of how the modems are able to transfer, and understand, data, or information, between themselves is important to the modems, but isn't important to us unsophisticated computer users.

What is important to you is that your iBook's modem is able to transfer information at a fast rate. Modem speed is given in *baud rate*, denoted by *bits per second*, or *bps*. Baud rates are in the thousands, so to shorten things up a bit one thousand is abbreviated as 1 K. Until recently, a baud rate of 33,600 (33.6 K) was considered pretty fast. As of this writing, the faster rate of 56,000 (56 K) is becoming standard. The iBook's modem operates at a speed up to 56 K.

A modem can be purchased as a separate device, or peripheral, and connected to a computer. Many computers, including the iBook, come with a built-in modem. You can't see the iBook's modem because it exists as electronic circuitry within the iBook. The only hint that a modem is indeed inside the iBook is revealed when you look near the rear of the left side of the computer. As shown in Figure 1-1 back in Chapter 1, among the ports along this side of the iBook is a modem port. The modem port accepts a standard telephone line connector.

Connecting a Telephone Line

To provide the iBook's modem with the ability to communicate with Internet-connected computers you begin by attaching a standard, active telephone line to the iBook's modem port. You don't need to have your local phone company add a separate phone line that will be dedicated to (reserved strictly for) your Internet use—but you may want to. A second line dedicated to the Internet means that your initial phone line remains free so that people who attempt to contact you by phone can get through. After you discover the simplicity of connecting to the Internet, and the variety of information available to you once you are connected, you might find yourself spending quite a bit of time online.

Setting Up Your Internet Account

You now have your iBook connected to an active phone line. But what number do you have the iBook modem dial in order to connect to the Internet? And once the Internet connection is made, how do you go about actually interacting with the Internet? Those two questions are addressed next.

Companies That Provide Internet Access

The phone line that's connected to your iBook modem (by way of the modem port on the iBook) is your means to accessing the Internet. The number that's to be dialed is dependent on just how you've elected to access the Internet. There are two types of businesses that are willing to let you use their facilities for the purpose of connecting to the Internet: Internet service providers and commercial online services.

Internet Service Providers

An *Internet service provider* (or *ISP*) is a company that is itself a part of the Internet—they maintain one or more computer's that are connected to other Internet-connected computers. Besides being a part of the Internet, an Internet service provider maintains thousands (or tens of thousands, or even hundreds of thousands) of modems which are each connected to the Internet service provider's own Internet-connected computer. To connect to the Internet you have your iBook dial up a special phone number that connects your iBook's modem with one of the Internet service provider's modems.

An Internet service provider exists solely as a means for computer users to access the Internet. So you can guess that the service they provide isn't free—

the ISP needs to charge a fee in order to maintain its computers and modems, pay its staff, and make a profit. Fortunately, the fee is what most people consider low—anywhere from $9 a month to $30 a month, with about $15 to $20 a month being the norm. In return for paying this fee you typically get unlimited Internet access. That is, there is no limit as to the number of times you can connect to the Internet, and there is no limit to the length of time you can spend online once your make a connection.

Commercial Online Services

Online services, such as America Online (AOL), Prodigy, and CompuServe, existed initially to provide users with an easy-to-use interface to some of the areas of the Internet, and also to provide their own, limited-access content. For instance, years ago, when accessing the Internet wasn't for the novice, America Online offered its users a software program that made it simple to connect to the Internet, send and retrieve e-mail, and download files from its own software collection. Computer users who weren't particularly computer-proficient, or weren't familiar with the intricacies of the Internet, found commercial online services such as AOL provided them with the means to join what was about to become the Internet revolution.

When the Web started to become popular, commercial online services started to focus on providing their members with access to the Web—along with access to other areas of the Internet (such as e-mail). Now, when you sign up with a commercial online service such as America Online you are also provided with the easy ability to access the Web.

Like Internet service providers, commercial online services survive by charging subscribers a monthly fee. This fee is typically $20 per month, and with it comes access to both the Internet (including the Web) and the commercial service's own content (such as areas dedicated to different interests, such as sports, computers, and news).

Internet Service Providers Versus Commercial Online Services

To connect to the Internet, you tell your iBook's modem to dial the phone number of a company that offers Internet access. That means you need to choose, and then subscribe to, a service provider that offers Internet access. When selecting a provider, you'll pick from one of the two above-mentioned categories: Internet service providers (ISPs) and commercial online services.

The preceding descriptions of ISPs and commercial online services may make it seem that commercial online services are always the route to take: they typically offer you Internet access *and* their own areas of content not accessible by non-members. The choice isn't quite that simple anymore, as ISPs have fought to gain users in a couple of ways.

Both online services and ISPs offer unlimited access options for a monthly fee. If you shop around, you'll find that there are many ISPs that offer monthly fees lower than online services—though the savings won't be huge. An online service that includes unlimited Internet access typically costs you about $20 a month, while an ISP that also offers unlimited Internet access can be found for about $12 or $15 a month.

The difference in the way services use the term *unlimited* is also a factor in choosing how you access the Internet. While a commercial online service such as America Online does say that you may connect to the Internet and remain connected for as long as you want, there is a catch. While connected, you must remain somewhat attentive to your iBook. Once you're connected, you need to do something (such as check for e-mail, visit a Web site, and so forth) occasionally or eventually America Online will automatically disconnect you and you'll need to redial the access number. This is done because with over 10 million subscribers, America Online doesn't have enough modems to ensure that all (or even a large percentage of) members can access AOL at any given time. If you're connected and aren't active, America Online disconnects you to free up the AOL modem your iBook was connected to. Internet service providers, on the other hand, mean it when they say their services are in fact unlimited. If you intend to stay connected to the Internet for extended periods of time, consider an Internet service provider.

Tip

Why *would* someone connect to the Internet, leave his or her computer unattended for perhaps long periods of time, and still want to remain connected to the Internet? Usually its people who receive a lot of e-mail that want this feature. People who use e-mail as their primary means of communicating with others (and many business people do in fact work this way) want to be able to get their messages at any time of the day. Some Web browsers and all e-mail programs have an option that flashes an icon on-screen when e-mail arrives, so a person connected to the Internet throughout the day always knows when e-mail has arrived.

Another possible advantage an Internet service provider may offer over a commercial online service is in the area of *Web page hosting*. In order to have your own Web page, you need to have space reserved for you on the hard drive of an Internet-connected computer. Both online services such as America Online and InTernet service providers offer yOu this space, but ISPs usually offer more space (meaning you can have more Web pages, or include more space-occupying graphics on your Web pages). If you're interested in having a Web page of your own (if you're able to connect to the Internet, the hard drive space is waiting for you!), read Chapter 14.

Setting Up Your iBook For the Connection

You've got your iBook connected to a phone Line, and you've decided upon a Means of accessing the Internet (that is, you've determined whether you'll use an Internet service provider or a commercial online service). There's one last step you may need to take in order to make that first connection, though. You've got to let your iBook know what your decision was.

Using a Commercial Online Service

If you're going to access the Internet through an online service such as America Online, you run that service's own software program and it walks you through the initial setup. While other services exist (notably CompuServe and Prodigy), I've mentioned America Online here because its software is included with the iBook, and because it's by far the most popular of the commercial services.

Tip

If you're serious about getting started with, and using, America Online, go back and read Chapter 5. Here, to give you an idea of how easy it is to use a commercial service, I'll just provide a quick overview of AOL.

When you run the America Online software for the first time the program asks you if you want to begin an automatic setup of an AOL account. If you're new to AOL, go ahead and leave that option selected (see Figure 6-1). Then click the **Next** arrow. If at any point in the process you decide you'd rather not become an AOL member, you'll have the option of canceling the whole setup.

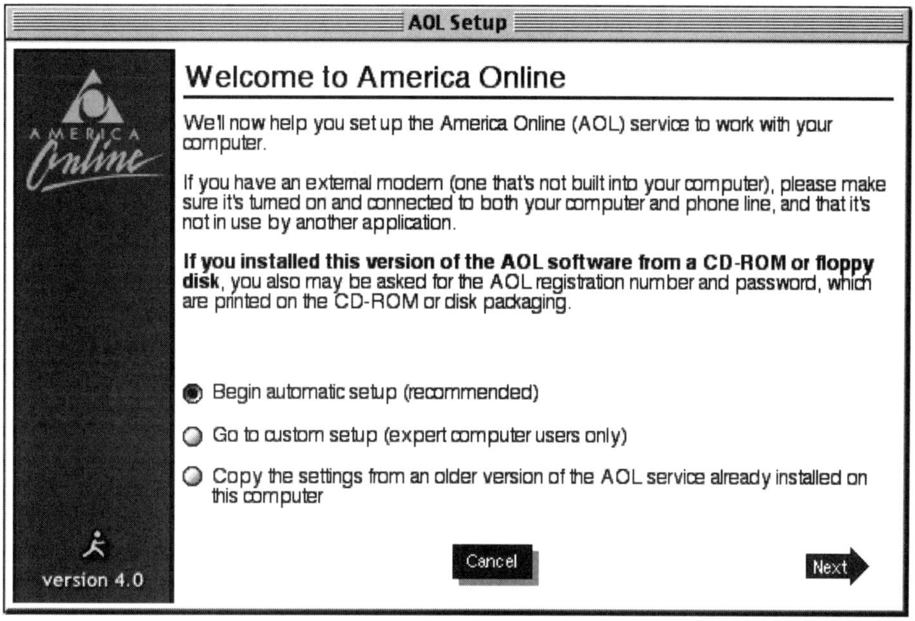

Figure 6-1 Signing up to be an AOL member.

The setup process begins with the AOL software determining the type of modem connected to your computer. After that the software asks you to answer a few phone-related questions, such as whether you have touch-tone service and your area code. The AOL software then returns one or more local phone numbers that you can use to log on to AOL. Then your first connection to AOL is made. The AOL software keeps track of which number to call and it automatically tells your iBook's modem to dial the number—so you don't have to worry about any of the log on details.

Once connected to AOL you need to agree to sign up for an account. Sorry, no free rides here! If you do agree, you'll be asked to enter your name, address, and telephone number. After that you're prompted to enter your payment method. If you choose a credit card type, you're then asked to enter the card information. After doing that, you're officially an AOL member. You'll choose a user name and a password, and from then on that's the information you use each time you want to log on to AOL.

Tip
If you'll be using America Online, refer to Chapter 5 to see how to use the AOL software to surf the Web, send e-mail, and do all sorts of other Internet-related stuff.

Using Apple's Internet Setup Assistant

The Apple Internet Setup Assistant software is designed to help you set up your iBook to either make use of an existing account you have with an Internet service provider, or to create a new account with an ISP. Double clicking on the Internet Setup Assistant icon on your iBook's hard drive starts up the assistant (you'll find this software on your desktop or in the Internet folder). At the opening screen you have the option of quitting or continuing on. If you carry on, then the assistant allows you to sign up with an Internet service provider (ISP) (the **No** button in Figure 6-2), or update the iBook so that it knows about an ISP that you are already signed up with (the **Yes** button in Figure 6-2).

Figure 6-2 The Internet Setup Assistant.

If you don't currently have service with an ISP, you'll click the **No** button and the assistant will start walking you through the process of signing up with an ISP named EarthLink. Just click the Setup button to begin (see Figure 6-3). You'll fill out a series of forms, such as the one shown in Figure 6-4. The information required of you is pretty self-explanatory, but the software goes a long way to making sure you don't become confused (it even *talks* you through the process).

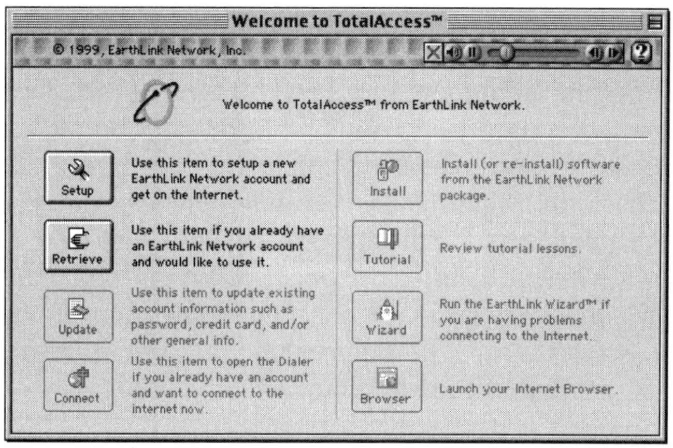

Figure 6-3 Starting the EarthLink sign up process.

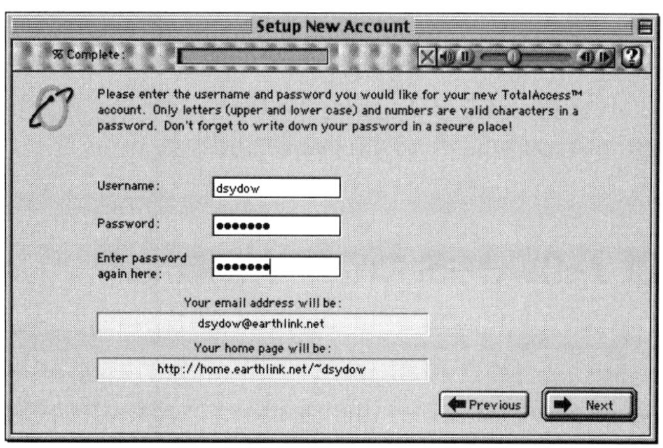

Figure 6-4 Entering information needed by EarthLink.

Eventually the assistant will automatically connect your iBook to the Internet in order to complete your registration with EarthLink. When finished, you'll have agreed to EarthLink's policies (and, of course, have given EarthLink your credit card information), and EarthLink will have made you a member and set up your iBook such that you can easily connect to the Internet via EarthLink at any time.

At this writing Apple has selected EarthLink to be the Internet service provider. It's important to note that if you don't currently have an Internet service provider, and you want one, you aren't obligated to use EarthLink. Apple's just made it very easy for you to get started with this particular ISP. If you already have an ISP, then you may still want to use the Internet Setup Assistant before first attempting to connect to the Internet. By using the assistant you can easily supply your iBook with the information it needs (such as the phone number to dial) in order to connect to your ISP. When you click the Yes button (back in Figure 6-2), the Internet Setup Assistant starts the processes of displaying and requesting information—all from its one window. After reading a window of information, click on the right-facing arrow icon at the window's lower right to view a new window of information. The questions that the assistant asks will require that you have information about your ISP handy—so get that information out before you begin.

If you do elect to sign up with EarthLink, the Internet Setup Assistant will see to it that your iBook Internet-related software is set up so that in the future connecting to the Internet is a snap. Any time you launch an Internet application (such as the Netscape Navigator Web browser or the Microsoft Internet Explorer Web browser) your iBook will automatically dial up the ISP's number and connect to the Internet. Optionally you can run the Remote Access Status application from under the Apple menu on your iBook to click a button to connect to the Internet. Quitting the Internet is easy to do as well—just click the Remote Access Status **Disconnect** button.

Internet Access Software

The Internet consists of a number of different areas—e-mail and the World Wide Web being the most commonly accessed. To access an area of the Internet you need to make use of the appropriate software. For the Web, you need to use a Web browser.

Moving About the Web

Every Web page has it's own, unique address. Once you're iBook is connected to the Internet, your tool to navigate the Web is the Web browser. Entering an address in a Web browser window causes the browser to find the specified Web page and display that page's contents in a the window.

Note

As you'll read in Chapter 8, very often you don't need to know the address of a Web page in order to move to that page. That's because one Web page is often linked, or associated, with another page by means of a hypertext link. A hypertext link is a Web page word, phrase, or picture that you click on in order to move to (display) a different Web page.

The Format of a Web Page Address

A Web page *address* is also referred to as the page's URL (Uniform Resource Locator). A URL is text that identifies a single Web page. There are three parts to a single URL: the protocol, server, and pathname.

Protocol The protocol specifies the format by which the Web browser should interpret the information on a page. The pages you visit will most often have information stored in the HyperText Transfer Protocol, or HTTP. A colon follows the protocol of a URL. For instance, in the URL `http://www.apple.com/support`, the `http:` part of the URL is the protocol.

Server The server identifies the computer system that holds the information that makes up the specified Web page. The server name is preceded by two slashes. In the URL `http://www.apple.com/support`, the `//www.apple.com` part of the URL is the server.

Pathname The pathname identifies the location of a page on the server. Because a server may (and almost always does) hold more than one Web page, this pathname is necessary to specify which page you're interested in viewing. Each segment of a pathname is preceded by a single slash. In the URL `http://www.apple.com/support`, the `/support` segment of the URL is the pathname. If a URL includes more than one occurrence of a single slash, then that URL's pathname includes one or more folders. For instance, the URL:

`http://www.apple.com/hotnews/features/jobsthinkingdifferent.html`

has a pathname of `/hotnews/features/jobsthinkingdifferent.html`. The `/jobsthinkingdifferent.html` segment of that pathname refers to a particular Web page name, while the `/hotnews/features` segment refers to a folder named `features` that itself is in a folder named `hotnews`. In summary (well, as summarized as possible), the information for the Web page that holds information about Steve Jobs' talk of a year of "thinking different" can be found in a file named `jobsthinkingdifferent.html`, and that file is located in a folder named `features` in a folder named `hotnews` on a server named `www.apple.com`.

Tip
Some URLs appear to not include a pathname. The URL `http://www.apple.com` is an example. When a URL doesn't have pathname listed, a Web browser knows to use a special file located on the given server. That special file is usually named index.html. That means entering a URL of `http://www.apple.com` or entering a URL of `http://www.apple.com/index.html` will result in the same Web page being displayed.

Browsers and Addresses

To move to a particular Web page (to display the contents of a particular Web page within a window of a Web browser), you enter thaT page's address, or URL, in the browser. Entering the URL involves clicking in an address box and typing in the URL. Exactly where the address box is located is dependent on the Web browser you're using. The same holds true for exactly what the address

Figure 6-5 Entering a URL in AOL, Navigator, and Internet Explorer.

In the America Online browser the address box isn't labeled. In Netscape Navigator the box is named **Go To**. Microsoft has given this same box the name **Address**. In all cases the address box works the same: click in the box, type in a URL, and then press the Return or Enter key on the keyboard. After that the browser finds the specified address (assuming your iBook is connected to the Internet at the time you're doing all this), retrieves the information at the located address, and displays that information in the browser's window.

Tip
Read Chapter 8 for more details on the above-mentioned browsers. Read Chapter 9 for more details on browsing the Web—regardless of which Web browser you use.

Online Services and the Web

If you join the commercial online service America Online, the act of logging on to AOL also connects you to the Internet. To browse the Web all you need to do is enter a URL in the address box located under the tool bar near the top of the monitor (refer back to Figure 6-5). Press the Return or Enter key and the AOL software opens a browser window (if one isn't already open) and fills that window with the information located at the address you entered. Figure 6-6 shows how an AOL browser window looks when displaying the information at the MacCentral Macintosh news Web site.

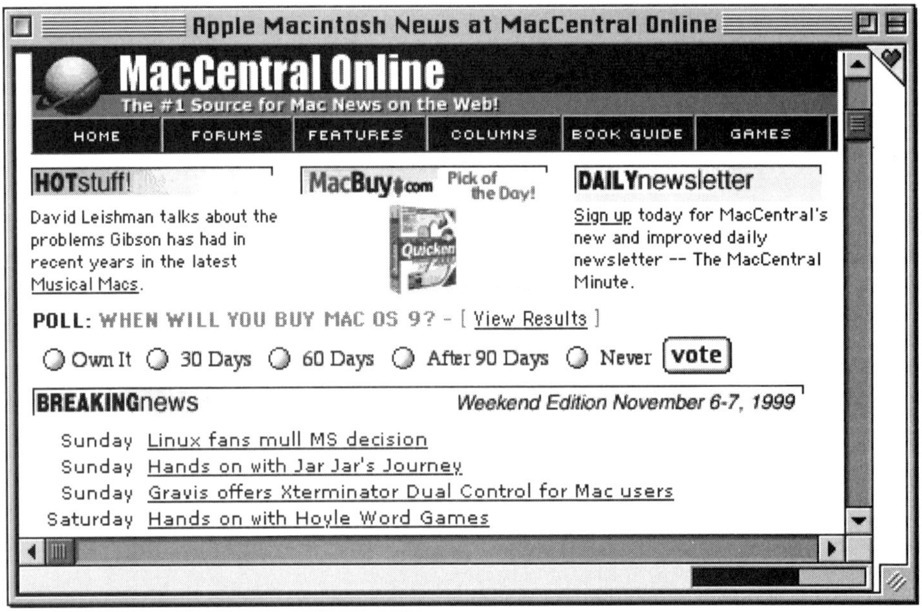

Figure 6-6 America Online's built-in Web browser.

Internet Service Providers and the Web

If you elect to connect to the Internet by way of an Internet service provider, then you have your choice of using either the Netscape Navigator or the Microsoft Internet Explorer browser. If you use Navigator, type a URL in the **Go To** box (refer to Figure 6-5) and press the Return or Enter key. If you instead choose Internet Explorer, then type a URL in the **Address** box and press the Return or Enter key. In either case the browser software will display the results in a browser window. Regardless of which browser you use—America Online's, Netscape's, or Microsoft's—the results will look very similar.

7

E-mail and ISPs

Of the many Internet functions, e-mail, or electronic mail, is the one that is most commonly used. When you access the Internet for the first time you *may* want to jump right in and start visiting World Wide Web sites. But it's equally as likely that you'll want to quickly create and send an e-mail message—even if only to prove to someone that you've arrived on the 'Net! If you're an America Online user, then you'll want to use the AOL software to send, receive, and organize your e-mail (refer to Chapter 5 for the information on AOL and e-mail). If you connect to the Internet by way of an Internet service provider, then you should consider using e-mail client software—a program dedicated to working with e-mail. Your iBook comes with such a program—Microsoft's Outlook Express. In this chapter you'll see how to use Outlook Express to receive and read messages sent to you. You'll also find out how to attach files to an e-mail message—a skill that's handy for distributing files to other and also to yourself (yes, yourself).

E-Mail

There are numerous programs that allow you to compose, send, receive, read, and organize e-mail. But if you aren't too familiar with these various programs, picking Microsoft's Outlook Express is a good choice. It came free with your iBook, and it's a more than adequate e-mail program.

Note
If you're an America Online user, you don't need or use a separate e-mail program such as Outlook Express. Instead, read Chapter 5 to see how to use the e-mail software that's built into the America Online program.

Internet E-mail Addresses

Just as you need to know a person's street address in order to send him or her US Mail, you need to know a person's e-mail address in order to send that person an e-mail message. Every e-mail address is composed of three parts. Consider the address `jimmymac@alpha.net` as you read about the three address parts.

Mailbox name This component of the address (also referred to as the user name, or user ID, or screen name) is the part of the address that precedes the `@` symbol. The mailbox name may consist of letters and numbers. It may not include commas, spaces, or parentheses. The mailbox name identifies one person on a particular system (both the @ symbol and systems are discussed next). For the address `jimmymac@alpha.net`, the mailbox name is `jimmymac`.

@ (the at symbol) The @ symbol always separates an address mailbox name from an address host name. And speaking of host name...

Host name The host name indicates on what system the recipient has his or her account. It also indicates the type of system. In our current example, `jimmymac@alpha.net` is a person with an account on a system known as `alpha`. The `net` in the host name `alpha.net` means that the host is a networking organization, and is no doubt the host name of an Internet service provider. If our friend `jimmymac` had an America Online account, then his e-mail address would be `jimmymac@aol.com`. Here `aol` stands for America Online, and `com` refers to the fact that America Online is a commercial organization (in short, a business). The last part of the host name is called the *zone*. As shown in the table on the next page, each zone is three characters in length and represents an organization of a specific type.

Zone	Organization Type
com	Commercial organization
edu	Educational institution
gov	Government body
int	International organization
mil	Military site (United States)
net	Networking organization
org	Organization that doesn't fit into any other zone

As you see in this chapter's Microsoft Outlook Express section, once you know a person (or company's) e-mail address, sending a message is easy.

Getting Started

When you first start Outlook Express you may see an alert window like the one shown in Figure 7-1. Before sending or receiving e-mail, Outlook Express needs to know about how your Internet Service Provider handles electronic mail. To give Outlook Express that information, choose **Preferences** from the **Edit** menu. Click on the E-mail item under the Accounts category to see the fields of information shown in Figure 7-2.

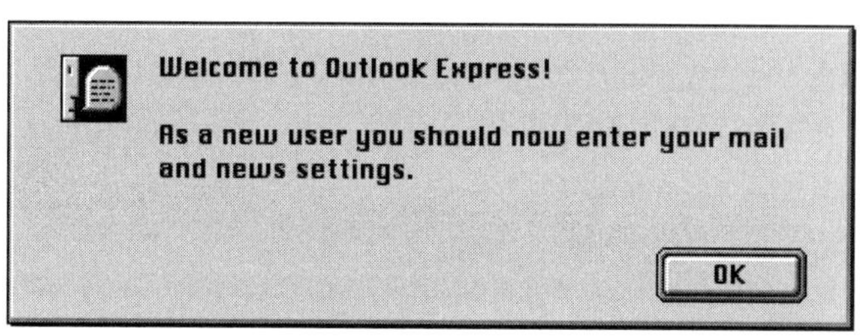

Figure 7-1 An introductory message from Outlook Express.

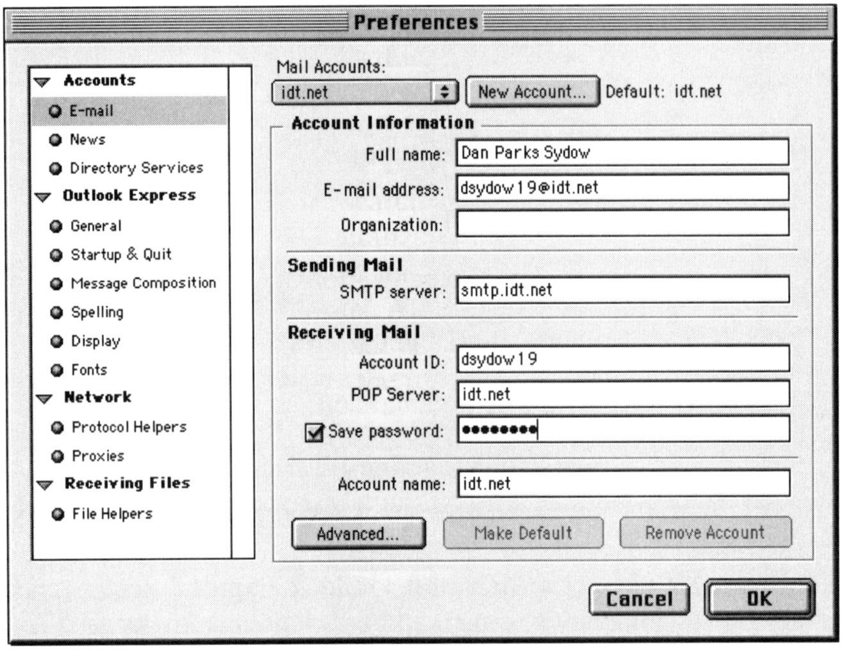

Figure 7-2 Configuring Outlook Express.

When you click on E-mail, you'll see a number of boxes that need to be filled in (see Figure 7-2). Or perhaps they won't need filling in. If you've entered the requested information for use in a different e-mail program, Outlook Express may find that information on its own and fill in the boxes for you. If not, you'll need to do the work yourself. Here's a summary of the needed information.

Full Name Here you type your first and last name (and, optionally, your middle name).

E-mail Address Type your complete e-mail address in this box.

Organization If you're sending e-mail from your office, you may want to fill in this box with your company's name.

SMTP server Your Internet service provider has a name for the mail server (computer) that the ISP uses for sending outgoing mail. This *Simple Mail Transport Protocol* name will have been provided to you by your ISP.

Account ID This box holds just the mailbox component of your e-mail address—the part of the address that precedes the @ symbol. For the address `jimmymac@alpha.net`, the Account ID would be `jimmymac`.

POP Server The Post Office Protocol is a way in which mail is transferred over the Internet. Your Internet service provider has a name it uses for its incoming mail (recall that the SMTP server is the server used by your ISP for *outgoing* e-mail). The POP name will have been provided to you by your ISP.

Save password box To receive your e-mail you need to enter your account password each time you run Outlook Express. Figure 7-3 shows the dialog box you're faced with when you attempt to retrieve new mail messages (note that your **Connect** to name and your **User ID** will differ from the figure's). This e-mail password is one that your Internet service provider gave you. If you want to avoid entering your password so often, check the **Save Password** check box in the Preferences window and then type your password. As you type the password, its characters are represented by dark circles to hide the password from anyone looking over your shoulder. If people other than yourself have access to your iBook, consider leaving the **Save Password** check box unchecked so that anyone who attempts to retrieve your new mail (including yourself) will face the dialog box shown in Figure 7-3.

Account name Provide a name for your mail account. There is no right or wrong value here—this name simply serves as an identifier. For instance, *My Email Info* will do just fine as an account name. Some people have more than one account, and for such people this account name serves as a reminder of which account they are currently working from. If you have just one account (most likely the case), you still need to supply an account name here.

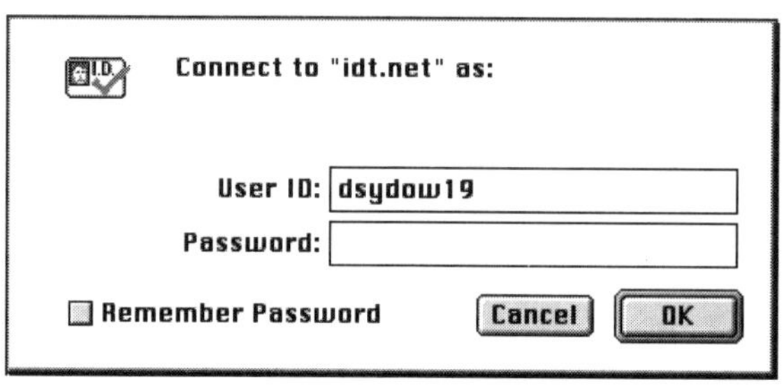

Figure 7-3 A password is required to retrieve e-mail.

The Preferences window is important to getting your E-mail account set up, but it's a window you'll encounter perhaps only one time. The main Outlook Express window (shown in Figure 7-4), on the other hand, is one you'll face the entire time you're running Outlook Express. This main window serves as a command post of sorts—from here you create new messages to send, retrieve and read messages others sent to you, and organize your mail.

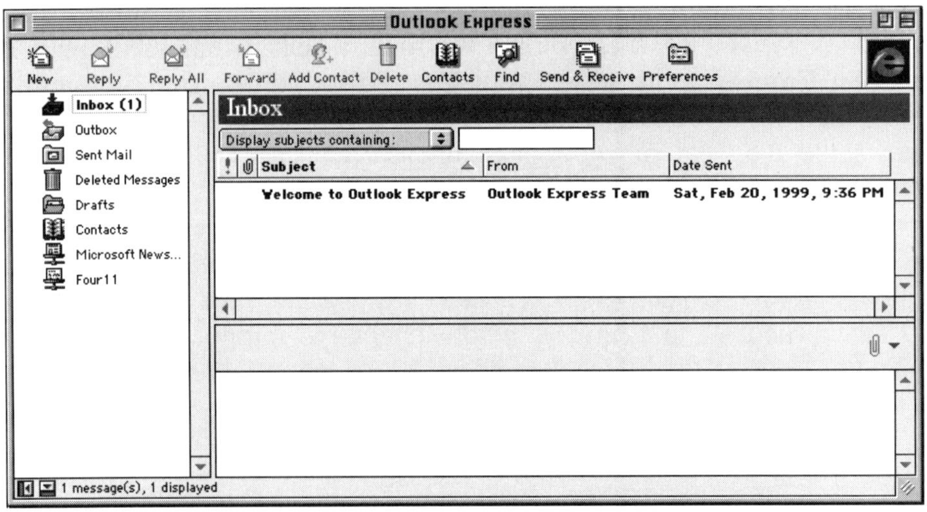

Figure 7-4 The main window of Outlook Express.

The main window includes a number of icons running along the top of it. The most important of these icons are the **New** icon (used for creating a new mail message) and the **Send & Receive** icon (used to send any new, unsent messages you've written and to retrieve any new, awaiting messages sent to you by others).

The left area of the main window holds a number of items. In your early stages of learning to use Outlook Express you can get by without knowing about these items, but a brief introduction to the most important ones may prove helpful:

Inbox Holds newly received messages.

Outbox Holds unsent messages that you've written.

Sent Mail Holds copies of messages you've sent.

Deleted Messages Holds messages you're finished with.

Important
When you're finished reading a message, it stays in the Inbox until you move it into Deleted Messages. If you want to save the message for future reference, don't place it in the Deleted Messages trash can. Simply leaving the read message in the Inbox is one way to save the message.

The upper of the two areas on the right side of the main window displays the messages that are held in one of several folders. The messages displayed here vary depending on which item is currently selected in the main window's leftmost list. In Figure 7-4 the Inbox is selected, so this upper-right area displays the contents of the Inbox (which the figure shows to be a single message titled *Welcome to Outlook Express*).

The bottom of the two areas on the right side of the main window displays the contents of a single message. To read a message, first display its title in the upper area (by clicking on the appropriate list item, such as Inbox). Then click on the message title in the upper area. Doing that displays the contents of the message. For example, to read the *Welcome to Outlook Express* message listed in Figure 7-4 I'd click on that message title.

Sending E-Mail

Before sending e-mail you need to create, or compose, a message. Begin by clicking on the **New** icon in the main window of Outlook Express. A new message window like the one shown in Figure 7-5 appears.

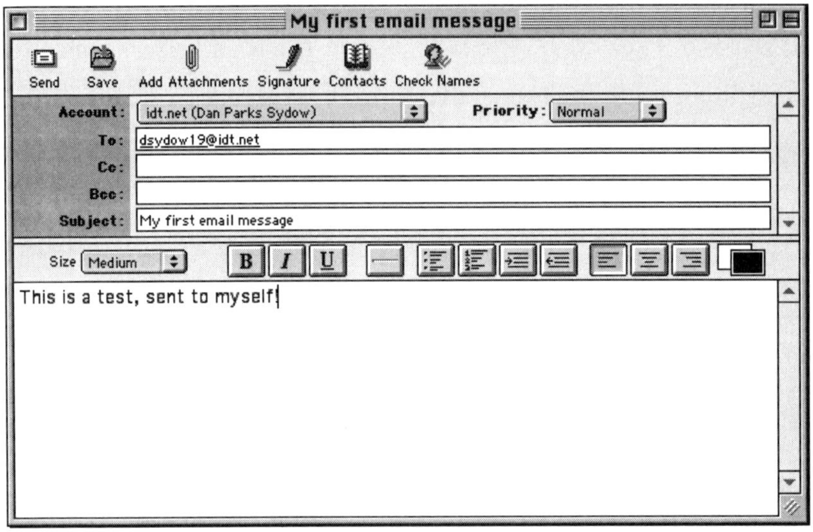

Figure 7-5 A new message window.

A new message needs to list the message recipient, so you'll need to know the recipient's e-mail address. There are a number of ways in which you'll have a person's e-mail address:

Memorized If you e-mail someone often, you may have that person's e-mail address committed to memory. Some e-mail addresses are simple to remember, some aren't. For example, Figure 7-5 shows that one of my addresses is `dsydow19@idt.net`. The address includes part of my name, but it isn't likely that someone will remember the address. One of my other addresses (I have more than one e-mail account) is much easier to remember. The address `dan@sydow.com` includes my first and last name.

Business card These days, a business card typically includes an e-mail address.

Prior e-mail contact If the person has sent e-mail to you in the past, an e-mail address will be included in the message. If you still have the message saved, reread it.

Contact list Once you know a person's e-mail address, use the Contacts feature of Outlook Express (discussed ahead) to save the address for future correspondence.

Internet search Use an Internet e-mail address search site (refer to Chapter 9) to find a person's e-mail address (note that not all addresses can be found by this means).

Once you have the person's e-mail address, type it in the **To** box of the message window. As a text, you might want to enter your own e-mail address in the To box in order to send yourself an e-mail message. Now click in the **Subject** box and type in an appropriate subject. Click in the main text area and type your message.

Outlook Express includes a number of text-formatting features. You can apply formatting to any portion of the text by selecting the text and then clicking the appropriate formatting button, such as the **B** button to make the text bold.

When you're satisfied with the text of your message, click the **Send** icon located at the top left of the message window. After doing that a Progress window appears to show you That the message is being sent. After the message is sent, the window disappears—your message has been transmitted to the specified recipient.

Receiving and Reading E-Mail

To "manually" check to see if someone has sent you e-mail, click on the **Send & Receive** icon located near the upper-right of the Outlook Express main window. Since I've mailed myself a message in the *Sending E-Mail* section of this chapter, I can test out the receiving of e-mail now by clicking on this icon. As shown in Figure 7-6, the title of a new, unread message appears in bold in the upper right area of the main window of Outlook Express (if it doesn't appear, click on the Inbox item on the left of the main window to make sure the upper right area is displaying new messages).

To read the message, click on its name. As shown in figure 7-7, the text of the message appears in the lower part of the main window.

If the message includes one or more attachments (files that the sender added, or attached, to the e-mail message), the paper-clip icon will be enabled. Attachments are described later in this chapter, in the *Attachments* section.

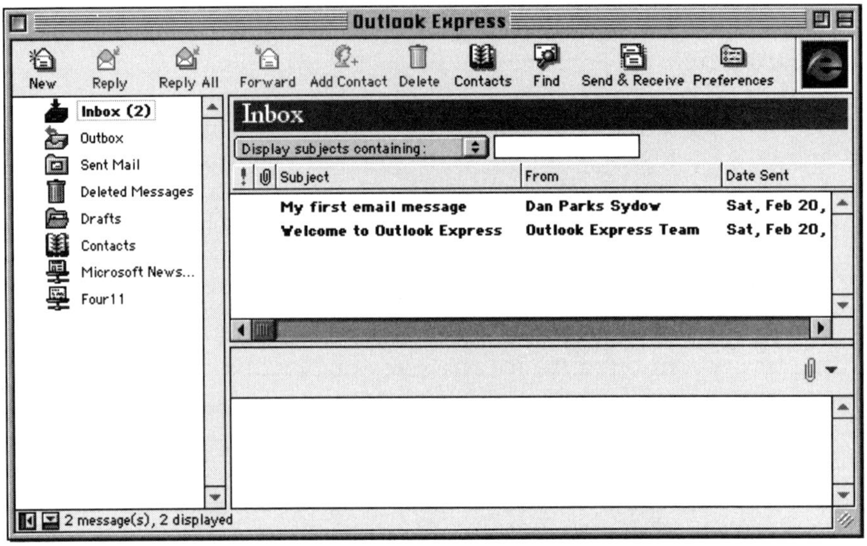

Figure 7-6 An unread message has a boldface title.

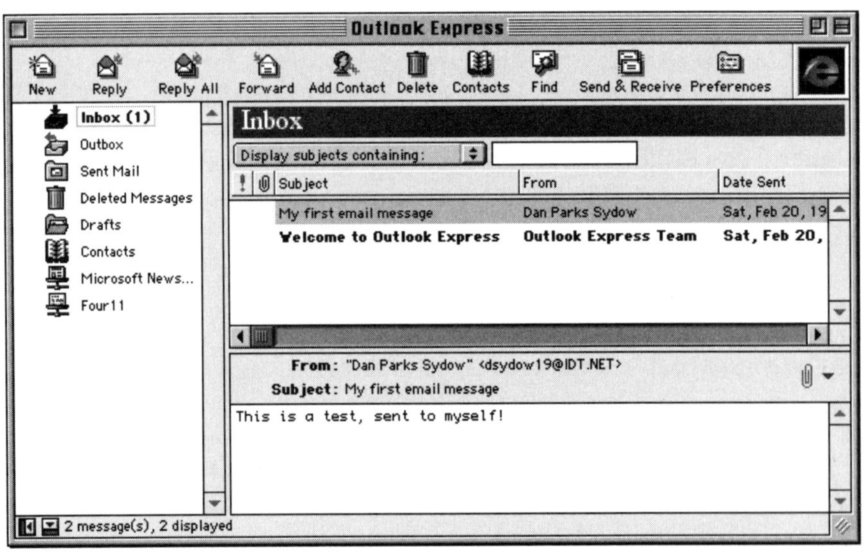

Figure 7-7 Displaying a message in the main window.

To get a better view of the text of a message you can double-click on the message title in the upper right area of the main window. Doing that displays a new window that holds the contents of the message (see Figure 7-8).

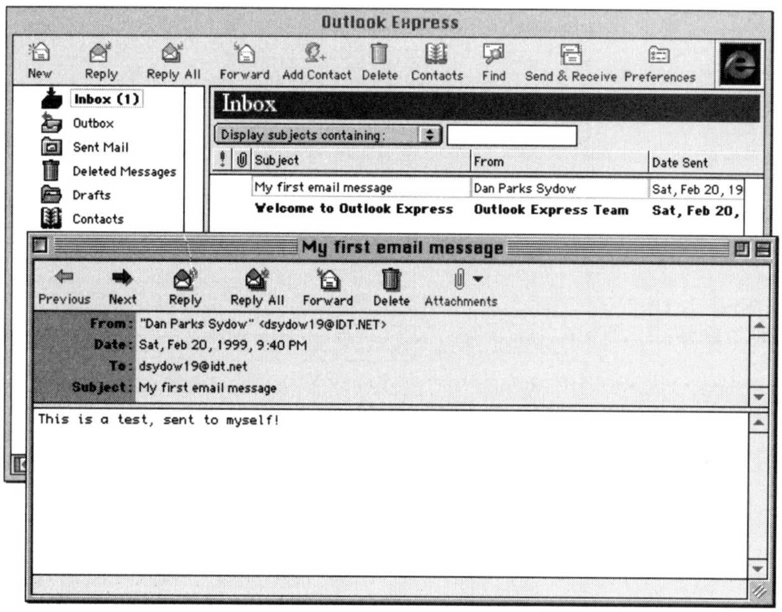

Figure 7-8 Displaying a message in its own window.

To set up Outlook Express to periodically check for new mail, choose **Preferences** from the **Edit** menu to display the Preferences window. Click on **General** under the **Outlook Express** category in the list in this window, as I've done in Figure 7-9.

Check the **Check for mail every x minutes** check box, then enter a number in the box. Since I have no real life, I spend hours sitting by my Mac waiting for e-mail. Thus I've entered a small number in this box so that Outlook Express frequently reports to me whether or not I have new mail! When Outlook Express does check for mail, a small Progress window appear for a few moments and then disappears.

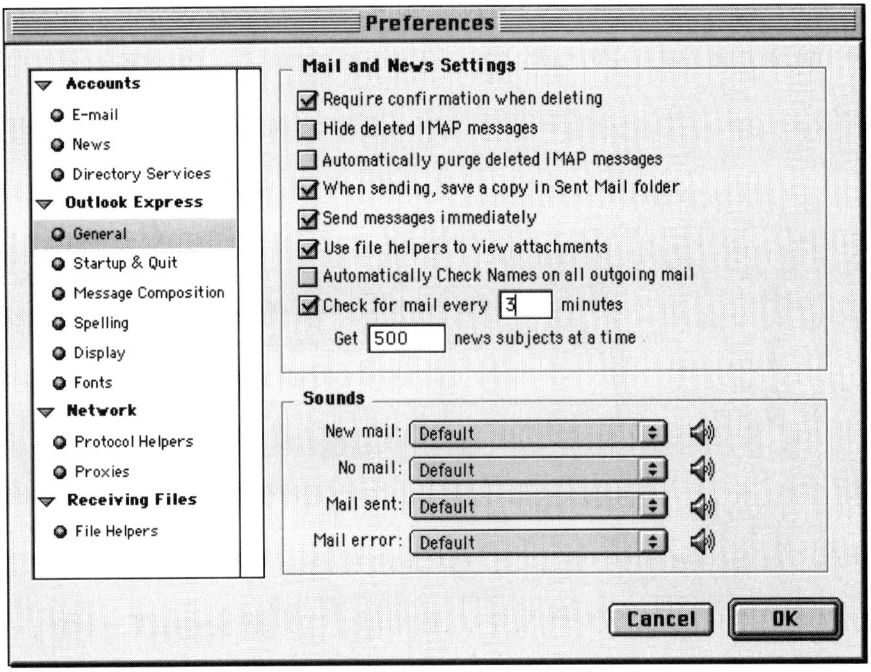

Figure 7-9 The General area of the Preferences window.

Replying to E-Mail

After reading an e-mail message, you may be inclined to reply to it. That is, you might want to send a message right back to the person who sent you the message you just read. As you read in this chapter's *Sending E-Mail* section, you could do this by clicking the **New** icon, typing the address of the intended recipient, typing the subject of the message, typing the text of your message, and finally clicking the **Send** icon. Or, you could click the **Reply** icon (see the top of Figure 7-10 for a look at that icon) and let Outlook Express do a little bit of the work for you. In Figure 7-10 you see that I've clicked on the subject of an e-mail message and am now reading that message. Normally I'd click the **Delete** icon when I encounter such a message, but for the sake of example I'll reply to this one!

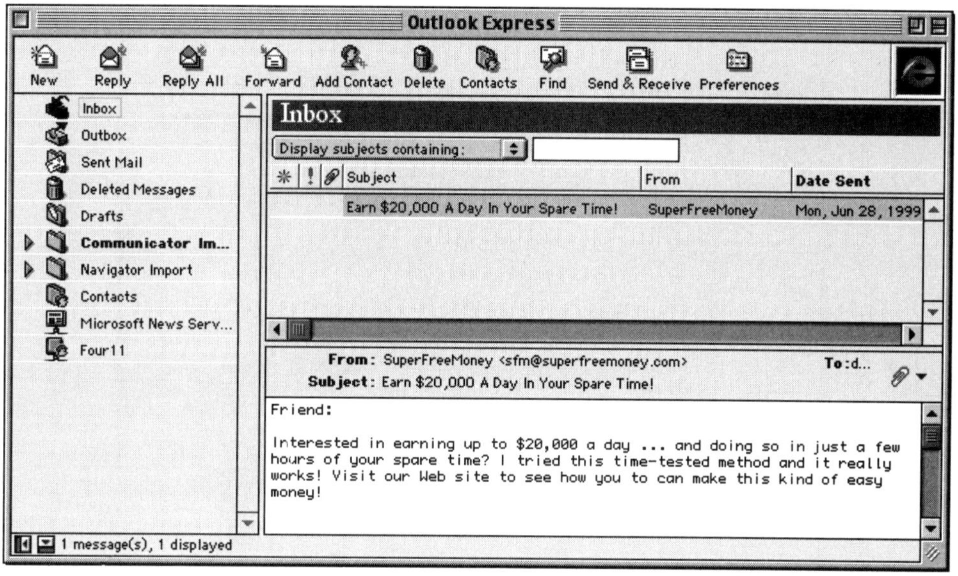

Figure 7-10 Reading an e-mail message.

To reply to a message, click the **Reply** icon. Doing that displays a new message window—just as clicking the **New** icon does. Now, however, Outlook Express fills in the address of the recipient and the message subject. Looking at Figure 7-11 you'll see that the **To** field and the **Subject** field are both filled in. I had nothing to do with that—Outlook Express handled those tasks.

There's one other thing that Outlook Express does in the new message—the program quotes the entire original message. That is, the text of the original message, with each line prefaced by the ">" character, appears in the body of your new message. This serves as a reminder to the recipient—he or she may not recall just what it is your writing back about unless you echo the message.

After adding your own text to this reply message, click the **Send Now** icon as you would for any other e-mail message you'd send.

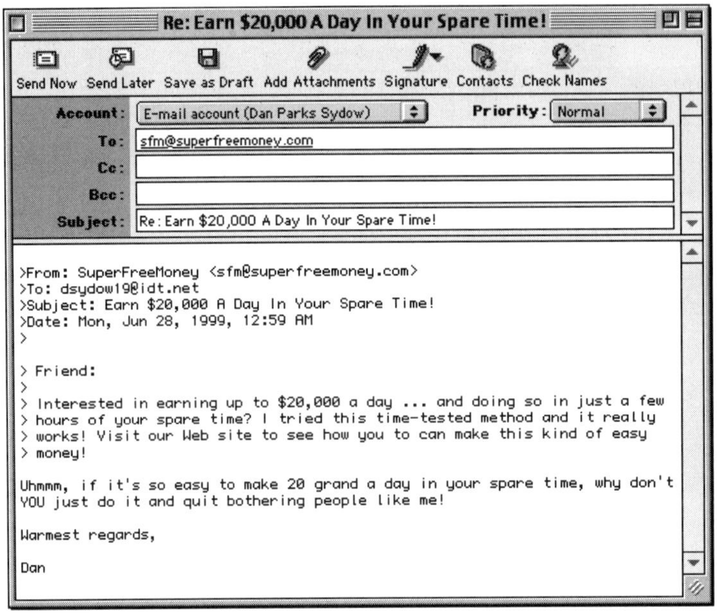

Figure 7-11 Replying to an e-mail message.

Attachments

You can add files to an e-mail message so that these files get sent along with the message. The recipient of the message then gets both the text of your e-mail message *and* the attached files. Outlook Express makes it easy to add attachments to an e-mail message you send, and to access attachments that are a part of an e-mail message you receive.

Adding Attachments to a Message to Send

To specify that a file be attached to an e-mail message, first create a new message by clicking the **New** icon in the main window of Outlook Express. Then click the **Add Attachments** icon in the message window to bring up the dialog box shown in Figure 7-12.

Use the pop-up menu at the top of the dialog box to move to the folder that holds the file to attach. Click on the file name, then click the **Add** button. The selected file appears in the list at the bottom of the dialog box. In Figure 7-12

I've selected a file named *1999.02.MonthlyReport* from the folder named *Reports*. Because years ago I quit my full-time engineering job to pursue a writing career, it's obvious that this is a hypothetical example—I have absolutely no one to deliver any kind of monthly report to. Still, the example accurately demonstrates how to attach a file to a message!

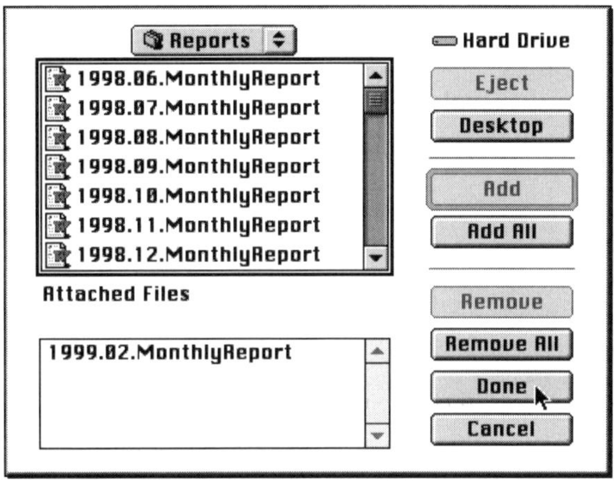

Figure 7-12 Specifying a file to attach to a message.

If you want to attach more than one file to an e-mail message, select the additional files in this same way. When finished, click the **Done** button. After clicking the **Done** button the dialog box disappears and the e-mail message window reflects the fact that an attachment has been made by displaying the attached file in the bottom of the message window. Figure 7-13 shows a message window after a single file has been attached (the Microsoft Word file named *1999.02.MonthlyReport*).

To send the e-mail message, complete with attachment, click the **Send** icon located at the top of the message window.

Encoding Attachments

When you send an e-mail message, you're typically sending text—written words. When you attach a file to a message, you may again be sending just text, or you may be sending information in other formats. For instance, if you attach a shopping list to a message, you may be just sending a text file—a file that holds only text. However, if you attach a Microsoft Word file, or a QuickTime movie file, or a program, or a file that holds a picture, you'll be sending information other than just text. This non-text transfer complicates matters because the Internet was established as a means of transmitting only text. Thus successfully transferring this more complex set of information across the Internet is a little trickier than successfully transferring plain old text. To greatly enhance your chances of having the recipient successfully receive a message's attachments, you'll want to *encode* that attachment.

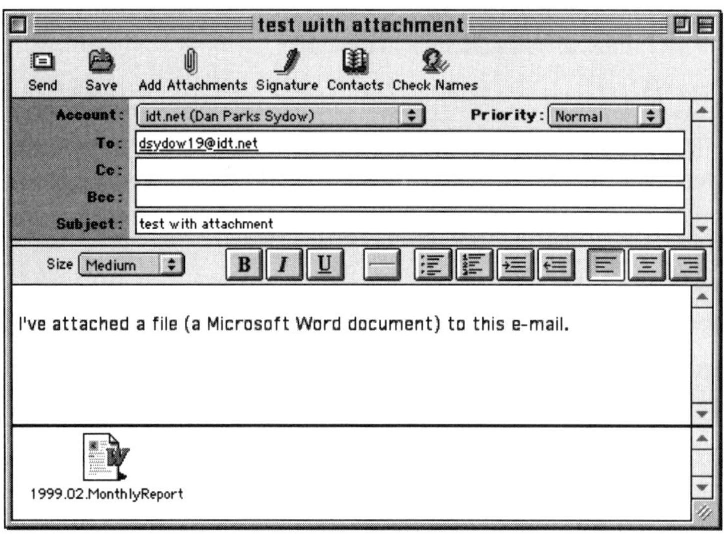

Figure 7-13 A message with a file attached.

Encoding is a means, or technique, of converting binary, or non-text, information into text—and of converting the altered information back to its original format. Converting a binary file, such as a picture file or a program into text, and then converting that text back to its original Form is very tricky stuff. Fortunately you and I don't need to know anything about how that's done—we only need to know that it's very possible to do.

There are several different types of file encoding, including Base64, BinHex, and UUEncode. Again, the specifics of each aren't important. What is important is that if successful encoding is to take place, then both ends of a message—the sender and the recipient—must have the ability to use the same type of encoding. So if you specify that an attached file be encoded using, say, the UUEncode format, then the recipient of your message must be using an e-mail program that is capable of working with UUEncode-encoded messages. This requirement used to mean that file attachment encoding caused innumerable problems. Now, e-mail programs have become very sophisticated, and most are capable of working with a variety of encoding formats. In Outlook Express you can choose from one of three encoding formats (or no encoding at all) for attachments. As shown in Figure 7-14, it's the Preferences dialog box that allows you to specify which encoding method to use.

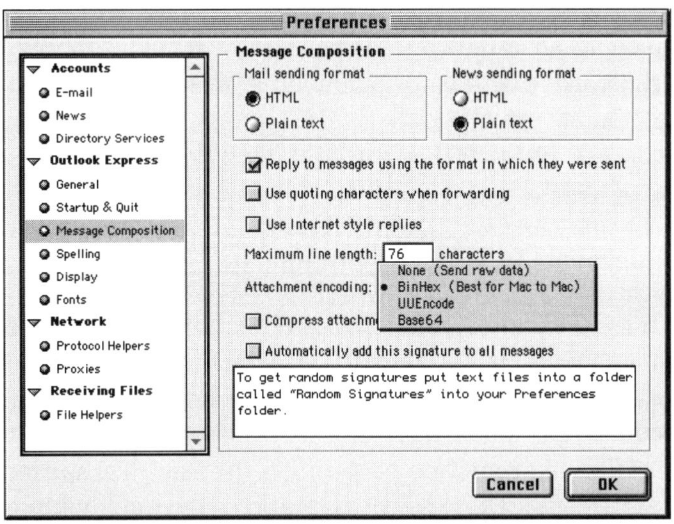

Figure 7-14 Choosing an encoding method.

To set encoding, choose **Preferences** from the **Edit** menu. Then click on Message Composition under the Outlook Express category. Now choose an item from the Attachment encoding pop-up menu (shown in Figure 7-14). Choosing an encoding type can be confusing, so consider the following points.

If you're sending a Macintosh file (since you're on an iBook, you are doing this much) to someone you know is on a Macintosh (in other words, the message will make a Macintosh-to-Macintosh journey), use BinHex as the encoding type. Macintosh file are often composed of two parts (a resource fork and a data fork, if you must know), and using the BinHex encoding method ensures that both parts of the one file get successfully transmitted.

If you *know* the recipient *isn't* using a Mac, or you *aren't sure* of the type of computer the recipient is using, choose either Base64 or UUEncode. Both of these encoding methods are very common in the PC world, so a PC user that receives an attached file stands an excellent chance of being able to decode the attached file. If the recipient happens to be using a Mac, then there is also a good chance that he or she will be able to access the attached file (assuming the recipient is using a good e-mail program such as Outlook Express!).

Accessing Attachments From a Received Message

When you receive an e-mail message, it may include one or more attachments. You can easily see if an attachment is present by looking to the left of the message title in the Outlook Express main window. If there is a little paper-clip icon just to the left of the title, then that message includes one or more attachments. Back in Figure 7-7 you can see that the first e-mail message I sent, the one cleverly titled *My first email message*, doesn't include an attachment (notice the lack of a paper-clip icon).

To access a message's attachments, begin by clicking on the message title to display the message in the bottom part of the main window. When you do this with a message that includes one or more attachments, you'll notice that the paper-clip icon in the lower-right of the window is enabled (yes, I'm now referring to a *different* paper-clip icon than the one that appears next to the message title). If you click on a message title in the main window of Outlook Express, and this paper-clip icon becomes enabled, that message has one or more attachments. You can find out just how many, and access them, by clicking on the paper-clip icon and holding down the mouse button. That displays a pop-up menu like the one shown in Figure 7-15.

Figure 7-15 illustrates the result of sending the message shown in Figure 7-13 back in this chapter's *Adding Attachments to a Message to Send* section. Recall that for that message I attached one Microsoft Word file named

1999.02.MonthlyReport to a message. Now, in Figure 7-15, you see that file name listed in the pop-up menu. If I had attached additional files to the message, they too would be listed in the menu.

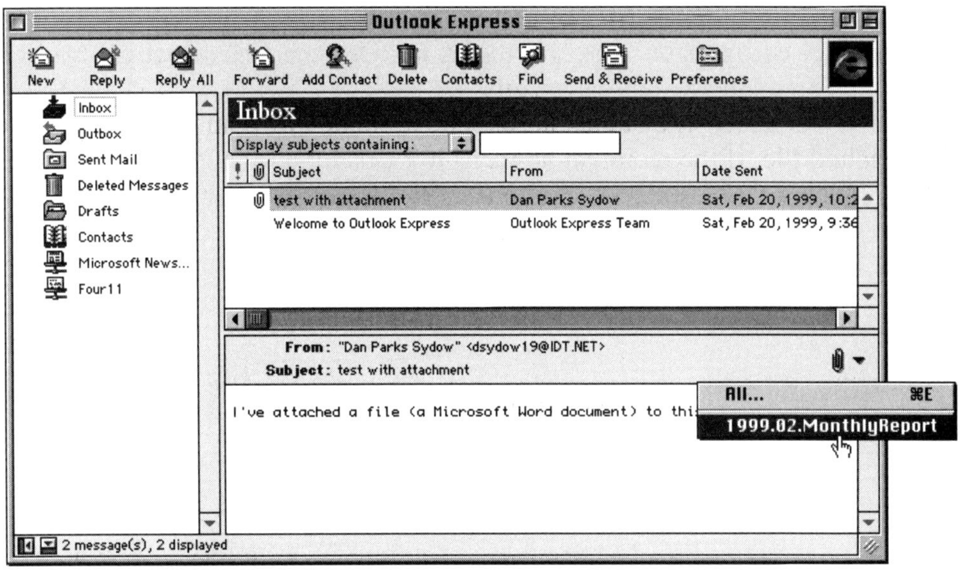

Figure 7-15 The attachments pop-up menu.

Tip

If you haven't already done so, create a new mail message, add one or more attachments to it, and then send it to yourself. If you haven't set up Outlook Express to automatically check for new e-mail (refer to this chapter's *Receiving and Reading E-Mail* section), then after sending the message you'll need to click on the **Send & Receive** icon located along the top of the main window of Outlook Express. Don't be alarmed if the sent message isn't immediately available—it needs to travel the phone lines to your Internet service provider's server, and then back to your iBook. This trip, however, takes as little as a few seconds and at most usually a few minutes.

To access an attachment, choose its name from the paper-clip pop-up menu. Doing that starts up the program that created the attachment and opens the attachment. So, for instance, choosing *1999.02.MonthlyReport* from the message in Figure 7-15 starts up Microsoft Word and opens that Word file.

If you'd rather not display the contents of a single file, but would rather have all of a message's attachments (even if there's only one) saved to a folder on your hard drive, choose **All** from the paper-clip pop-up menu. As shown in Figure 7-16, doing that brings up a dialog box that lets you select a folder into which the attachments will be saved.

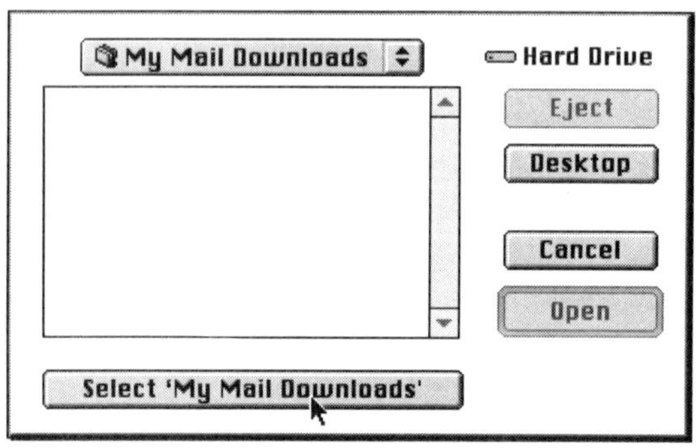

Figure 7-16 Specifying where attached files should be saved.

Tip

Prior to saving the attachments you may want to create a new folder on your desktop or hard drive. So that you can always quickly find saved attachments you can use this folder specifically for holding such files. In Figure 7-16 you see that I did exactly this—I created a folder named *My Mail Downloads*, and in that figure I'm selecting it as the destination for saved attachments.

Compressing Attachments

If you attach one or two small files to an e-mail message, the sending of the message won't take long. However, if you attach several files—especially ones that consist of lots of graphics, sounds, or movies—to a message, then the sending of that message may take a while. In such a case Outlook Express can't just burst a few bytes over your phone line—the program needs to transfer all the possibly several megabytes of data. If you're attaching a large file to an e-mail message you'll want to consider compressing that information.

File compression is a means of shrinking the size of a file. Like file encoding (which is the conversion of binary information such as that which makes up a graphic image to text), file compression involves converting the contents of a file. Again like file encoding, you don't have to know the details of file compression—you only need to know that it works!

To have Outlook Express compress the files that are currently attached to a message you're about to send, make sure the **Compress Attachments** item in the **Message** menu is checked. If this item isn't checked, choose it (you can then drop down the **Message** menu to confirm that this item is now indeed checked). When you click the **Send** icon in the message window, Outlook Express will take care of compressing all attached files.

If you want to always specify that attached files be compressed, choose **Preferences** from the **Edit** menu. Then click the **Message Composition** item under the Outlook Express category. Finally, click the **Compress attachments** checkbox—as I'm doing in Figure 7-17.

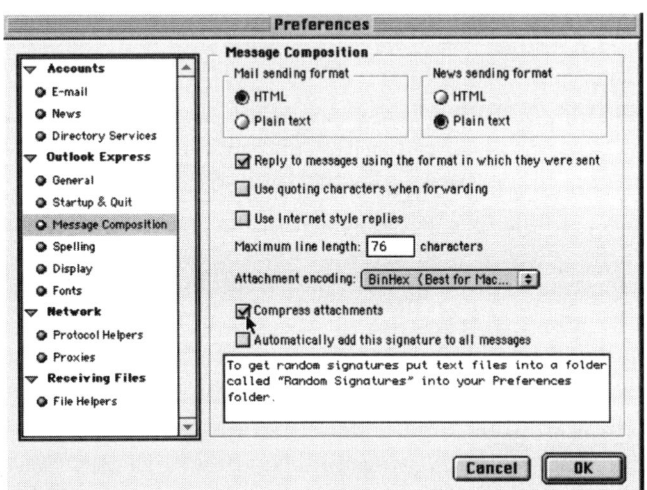

Figure 7-17 Setting Outlook Express to compress attachments.

Using Attachments to Transfer Files

The iBook has no floppy drive! You may have heard from iBook opponents that this omission is the computer's major handicap. How on Earth will an iBook user transfer a file from, say, his iBook at home to his computer at work or school? Welcome to the Internet age. The *i* in *iBook* stands for Internet. Anyone who uses an iBook is expected to either be, or eventually become, at least somewhat proficient at accessing the Internet. Once you have Internet access capabilities on your iBook and the destination computer (the computer that is to receive the file or files you wish to transfer), file transfer is simple. Just e-mail the files to yourself.

In this chapter you've already seen how to attach one or more files to an e-mail message, send that message, receive that same message, and access its attachments. In this chapter's examples I've purposely e-mailed messages to myself—in the hopes that as you followed along you'd do the same. If you have done that, then you already know how to transfer files from an iBook to another computer, and vice versa.

To transfer a file, attach it to an e-mail message and then send that message to yourself (to your own e-mail address). Quit Outlook Express and go to the computer that the file is to be transferred to. Connect to the Internet and check your e-mail. The just-sent message—complete with attached file—will be there. Access the attachment and you've now got the file on your other Mac.

Tip

If your desire is to transfer files between your iBook and another Mac located in the same room, consider setting up a small, simple network. Connecting two Macs together is the topic of Chapter 11.

Tip

You don't *have* to use the Internet as your file transfer medium, of course. Alternatively you can use a removable media drive to move a copy of a file from one Mac to another. That's assuming that both your iBook and the computer that will be the eventual recipient of your files are equipped with a similar drive. Chapter 10 discusses such removable media drives, including the Imation SuperDisk and the Iomega Zip.

Contacts

It's not easy to remember the e-mail addresses of all your friends, relatives, and business associates. So it's a good thing you don't have to! The Contacts feature of Outlook Express is a means of keeping track of anyone you contact via e-mail.

To view a list of contacts, click the Contacts icon located at the top of the main window of Outlook Express. The list will initially be empty, so click on the New icon at the top-left of the Contacts window to display a window that allows you to enter information about one contact. Figure 7-18 shows this window.

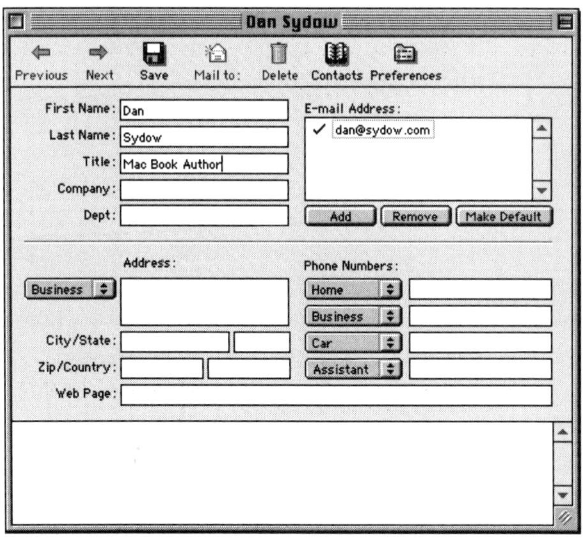

Figure 7-18 Entering a new contact.

For any one contact you can enter as little or as much information as you want. If you have a separate address book (either an electronic one or a "real" one) that you use to keep track of the addresses and telephone numbers of acquaintances, then you might not want to repeat all this information in Outlook Express. Instead, you'll probably opt to use Contacts as a means of keeping track of the e-mail addresses of people. In such a scenario just enter the contact's name and e-mail address, and perhaps a little descriptive information about the contact—as I've done in Figure 7-18. When finished, click the Save icon at the top of the window, then close the window by clicking on the close box in the window's title bar. The newly entered contact is listed in the Contacts window, as shown in Figure 7-19.

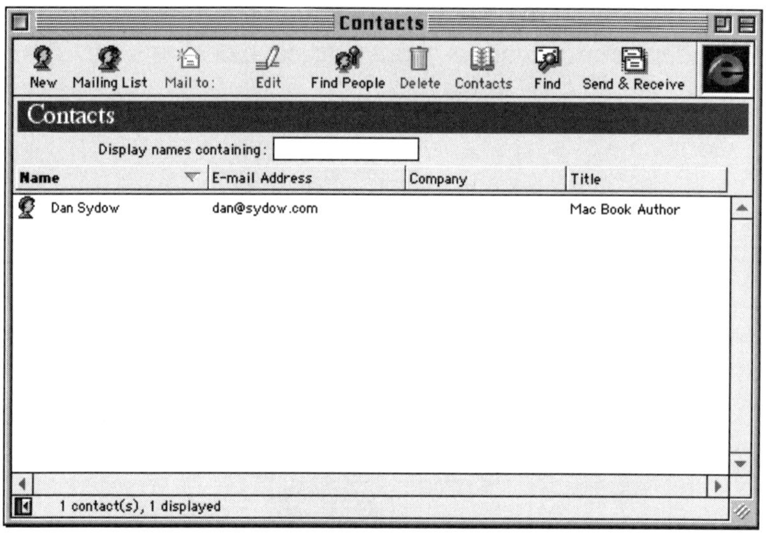

Figure 7-19 The list of all contacts.

The headings that appear above the list (Name, E-mail Address, Company, and so forth) coincide with the categories of information in the window that allowed for contact information entry. If you want to change which headings are listed, click on **Columns** in the **View** menu. That brings up another menu—the one shown in Figure 7-20.

To display a heading, make sure its name is checked in the menu (choose it if it's not checked). To instead hide a heading, make sure its name is unchecked (yes, in this case you choose it if it is checked). Back in Figure 7-19 you see that I've used the **Columns** menu to set up my Contacts window to display just four headings (Name, E-mail Address, Company, and Title).

To send mail to someone in your Contacts list, first click on the contact in the Contacts window. Now click the Mail to icon located along the top of the Contacts window. Doing that brings up a new message window with the To field filled in—there's no need to enter (or remember) the contact's e-mail address!

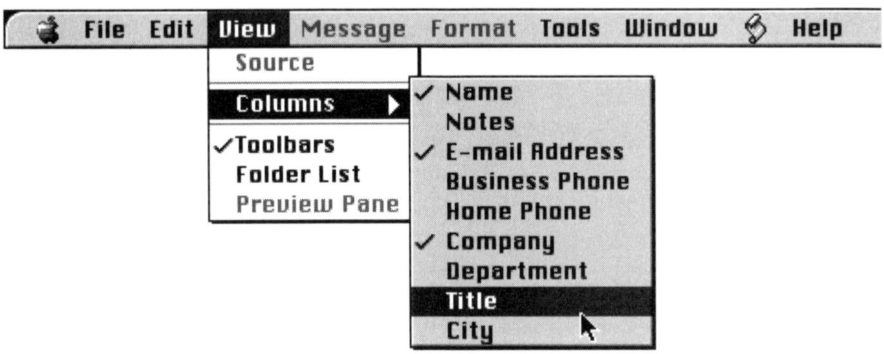

Figure 7-20 The Columns menu.

8

Working With Web Browsers

The word *Internet* is a term for a huge communications network that has a number of services (or functions, or parts, or resources). Each service has to do with transferring information. *FTP* (for *File Transfer Protocol*) is the part of the Internet that's used to transfer files to (upload) and from (download) the Internet. *Usenet* is the part of the Internet that holds newsgroups—areas where surfers post and read public messages on select topics. The most well-known service of the Internet is *e-mail*, the part of the Internet that handles personal messages. The *World Wide Web* (or, more often, simply the *Web*) is the part of the Internet that displays "pages" of text, images, and multimedia content viewable with a Web browser. This chapter focuses on the World Wide Web.

In the past, different programs were needed in order to access the different services of the Internet. Of late, surfers have the luxury of selecting only one program to access most of the Internet. If you're a member of America Online, you'll most likely use your AOL software to download files, access newsgroups, send e-mail, and browse the Web (refer to Chapter 5). If you use an Internet Service Provider (ISP) to connect to the Internet, you can use the Netscape Navigator or Microsoft Internet Explorer software to transfer files and browse the Web. In this chapter, you'll see how to make the most of whichever one of these Internet software tools you use.

Netscape Navigator

Your iBook came equipped with version 4.6 of Netscape Communicator. Communicator is Netscape's Navigator Web browser combined with Netscape's Internet mail and other tools. The whole package is accessed by double-clicking on the Netscape Communicator icon in the Netscape Communicator folder. Here I'm talking about browsing the Web—so I'll be referring to Navigator. Keep in mind that "Navigator" and "Communicator" are names people use interchangeably.

Tip
If you're an AOL member, you probably use the Web browser that's built into the America Online program. That's fine—but you should know that you can instead use either Navigator or Microsoft Internet Explorter. Once you're connected to AOL, simply double-click the preferred Web browser icon on the desktop. Doing that while connected to AOL means you'll be able to access the Web from that browser.

Getting Started With Navigator

The main function of a Web browser is to make it easy to navigate the Web. When you connect to the Internet and then start up Navigator, you'll be taken to a preselected Web site (in this section's *Changing Your Home Page* subsection you'll see how to have a different Web site appear when you start Navigator). If you know the Web address of the Web site you'd like to visit, you can click in the **Go To** box and type it in. In Figure 8-1 you see that I'm about to visit Apple's home page. After you press the Return or Enter key, Navigator is responsible for traversing the Web to locate the address, gathering the information on the found Web site, and displaying that information in a window.

Figure 8-1 Entering a Web page address in Navigator.

It's not always necessary to know the address of a Web site in order to visit it. In fact, more often than not you won't know the site's URL. Instead, one Web site may include mention of interesting information at some other Web site or at some other page of the site you're at. A site will often include a hypertext link to the mentioned page. A *hypertext link*, or simply a *link*, is a highlighted word or picture (either by color, or underlining, or both) that serves as a shortcut to another area of the Web. All you need to do in order to visit the mentioned site is to move the cursor over the link and click the trackpad button. Navigator then takes care of determining the address to visit, going there, and replacing the contents of the window with the information at the new site.

After moving to a new page and checking out its content (its information), you may want to return to the location from which you started (the page that held the hypertext link). The green Previous arrow near the upper left of a Navigator window makes it easy to return to the page where you were previously. After returning to the previous page, you can again jump ahead to the page you just came from by using the Next arrow located to the right of the Previous arrow.

Keeping Track of Where You've Been

As you move from one Web site to another, you'll find that you'll soon lose track of where you've been. You may remember the name of a particular site you visited, but you won't likely remember that site's address. Navigator provides you with a couple of features that make it easy to revisit a Web site of interest—without having to memorize that site's URL.

Using the Go Menu

When you visit a Web page, Navigator automatically creates a new menu item in the **Go** menu (see Figure 8-2). Every Web page that you visit has a title—you'll find it in the title bar of the browser window that displays the page's content. It's this title that Navigator uses as the name of the new menu item. The contents of the **Go** menu, then, grow as you surf the Web. The **Go** menu thus reflects where you've been, providing a history of your travels about the Web. To return to any of the pages you've recently visited, just select the page's title from the **Go** menu.

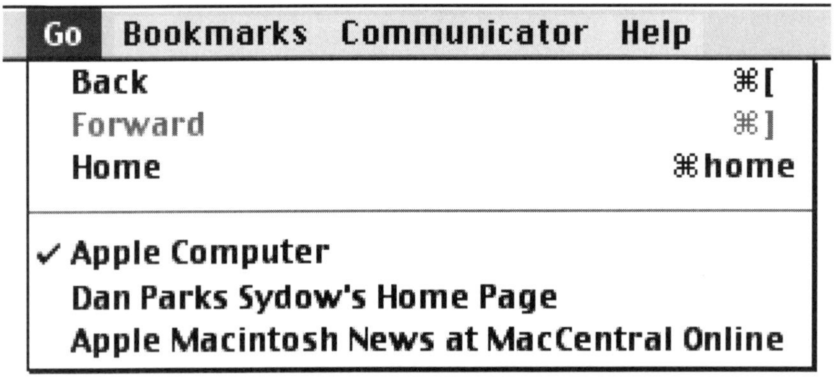

Figure 8-2 The Navigator Go menu.

The **Go** menu displays a single *lineage* of history items. That means that if you follow links from one page to another, then backtrack and follow a different set of links (effectively creating a "fork in the road"), only the most recently traversed path is saved to the **Go** menu. In any event, quitting Navigator (or closing the currently open browser window) clears the **Go** menu. That's not a shortcoming of Navigator: it's the nature of the **Go** menu to provide you only with feedback on your current Web travels. To permanently save the addresses of Web pages of interest, read the next section—*Using the Bookmarks Menu.*

Using the Bookmarks Menu

The **Bookmarks** menu also keeps track of where you've been, but in a way different than the **Go** menu. Rather than a page being automatically added to the **Bookmarks** menu, you must carry out this task manually. When you pull down the **Bookmarks** menu, you'll find that it contains the titles of a number of Web pages. To display the contents of any page, just select the page's title.

Bookmark items offer a more permanent means of page retrieval than do items in the **Go** menu. When you add a bookmark to the **Bookmarks** menu, the item remains in the menu—even after you quit and then restart Navigator. Thus, bookmarks are a good way to store the locations of Web pages you intend to often revisit.

To bookmark a Web page, first visit the page. Once there, choose **Add Bookmark** from the **Bookmarks** menu. That's all there is to it. Clicking on the **Bookmarks** menu now reveals a new item at the bottom of the list.

If you spend a little time learning about bookmarks now you'll be guaranteed of having more productive Web-surfing sessions in the future. After adding a few bookmarks you'll want to organize the items in the **Bookmarks** menu. To do that, choose **Edit Bookmarks** from the **Bookmarks** menu. The Bookmarks window that appears lets you work with any one bookmark. Here are a few of the organizational tools at your disposal:

Change the order of bookmarks Click on the name of a bookmark and drag it to a different location in the Bookmarks window.

Remove a bookmark Click on a bookmark name and choose **Cut** from the **Edit** menu.

Rename a bookmark Click on its name and choose **Get Info** from the **Edit** menu.

Add a folder To add a folder to the **Bookmarks** menu choose **New Folder** from the **File** menu, then drag the folder to wherever you want in the Bookmarks window. Add bookmarks to the folder by dragging each to the new folder.

Where to Go and What to Do

Netscape Navigator provides a **Guide** submenu under the **Bookmarks** menu. Click on **Guide** and you'll see the submenu shown in Figure 8-3. With the exception of the bookmark named **Live Home Page**, the items in this menu are pretty much self-explanatory. The site at the bookmark **Live Home Page** is shown in Figure 8-4. Here you can use a search engines to search the Web, or click on any one of dozens of links to go to a topic of interest. This site can serve as your home page (the site displayed in a window when you start up Navigator)—but it doesn't have to. In the next section, *Changing Your Home Page*, you'll read how to change your home page. If you do that, you might just forget how to reach the Live Home Page. Now you know how you can reach this handy, general-purpose site—just choose **Live Home Page** from the **Guide** submenu of the **Bookmarks** menu.

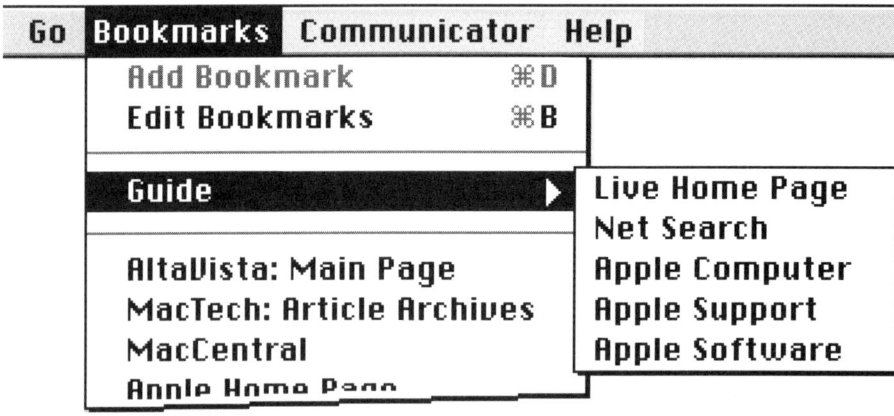

Figure 8-3 The Navigator Guide submenu.

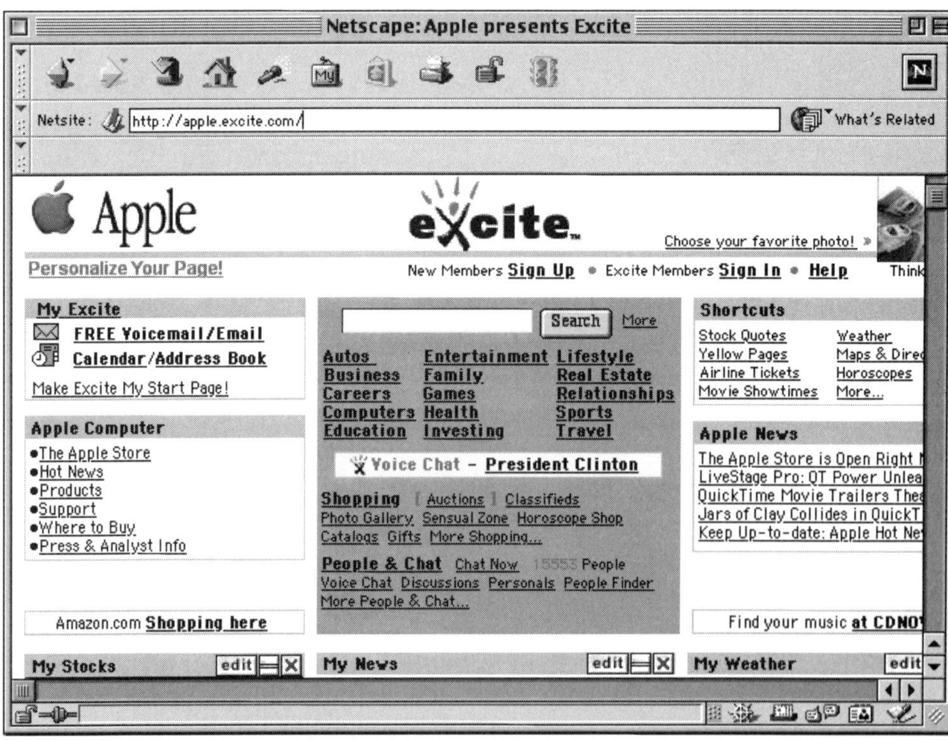

Figure 8-4 Netscape's Netcenter Web page.

Changing Your Home Page

When you run Navigator, a browser window opens and the information from a Web site appears in that window. Netscape calls this *default* page that the browser opens to the browser's *home page*. While Netscape initially determines which site serves as your home page, you aren't required to keep things in that state. Instead, you can select any Web page to be the browser's home page.

To change the home page, begin by choosing **Preferences** from the **Edit** menu. Next, click on *Navigator* in the *Category* list that appears on the left side of the Preferences window. Move the cursor over the end of the currently specified home page address in the **Home page location** edit box, click the trackpad button, then backspace to delete the address. Now type in the address of the page you want to serve as your home page. In Figure 8-5, I changed the Navigator home page to the MacCentral Web site so that each time I start up Navigator, the first thing I see is updated news on Apple and the Macintosh.

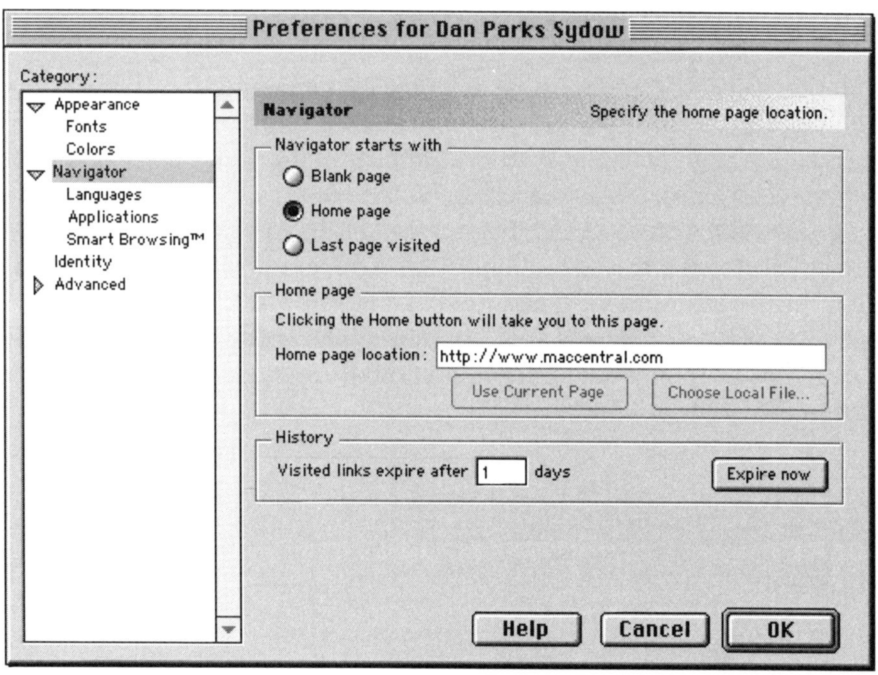

Figure 8-5 Changing the Navigator home page.

Microsoft Internet Explorer

Your iBook's hard drive has version 4.5 of Microsoft's Internet Explorer Web browser installed on it. Here you'll see how to get started surfing the Web with Microsoft Internet Explorer (or, as sometimes referred to, Microsoft IE).

Tip

If you're an America Online subscriber, you probably use the Web browser that's integrated into the AOL program. Be aware that you have the option of instead using Netscape Navigator or Microsoft Internet Explorer. After logging on to AOL, simply double-click the preferred Web browser icon on the desktop. Launching a Web browser while connected to AOL sets that browser to work—it's able to access the Web without any extra work on your part. After that, read the appropriate section in this chapter (either this Microsoft Internet Explorer section or the previous Netscape Navigator section) for some instructions on using the browser.

Getting Started With Internet Explorer

A Web browser's primary purpose is to make navigating the Web easy. After you connect to the Internet and start up Internet Explorer, a browser window appears and the contents of a Web page appear in the window (in this section's *Changing Your Home Page* subsection you'll see how to have a different Web site appear when you start Internet Explorer). If you know the address of a Web page you'd like to visit, click in the **Address** text box and type in that address. In Figure 8-6, I've typed in the address of Apple's home page. After you press the Enter or Return key, Internet Explorer traverses the Web to find the desired page, gathers the information on the page, and displays that information in the browser window.

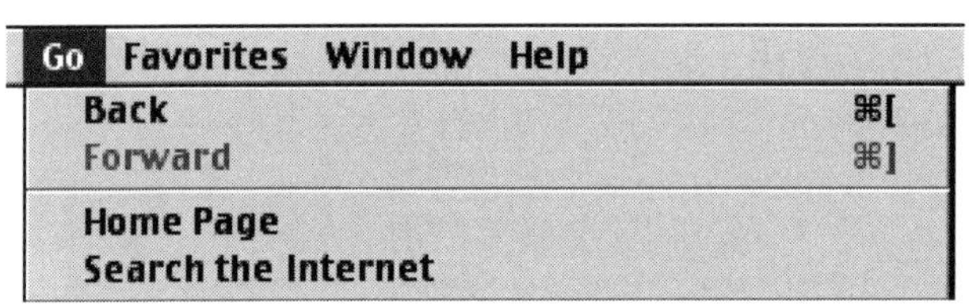

Figure 8-6 Entering a Web page address in Internet Explorer.

Web page addresses can be long and complicated, so it's not practical to memorize more than a handful of the pages you'll frequent. Not knowing a page's URL isn't a big drawback, though. That's because you'll often learn about one Web page when you're visiting another—one Web site may include mention of some interesting information at some *other* Web site, or at some *other* page of the site you're at. To make it easy for you to visit another page, a Web site developer will generally include a hypertext link to the page. A *hypertext link*, or more simply a *link*, is a highlighted word or picture (highlighting can be in the form of coloring, underlining, or both) that acts as a shortcut to another page on the Web. To visit the linked site all you need to do is position the cursor over the link and click the trackpad button. Internet Explorer then determines the address to visit, moves there, and finally replaces the contents of the browser window with the information at the new page.

After linking to a new page and visiting for a while, you may want to return to the point from which you started (the page that held the hypertext link). The Previous arrow near the upper left of the Internet Explorer window is used to quickly return to the page you were previously visiting. After returning, you can again jump ahead to the page you just came from by using the Next arrow located to the right of the Previous arrow.

Keeping Track of Where You've Been

Surfing from Web page to Web page isn't always a focused, orderly trip—you'll soon find that that it's easy to lose track of where you've been. You might recall the name of a particular page you visited, but it's unlikely that you'll also remember that page's address. Internet Explorer offers the Web surfer a couple of menus that make it simple to revisit Web pages of interest, and without having to know the addresses of those pages.

Using the Go Menu

When you encounter a Web page, Internet Explorer automatically adds a new menu item to the Internet Explorer **Go** menu (see Figure 8-7). You've probably noticed that each Web page has its own title in the title bar of the browser window, where the page's content is displayed. This title is what Internet Explorer uses as the name of the new **Go** menu item. Because Internet Explorer adds a new menu item at each stop you make on the Web, the contents of the **Go** menu grow as you surf the Web. The **Go** menu serves as a list of where you've been—it provides a history of your journey across the Web. All you need to do to revisit any of the pages you've recently stopped at is to select the page's title from the **Go** menu.

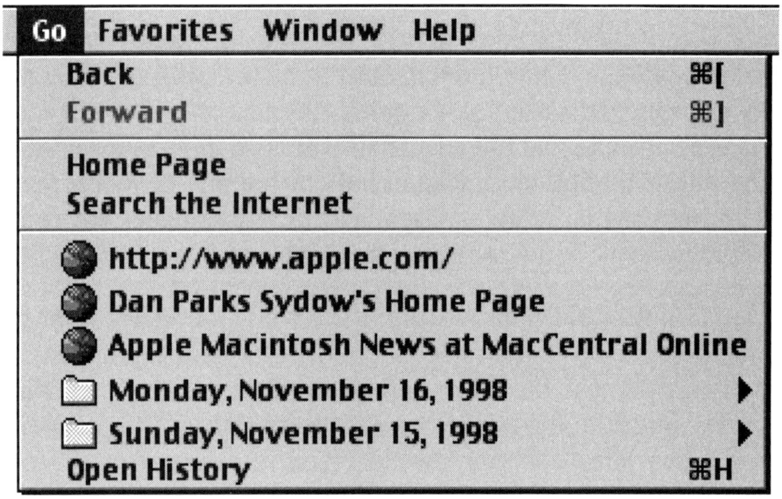

Figure 8-7 The Internet Explorer Go menu.

The **Go** menu displays what's referred to as a single lineage of items. If you use hypertext links to move from one Web page to another, and then backtrack and follow a new set of links, only the most recently traveled path is stored in the **Go** menu. If you run Internet Explorer again the next day, you'll find that Internet Explorer has taken all of the previous day's visited sites and placed those addresses in a new folder (see Figure 8-7). To permanently save the addresses of Web pages of interest, and to keep them in a preferred order, read the next section—*Using the Favorites Menu.*

Using the Favorites Menu

Like the **Go** menu, the **Favorites** menu is used to keep track of where you've been. Rather than a page being automatically added to the **Favorites** menu, though, you're in charge of carrying out this chore. Clicking on the **Favorites** menu reveals the titles of a number of Web pages. To visit a page that's listed in this menu, simply select the page's title.

Favorite items (some people refer to them as bookmarks, which is the term used by the Netscape Navigator Web browser) offer a more permanent means of page retrieval than do items in the **Go** menu. When you add a bookmark to the **Favorites** menu the item remains in the menu—it doesn't end up automatically going into a dated folder. Thus, bookmarks are a good way to store the locations of Web pages you intend to often revisit.

To add a Web page to the **Favorites** menu (to "bookmark a Web page," as some would say), first visit the page. Once there, choose **Add Page to Favorites** from the **Favorites** menu. That's all there is to it. Clicking on the Favorites menu now reveals a new item at the bottom of the list.

After adding a few favorites, you'll want to organize the items in the **Favorites** menu. To do that choose **Organize Favorites** from the **Favorites** menu. The Favorites window that appears lets you work with any one favorite. Here are a few of the organizational tools at your disposal:

Change the order of favorites Click on the name of a favorite and drag it to a different location in the Favorites window.

Remove a favorite Click on a bookmark name and choose **Cut** from the **Edit** menu.

Rename a favorite Click once on a favorite and then type in the new name.

Add a folder To add a new folder to the **Favorites** menu, choose New Folder from the Favorites menu. Then type in a name for the new folder and drag the folder to wherever you want in the Favorites window. Add favorites to the folder by dragging each to the new folder.

Practice adding, deleting, and organizing Web pages in the **Favorites** menu. Once you're proficient in the use of this menu your Web-surfing sessions will become more productive.

Where to Go and What to Do

Internet Explorer offers a number of pre-set favorites in the Favorites Bar (the lower of the horizontal strips running along the top of a browser window, and the strip picturing a number "world" buttons). Of these the Microsoft

MacTopia and the Live Home Page favorites may be the most useful. Clicking on Microsoft MacTopia takes you to a site that holds, among other things, links to Macintosh and Mac product news (note that this Web page is a part of Microsoft's Web site, so the information unquestionably leans towards Microsoft products). The Live Home Page favorite delivers you to a page that holds all sorts of information, including daily weather, horoscope, sports scores and more. This is the same page shown back in 8-4.

Note
The Chapter 9 section *Web Sites of Interest* provides the addresses of a number of interesting sites you'll want to visit. Look to Appendix A for still other sites and addresses.

Changing Your Home Page

When you run Internet Explorer, the browser visits one of Microsoft's Web pages and displays that page's content in a browser window. This page that appears upon starting Internet Explorer is referred to as the browser's *default* home page. Internet Explorer comes with a Microsoft page as the home page, but you don't have to keep things that way. You have the option of selecting any Web page to be the browser's home page.

To change the home page, begin by choosing **Preferences** from the **Edit** menu. If you don't see a number of items displayed under **Web Browser** in the list on the left of the preferences window, click on the little triangle by **Web Browser** now (refer to Figure 8-8). Then click on **Home/Search** in the displayed list. The contents of the right side of the window will change to include a Home Page section. Type the address of the Web page you want to use as your new home page. In Figure 8-8, I've entered the URL of MacCentral so that I can begin each Web session with an update on what's going on in the world of Apple and the Macintosh. Click the **OK** button and you're all set.

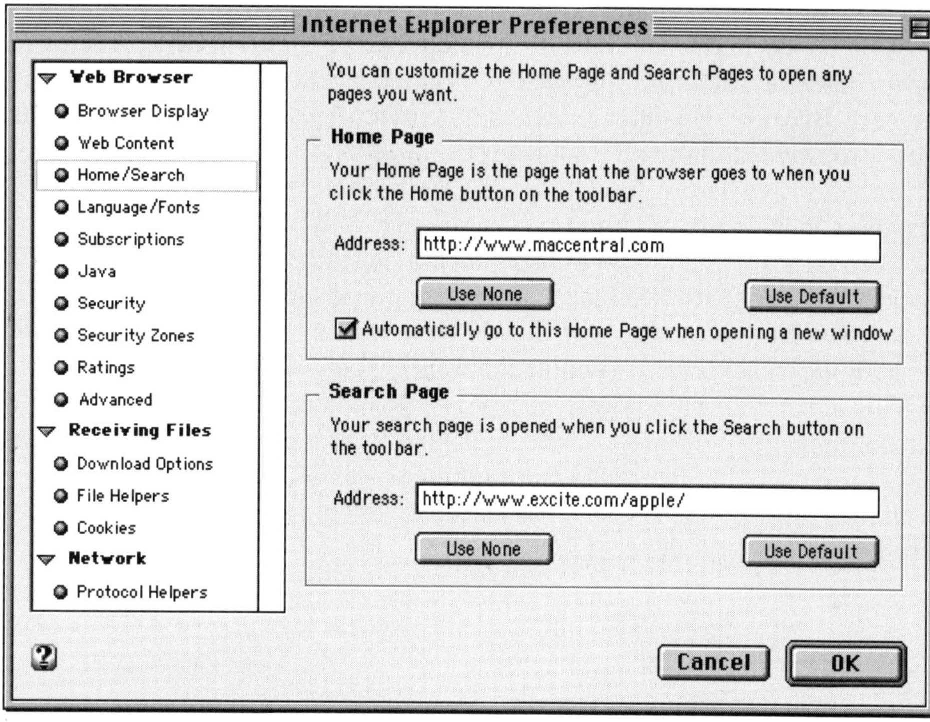

Figure 8-8 Changing the Internet Explorer home page.

Web Browser Plug-Ins

The Internet and the World Wide Web have seen—and continue to see—explosive growth. It seems that every few days there's some new Internet-related technology being announced. How does a software company that makes a Web browser keep up with these rapid changes? One way is to constantly work on the next, improved version of the Web browser. As you wait for this new and improved version of the browser you use, though, how can you take advantage of the already-here, waiting-to-be-used, Web enhancements? By making use of Web browser plug-ins.

A plug-in is a software component (a miniprogram, if you will) that a Web browser can use. Consider a plug-in an extension of the Web browser. A plug-in is designed to deliver some specific type of information from a Web page to a Web browser. Consider Apple's QuickTime plug-in. You have programs on your iBook that know how to display and play QuickTime movies (the SimpleText text editor, surprisingly, is capable of playing QuickTime movies). Because they have QuickTime movie-playing code built in to them, those programs don't need a QuickTime plug-in. But your Web browser, on its own, *doesn't* know how to play QuickTime movies. Some Web page designers include QuickTime movies on their Web pages. So what does your Web browser do when it encounters such a page? It displays the *other* information that's on that page (such as text, graphics, and hypertext links), but it doesn't display the movie! *Unless* you already have a QuickTime plug-in on your iBook's hard drive. If you have the necessary plug-in, your Web browser will, in a sense, incorporate that plug-in's capabilities and play the movie it's encountered. Fortunately, the technical details of how a Web browser makes use of a plug-in aren't of importance to us Web surfers. We only need to know a little bit about what plug-ins are available and how to go about getting them.

Popular Plug-Ins

There are hundreds of plug-ins available for browsers, with new ones being developed every day. Which of these are the most important? This section provides a look at some of the most popular plug-ins.

RealPlayer by RealNetworks

Your Web browser can play a sound it encounters on a Web page by loading that sound into your iBook's memory and *then* playing the sound. Getting the sound into memory is necessary before the sound can be played. For a short sound, the time it takes to make this transfer of information is quick and unnoticeable. This technique works well for short sounds, but *isn't* efficient for longer audio clips, such as a two-minute speech by your favorite politician. That may be a poor example, since you may not *have* a favorite politician, and since there may be no speeches of such a short duration by *any* politician, but you get the point. Having to load into memory a lengthy sound would be time consuming, and would break the continuity expected of a Web page. That is, if you clicked on a **Hear Speech** button on a Web page, you'd expect to hear speaking now—not seconds, or possibly minutes, later when the downloading completed.

The solution to this dilemma is *streaming audio*. In essence, streaming audio loads into memory a very short part of a sound, plays that portion of the sound, and then repeats the process with the next part of the sound. As you can imagine, streaming audio is designed so that the loading and playing cycle is smooth—there are no pauses between the playing of "sections" of a sound.

The pioneer and leader in streaming audio is RealNetworks. This software company has come up with RealAudio and RealPlayer. RealAudio is the software technology that enables a Web page designer to include streaming audio on his page. RealPlayer is the software technology that allows a Web browser to play streaming audio when it encounters it on a Web page. RealPlayer is also capable of playing RealVideo, the video companion to RealAudio.

You can get the most recent version of the RealPlayer plug-in at RealNetworks site `www.real.com/products/player/`.

Shockwave by Macromedia

Macromedia is another contender in the Web browser streaming audio market. Like RealNetworks's RealAudio technology, Macromedia's Shockwave technology delivers streaming audio from Web pages to Web browsers. Shockwave, however, is best known for delivering streaming high-resolution images and graphics to Web browsers. The designer of a Web page uses Macromedia's Director, Flash, or Authorware software to create multimedia contents, and Web surfers use the Shockwave plug-in to display this content in their Web browsers. Like the loading to memory of long sounds, the loading to memory of detailed graphics is time consuming. Shockwave uses a streaming technique to load to memory graphics information piecemeal, successively displaying parts of a single image to make for a smooth display.

To download the most recent version of the Shockwave plug-in, visit `www.macromedia.com/shockwave/download/`.

QuickTime by Apple Computer

Apple's QuickTime plug-in allows your Web browser to display QuickTime movies, QuickTime music, and QuickTime virtual reality panoramas. Like several other multimedia technologies, QuickTime employs streaming so that when your Web browser encounters a QuickTime-enhanced page, the QuickTime information on that page is displayed as it loaded into memory.

You can get more information about the latest version of the QuickTime plug-in at `www.apple.com/support/quicktime/`.

Acrobat Reader by Adobe

When you buy new software, there's a good chance that the program's documentation (user manual, reference manual, and so forth) will not be a book, but rather a file on a CD-ROM. If you don't like reading a lengthy document on your monitor, you can print out the documentation. This relatively new documentation distribution method has brought with it a number of problems. Chiefly, the display of a page of text on screen wasn't crisp, printed versions of documents often didn't match page-for-page what was displayed on screen, and documents weren't portable, or cross-platform (that is, the same document couldn't be viewed on both a Mac and a PC). Adobe pretty much solved these problems with its Portable Document Format (PDF) files. If you snoop around on your hard drive, you'll encounter a number of files with names that end with *.pdf*. Such a file is an Adobe PDF file, and can be viewed with Adobe's Acrobat Reader software (a version of which is included with your iBook).

A number of Web pages offer you the opportunity to download documents in PDF format. For instance, if you want to know the technical details of the iBook, Apple offers a PDF document for downloading at `www.apple.com/ibook/specs.html`. If you want your Web browser to also be able to display a PDF document in a browser window, the Acrobat Reader plug-in is the ticket.

The latest version of the Adobe Acrobat Reader plug-in is available at Adobe's site at `www.adobe.com/prodindex/acrobat/readstep.html`.

Getting Other Plug-Ins

The previous section describes a few of the most popular plug-ins, but how do you learn about others? You could spend a lot of time searching the Web for information on what's available, but there's a much easier way to handle the plug-in issue: do nothing! *Making use* of a plug-in is meant to be easy. When your browser needs to use a plug-in from your hard drive, it should do so seamlessly and transparently. *Getting* a plug-in should be a similar experience—and it is.

You don't need a particular plug-in until you encounter a Web page that is enhanced by that plug-in's technology. For example, if you surf the Web but *never* encounter a page that includes a RealAudio sound, you don't need the RealPlayer plug-in. Because there are hundreds of plug-ins available, you can see why it isn't feasible or necessary to download a substantial number of them. So how do you determine which plug-ins you need? You don't—your browser does that for you. If you visit a Web page that's enhanced by a technology for which your browser *doesn't* have a suitable plug-in, your browser will make you aware of the fact.

When you encounter a Web site that requires a plug-in that you don't have, your browser will display a window that gives you the opportunity to download the needed plug-in. Go ahead and do that. The act of downloading a plug-in isn't enough to get your browser to recognize that you now have the plug-in, though. Downloading a plug-in places an installer program on your hard drive. Run that installer to move the plug-in into a folder within your browser's folder.

9

Where to Go on the Web

By now you certainly know how to connect to the Internet and browse the Web. In the event that you *don't*, read Chapter 5 if you're an America Online member, or Chapter 6 if you want to use an Internet service provider to get connected. Now that you're connected, you have the ability to freely traverse the Internet. But where, exactly, should you be *going*? In this chapter you'll find listed a number of Web sites that many people find interesting. The addresses supplied here will get you started, but, of course, they aren't tailored for your own tastes and interests. So you'll want to know how to go out and find the sites that do hold exactly the information or entertainment you're interested in. To do that you'll need to know how to search the Web—another topic included in this chapter. As you visit newly discovered Web sites, you'll want to ensure that you protect your privacy. And if you have children you may want to limit their time online or the types of sites they have access to. Those Internet precautionary topics are also covered.

Web Sites of Interest

Every day thousands of new pages are added to the Web. That's right—*thousands*. So, of course, I can't possibly hope to list all the best here. By providing descriptions of some popular sites in some popular categories, though, I can get you jump-started on your Web browsing quests.

Tip
Consider this section a list of highlights. Appendix A lists more categories and more sites of interest, but no site descriptions.

Business News

If you want to get your business news throughout the day, rely on a Web business newspaper rather than a "hardcopy" paper.

Wall Street Journal

`www.wsj.com`

This is the site to visit for business news. Be forewarned, though, that in order to access this site you need to subscribe to it. For the in-depth business and technology coverage you get, sixty bucks a year isn't bad—but it's still sixty bucks.

Government

The United States government has a significant online presence. If you need information from a government agency, be sure to see if that agency has a Web site (refer to Appendix A for the addresses of plenty of other agencies).

Education, Dept. of

`www.ed.gov`

Here you'll find information regarding a variety of educational programs and services, including student financial assistance information.

Health and Human Services, Dept. of (HHS)

`www.os.dhhs.gov`

This is a branching-off point to go to any one of the dozen or so HHS agencies, including the National Institutes of Health (NIH) and the Administration on Aging (AOA).

Internal Revenue Service (IRS)

`www.irs.gov`

Forms, forms, and more forms. Save a trip to the library and instead download those forms here. Forms are all "official" so you can print one, fill it out, and mail it in (don't forget to attach your check!).

Social Security Administration (SSA)

`www.ssa.gov`

Benefit publications, disability information, and downloadable versions of all the forms you'll ever need (application for a new or replacement Social Security card, and so forth) can all be found here.

Macintosh News

What is Apple up to now? In particular, what's Steve Jobs up to now? Find out by checking in at an online site that offers news and rumors regarding Apple and the Macintosh.

Apple, Inc

`www.apple.com/hotnews`

This link from Apple's main page `www.apple.com` offers up information about some of the latest happenings at Apple. It's Apple's own Web page, though, so don't expect to find any rumors here.

MacCentral

`www.maccentral.com`

With one hundred and fifty *thousand* visitors a day, MacCentral (see Figure 9-1) is the most frequented site of surfers interested in obtaining daily Apple and Macintosh news. It's updated several times a day, so check out MacCentral for late-breaking Mac stories. Here you'll also find columns by the top Mac experts, including Andy Ihnatko and Bob LeVitus

MacToday

`www.mactoday.com`

You've seen MacToday on your supermarket's magazine rack—now see its online companion. MacToday (shown in Figure 9-2) provides you with current Apple news, Mac gossip, Mac program tips and tricks, software reviews, and more.

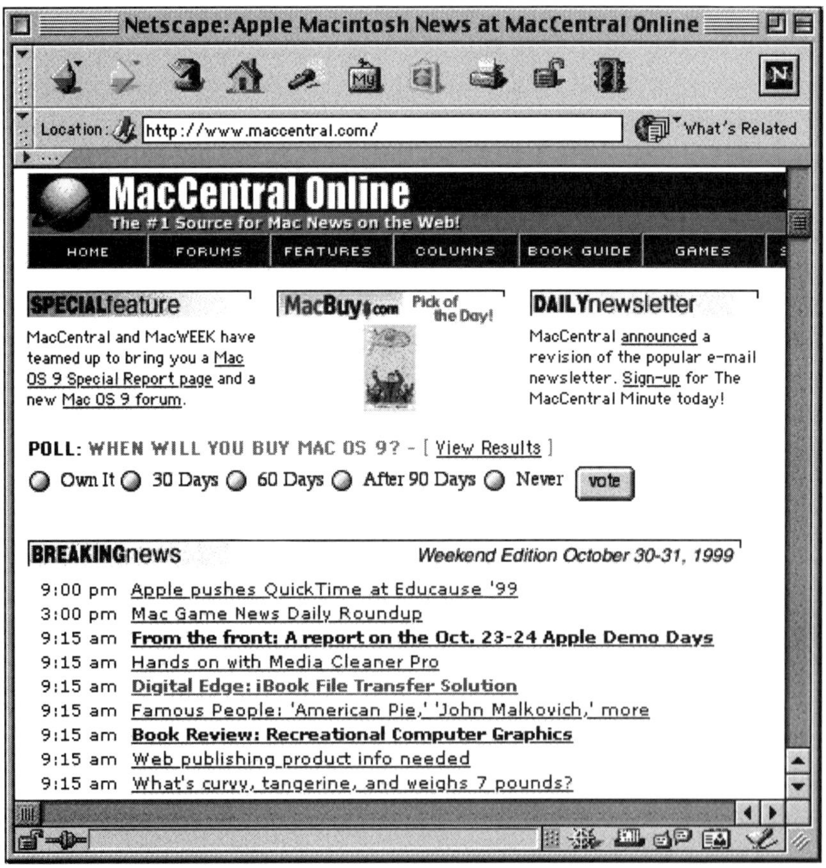

Figure 9-1 The home page of the Mac news Web site MacCentral.

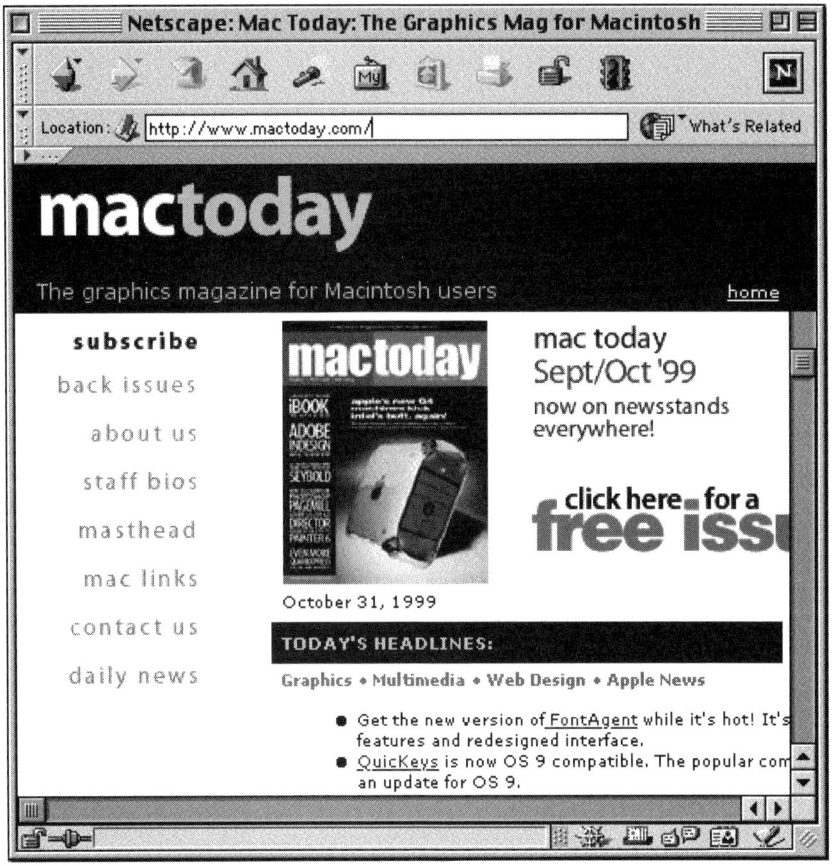

Figure 9-2 The home page of the Mac magazine MacToday.

Macintosh Programming

Interested in moving to the next level of working with a computer? I didn't think so. But if you *are* crazy enough to attempt to write your own Macintosh software, check out these sites.

Apple Developer Site

`www.apple.com/developer`

This is Apple's Web site just for programmers. Programming information and tools are located here.

Apple Intro to Macintosh Programming Site

`developer.apple.com/macos/intro.html`

This page is for those new to Macintosh programming. Here you'll find a list of books for getting started, sample code, and more.

MacTech Magazine

`www.mactech.com`

MacTech Magazine is the magazine for Mac programmers. This Web site is the magazine's online companion. Articles from past issues, code examples, and Macintosh headlines are all found here. Here you'll find my own Getting Started monthly column for beginner-level Mac programmers.

Newspapers

Didn't get a chance to read this morning's paper? Don't worry—just go online. Many of the nation's top newspapers have an online version that's free for the browsing.

USA Today

`www.usatoday.com`

This national newspaper is also available worldwide at `www.usatoday.com`.

Washington Post

`www.washingtonpost.com`

Many people rate this online paper Number One. You'll find the Washington Post's online site well-organized and easy to search.

Sports

Whatever sport is your favorite, there are Web pages devoted to it. The following are a few select sites of interest.

ESPN

`ESPN.SportsZone.com`

Just about all the sporting information you'd find on the ESPN cable station can be found on their Web site as well. There are football, baseball, basketball, and hockey scores, interview audio clips with big-name players (download a short interview and play it on your iBook anytime you want), and more.

NFL

`www.nfl.com`

News, schedules, stats, and links to each pro football team's own site. Football is the only pro sport I've listed in this chapter (okay, so I'm biased . . .), but of course there are sites for nearly all other sports, major and minor. Check Appendix A for the addresses.

World Wrestling Federation

`www.wwf.com`

Who am I to say that wrestling isn't a sport? The WWF site provides you with information about upcoming matches, pay-per-view events, photos, and all sorts of other goodies—if you're a wrestling fan, of course!

Women's Interests

Can a worldwide network that is a collection of the ideas, opinions, interests, and whims of millions of individuals be a medium that serves only one select group of people? Of course not. But there's no denying that the Internet was built mostly by males, and that now, several years later, best serves males. Sites that are chiefly of interest to men dominate the Web. All Web sites don't intentionally cater to men, but it's safe to say that there are a huge number of sites that, by the nature of their topics, appeal far more to men than they do to women. I don't have the statistics on visitors to `www.worldwrestling.com`, but I'm guessing that it's mostly men who stop by here for a visit. Contrast that with sites set up to serve women, such as...such as... ahem. It seems there really aren't too many that come to mind. In the last few years, the percentage of women making use of the Internet has been rising. Obviously, a change will come about to end this dearth of women-oriented sites. That change may, in fact, have started to take place—thanks to a new site named GoddessGear.com at, of course, `www.goddessgear.com`.

GoddessGear.com is a site set up by women, for women. One of its goals is to serve as a Web *portal* for women. A portal is a site that acts as a collection of links to other sites of interest. A portal is thus a hub from which one branches off to various places of interest. From the portal you visit one site, click your browser's Back button to return to the portal, and then visit another site. When you visit the GoddessGear.com site (Figure 9-3) you'll see that it includes links to sites that appeal to women—sites that specialize in a range of topics for a woman's mind, body, and soul.

GoddessGear.com's foreground is women, and its background is women and Macintosh. GoddessGear.com isn't a part of Apple, but it was founded, and is run, by Michelle Sain and some of her fellow ex-Apple colleagues. This group understandably felt that women's interests weren't adequately represented on the Internet, and their GoddessGear.com site serves as a cornerstone in the building of an Internet that will eventually serve the needs and interests of all groups of people.

Note

Women are pretty clever at gift buying—so it shouldn't surprise you that an increasing number of women are purchasing gifts on the Internet. If I'm representative of men, then it seems men struggle more with the gift buying process (unless, of course, it comes to buying gifts for ourselves, such as fishing equipment, imported beer, sports memorabilia, guns, and so forth). Men would be wise to take a cue from women and use the power of the Internet to look for gifts. Because it holds pointers to a vast collection of services, items, and ideas that appeal to women, a site such as GodessGear.com is a good place to get gift ideas. I'll be returning to GoddessGear.com often in the hopes that soon they'll direct me to the best buy on that set of power tools that I just *know* my wife wants for her next birthday...

Figure 9-3 The GoddessGear.com site.

Searching the Web

You've now been provided with a number of sites that may be of interest to you. But it's pretty darn unlikely that I covered them all. Read this section to find out not only how to find many more interesting and useful sites, but also how to find very specific information.

Searching for Web Page Topics

You can look for all sorts of information on the Web, including the whereabouts of people (see *Searching for a Person or Business*) and even detailed street maps (see *Other Searches*). But more than likely you'll search the Web for sites that present information about some topic that is of interest to you. You may have heard of a new book, video, or computer program that sounds interesting, but before buying it you'd like to read a few reviews of it. You may have just been given a school assignment to write a report on the Byzantine Empire and, while quite embarrassed to acknowledge it, know yourself to be the only one who *isn't* a renowned expert on that topic. Where to turn? The Web, of course. There are hundreds of millions (yes, *millions*) of Web pages, though, so you'll need a little assistance in finding the pages that hold the information you seek.

Search Engines

An Internet search engine is a site dedicated to searching the Web for pages that match your specified criteria. To make use of a search engine, you first visit the search engine's site. Once there, type in one or more *keywords*. A keyword is a word that is key to what you're interested in—a word that must be included on a Web page in order for the search engine to consider that page a match.

The best-known search engine site may be Yahoo!, but there are actually thousands of such sites! The following is a summary of the most popular search sites.

AltaVista At `www.altavista.com`, AltaVista provides you with a powerful, flexible means of searching the Web. Refer to the next section, The AltaVista Search Site, for more.

Excite Go to `www.excite.com` to make use of a search site that allows you to search either by keyword or by category.

InfoSeek Housed at `www.infoseek.com`, InfoSeek lets you search by keyword or by category. InfoSeek helps narrow things for you by including their own list of "InfoSeek Select Sites."

Lycos At `www.lycos.com`, Lycos offers keyword or category searching and provides a custom search option as well. Figure 9-4 shows the Lycos site, including its list of search categories.

WebCrawler At `www.webcrawler.com`, this search site is another one allows you to search by keywords or by clicking on a topic.

Yahoo! Located at `www.yahoo.com`, Yahoo! runs searches that are quick, and generally turn up an adequate number of pages that match your criteria. For a more comprehensive search of the entire Web, instead try AltaVista.

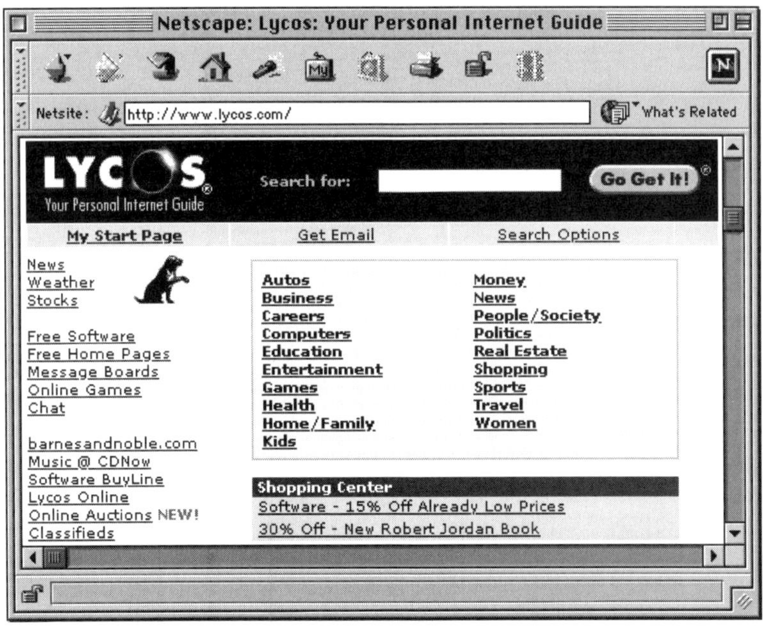

Figure 9-4 The Lycos Web search site.

Note

A search site keeps, and frequently updates, a database of Web sites. When you perform a search, the search engine actually examines this database rather than the entire World Wide Web.

The AltaVista Search Site

Yahoo!, at `www.yahoo.com`, gets much of the publicity, but just as good (or better) is the AltaVista search engine at `www.altavista.com`.

Using AltaVista, here's how a typical search goes (other search sites work in much the same way). Enter one or more keywords in the provided edit box. If you enter two words, the search engine will seek out all Web pages that include *either* of the words. If instead you want the search engine to return a list consisting of Web pages that include *both* words, precede each word with a plus sign (+) to tell the search engine to find pages that include "this word plus that word." Figure 9-5 shows such a search about to be conducted. Only a page that includes both of the specified words (*ibook* and *networking*) will be searched for.

Click the **Search** button and AltaVista returns a list of sites—each of which includes reference to your keywords. Each name in the list is a hypertext link, so clicking on a name takes you to that site. Figure 9-6 shows a couple of the links that resulted from the search criteria specified in Figure 9-5.

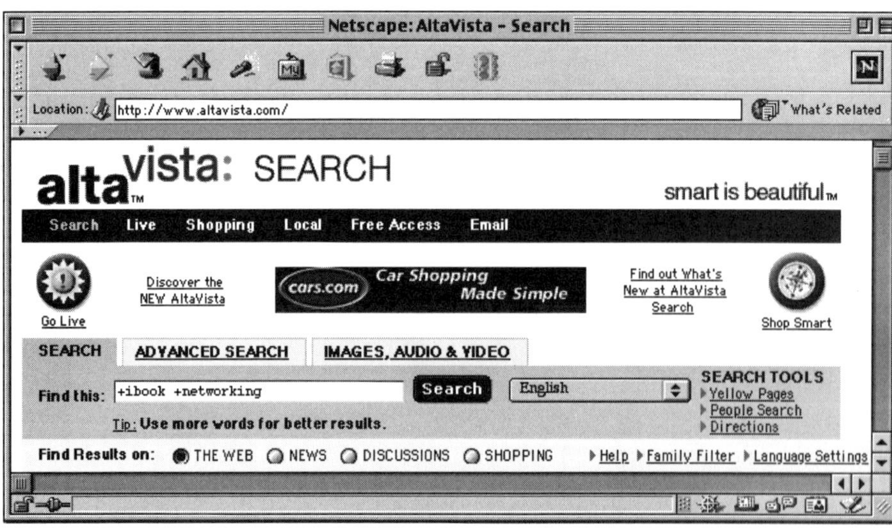

Figure 9-5 Getting ready to search with AltaVista.

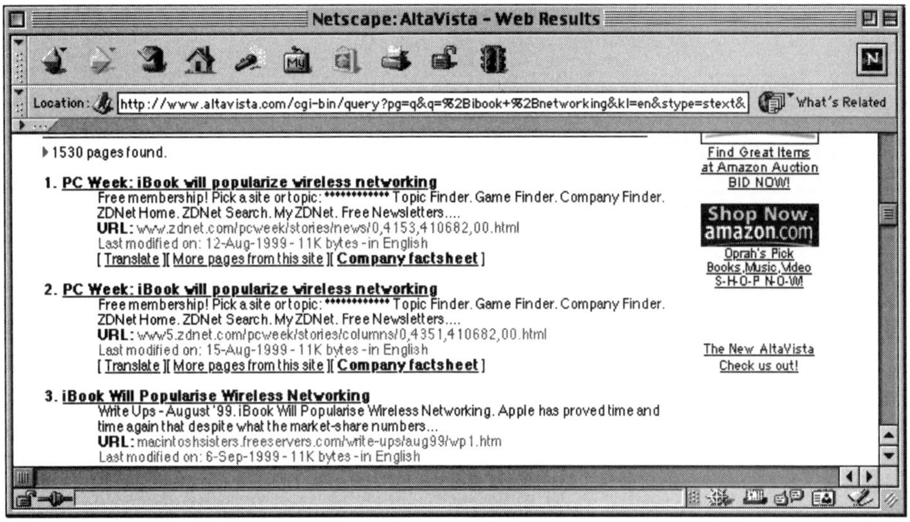

Figure 9-6 AltaVista returns a list of keyword-matching sites.

Search Pages

If you don't want to limit yourself to one search engine, consider making use of a Web site that allows access to numerous engines. Netscape has set up an "all purpose" searching page at `home.netscape.com/escapes/search/` that consists mostly of links to search engines and other lists of links organized by topic. Figure 9-7 shows this page when Lycos is selected from the search engine list on the left side of the page.

Sherlock

Find File used to be the Macintosh searching utility that would appear on the screen when you selected Find from the File menu. Apple upgraded that handy utility and named the improved file-finder Sherlock. With Mac OS 9 comes the new, improved Sherlock—referred to as Sherlock 2. Sherlock 2 makes finding misplaced files easy. It also is a handy tool for searching the Internet. When you choose **Find** from the **File** menu (or **Search Internet** from the **File** menu, or **Sherlock 2** from the **Apple** menu), you'll see the Sherlock 2 window—as shown in Figure 9-8.

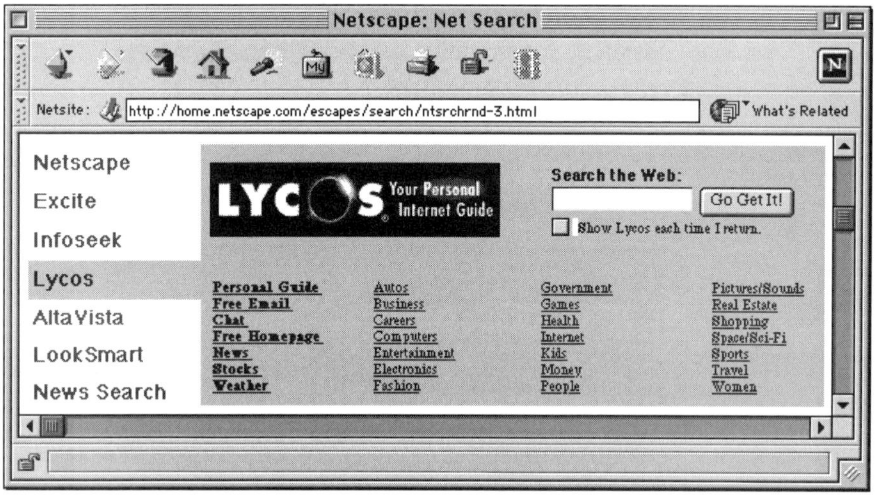

Figure 9-7 Netscape's Web search page.

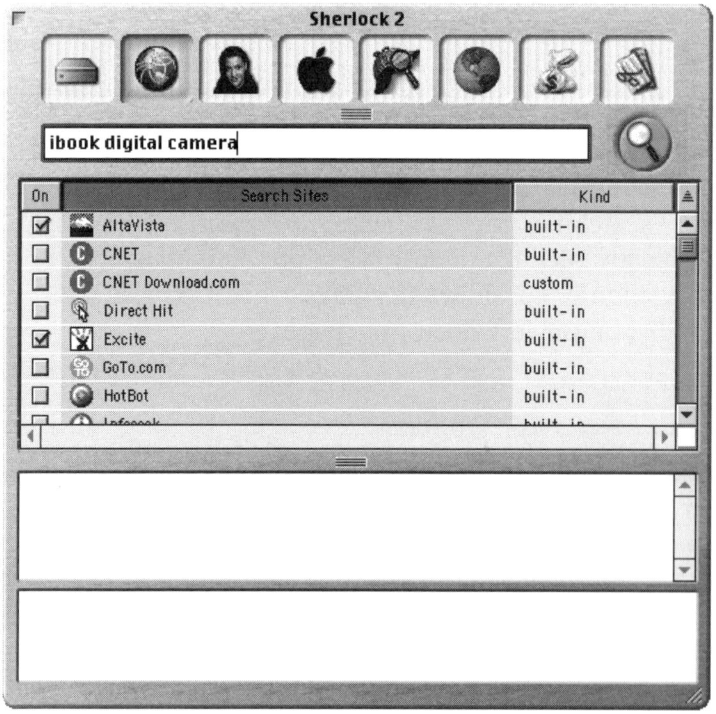

Figure 9-8 The Sherlock window.

Sherlock lets you search didn't types of things by the use of what Apple calls channels. The File Channel, for instance, let's you search for a file—or words or phrases in a file—on your iBook's hard drive or on CD discs. The Internet Channel is used to search the Internet for Web pages of interest. One of the best features of Sherlock is its ability to make use of multiple search engines to search the Internet. Enter one or more keywords to search for, click on the search engines to use, and then click the Find icon. In Figure 9-8 I've selected the Internet Channel (the second picture button along the top of the Sherlock window), and have entered the keywords ibook, digital, and camera. I've opted to use the AltaVista and Excite search engines. After clicking the Find icon, a list of Web pages that hold these keywords is returned (see Figure 9-9). Click on the name of a Web page and a description of the page, along with a link to it, are displayed in the Sherlock window. Clicking on a link tells your Web browser to display that page.

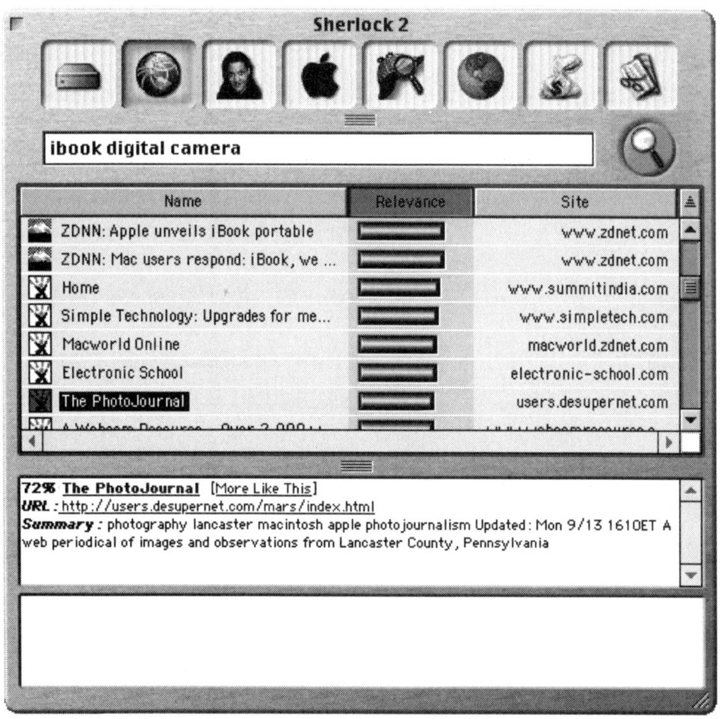

Figure 9-9 Using Sherlock to search the Internet.

Note
The first iBook computers shipped with Mac OS 8.6 installed. That operating system came with Sherlock (not Sherlock 2). If you own one of the first iBooks, then your Sherlock window will look different than the one pictured here. You can, however, use Sherlock in a similar manner to search the Internet.

Searching for a Person or Business

If you'd like to get in contact with a person or business, but don't know or don't recall how to go about doing that, use the Web to search for the means of making contact. There are several people/business search sites, a few of which are listed below. Figure 9-10 shows InfoSpace—one of the most popular sites.

Search site	Web address
555-1212 People Look up	`www.555-1212.com`
Excite Reference	`www.excite.com/Reference`
InfoSpace	`www.infospace.com`
Switchboard	`www.switchboard.com`
World Pages	`www.worldpages.com`

Searching for a person or business involves nothing more than a few mouse clicks and a little typing. At InfoSpace, for instance, searching for someone's phone number begins by clicking on a *White Pages* tab (see Figure 9-10). Doing that displays a few text boxes where you enter as much information as you know about the person. Clicking the Find button then reveals a list of possible matches. Note that if you don't know where the person lives, the search can still be conducted—you'll just have more names to sort through as you determine which *Smith* or *Jones* is the one you're looking for.

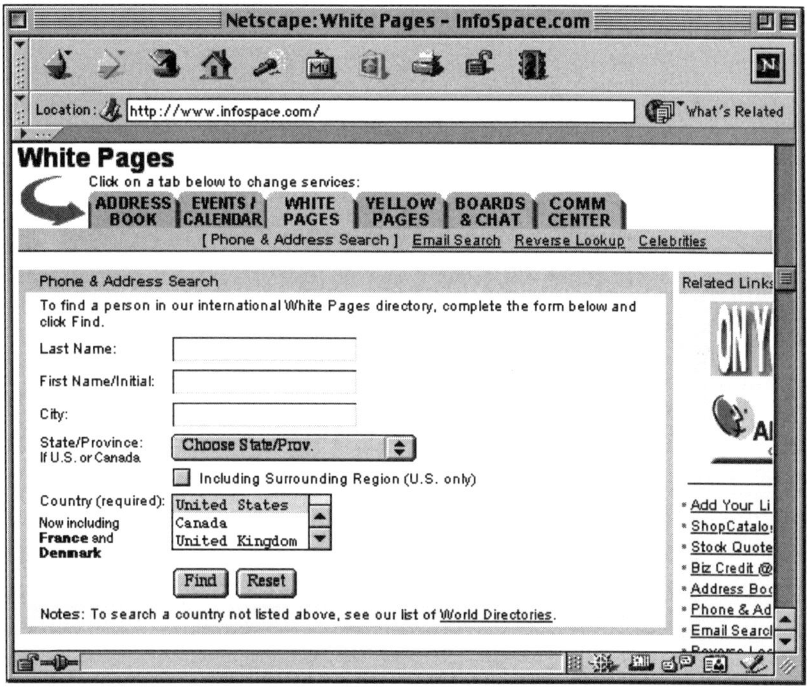

Figure 9-10 InfoSpace searches for people and more.

Note
None of these search sites are infallible. If someone doesn't want to be found, you may not find him or her. For instance, if your home phone number doesn't appear in your local telephone directory, then it won't show up if someone attempts to find it online. Your e-mail address isn't so private, though, and someone searching for it may be successful—whether or not you want to be found!

Note
Use Sherlock 2 to search for people on the Internet. First click the People Channel (the third picture button from the left along the top of the Sherlock window), then enter a name to search for. Choose the Internet search engines to use, then click the Find icon to see your results.

Other Searches

A few other searches you may be interested in are for street locations, zip codes, area codes, and 800 numbers.

Street Maps

If you're planning to go to someone's house or place of business, and you aren't familiar with the neighborhood, try a map-displaying site such as Maps On Us at `www.MapsOnUs.com`. After you enter a street name, city, and state (or a zip code), Maps On Us displays a map of that street and its surrounding streets (see Figure 9-11). To see more or less of the surrounding area, use the zoom buttons that are also displayed on the map page.

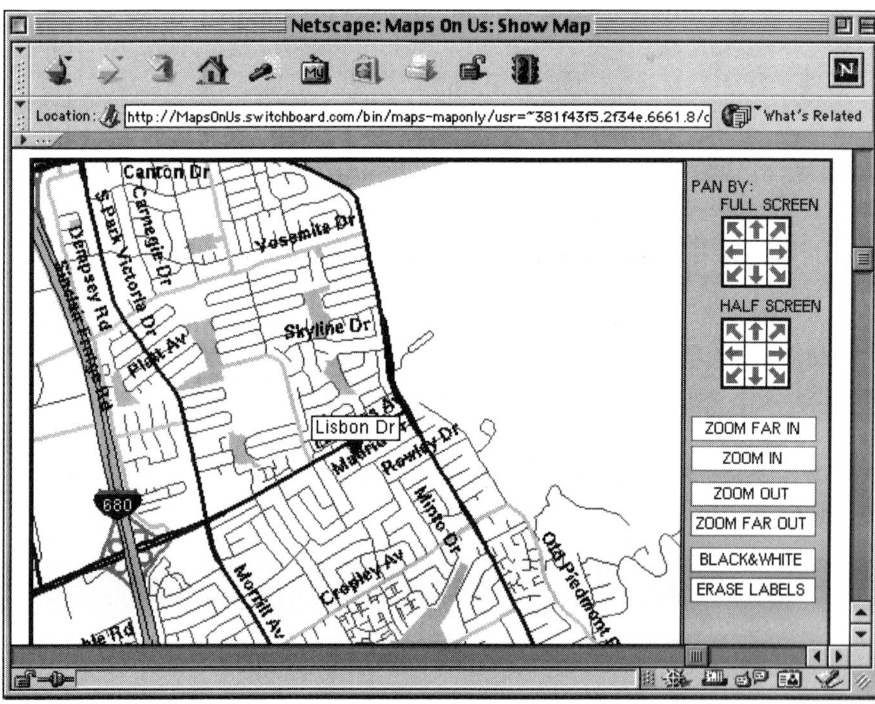

Figure 9-11 Maps On Us displays detailed street maps.

Zip Codes

For ZIP code information, check out the Postal Service's ZIP Code Lookup and Address Information page (of course it has a long title—it's a government Web page!). When you go to `www.usps.gov/ncsc` you'll find links to a page that returns a ZIP+4 code for the address you enter and also to a page that associates a ZIP code with a city you inquire about (or vice-versa).

Area Codes

To find the area code or codes associated with a city, or the city or cities associated with an area code, go to the Area Code Lookup Web page at `www.555-1212.com/area_codes.cfm`.

Storing Information on the Internet

The Web is primarily thought of as a place to view and retrieve information. If you think of the Internet only as a means of getting information, though, you're missing out on one of the 'Nets more powerful and overlooked uses—information storage.

The Internet is a huge network of server computers, most with high-capacity storage capabilities. For a small (usually monthly) fee, some Internet sites will reserve a portion of their drive space just for you. With several gigabytes of hard drive space conveniently located *on* your iBook, why would you want to rent more drive space *away* from your computer on the Internet? For exactly that reason—this additional storage space is not a part of your iBook.

If files that you've saved on your iBook's hard drive inadvertently get deleted, or inexplicably become corrupt, you'll need to rely on backup copies of those files. Hopefully you've taken precautions and saved copies of those valuable files on removable media, such as on a Zip disc. That way, a severe problem (such as a broken or stolen iBook) won't mean you've lost your backup files *and* your original files. What if an even worse scenario occurs, though? What if the problem that caused you to lose the original files also causes you to lose your backup files as well? The ideal backup solution is to store your duplicate files off sight. That is, keep copies of valuable files far from your iBook to greatly decrease the likelihood that a single problem won't destroy both an original file and its backup copy. The perfect off sight storage facility is the Internet.

There's a second reason you might want to store information on the Internet—easy, convenient accessibility of that information from any location and any computer. Because your iBook is a portable computer, you may be confident that all the information you need will be with you wherever you go. That typically isn't the case. Many people who own a notebook computer also own a desktop computer. If you store information such as a calendar or daily "To Do" list on your desktop Mac, and then leave home with your iBook, you've just left behind what may be very important information that you'll need later that day. To avoid having to keep track of what information is where (is that file on my iBook, or on my desktop Mac at home, or on my computer at work?), store such often-accessed and often-updated information on the Internet.

BackJack.com

When you're speaking to someone who always repeats the same old stories, you're talking to someone who's *redundant*. Redundancy may be bad in social life, but it's very, very, very (oops, there I go repeating myself) important in computing life. *Electronic media*—whether it's the disc from a CD-ROM drive, a hard drive, or a removable media drive such as a Zip—is not infallible. Files, or even entire discs, can, on rare occasions, become corrupt. Some part of the disc becomes damaged, and the files on that disc can't be opened or viewed from your computer. Here, damaged doesn't necessarily mean obviously physically damaged. You don't need to break a CD-ROM disc in half to damage it. The disc may look fine, but when you put it in the iBook's CD-ROM drive, your CD-ROM drive may spin a bit, and then the iBook could report on screen that the disc is unreadable. Discs store information by arranging particles in a particular, exact, order. If something disrupts this order (the presence of a strong magnetic field is one such "something"), then the information becomes unreadable by the drive that's supposed to be able to read it.

Sometimes a file becomes problematic not by a force of nature, but rather by your actions. You may accidentally discard that word processor document that holds your term paper in the Trash on your iBook's desktop. Or you might inadvertently change some important numbers in the spreadsheet document that holds your company's quarterly report.

Whether you have a corrupt, missing, or accidentally altered file, you'll want to rely on a backup copy of the file. If you play it safe—and you must—then you'll have a copy of that file in a backup folder on your hard drive, and hopefully another backup copy of that same file on a disc that is removed from your iBook (such as a Zip disc). When you encounter a problem, copy a backup version to your iBook's hard drive and open that file.

Now you've got this backup system pretty well handled. There is one other very important element to this file protection scheme, though. Offsite backup. In addition to the backup copies that you keep locally, onsite, you should keep a backup copy of your most important files away from your computer. Far away from your computer. If your basement office floods, or all your computer equipment gets stolen, or that backup copy you just *know* you made is missing, or some other "it won't happen to me" event occurs, you'll want to know that your key files can be retrieved and worked with. One of the most convenient areas for storing and retrieving files offsite is...the Internet.

To use the Internet as your file backup storage area, you rent space on a company's Internet-connected computer. Anytime, day or night, you can upload to, and download from, this computer. One company dedicated to Internet file backups is BackJack at `www.backjack.com` (note when typing in that address that there's no letter *L* in the name—it's *BackJack*, not BLackJack.

When you subscribe to BackJack you're given a software program that is used for file encryption (password-protect), file compression (make small smaller), and file transfer (move the files back and forth). You can use the BackJack program to store and retrieve your files anytime. You can also optionally set up the software so that your files get backed up automatically at a regular interval (such as, say, every day at 3:00 a.m. when you aren't using your iBook).

To make use of BackJack you need a Macintosh computer that holds the files to backup (your iBook), an Internet connection (by way of any Internet service provider), and the BackJack software (available for downloading from BackJack). BackJack offers a free 15 day trial period in which you can freely download and use the BackJack software. Try out their file-storing system and, if satisfied, subscribe to their services. BackJack offers a varied pricing structure (to account for users with more than one computer, users that require a lot of storage space, and so forth), but for only about $10 a month you will be able to backup all the important files on your iBook.

iMagicalDesk

Magically, Inc., describes iMagicalDesk at `www.imagicaldesk.com` as a *webtop*, or *virtual desktop*—a personal desktop on the Internet. You've got a nice desktop courtesy of the Macintosh operating system and your iBook, so why do you need another one? For accessibility. Yes, even though your iMagicalDesk virtual desktop "exists" in a place far, far, away, on a server in some other state or some other part of the world, it will greatly aid you in organizing and accessing information that you normally store on your computer.

As you'll see in this book's networking chapter, transferring information between an iBook and a desktop Macintosh is fast and easy. So before you leave home or work with your iBook, you can quickly and easily move your daily files from your desktop Mac to your iBook. And shortly after you bought your iBook you most likely copied all your often-used applications, folders, and files to your iBook's roomy hard drive. So you're all set for a days work on the road, right? Maybe. And maybe not. What if you download a file from the Internet to your iBook, and then realize the application that's needed to open that file is back on your desktop Mac? Or, what if you're sure you have your calendar or To Do list up to date, but now realize that the version on your iBook doesn't include today's appointments? Don't feel bad, these kinds of things happen to all of us! I've learned, and you will too, that it makes sense to store some information on the Internet so that you always have access to it—regardless of which computer you're using. The folks at iMagicalDesk have made the process of storing and retrieving such information very, very easy. Perhaps best of all, they've made this service free!

To make use of iMagicalDesk, you visit `www.imagicaldesk.com` and sign up for their service. Then, each time you want to go to your own personal area (your virtual desktop) within iMagicalDesk, you do so by visiting `www.imagicaldesk.com` and entering your username and password. That causes your browser to display a desktop like the one shown in Figure 9-12.

From the desktop you can easily access any of several iMagicalDesk functions, such as the address book, or e-mail. To do that, just click on the appropriate icon. For instance, if you click on the Calendar icon (refer back to Figure 9-12), you'll see a calendar that displays the current month—as shown in Figure 9-13.

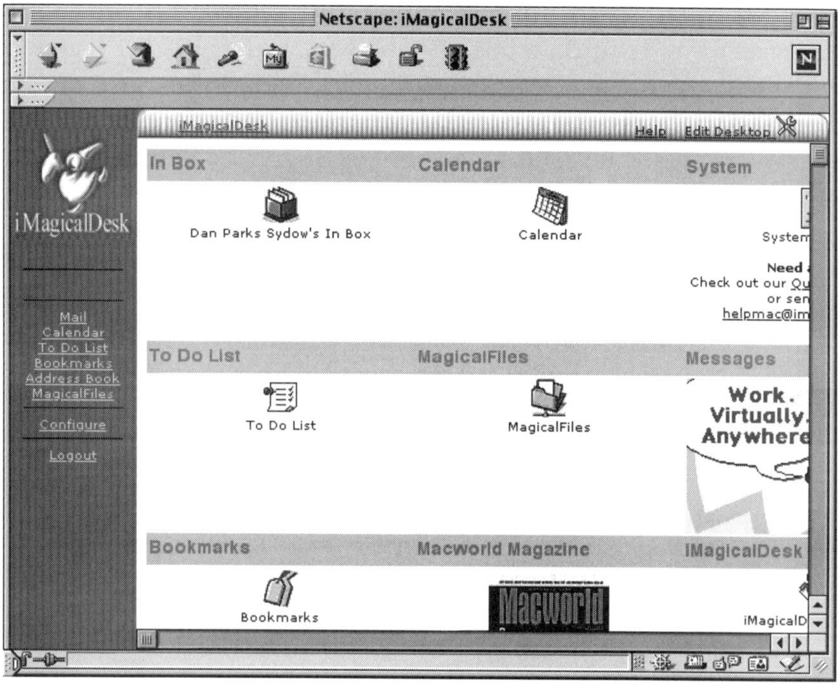

Figure 9-12 The iMagicalDesk desktop.

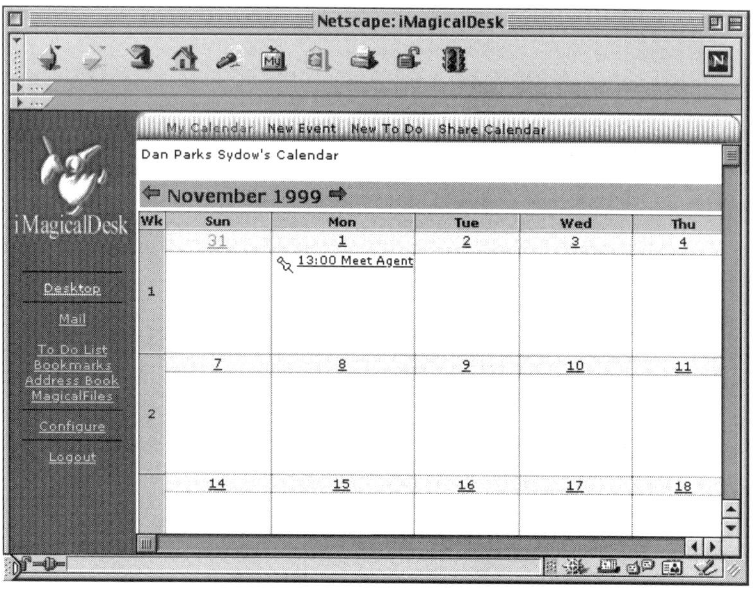

Figure 9-13 The iMagicalDesk Calendar.

In Figure 9-13 you see that at 1:00 p.m. on November 1st I'm to meet my agent. Because you're reading this *after* November 1st, 1999, I'll end the suspense and tell you that yes, thanks to iMagicalDesk, I did make the appointment! To add an entry in the Calendar, you click on **New Event** in the menu bar that runs along the top of the Calendar. Doing that displays an event entry screen—as shown in Figure 9-14.

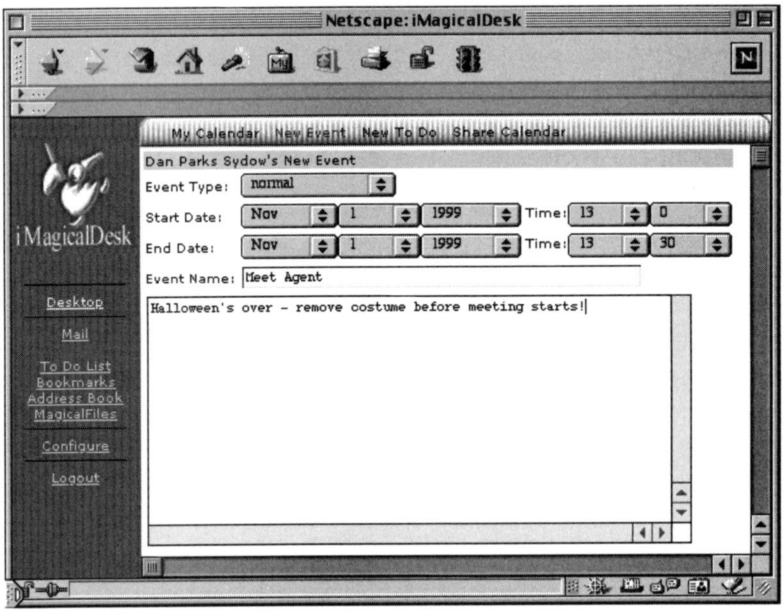

Figure 9-14 Adding an item to the iMagicalDesk Calendar.

Another function of iMagicalDesk is the To Do List. If you prefer entering your appointments or things to do in a list rather than a calendar, just click on the To Do List icon on the desktop (refer back to Figure 9-12) to visit a To Do list like the one in Figure 9-15.

Adding an item to the To Do List is accomplished in a manner similar to adding an entry to the Calendar. In the To Do List you click on New To Do in the menu bar, than fill in a short form that defines the item to add to the list.

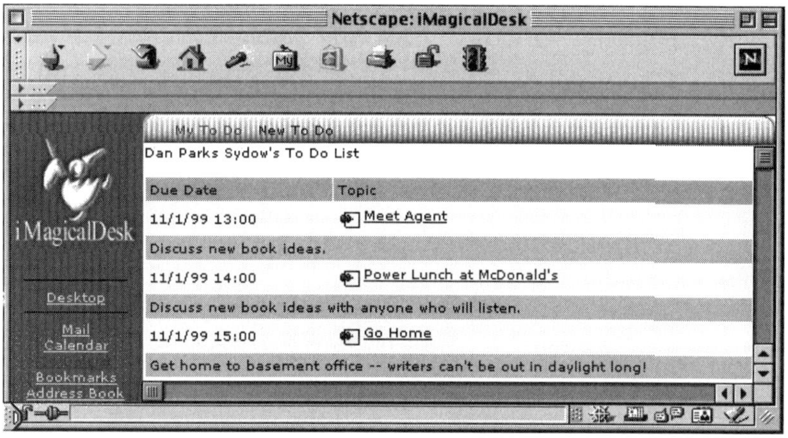

Figure 9-15 The iMagicalDesk To Do List.

I've briefly described the Calendar and the To Do List, but iMagicalDesk offers other functions as well. Here's a summary of the main components that make up the iMagicalDesk suite of Internet-based services:

Desktop Colors iMagicalDesk claims they support the Mac. Here's the proof that they do. With a single click you can change the virtual desktop color scheme to any one of five flavors. Of course those five flavors correspond to those of the iMac and iBook computers.

Disk Space When you sign up with iMagicalDesk you get 5 MB of disk space on the iMagicalDesk server. Use this space to store backup copies of important files, files that you may be accessing from a variety of locations, or files that you want to share with friends or co-workers. The 5 MB of disk space is free—if you want additional space you get it for a

E-mail iMagicalDesk provides you with a free e-mail address. Any messages you receive at this address are stored on iMagicalDesk's central Internet server computer. Having Web-based e-mail is nice because you can access it from any computer that has Internet access. For instance, if you're using the computer of a friend or co-worker, and that computer is connected to the Internet using that person's account rather than your own, you can still check your e-mail (by going to iMagicalDesk and entering your username and password.

Sherlock Plug-ins A very useful feature of iMagicalDesk's e-mail service is the set of iMagicalDesk Sherlock plug-ins. Download these three plug-ins and you can use your iBook's Sherlock (Find from the File menu) search engine to perform searches on all your iMagicalDesk e-mail. As you might expect the plug-ins allow you to easily search for keywords in the subject and sender lines of your e-mail messages. Better yet, the plug-ins let you perform keyword searches in the body, or content, of your e-mail messages.

Bookmarks You've probably got a nice list of bookmarks that you've created and saved in your Web browser's Bookmarks or Favorites menu. What happens, though, if you're accessing the Internet from someone else's computer? It's a good idea to save your most commonly used bookmarks on the Internet so that you can access them anytime, anywhere. The iMagicalDesk Bookmarks feature does just that. It comes set up with dozens of Mac-related bookmarks, and you can easily add any number of your own personal bookmarks.

Address Book Just as it's nice to have a set of often-used bookmarks stored on the Internet, so to is it helpful to keep important addresses on the Internet. Need to e-mail or phone someone, but your address book is on your desktop computer or back at home on your real desk? Just log on to iMagicalDesk and look up the information.

Calendar Described above, the Calendar makes it easy to keep track of upcoming events in calendar format.

To Do List Also described above, the To Do List is another means of organizing your work and social life.

Magical Files If you've ever encountered a file that you couldn't view because you didn't have the parent application (the program that created the file), then you'll appreciate the MagicalViewer function of iMagicalDesk. With the MagicalViewer service, you can open and view files of over 250 different applications—without having any of those applications on your computer. The other iMagicalDesk functions I've discussed are free, but the Magical Files function is considered a premium service and is thus available for a very modest monthly fee.

If you use your iBook while you're on the go (of course you do!), or use someone else's computer, then you're bound to encounter situations where information you need is back at your home or work computer and is inaccessible. Using the many features of iMagicalDesk to store and organize all sorts of information and files can save you a lot of aggravation. The iMagicalDesk service is convenient, easy to use, and free—so you'll no doubt consider the features of iMagicalDesk worth checking out.

Internet Precautions

Imagine this. *Thousands* of high-capacity server computers loaded with information, and all linked together. *Millions* of people sitting at home computers, accessing that information on those thousands of computers. Those same *millions* of people, corresponding with businesses. Those same *millions* of people, corresponding with each other. This wonderful, powerful, communication medium is, of course, the Internet. And while most people who use the Internet do so in good faith, some don't. And it takes only a very small number of people acting in bad faith to cause problems for the majority of people who are acting in good faith. It sounds like a scary scenario. And, potentially, it is—but it doesn't have to be. Armed with just a little Internet security knowledge and some common sense, any one who accesses the Internet can do so in a manner that's personally and financially safe.

Personal Information and the Internet

When you visit a Web site, you may not have access to all of the information stored at that site. That's because the site owner has the right to make available as little or as much information as desired. As a visitor to Web sites, you have that same right.

Keeping Private Information Private

Personal information about yourself or your family is just that—personal. Any personal information, such as your name, age, home or business addresses or phone numbers, Social Security number, credit card numbers, or online passwords assigned to you is all private *unless you voluntarily divulge it.*

If you receive e-mail (or, on America Online, an unsolicited Instant Message) or you visit a Web site that asks you (directly or indirectly) to disclose personal information, consider who requested the information. If there's some incentive to providing personal information, such as access to downloading a free program, consider carefully why the request to reveal personal information is necessary.

Important
Your Internet service provider or America Online will never request that you reveal your password. If someone sends you a message saying they work for your ISP or America Online, and that message asks you to "verify" your password (perhaps due to some supposed problem with the password), that person does not in fact represent that organization.

Why would anyone want information about you? There are a variety of reasons. The recipient of your personal information may want to use that information for general marketing purposes, to attempt to directly sell you something, to place you on a list to receive unsolicited e-mail (spam), to fraudulently represent themselves as you, to make use of your credit card, or even to personally harass you or your family. Likely? No. Possible? Of course.

Important
You may intend e-mail you send to be private—something to be shared only by you and the receiver of the e-mail message. But there's no guarantee that information you e-mail to another will remain private. There's nothing to stop the recipient of an e-mail message from forwarding a message's content to others, or even from posting a message's information on some public area of the Internet (i.e., accessible and readable by anyone connected to the Internet).

Cookies

If you move a file from one folder to another on your iBook's desktop, shut down your computer, and then restart it, the iBook will "remember" that you moved the file. The iBook keeps track of the *state* of the hard drive from one "session" to the next. The Web *isn't* set up in such a way. When you connect to the Internet, visit a site, disconnect, reconnect, and revisit that same site, the site *doesn't* know about your previous visit. A *cookie*, or *magic cookie*, allows a site to keep track of information about you or your computer from one visit to another.

A cookie is a small file that a site creates and automatically downloads to your computer. Cookies weren't invented in order to spy on you, though that's the impression some people have. The information in the cookie file on your hard drive is accessible only to the site that created the file. Other than information about your computer (such as the operating system it uses), a cookie file contains only information that you have supplied to the site. Cookies are harmless. If you have doubts about that, your browser does include an option to allow you to disable your iBook from accepting cookies. (Note, however, that some Web pages won't work properly if cookie-acceptance is disabled).

Keeping It Safe For Kids

The biggest risk a child faces on the Internet is wasting a lot of time in unproductive browsing! The likelihood of any problem more dire than that occurring is slight. However, since a worse problem carries such grave consequences, the issue needs to be addressed.

Risks For Kids

There are three primary risks children and teenagers face on the Internet: viewing of inappropriate material, indirect harassment, and direct abuse.

Inappropriate material There will always be a fringe element that abuses freedom of speech. The Internet isn't immune from the downside to the liberty to express ourselves. Material of a sexual, violent, and illegal nature exists on the Web. Who's to say what's appropriate and what's not? Parents. Parents can *filter*, or block, selected sites from access by children. Parents can discuss the topic with teenagers—though it's unlikely that parents can block sites from access by teenagers, since they usually are more proficient than adults at using the computer!

Indirect harassment A child who corresponds with people unknown is potentially subject to receiving messages that are harassing, mean-spirited, or vulgar. While there may be no direct threat involved, the encounters can be upsetting or demeaning.

Direct abuse How could physical harm come to a child just by that child connecting to the Internet? It can't happen without the child unwittingly aiding the potential perpetrator. By supplying personal information, such as a home address, or by agreeing to a personal meeting, a child who corresponds with strangers potentially subjects himself or herself to trouble.

Rules For Safety

For comprehensive information and guidelines for ensuring that a child has the best possible experience online, visit the SafeKids.com Web site at `www.safekids.com`. The Rules for Online Safety (for kids) link at this site provides a list of well-thought-out Internet guidelines that kids can understand and relate to. Below are a few summarized points made on that list. Click on the `www.safekids.com/myrules.htm` link at the SafeKids.com main page to see the complete list.

- Do not give out personal information, such as your address or telephone number, or your parents' work address or telephone number, without your parents' permission.
- Tell your parents right away if you come across any information that makes you feel uncomfortable.
- Never agree to get together with someone you "meet" online without first checking with your parents. Even if your parents agree to the meeting, one or both of your parents must go along.

Limiting Internet Search Results

For kids, one of the biggest uses of the Web is in searching out information. A parent's hope is that what kids try to uncover is school-related. But search sites such as Yahoo! and AltaVista don't monitor the Web, they just return lists of sites that match search keywords. A search site can first check Web sites before placing them in its database, and a number of search sites do just that. Because the content of each database site must be checked, by nature such a search site has a much smaller pool of Web sites from which search results are returned. But some of these "content-verified" search sites have large databases and as such are very helpful in returning information. For instance, Education World at `www.education-world.com` is a database of over 100,000 Web sites that have been checked and found to be free of sexually explicit, violent, or hateful content. A list of similar search sites can be found at SafeKids.com `www.safekids.com/search.htm`.

Limiting Internet Access

The SafeKids.com site has a link to a list of Internet filter software. A filter is a program that blocks access to some Web sites so that the ability to browse the Web becomes limited. Go to `www.safekids.com/filters.htm` to find names, and sources, of dozens of filters.

You already have one such Internet filter—Apple includes a copy of the EdView Internet Safety Kit Family Edition software with every iBook. The EdView kit has two components: the EdView Smart Zone Web site and the EdView Channel Lock software.

The EdView Smart Zone is a Web site that serves as a portal, or starting point, where kids can search the Internet for other sites of interest. From the Smart Zone (shown in Figure 9-16), kids can gain access to only a limited number of pre-approved Internet sites.

The EdView Channel Lock is a small password-protected program that runs on your iBook. When enabled, this software prevents a user from visiting sites that haven't been approved. In short, a user is essentially forced to visit the Smart Zone Web site and then from there traverse the Internet. The Channel Lock software and Smart Zone site prevent a child from visiting unapproved sites. While Internet access becomes restricted, you won't have to worry about the power of the Internet being crippled—there are still millions of Internet pages of educational resources, sports, entertainment, and news that are accessible. Among the features of the EdView Safety Kit are:

- Locks children into an educational and fun area of educator-reviewed Internet sites
- Can be turned on and off by parent, guardian, or teacher.
- Displays a "Sorry" page when an unapproved site is
- Ability to add additional parent/guardian-approved sites
- Allows searching by category or keywords

Another example of an Internet filter is The Learning Company's Cyber Patrol (`www.cyberpatrol.com`) program—currently the most popular filter. Cyber Patrol is configurable, meaning that it has a variety of settings that a parent can use to limit Web browsing options. For instance, both the time of day that the Internet can be accessed and the total daily time spent online can be set. Individual sites and groups of sites can be completely blocked from access. Since there are potentially thousands of sites that a parent may want to prevent a child from accessing, The Learning Company offers a CyberNOT List, a listing of researched Internet sites containing materials which parents may find questionable. The Cyber Patrol software can be easily set to block access to some or all of the sites in the CyberNOT List.

Note

You can download a demonstration copy of Cyber Patrol from `www.cyberpatrol.com/cp_dlml.htm`. The demo software is active for seven days, which is ample time to test it out to see if it's worth the $29.95 registration price, and the subsequent $29.95 yearly fee to get continuous updates to the CyberNOT List.

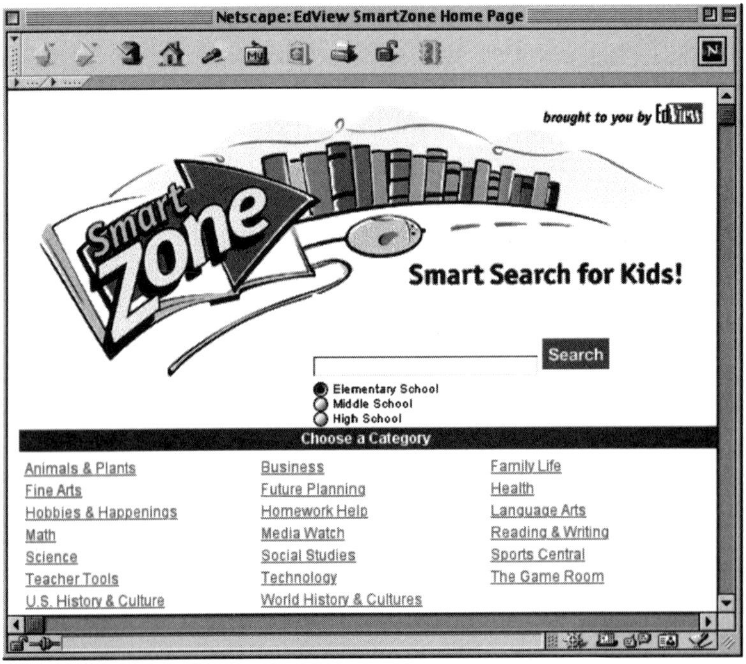

Figure 9-16 EdView's Smart Zone site.

Limiting America Online Access

As well as supplying users with Internet access, America Online has its own huge area of content. The AOL software allows parents to block access to some Internet sites and some of AOL's own content. To make use of America Online's parental controls, log in to AOL and then use the keywords Neighborhood Watch. The window that appears provides information on what can be blocked, and how to go about blocking it. To go to AOL's Web-blocking controls, follow these steps.

1. Choose **Parental Controls** from the **My AOL** menu.
2. Click on the **Fine-tune with Custom Controls** button in the Parental Controls window.
3. Click on the **Web** button in the Web window.
4. Click on the **Web Controls** button in the Web window.

After completing these steps, you'll finally face the Web Controls window. Parental controls are adjustable for each screen name. If a child doesn't have his or her own screen name, create one (to do that choose **Screen Names** from the **My AOL** menu and then double-click on **Create a Screen Name**). For each screen name you choose which level of Web access is to be allowed. Select the appropriate level for the child, then have the child use that screen name each time he or she logs on to America Online.

Note
The AOL-defined age groups are only guidelines. Children's maturity levels vary, so it's up to the parent to choose which level is right for each child.

10

Peripherals

Before the iMac, you'd connect a *peripheral*, or *device* (such as a printer, trackball, or external hard drive) to a Macintosh by plugging the peripheral's cable into the Mac's serial port, or ADB port, or SCSI port. With the iMac, this assortment of ports was eliminated. To connect a peripheral to an iMac, you plug the device's cable into one of the iMac's two *Universal Serial Bus*, or *USB,* ports. The iBook carries on with what will become tradition for Apple—Universal Serial Bus. USB has made some inroads in the PC world, but it's relatively new to the Mac world. In fact, the iMac was the first Macintosh model to use it. So whether you've used or owned, a Mac before, USB is most likely new to you.

This chapter introduces you to Universal Serial Bus: what it is, what its advantages are, and how you make use of it on your iBook. Different devices have different means of connecting, or interfacing, with a computer. Universal Serial Bus is a relatively new technology, so not all devices support it. That is, you can't just purchase any hard drive or printer and plug it into a USB port on your iBook. Fortunately, a Number of peripheral manufacturers are now supporting USB and are shipping products that are iBook-ready. In this chapter, you'll see descriptions of a number of such peripherals. If you have existing Mac peripherals that aren't USB devices (perhaps you own a desktop Mac that's a couple of years old, or older), and you'd like to connect one or more of them to your iBook, first read the start of this chapter to get an overview of USB. Then read the second part of this chapter to learn about a host of iBook connectivity solutions.

Introducing Universal Serial Bus (USB)

The *i* in *iMac* stands for Internet, but it could just as well stand for *innovative*. Apple's decision to drop altogether its long-standing reliance on three peripheral connection technologies (serial, SCSI, and ADB) in favor of USB certainly qualifies as innovative. Now, just a year after the introduction of the iMac, comes another innovative machine—the iBook. And like the iMac, the iBook relies on USB for the connecting of peripherals.

Pros and Cons of USB

In being the first Macintosh model to drop serial, ADB, and SCSI ports in favor of the USB port, the iMac generated some controversy. This controversy didn't last for long. The iMac was the first, but certainly not the last, USB Mac. Apple plans to migrate *all* Macintosh computers to USB—and the iBook demonstrates that commitment. Apple's decision wasn't arbitrary, of course—there are a number of advantages USB holds over other methods of connecting devices to a computer. This section outlines those pluses. No technology is perfect, however, and with change there always comes some drawbacks. So this section also describes the (fortunately) few aspects of USB that may be considered minuses.

Advantages of USB

Among the many advantages of USB the two greatest may be that it offers hot-plugging and it is auto-configuring.

Hot-swappable In the past, to add a peripheral to a Macintosh, you shut the computer down, connected the peripheral, then restarted the computer. Because USB is *hot-swappable*, these steps aren't necessary with an iBook. Hot-swappable, or hot-plugging, are terms that mean the same thing: that you can plug in and unplug devices *on-the-fly*. That is, you can interchange peripherals while the computer is running (while the computer is *hot*, so to speak). Without USB, the connecting or disconnecting of a device to a running Mac was strongly discouraged—doing so could freeze the system and possibly even damage the peripheral.

Autoconfiguring Most peripherals rely on a *SCSI* (*Small Computer Systems Interface*, and pronounced *scuzzy*) to connect to a Macintosh. Connecting a peripheral to a SCSI port is simple—you just plug the end of the peripheral's cable into the SCSI port on the back of the Macintosh. It's the configuring of the peripheral that can cause headaches. Each SCSI device must have an ID that is unique to the computer the device is connected to. That means that before connecting a new SCSI device to a Mac you need to know the ID of each SCSI device that is already connected to that same computer. While not an overwhelming processes, avoiding SCSI ID conflicts takes a bit of effort, and forgetting to verify that there are no conflicts is often a source of major headaches for new Mac users. If you haven't already guessed, now you know: USB devices don't need unique IDs. USB is an auto-configuring technology. Just plug a USB peripheral in and the device and the computer resolve the problem of how the two communicate without interfering with other existing USB devices.

Together, hot-swappable and auto-configuring are especially beneficial for those who don't have a complete, static, system set up. If you perform some task so infrequently that you can't justify buying a certain peripheral, you might occasionally borrow one from someone. Or, you may have a small workspace and choose to only plug in a certain device on those very few occasions when you need it. With the iBook and USB, these situations go smoothly. For instance, you could plug in a scanner and scan a picture, unplug the scanner and plug in a Zip drive, backup the scanned image to a Zip disk, and then unplug the Zip drive. Most importantly, your iBook could remain running throughout this process—there'd be no need to shut it down and restart between any of the steps.

Hot-swappable and auto-configuring are two chief USB advantages, but there are others as well. Briefly, these pluses include:

Support for many devices With USB, you can connect up to 127 devices to a single computer.

Cross-platform standard The fact that USB is the same on PCs and Macs is a direct advantage to peripheral manufacturers and an indirect advantage to iBook users. Developers need to design a peripheral to only one specification. The resulting product works on both PC and Mac computers. Because the installed base of Mac users is smaller than the installed base of PC users, in the past some manufacturers were leery of developing hardware for the Mac. Now they don't have to—their products will work on either type of machine. This means that soon there will be an abundance of peripherals for you to choose from.

Soon-to-be standard USB isn't the number one method of interfacing—now. But it soon will be. Newer Macintosh computers, such as the G4 Macs, the iMac, and the iBook, along with several PCs, feature USB now. Many PC manufacturers are making the USB transition, as is Apple. By the year 2000 over 90 percent of desktop computers are expected to feature USB. In the past, Apple has been criticized for using too many *proprietary standards*—technologies that are Apple's alone and are not used by PCs. Whether an Apple standard is better or not doesn't matter—such a standard isolates the Mac and makes it less profitable for peripheral manufacturers to develop Macintosh hardware.

Simplicity Hot-swappable and auto-configuring make the connection of USB devices simple. Add to that the standardized plugs used for USB devices. There is only one type of USB cable, so iBook users don't have to worry about determining which cables are needed for different peripherals.

Data transfer speed The whole purpose of a peripheral is to transfer data. A printer transfers data from the computer to the printer and onto paper. A modem transfers data from the computer to the modem and then to a phone line. USB technology transfers data far more quickly than serial or Apple Desktop Bus (ADB) technologies. In the past, Mac printers and modems used serial technology, while keyboards and input devices such as the mouse and trackball used ADB technology. Some peripherals will take advantage of the USB data transfer rate of 12 Mbps (megabits per second). Note that you should see the next section, *Disadvantages of USB*, to see how USB transfer speed is also a minus!

Disadvantages of USB

The advantages of Universal Serial Bus far outweigh any disadvantages, but USB does have a couple of shortcomings.

Software drivers In the preceding *Advantages of USB* section, I mentioned that because USB is a cross-platform standard, there is a plethora of devices available for iBook owners. That's because the same USB device that connects to a PC can connect to an iBook. The shortcoming here is that while the physical device is the same, different *driver software* is needed, depending on whether the device is being connected to a Mac or a PC. A driver is a small program that makes it possible for a device (such as a printer) to *interface*, or communicate, with a computer's operating system (such as the Mac OS). The Mac OS and Windows are different from one another, so if a peripheral requires a driver, different drivers are needed. Many manufacturers that have a USB device in production haven't written the appropriate Macintosh driver software for that device. That's understandable—in the past there were no USB Macs to which the device could connect. Writing a driver isn't a terribly daunting task, so in the near future expect to see driver software available for many USB devices. When that happens this disadvantage of USB will disappear.

Data transfer speed The USB data transfer rate of 12 Mbps is far superior to the transfer rates of serial and ADB technologies. But it is less than one-third the speed of the data transfer rate of SCSI. Apple is betting on two factors to lessen the importance of this USB/SCSI transfer speed difference. The first is the Internet and networks. Users who choose the iBook are expected to lessen their dependency on, or forego altogether, external storage devices. With the iBook, Apple is encouraging computer users to take advantage of either the Internet or of networks both to transfer data from one computer to another and to backup data. The second factor that lessens the impact of USB's slow speed relative to SCSI is a technology called FireWire. This already-developed Apple data transfer technology may soon be incorporated into new iBooks. FireWire is much faster than either USB or SCSI. In the near future, look for both USB and FireWire to be incorporated in all new Macintosh models, including the iBook.

Connecting USB Devices

If you don't know anything about connecting peripherals to a Mac, don't worry. Connecting a USB peripheral—whether a keyboard, mouse, printer, or game controller—is simple and doesn't rely on having knowledge of any other peripheral connection technology. And if you do know something about connecting peripherals to a Mac, don't worry about getting confused by having to learn about still one more technology—USB is really that simple.

Cables

Each USB cable has two types of connectors. Figure 10-1 shows the two connectors you'll find on any USB cable.

Figure 10-1 Both ends of a single USB cable.

The USB Type A plug (pictured on the left in Figure 10-1) always connects to a USB port such as the one port on an iBook. The Type B plug (shown on the right in the figure) connects to the USB device. For devices that don't have a removable cable (such as, typically, a USB mouse), the Type B plug isn't evident because the device-end of the cable is soldered directly to the device.

A USB cable's connectors will be marked with the standard USB symbol (shown in Figure 10-2) to make it obvious that the cable is to be used with USB devices. You'll notice on the cable pictured in Figure 10-1 that this is the case.

Figure 10-2 The USB symbol.

Data Flow Directions

When data is transferred from a peripheral to the iBook, the data is said to be going *upstream*. Conversely, data transferring from the iBook to a peripheral is thought of as moving *downstream*. Figure 10-3 elaborates on this concept

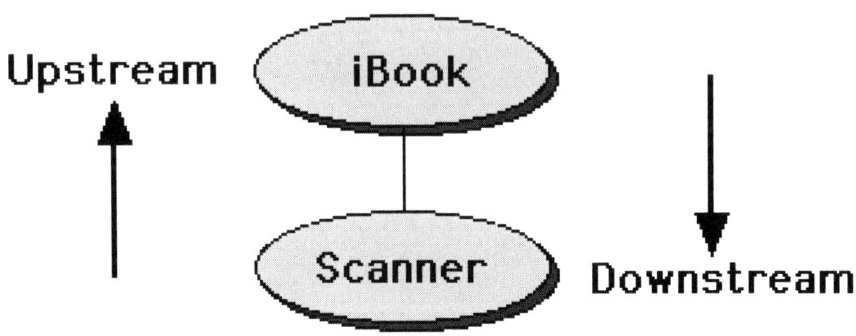

Figure 10-3 Data flow between an iBook and its USB peripherals.

In Figure 10-3, a scanner is connected to the iBook's USB port. In the device chain, or connection ordering of peripherals, the scanner is downstream from the computer. If the scanner had a USB port (some peripherals have an extra, available USB port built into them), and you plugged a second peripheral into that port, then both the newly added peripheral *and* the scanner would be considered downstream from the computer.

Hubs

There is only one USB port on an iBook, yet the iBook can support up to 127 USB devices. The means to achieving this feat is the *hub*. A hub, like the one pictured in Figure 10-4, allows a number of USB devices to be plugged into it. The hub, in turn, is then plugged into one of the USB port on the iBook. The hub shown in Figure 10-4 is a four port hub, so up to four peripherals could be plugged into it.

Figure 10-4 A typical USB hub (a four-port Peracom model).

Hubs come with different numbers of ports, with four and seven ports being common. Figure 10-5 provides a look at how a hub makes it possible to connect a few devices to an iBook using just the iBook's one USB port. The figure also includes a reminder that peripherals are downstream from the iBook (or that the iBook is upstream from the peripherals).

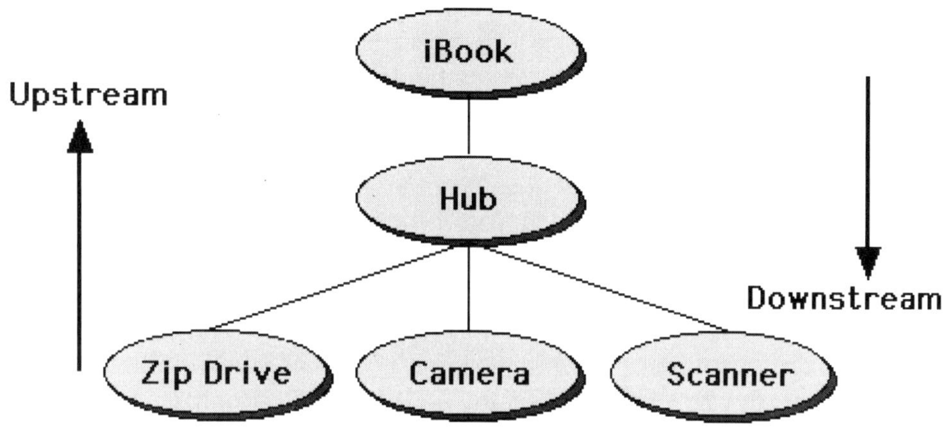

Figure 10-5 Data flowbetween an iBook and several USB peripherals.

Since a hub typically provides seven or fewer ports, you may be confused as to how a hub makes it possible to connect up to 127 devices to a single iBook. Consider that a hub is simply another device—just as peripherals such as printers, keyboards, and external drives are devices. So *another hub* can be plugged into a port on an existing hub.

If you aren't familiar with networking (where the use of hubs is common), you may think that there is something mysterious or complex about a hub. There isn't. A hub can be likened to the powerstrip that people plug computer equipment or stereo components into. Just as a powerstrip enhances the capacity of a wall outlet, so does a hub enhance the capacity of an iBook's one USB port.

Making the Connection

Connecting a peripheral involves little work. For a peripheral like a mouse or keyboard, you usually simply plug the device into an available USB port. The connections of some peripherals require just a little extra one-time effort.

Driver software Some peripherals require a driver—a piece of software that gets installed on the iBook and makes it possible for the iBook to properly communicate with the peripheral. If your device came packaged with a CD-ROM, then there may be driver on that disc. Because driver software is so small in size, a manufacturer may make the driver available for downloading at its Web site (thus saving the manufacturer the cost associated with packaging a CD-ROM with the peripheral). In all cases, there will be no guessing—*the instructions that accompany your peripheral will tell you whether driver software is necessary*. If it is, then you'll place the software on your iBook either by running an included installer program or simply by dragging the icon of the driver software to your System Folder. Again, the instructions will provide the installation details. Once installed, you don't ever need to manually run the driver software. That is, you don't run it as you would some other program. Instead, when you connect the peripheral the iBook senses the connection and automatically runs the driver software.

Provide power Some peripherals are powered by the iBook, while others require external power. A Zip drive, for instance, must be plugged into a powerstrip or wall outlet.

Plug into a port All USB devices need to be connected to a port. Back in Figure 10-1 you saw the two types of plugs that are present on one USB cable. If the device doesn't have a cable permanently attached to the device, plug the Type B connector into the device (the connector plugs into the device only one way, so you can't get it wrong). Plug the Type A connector of the cable into an available USB port (again, there's only one way this plug fits into a port so you can't make a mistake). The port on the iBook is located to the left of the round headphone jack (the port marked with what looks like a small speaker). If you have a USB hub already connected to your iBook, then you can instead plug the peripheral cable's Type A connector into an available port on that hub. Note that some devices (such as a keyboard) include one port. If you have such a device with a free port, you can optionally plug the Type A connector of the new peripheral into this port (as you did if you plugged your mouse into the keyboard).

Note

As mentioned above, some devices come with driver software. Once installed, you forget about the driver. That is, if you unplug the devicel, you don't need to remove the driver software. And if you later plug in the peripheral again, you don't need to reinstall or rerun the driver software.

Important
The entire USB system is controlled by a *host*. For a USB system centered on the iBook (remember, a Windows-based system can be USB, too), the iBook computer itself is the host; the iBook has built-in USB controller chips. Because there can be only one host for any given USB system, USB can't be used as a means of networking computers (there'd be competing hosts in such a case). That's why the iBook has built in Ethernet—Ethernet is the networking medium for the iBook. When multiple iBooks are networked via Ethernet, each iBook is the host of its own USB system and each iBook controls its own USB peripherals. See Chapter11 for more on networking.

Connection Problems

Connecting a USB peripheral is easy. But we're dealing with computers, so no matter how simple the task, there's always the possibility of something going wrong! If you connect a peripheral to your iBook and it doesn't seem to be working properly, consider the following possible solutions:

Electrical outlet Some peripherals need to be plugged into an electrical outlet. Of course, you probably don't have the device unplugged, with its power cord dangling in your lap. But it could have come unplugged without your knowledge, or the outlet or powerstrip to which it's plugged in may have lost power (blown fuse, overloaded circuit breaker, child under desk with paper clip inserted in outlet, and so forth). Check the device's power cord!

Bus-powered hubs A four-port or seven-port hub (like the ones described later in this chapter) is externally powered—you plug it into a wall socket or powerstrip. Some hubs are bus-powered—they derive their needed electricity from the iBook's internal power bus. Such a hub shares the power that the iBook uses. The iBook is a friendly enough machine, but it only has so much power it can give up; it can't support an unlimited number of unpowered hubs. The rule is that you can't connect one bus-powered hub to another bus-powered hub. Instead, you need to connect a bus-powered hub to one that is directly connected to a power source.

Driver software If a peripheral requires a software driver, and you failed to install that driver, the peripheral won't operate. The iBook, via a descriptive alert on the screen, will remind you of this. Disconnect the device from the port it's connect to and install the driver (refer to the peripheral's instructions to determine how to install the associated driver onto your iBook). Then reconnect the peripheral. This disconnecting and reconnecting of the device are necessary steps—failing to do so prevents the driver software from running. When you reconnect the peripheral, the iBook senses that a device has been added and runs the newly installed driver (installing the driver doesn't run it—it only places it on your iBook's hard drive).

Tip

The About.com at `www.about.com` is a Web site that employs hundreds of people to maintain lists of Web sites of interest to . . . just about everyone. Click on a channel (a topic) such as business/careers to see links to related subtopics, articles, and forums. The Macintosh area of About.com at `machardware.about.com/compute/hardware/machardware/` holds a number of links to Mac-related topics, including a link to USB information (and, incidentally, a couple of links to iBook information). Here you'll find links to manufacturer support pages for many of the USB peripherals discussed in this chapter.

USB Peripherals for the iBook

As USB becomes more popular on the Windows side, manufacturers are creating more and more USB peripherals. That's good for Window users—it gives them more hardware choices. And, for once, something good for Windows users becomes something good for Mac users. That's because the Universal in Universal Serial Bus means just that: a USB device is universally available for systems that support USB. The same USB peripheral, such as a printer or external storage drive, that can be used on a PC, can be used on an iBook.

Cross-platform peripherals are good news, but there is one caveat—some peripherals require specialized drivers. As mentioned in the *Disadvantages of USB* subsection of this chapter's *Pros and Cons of USB* section, a driver is a small program that makes it possible for a device (such as a printer) to interface, or communicate, with a computer's operating system (such as the Mac OS). Some USB peripherals will come in both Mac and Windows flavors. While the device itself will be the same, the accompanying driver software will differ. In some cases, a manufacturer will make drivers available for free download from its Web site.

How will you know if a USB device you're considering is iBook-ready? The device's box or the promotional information for the device on the manufacturer's Web site should specifically mention the fact (visit the Macally site at `www.macally.com` for an example). Another way to gain assurance that a particular peripheral is ready to be hooked up to your iBook is to read this chapter—the devices listed here are iBook-connectable!

Printers

You'll want to see, hold, and share the fruits of your computer labors—so a printer may be the first peripheral you obtain. This section is brief because it describes a type of printer that is in limited supply—the USB printer. Your options aren't, however, as constrained as you might imagine. That's because there exist enough types of printer *adapters* to make it possible to connect a huge variety of existing, non-USB printers to an iBook. For more on printer adapters, refer to this chapter's *Connecting Non-USB Peripherals* section.

Note
If your iBook is connected to a network that includes one or more printers, you're all set—just make sure one of the printers is shared. To do that, select it in the Chooser (under the Apple menu) of the machine it's connected to, click the **Setup** button, and check the **Share this Printer** checkbox. Then choose the printer from the Chooser under the Apple menu of the iBook.

Epson Stylus 740i Color Printer

Epson has several printers in its Stylus series, including two USB printers that are iBook-ready.. The Stylus 740i is an ink jet printer that delivers approximately six pages perminute (6 ppm). Dots-per-inch (dpi) resolutions for the Stylus 740 are 1440 x 720, 720 x 720, 360 x 360, and 180 x 180. The 740i comes standard in an iBook-matching blueberry, or you can outfit it with an optional tangerine printer cover if that's the flavor of your iBook.

Right out of the box the Epson Stylus 740i Color Printer is ready to connect to an iBook. Refer to Chapter 8 to read about the Epson USB/Parallel Printer Adapter Kit that allows you to connect a number of other Epson printers to an iBook.

Removable Media Drives

Apple has intentionally eliminated the floppy drive to encourage users to follow the trend of transferring files via networks and the Internet, and to keep down iMac production costs. If your work habits demand a floppy drive, though, don't despair—USB solutions exist. And if you're used to backing up or transferring your files by way of a high-capacity removable drive (such as a Zip drive), you're again in luck—a few USB solutions are on the market.

Imation 120 MB/1.4 MB SuperDisk Drive

Imation's USB SuperDisk is a drive that supports both large capacity discs (120 MB) and the much smaller, standard Mac- and PC-formatted 1.4 MB floppy disks. It even recognizes older 720 KB PC-formatted disks. If you need to make even occasional use of floppy disks, then the SuperDisk drive is definitely worth considering. Imation designed the SuperDisk specifically for the iMac—the color of its case even matches the iMac's colors. So, of course the SuperDisk also matches the colors of the iBook. The SuperDisk requires no adapters—it's a true USB device. Just plug the drive's cable into the USB port on your iBook and you're ready to backup any of your files.

Iomega 250 and 100 MB Zip Drive

Iomega's 250 MB Zip drive is the de facto standard in terms of large capacity removable media—several Mac models even come equipped with a built-in Zip drive. Now, Iomega is making sure that iBook owners aren't left out. Iomega's new USB Zip drive connects directly to your iBook's USB port and works with both the traditional 100 MB Zip disk cartridges that have become so common and the newer 250 MB Zip disk cartridges. If you don't need that much capacity, and you Want to save a few bucks, Iomega also makes a 100 MB-only Zip drive that's USB and ready to connect to your iBook.

VST Floppy Drive

Many computer users consider the floppy disk to be dated—but you may find yourself in a position where you need to be able to transfer files by floppy disk. VST Technologies at www.vsttech.com provides Mac users with both USB hard drives (see this chapter's Hard Drives section) and a floppy drive. Their external USB floppy drive is capable of reading and writing 1.4 MB Mac or PC formatted floppy disks.

Speakers

The iBook comes with just a single built-in speaker (of only marginal quality, too). If you're serious about sound, you'll want to invest in external stereo speakers to plug into your iBook's headphone jack.

CoZo speakers

CoZo speakers come in iBook-matching translucent tangerine and blueberry colors. These power amplified speakers are designed with the iBook in mind (though they'll work just as well with a G3 or G4 Macintosh computer). You can get more information on this $60 pair of speakers at `www.cozo.com`.

Microphones

The iBook doesn't come equipped with a microphone port, but there's an easy way to get around that. Griffin Technology, at `www.griffintechnology.com`, offers iBook owners the iMic Audio adapter. Plug this adapter into the iBook's USB port, then plug virtually any inexpensive microphone into the adapter. The iMic provides professional quality sound input—supporting stereo input at up to 48 Khz.

Video Input

Your iBook comes with a nice sized, high-resolution screen for the output of images—but what do you do if you want to input video? Unlike many Mac models, the iBook doesn't come equipped with a video input port. If you want to get video into your iBook, though, there is a solution.

Eskape Labs MyTV

Eskape Labs, at `www.eskapelabs.com`, has recently released MyTV. Connect the MyTV box (shown in Figure 10-6) to your iBook's USB port, and you're all set to now plug in a video source such as a camcorder or a VCR. Do that and you can "capture" the output from this video source and watch it in a window on your iBook, or save it to a file on your iBook's hard drive. The MyTV has a built-in 125 channel cable ready TV tuner too—plug your cable line into the device and you can watch cable TV in a window on your iBook.

Figure 10-6 The MyTV device.

Video Output

Your iBook has a built-in monitory, so you're all set when it comes to viewing images—right? Maybe. If you want a second monitor, or TV, to "mirror" the image that's on your iBook monitor, you'll need a video out device—an adapter that plugs into the iBook's USB port to supply the iBook with the video output port that doesn't come standard on the iBook.

AVerMedia MicroSystems' USBPresenter Video Output Adapter

Want people across the room to be able to view an on-screen demo or presentation? If so, you need the ability to attach a big screen to your iBook. AVerMedia Microsystems, at `www.vermedia.com`, provides you with that adapter in the form of their USBPresenter device. Plug the USBPresenter into your iBook's USB port, then plug your video device (such as a television) into the USBPresenter. Now, anything displayed on the iBook screen is mirrored (displayed) on the video device. You can also plug a video capture device (such as a VCR) into the USBPresenter in order to save an on-screen demo or presentation for later playback on the video capture device.

Mice and Trackballs

If you don't care for the trackpad and trackpad button that come built into your iBook, you may want to instead use a conventional mouse or trackball. You can do that by simply plugging a USB replacement mouse or trackball into the iBook's USB port..

Macally iMouse

Macally has come out with a host of devices specifically designed for the iMac and iBook. One of those products is the iMouse. As shown in Figure 10-7, the iMouse has a shape more closely reminiscent of a traditional mouse than the iMac-supplied mouse does. What isn't conveyed in the monochrome figure is the fact that the iMouse matches the iMac and iBook color-schemes.

Macally iBall Trackball

Macally's covered all the iMac and iBook data-input bases. Besides the iMouse mouse, Macally offers the iBall trackball. Like the iMouse, the iBall case matches the coloring of the iMac and iBook. Figure 10-8 provides a look at this device.

Figure 10-7 The Macally iMouse.

Figure 10-8 The Macally iBall.

ITAC evolution Trackball

When it comes to USB trackballs, you've got a choice. Besides the Macally iBall, there is the ITAC evolution trackball, which is shown in Figure 10-9. This device doesn't share the iBook color scheme, but it has advantages that far outweigh that slight drawback. The evolution trackball's somewhat odd shape reflects the device's ergonomic design—the trackball provides hand support for stress reduction. The evolution's light ball movement force also contributes to reduced user-effort. The trackball comes with six large keys that lie to either side of the trackball's ball.

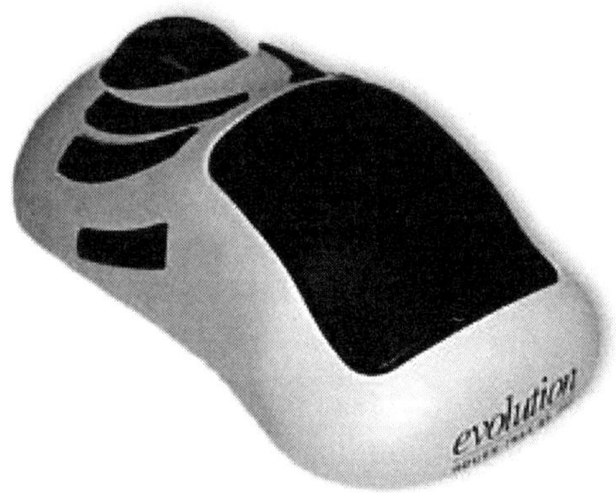

Figure 10-9 The ITAC evolution trackball.

Keyboards

Your iBook's built-in keyboard is very adequate—but if you're an experienced computer user, you may have a preference for a different style of keyboard. With the exception of the keyboard that comes with the iBook, Apple's keyboards are ADB devices rather than USB devices. There are, however, a number of USB keyboards normally used with PCs. A USB-compatible keyboard will be advertised as such.

Note
If the keyboard you use isn't designed specifically for a Macintosh, then it won't have a key with the "four leaf clover" Command key symbol on it. You'll need to get used to using the key that takes its place on a PC-style keyboard, located between the CTRL and ALT keys. If the keyboard was specifically designed for Windows, there'll be a Windows key that can serve as the Command key. Also, you'll notIce that there's no power key on a PC-style keyboard. Just use the power button on the iBook to turn your computer on.

Microsoft Natural Keyboard elite

You can see in Figure 10-10 that Microsoft's Natural Keyboard elite certainly doesn't look like a conventional keyboard. The layout of keys on a typical keyboard forces a typist to position his or her hands at angles that aren't natural. An ergonomically designed keyboard attempts to have the keyboard provide a better hand-to-keyboard "fit. There are other ergonomic keyboards, but for what it's worth, Microsoft's Natural Keyboard elite is the best-seller.

Macally iKey Keyboard

Like the other Macally iBook-related peripherals (the iMouse, iBall, and iHub), the colors of the iKey keyboard (Figure 10-11) closely match the color-scheme of the iBook itself. The blueberry keyboard has a curved design and the black keys have a quiet, soft touch.

Figure 10-10 The Microsoft Natural Keyboard elite.

Figure 10-11 The Macally iKey.

Game Controllers

You bought an iBook for productivity purposes only, right? You probably had no plans of ever playing cool games such as Quake or Riven, right? But since the 3D Nanosaurous and Bugdom games were included for free, you really should make sure that you get the most out of them. To do that, you'll want to use a game controller in place of your mouse and keyboard.

Gravis GamePad Pro USB

GamePad Pro USB, shown in Figure 10-12, is Gravis's first USB device. If you're tired of using the arrow keys on your iBook keyboard to try to escape from the enemy, consider getting a GamePad Pro. This gamepad has a thumb-controlled directional pad and ten programmable action buttons.

Figure 10-12 The Gravis GamePad Pro USB.

ThrustMaster Top Gun USB Joystick

ThrustMaster has long supported the PC. Now they're entering the Mac market. And their first Macintosh-supported product is just for you—a USB device that's all ready to be connected to an iBook. Figure 10-13 shows the Top Gun joystick, which includes a 4-way hat switch, three action buttons, and a quick-action trigger.

Figure 10-13 The ThrustMaster Top Gun USB joystick.

Cameras

Descriptions of digital cameras often include the term *mega pixel.* A mega pixel image is composed of a million or more pixels. The more pixels that make up an image, the higher that image's resolution, and, consequently, the more clarity that image has. There are severa mega pixel, high quality USB digital cameras available now, with more coming.

Kodak Digital Science DC220 and DC 260 Digital Cameras

Both the Kodak Digital Science DC 220 and DC 260 cameras (shown in Figure 10-14) are USB devices that feature mega pixel resolution, an autofocus 3x zoom lens, time lapse, and audio recording. With 1.6 million pixels devoted to each image, expect photo-realistic quality for pictures up to 8 x 10 inches in size.

Connectix/Logitech QuickCam VC Video Camera

The Logitech QuickCam (which used to be the Connectix QuickCam before Connectix sold its hardware division to Logitech) is a new USB version of Logitech's popular digital video camera. Plug this color camera's six-foot cable into your iBook's USB port and you can shoot 15-frame-per-second live-action video—perfect for videoconferencing (videoconferencing software included). The QuickCam, shown in Figure 10-15, can also be used to capture still images.

Figure 10-14 The Kodak Digital Science DC260 digital camera.

Figure 10-15 The Logitech QuickCam VC USB video camera.

Scanners

Resolution refers to how much data can be displayed in a given area. So, resolution refers to clarity. For scanners and cameras, higher resolutions are better: a higher resolution means the device will create an image that displays more detail in a given area. Resolution may be given in dpi (dots-per-inch) or ppi (pixels-per-inch). "Dots" and "pixels" are terms that are interchangeable, so if one device claims it has a resolution of 1200 x 600 dpi (a one inch by one inch image will be created using 1200 dots in one direction and 600 dots in the other) and another device claims a resolution of 1200 x 600 ppi, then their resolutions are the same. There are a few high resolution USB scanners available now, with more in the works.

Agfa SnapScan 1212u USB Color Scanner

The 1212u is a USB color scanner that can capture images up to 8.5 x 11.7 inches in size, with a resolution of 1200 x 600 dpi (dots-per-inch). The scanner comes with Agfa's own scanner control software that automatically calibrates the scanner for each scan.

Epson Perfection 636U Color Scanner

Epson, at `www.epson.com`, offers iBook owners this 600 x 2400 dpi color scanner that they say is a "professional quality scanner."

UMAX Astra 1220 USB Scanners

The Astra 1220U USB scanner from UMAX Technologies scans any document up to an 8.5 x 11.7 inches in size and produces an image with a resolution of 600 x 1200 dpi. The Astra is a USB device, and was designed with the Macintosh in mind, so it comes with a good Macintosh software bundle that makes iBook scanning, and working with the resulting images, easy.

Hard Drives

Your iBook's hard drive should serve you well—its several gigabytes of storage space is enough to hold a lot of programs, documents, and image files. If the time comes when you do need more fixed storage (as opposed to removable media, such as that offered by Iomega's Zip drive and its Zip cartridges), you have a couple of choices.

Apple Drives

Direct from Apple comes a USB hard drive available in a number of storage capacity sizes, including 2, 3, 4, 6, and 9 GB. This compact, external drive can be placed next to your iMac in either a vertical or horizontal position. (Note that while this drive is from Apple, and is a USB device, its case doesn't match the iBook color scheme.)

VST Hard Drives

VST Technologies at www.vsttech.com offers this external USB hard drive in 4 GB and 6 GB sizes, and comes in iBook-matching colors.

USB Hubs

This chapter's Connecting USB Devices subsection of the Introducing Universal Serial Bus section discusses hubs in depth. In short, a hub gives your iBook additional USB ports; if you're connecting more than a couple of USB devices to your iBook, you need a hub. A USB hub is a relatively simple device—look for more and more manufacturers to be marketing inexpensive ones.

Macally iHub

Macally makes peripherals, including a keyboard, mouse, and trackball, that match the iBook. They also make a translucent blueberry four-port USB hub (see Figure 10-16).

Figure 10-16 The Macally iHub.

Peracom USB Quad Hub

The Peracom USB Quad Hub is a four-port hub. For a look at this hub, refer back to Figure 10-4.

Entegra Hubs and Cables

Entegra is one of the first companies to become deeply involved in USB. Entegra makes four-port and seven-port hubs, and a variety of USB cables. Their hubs are designed to be easily stacked, to minimize desktop use.

Keyspan USB Hub

The Keyspan USB Hub provides four bus-powered or self-powered powered USB ports. Keyspan also makes a USB Card (to provide USB ports to Mac computers that don't have USB) and USB-to-serial adapter. Both of these products are discussed later in this chapter.

Connecting Non-USB Peripherals

The iBook has a Universal Serial Bus (USB) and an Ethernet port. Other older Macs have some combination of serial, parallel, Apple Desktop Bus (ADB), Ethernet, and infrared ports. Existing, "pre-USB Mac" peripherals have one or more of these ports as their means of interfacing with a Mac. If you already had a Mac when you bought your iBook, you are now no doubt interested in connecting some or all of your existing peripherals to the iBook. Or, you may know of a source of inexpensive, used Macintosh-compatible hardware. With all those different types of ports and cables, what's a poor iBook owner to do? Why, read this chapter of course.

The iBook's USB port and its Ethernet port are intended to be the main means of adding peripherals. USB is fairly new to the Mac, so the likelihood that you have any USB peripherals connected to older Macs is pretty slim. If you're a home user, then it's unlikely that your Mac is a part of an Ethernet network, which also makes it unlikely that you have a lot of peripherals with Ethernet ports. It should be obvious that when it comes to connecting old peripherals to a new iBook, *adapters* is the name of the connection game. A large part of this chapter deals with the various adapters that are available to make possible the interconnection of the old and the new.

Non-USB Macs have one or more serial ports. Both the modem port and printer port (some Macs have these two ports combined into a single port) are serial ports. The iBook doesn't have a serial port, but in this chapter you'll read about several relatively simple solutions for connecting many types of serial devices (such as printers) to the iBook.

If you have a Mac with a number of SCSI and ADB devices, you may be a bit disappointed that Apple has gone with USB for the iBook. Don't be. Apple, along with most of the personal computer industry, is (or will soon be) migrating to USB. Future Macintosh computers will all be USB-only machines. iBook or not, get ready for USB.

Connecting Printers

Many Mac users stick with Apple peripherals. So a lot of iBook owners may have Apple printers. While no earlier Apple printer came equipped with a direct means to connect to a USB port, your printer investment is unlikely to be lost. For Apple printers, and a handful of printers by other manufacturers, a few connectivity solutions exist.

If you have an Apple printer, read either the *Connecting an Apple StyleWriter* or the Connecting an Apple LaserWriter sections. I won't attempt to explain how to connect every type and model of Apple printer to an iBook—the possibilities are extensive. Instead, I'll defer to a very useful Apple Web page. Regardless of the type of Apple printer you have, read the *Using the Apple Connectivity Web Site* section to get a feel for how Apple's Web page works, and to possibly find additional details regarding your specific printer. If you've got a non-Apple printer, then the *Connecting Other Third-Party Printers* section holds the most important pages for you.

Using the Apple Connectivity Web Site

Want to connect an Apple printer to your iBook? If so, stop in at the iMac Connectivity Page support.info.apple.com/support/imac/connectivity/connectivity.taf. That's right, the address of this page includes a reference to the iMac—not the iBook. The iMac was the first USB-equipped Mac, so Apple took great pains to provide Web support for those interested in learning how various USB and non-USB devices could be connected to their new iMac computers. Because the iBook is the "iMac to Go", the connectivity solutions that apply to iMacs generally apply to iBooks. In fact, the just-mentioned Web site used to be titled iMac Connectivity. Now it has the more general (as in, pertaining to both iMacs and iBooks) title of USB Connectivity. When you go the this site, you'll see a page that looks like the one shown in Figure 10-17.

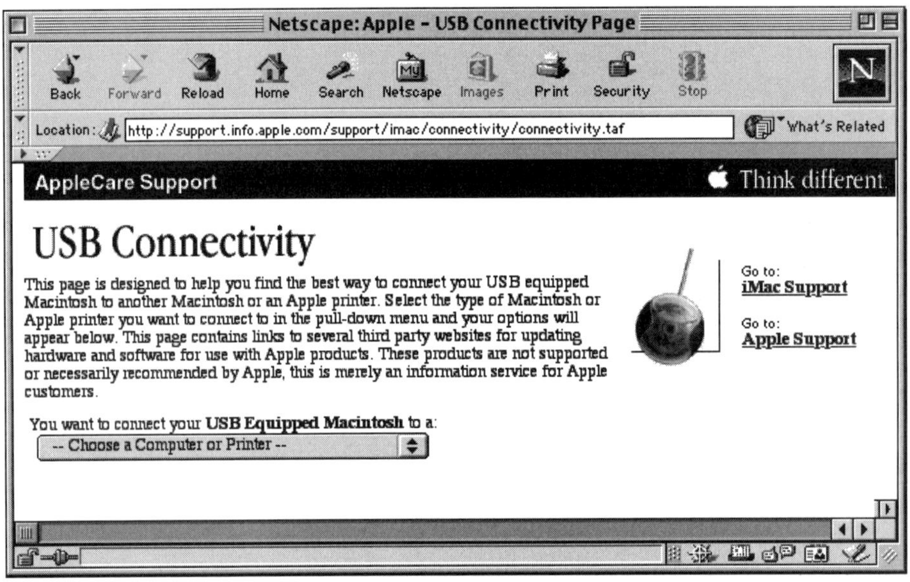

Figure 10-17 The main page of Apple's USB Connectivity Web site.

Tip

From the title of the pop-up menu in Figure 10-17, you can see that if you need to connect another Macintosh computer to your iBook, then this USB Connectivity Page is still the place to be. Refer to Chapter 11 for more information on using this site for that purpose.

Click on the **Choose a Computer or Printer** pop-up menu to reveal a list of items that may be connected to the iBook. Figure 10-18 shows the contents of this menu.

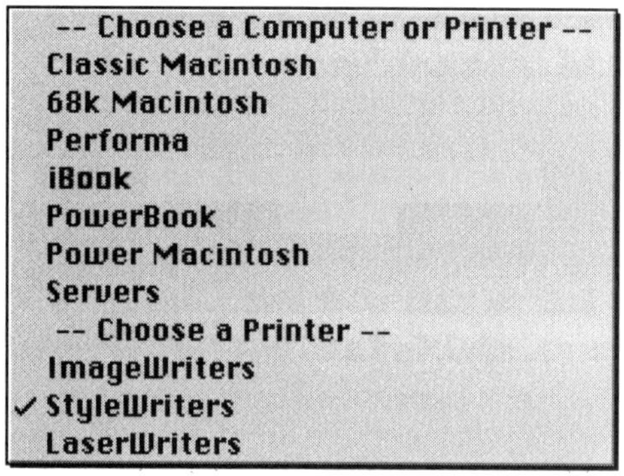

Figure 10-18 Selecting a type of device to connect to the iBook.

Select the category of printer you're interested in connecting to your iBook. Doing that changes the title of the pop-up menu (to the selected item), and adds a new pop-up menu to the right of the original one. Figure 10-19 shows the results of choosing **StyleWriters** from the **Choose a Computer or Printer** pop-up menu.

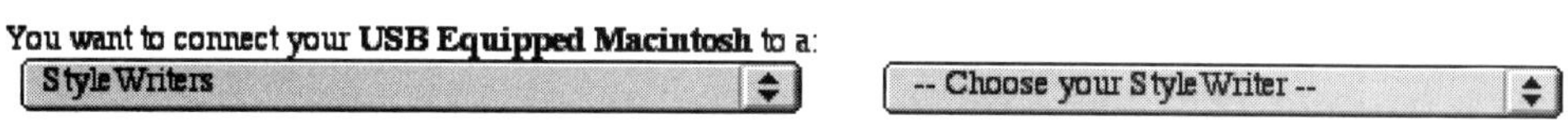

Figure 10-19 A second menu is displayed on the Connectivity page.

Finally, choose the particular printer model from the new pop-up menu. Figure 10-20 shows the StyleWriter models to choose from. If you select a different type of printer (namely, **ImageWriters** or **LaserWriters**) from the first pop-up menu, you will, of course, see a different list of printer models.

Choosing a printer model brings up information about connecting that one specific model to an USB Macintosh such as an iMac or iBook. I chose the StyleWriter 2500 option and a part of the resulting display of information is shown in Figure 10-21.

Figure 10-20 Selecting a device from the second pop-up menu.

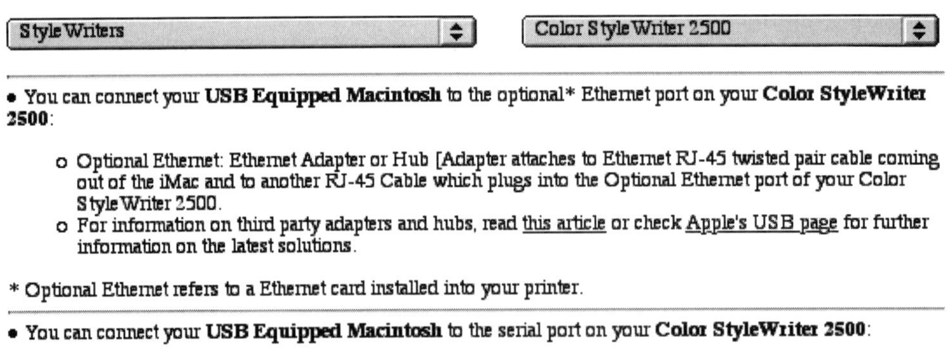

Figure 10-21 Connectivity information for a particular device.

Figure 10-21 shows that Apple provides you with some pretty specific instructions for connecting a particular printer to an iBook. You can get still more information on this topic by reading the next section.

Connecting an Apple StyleWriter

All StyleWriter models can be connected directly to the serial port found on the back of most Macintosh computers. *Some* StyleWriter models can optionally become part of a LocalTalk network by connecting the printer to a LocalTalk connector and then plugging that connector into the Mac's serial port. Whether your StyleWriter is "serial-only" or "LocalTalk capable" determines the iBook connectivity solution you'll employ. Find your printer model in the following two lists, then read the appropriate section of the two that follow the lists.

StyleWriter I, II, 1200, 1500, 2200, 2400, 2500 read the *Serial-Only StyleWriters* section.

StyleWriter 4100, 4500, 6500 read the *LocalTalk StyleWriters* section.

Some StyleWriters connect only *directly* to one of the Mac's serial ports, either the printer port or the modem port—they can't connect first to a LocalTalk connector box to become a part of a LocalTalk network. For such a StyleWriter, you have a few iBook-connection options.

If you want to connect a serial printer to a USB port on your iBook, consider the USB Serial Adapter from Keyspan. Plug the adapter into the USB port on your iBook. Then just plug one end of a standard Apple serial cable into the printer's serial port and the other end into the adapter. The Keyspan USB Serial Adapter offers a plus in that the adapter has two serial ports on it, so you can optionally, and easily, connect a second serial device to the same iBook. The Keyspan adapter isn't for peripherals that rely on MIDI, Geoport, or LocalTalk technologies, but for Apple StyleWriters that aren't a part of a LocalTalk network, or for graphic tablets or PDAs (Personal Digital Assistants), it's a great iBook connectivity solution.

A third serial printer solution is Farallon's EtherMac iPrint Adapter SL. This serial-to-Ethernet adapter is pictured in Figure 10-22.

Figure 10-22 The Farallon EtherMac iPrint Adapter.

Normally, you connect a StyleWriter to a Mac by running a serial cable from the StyleWriter's serial port to the Mac's printer or modem port. To connect a StyleWriter to an iBook, you connect the printer to the iPrint adapter and the adapter to the iBook. Just follow these steps:

1. Plug one end of the serial cable into the StyleWriter printer's round serial port, just as you've always done.
2. Plug the other end of the serial cable into one end of the iPrint adapter.
3. Plug one end of a standard 10Base-T Ethernet cable into the remaining port on the adapter.
4. Plug the other end of the Ethernet cable into your iBook's Ethernet port.

The iPrint adapter is nothing more than a means of connecting a serial device (the printer) to an Ethernet port. The adapter kit includes the adapter and both of the needed cables, so all you need to do is plug away!

Some StyleWriter printers can optionally connect to a serial port via LocalTalk. For such printers, the simplest iBook connection solution may be Farallon's EtherMac iPrint Adapter LT. Figure 10-22 shows the adapter. To make use of this adapter, you'll also need a couple of LocalTalk connection kits. A connection kit consists of a connector box, a standard LocalTalk cable, and possibly a terminator (used to terminate, or "plug up," an unused jack in the two-jack connector box). Farallon, the maker of the iPrint adapter, also makes LocalTalk connector kits. Figure 10-23 shows what the Farallon PhoneNET Connector kit looks like. Apple and other manufactures sell LocalTalk connector kits as well.

Figure 10-23 A Farallon PhoneNET connector kit.

Important

There's a similarly named Farallon adapter for connecting other select StyleWriter models to the iBook. The EtherMac iPrint Adapter LT (*LT* for *LocalTalk*, discussed next) is for LocalTalk rather than serial StyleWriters. You want the SL (*SL* for *serial*) adapter, not the LT adapter.

Normally, you connect a LocalTalk StyleWriter to a Mac by plugging a connector box into the printer's serial port, plugging a connector box into the Mac's serial port, and then joining the boxes with a LocalTalk cable. To connect a LocalTalk StyleWriter to an iBook, follow these steps instead:

1. Plug the serial cable attached to the LocalTalk connector box into the StyleWriter's serial port—just as you'd do if connecting the printer to an ordinary Mac.
2. Plug one end of a standard LocalTalk cable into one of the jacks on the LocalTalk connector box.
3. Plug the other end of the LocalTalk cable into the jack located at one end of the iPrint adapter.
4. Plug one end of a 10Base-T Ethernet cable into the remaining port on the adapter
5. Plug the other end of the Ethernet cable into your iBook's Ethernet port.

The iPrint adapter, along with a LocalTalk connector box, serves as the means of connecting a LocalTalk device (the printer) to an Ethernet port.

Connecting an Apple LaserWriter

This chapter's *LocalTalk StyleWriters* section introduced the concept of using an Ethernet-to-LocalTalk adapter to connect a LocalTalk device (such as one of the high-end Apple StyleWriter printers) to an Ethernet port (like the one located on the iBook). Like connecting a LocalTalk StyleWriter to an iBook, connecting an Apple LaserWriter to an iBook also involves the use of an Ethernet-to-LocalTalk adapter. If you haven't read the short *LocalTalk StyleWriters* section, jump back just a bit and do so now. Then return here for descriptions of the adapters you can choose from.

Farallon iPrint Adapter LT In the *LocalTalk StyleWriters* section, you read about Farallon's EtherMac iPrint Adapter LT. The Apple LocalTalk StyleWriters are only one type of printer this adapter supports. Because Apple LaserWriter printers support LocalTalk, this same Farallon adapter can also be used to connect an Apple LaserWriter to an iBook. Again, if you purchase this adapter, make sure to get the LocalTalk (LT) adapter rather than the serial (SL) adapter.

Asante AsanteTalk One end of the AsanteTalk adapter (shown in Figure 10-24) plugs into any Apple LaserWriter printer, while the other end plugs into the Ethernet port of your iBook. The result is an iBook that can print to the LaserWriter. The AsanteTalk kit comes with the AsanteTalk Ethernet-to-LocalTalk adapter, all necessary cables, and set-up documentation.

Sonic Systems microPrint The microPrint adapter from Sonic Systems makes the connection of an Apple LaserWriter to an iBook simple. The microPrint/2 (see Figure 10-25) allows two LocalTalk devices to be hooked up to a single iBook through the Ethernet port. There's also a microPrint/12 model that makes it possible to connect—you guessed it—up to a dozen LocalTalk peripherals to an iBook.

Figure 10-24 Asante's AsanteTalk Ethernet-to-LocalTalk adapter.

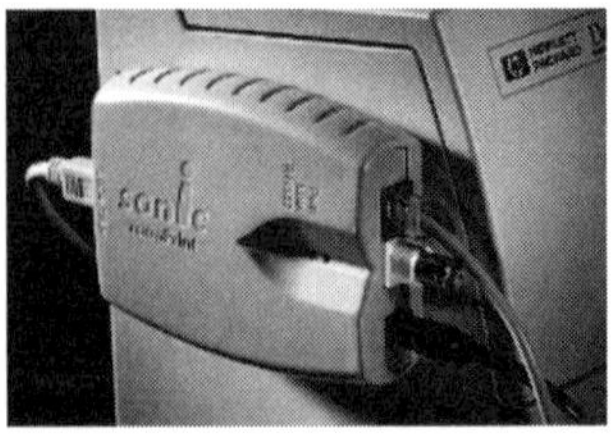

Figure 10-25 Sonic Systems microPrint Ethernet-to-LocalTalk adapter.

Connecting Other Third-Party Printers

To this point, the *Printers* section has focused on Apple printers. But if you have a printer manufactured by a third party (a company other than Apple), you'll find that you, too, should be able to hook up your existing printer to your iBook. A number of companies have come out with, or will soon come out with, adapters that make this possible. As you look over the following sections, you may notice that your particular printer isn't discussed. Don't worry! The manufacturer of your printer may not have come out with an iBook adapter yet, but there is no doubt a general-purpose adapter available. Read the paragraph below that's associated with your type of printer for some general tips on getting connected.

Serial printers Any serial printer that has a LocalTalk option can be connected to an iBook's Ethernet port using a LocalTalk-to-Ethernet adapter. Farallon's EtherMac iPrint Adapter LT (discussed in this chapter's *LocalTalk StyleWriters* section) is one such adapter that works for a variety of Apple and third-party serial printers.

Laser printers A laser printer that has a LocalTalk option can be connected to an iBook's Ethernet port using any of the three Ethernet-to-LocalTalk adapters (Farallon iPrint Adapter LT, Asante AsanteTalk, and Sonic Systems microPrint) mentioned in the preceding *Connecting an Apple LaserWriter* section.

Ethernet printers An Ethernet printer can connect directly to an iBook. Connect a standard Ethernet crossover cable from the Ethernet printer to the iBook's Ethernet port. From the iBook, select the Chooser from the Apple menu and click on the Ethernet printer icon in the Chooser's list of printer icons. You're all set.

There are several Mac-ready USB printers available—the following are descriptions of a couple of them.

Hewlett-Packard DeskJet 670C and 690C Series Printers The Hewlett-Packard DeskJet 670C series and 690C series printers weren't specifically designed to work with Macintosh computers. These HP printers connect to a parallel port—a port not present on Macs. Hewlett-Packard and Apple have recently aligned more closely, and as a part of this alliance, HP has introduced the HP Printer Cable Kit. The main component of this kit is a USB-to-parallel conversion cable that allows any of the numerous printer models in the 670C and 690C series to be easily hooked up to the USB port on an iBook.

EPSON Stylus Color 440, 600, 640, and Photo EX Printer Epson isn't a huge name in Macintosh printing. Most of Epson's printers also connect to a parallel port, which is not found on a Mac. With the release of the EPSON USB/Parallel Printer Adapter Kit, though, Epson's Mac-marketshare might just improve. The cable that is the primary component of this adapter kit connects to an Epson printer's parallel port and to the iBook's USB port. As of this writing, the adapter kit allows for the connection of one of three EPSON Stylus Color models (440, 600, or 640) or an EPSON Stylus Photo EX printer to an iBook. These models represent a large range in printer resolution and price, so if you don't yet have a printer, you might want to further investigate the details of these models.

Connecting Other Peripherals

Printers may be the most common legacy hardware that users will want to connect to an iBook. But there are other peripherals sitting around just waiting to be put to use by the iBook.

ADB (Apple Desktop Bus) Devices

The iBook's USB port replaces the ADB (Apple Desktop Bus) port, and a few other ports found on all pre-iBook Macintosh computers. So, if you want to buy a new input device for use on your iBook, you'll probably go with a USB device. Refer to the previous sections of this chapter for the details on USB keyboards, mice, trackballs, and so forth. If you already own a non-USB input device that you'd like to use on an iBook, then read this section.

In the past, Macintosh input devices were typically connected to the ADB port. The iBook doesn't have an ADB port, so to make use of an existing ADB product you'll need a USB-to-ADB adapter. Fortunately, just such an adapter exists.

Griffen Technology iMate USB-to-ADB Adapter The iMate USB-to-ADB adapter was designed by Griffen Technology specifically for the iMac—but you can guess that from the adapter's name as well as from its translucent plastic case. The iMate works equally well when connected to an iBook. Just plug one end into your ADB device (such as a trackball) and the other end into an iBook USB port and you're all set.

SCSI Devices

If you already had a Mac when you bought an iBook, you probably have existing peripherals that are *SCSI* (pronounced *scuzzy*, which stands for *Small Computer Systems Interface*) devices. Many Macintosh hard drives and removable media drives (such as the Zip drive) are SCSI devices. If you have such devices, you may be content to leave them on your old Mac and buy new devices for your new iBook. If so, check out this chapter's *USB Peripherals for the iBook* section. If, however, you want to be able to use an existing SCSI device on the iBook, you can either connect your new iBook to your older Mac to create a simple network that allows you to share the SCSI devices between both Macs (refer to Chapter 11), or you can get a USB-to-SCSI adapter.

Microtech USB Xpress SCSI USB to DB25 Adapter Microtech, at `www.microtech.com`, offers this adapter as a way to connect SCSI devices such as scanners and hard drives to your iBook's USB port.

Digital Cameras

If you're interested in digital photography, you'll be glad to hear that there are a host of new USB digital cameras available for the iBook—earlier in this chapter you read a few of the details. If you already own a digital camera, there may be an iBook connectivity solution already available.

Connectix QuickCam The new QuickCam VC (which is now the Logitech QuickCam VC, thanks to Logitech's acquisition of the Connectix hardware division) is a USB device. But if you already own a different Connectix QuickCam model, you can make do without having to buy a new digital video device. Instead, Grayscale QuickCam, Color QuickCam, and even QuickCam VC used on a Windows machine, can all be made to work with an iMac simply by downloading the appropriate software update from `www.connectix.com/html/quickcamvc_mac.html`.

Momentum uConnect Serial Port Adapter If your digital camera connects to a Mac serial port, then you can use the Momentum uConnect adapter instead to connect the camera to one of the iBook's USB ports. Momentum lists digital cameras by Kodak, Olympus, Apple, Connectix, Agfa, Casio, Canon, Chinon, Epson, Ricoh, and Sony as ones that work with the uConnect adapter.

Important

The uConnect adapter works with many PDAs (Personal Digital Assistants)(such as the PalmPilot and Newton) and graphic tablets (such as Wacom's), as well as with digital cameras. The uConnect adapter *doesn't* support LocalTalk, though, so it isn't a USB-to-serial printer solution. Momentum does make a uConnect model just for printers. Refer back to the *Connecting an Apple StyleWriter* section earlier in this chapter for information on the uConnect for Printers adapter.

11

AirPort, Ethernet, and Networking

The iBook is the first Macintosh that comes ready for the AirPort card and AirPort base station—optional equipment that provides for easy wireless Internet access or wireless Ethernet networking. In this chapter you'll see how to make use of AirPort. If you don't have AirPort, and aren't interested in adding this technology to your iBook, but you still want to make your iBook a part of a network, you've come to the right place. While AirPort is interesting, it isn't a requirement to make iBook-networking possible—you can use the built-in Ethernet capabilities of the iBook to easily make your portable computer a part of a small or large network.

If you already were in possession of a Macintosh when you bought your iBook, you may want to consider networking the two computers together. Networking is a term that scares many computer users, but it needn't. While large-scale networks can be complicated to set up and administer, the connecting together of a couple of Macs is actually, yes, easy! By networking your iBook with other Mac-compatible hardware (such as another Mac and a printer), you make it possible for your iBook to easily transfer files between computers and to share all the peripherals (most notably, but not limited to, a printer) that are already connected to your other Macintosh. And when it's time to take your iBook with you, you can easily remove it from the network—and just as easily return it to the network at any time.

A simple Macintosh network requires very little hardware, very little time, very little expense, and very little knowledge. Reading this chapter also takes very little time, so what are you waiting for—read on and get your own Mac network set up!

Important
If you've never been involved in setting up a network, you may be ready to call it quits right now. Don't! You will certainly want to read at least this chapter's Networking an iBook and Ethernet Peripherals section. There you'll learn how to implement an ideal solution for transferring files between your iBook and a desktop Mac. The network described in that section involves a single $15 cable and only about 15 minutes of your time for a one-time-only setup of the networking software. The cable is available at just about any computer store (it's not a Mac-only item—it's for any Ethernet network). The software you need already exists under the Apple menu of both your desktop Mac and your iBook.

AirPort: Going Wireless

AirPort is a new technology that allows a Macintosh to wirelessly communicate with a modem or an Ethernet network. This means you can use AirPort for a wireless connection to the Internet, or for wireless connection to a LAN (local area network). Your iBook may already have wireless capabilities—purchasing an iBook equipped with an AirPort card is one configuration sold by many dealers. If your iBook doesn't have AirPort, you can easily add this technology to your computer.

AirPort Basics

AirPort uses radio frequencies (RF) as its means of communication. Using radio frequencies means that AirPort works through solid objects—your iBook can be up to 150 feet from the point to which it's communicating, and there can be a wall or walls (or floors) between the iBook and the point of communication.

To make use of AirPort you'll need the AirPort card. Depending on how you plan on using your iBook, you may also need the AirPort base station. Figure 11-1 shows the small, credit card sized AirPort card.

Figure 11-1 The AirPort card.

Chapter 12 describes just how the small AirPort card is installed in an iBook. In short, you'll do the following:

1. Lift the iBook keyboard
2. Plug the AirPort antenna into the AirPort card (the antenna is present in all iBooks)
3. Plug the AirPort card into the iBook
4. Replace the keyboard

Figure 11-2 shows where the AirPort card rests in an iBook. In that figure I'm pointing to where the card plugs into the iBook (the connector is just under the trackpad).

The AirPort card communicates with another AirPort card or with an AirPort base station. Figure 11-3 shows the back of the AirPort base station.

As of this writing the AirPort card has a list price of $99, while the AirPort base station has a list price of $299.

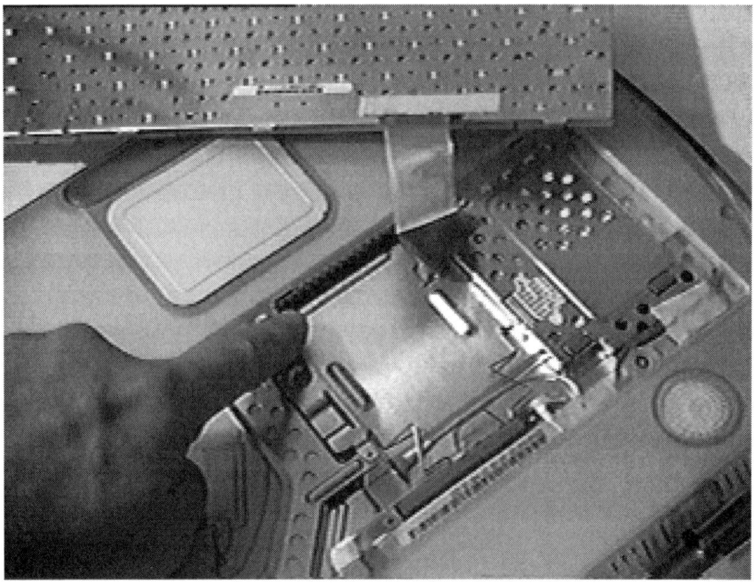

Figure 11-2 The AirPort card goes under the keyboard.

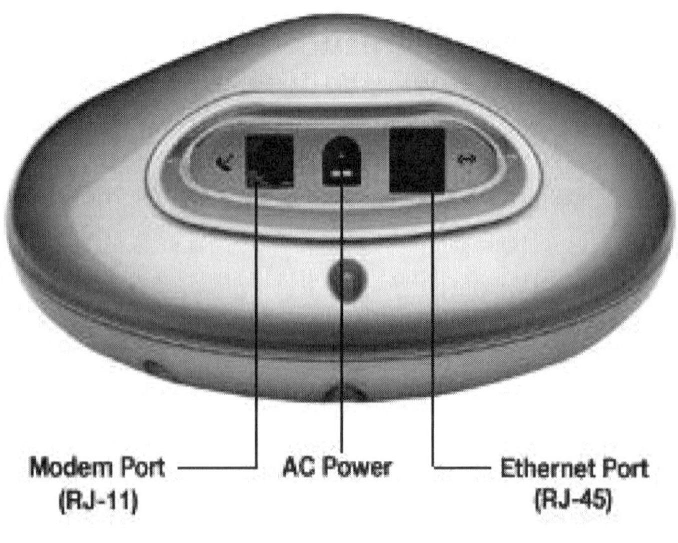

Figure 11-3 The AirPort base station (back).

Using the AirPort Base Station

The AirPort base station has a 56K modem built into it. As shown in Figure 11-4, to connect to the Internet, you plug your phone line into the modem port of the base station (as opposed to plugging the line into the modem port of your iBook, as you'd do if you weren't using AirPort). AirPort doesn't replace your need to have an account with an Internet service provider and to be in the vicinity of an active phone line. Instead, it replaces the need to have your iBook directly plugged into a phone jack.

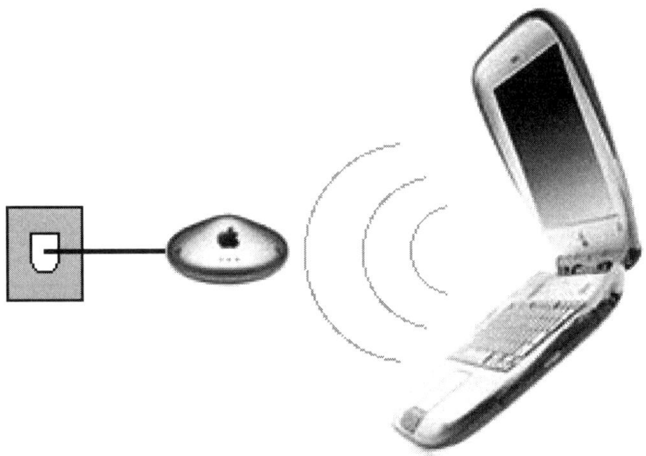

Figure 11-4 Using AirPort to connect to the Internet.

The AirPort base station also contains a 10/100Base-T Ethernet port. Later in this chapter you'll read much more about Ethernet, 10/100Base-T, and networks. For now, just know that the Ethernet port on the AirPort base station makes it easy to add an iBook to a network. To do that you'll plug an Ethernet cable into the AirPort Ethernet port and into the hub of an Ethernet network. After that, your iBook is a part of the network! Figure 11-5 shows this scenario for a small network consisting of two iMacs that are physically connected to one another and one iBook that's wirelessly "connected."

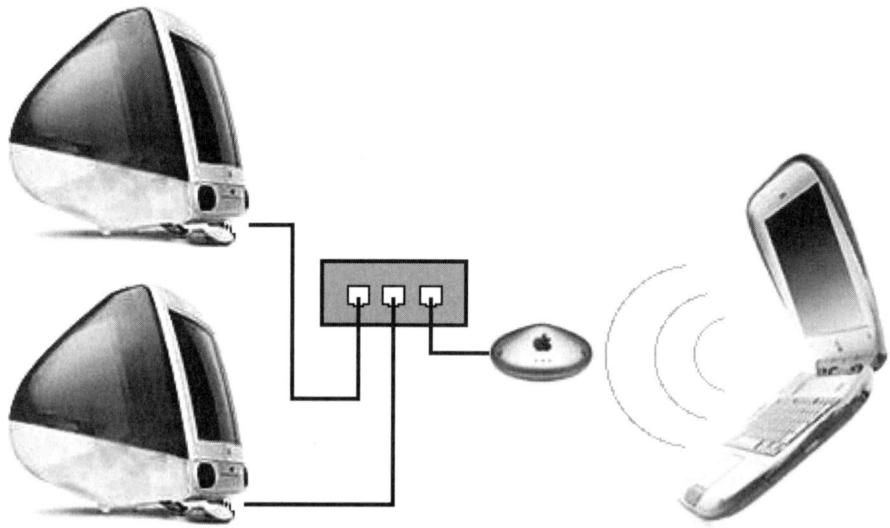

Figure 11-5 Using AirPort to connect to a network.

A single base station can be used to connect up to ten iBooks to one Internet connection or to one network. For instance, two people, each with their own iBook, could independently surf the Internet at the same time by way of the base station's single 56K connection to the Internet (see Figure 11-6).

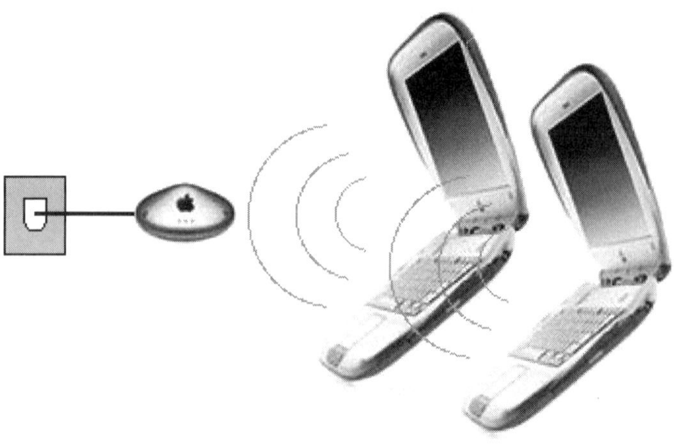

Figure 11-6 Multiple iBooks using one base station.

Computer-to-Computer AirPort Communication

While for most users a base station will be needed for wireless connections, there are situations where no base station is needed. Two AirPort card-equipped iBook's can, via their cards, communicate wirelessly with one another. If you're goal is the transfer of files between two iBook computers, then you could equip each with an AirPort card and forego the base station.

With a computer-to-computer AirPort setup you could also have one of your two iBook computers maintain a wireless Internet connection. To do that you'd use one AirPort-equipped iBook to connect to the Internet as you'd do if it didn't have an AirPort card. That is, you'd plug your phone line into the modem port of that iBook. After connecting to the Internet in this manner the second AirPort-equipped iBook could connect to the Internet by simply communicating with the first iBook—as shown in Figure 11-7. Note that for such a situation you need only one account with an Internet service provider and only one connection to that account. Both iBooks will, however, be able to act independently on the Internet (that is, both users could simultaneously visit different Web sites or simultaneously send e-mail to different recipients).

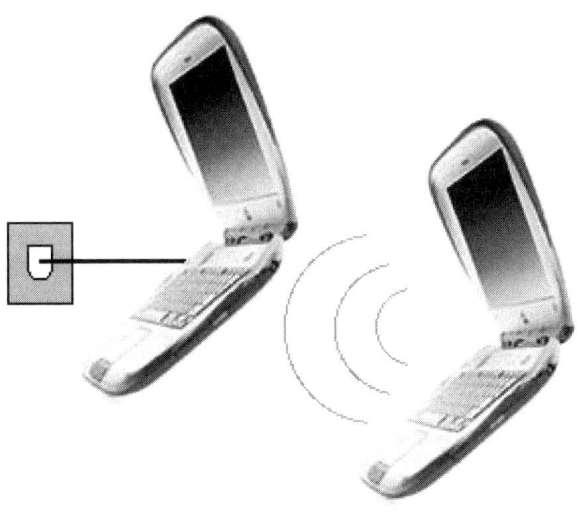

Figure 11-7 Multiple iBook's using one Internet connection.

AirPort Software

Along with the AirPort card AirPort software. The AirPort Setup Assistant is a program that walks you through the process of getting your AirPort-equipped iBook to function properly. You should need to run this assistant just one time. The Wireless Control Strip Module is a module that appears in your iBook's control strip. Click on it to see which networks are in the range of your iBook.

Tip
You can also get AirPort information and help from the **Help** menu that's always present on your desktop. Choose **Mac Help**, then enter airport as the keyword to search for.

About Networking

A network consists of two or more computers connected to one another in a manner that allows some or all of the files on one computer to be accessed from the other computer or computers. A network usually will (but isn't required to) include a printer that is shared by some or all of the computers in the network. There are several advantages to networking computers, including:

- Easy file transfers (eliminating the need for a floppy drive and the use of low-capacity floppy disks)
- Eliminating the need to purchase duplicate hardware (such as printers) for each computer
- Eliminating the need to buy extra storage devices (such as hard drives)

Physically connecting two computers together is easy: it typically takes just a single cable running from one computer to the other. Getting the two connected computers to then be able to effectively communicate (transfer files and share information) used to be the more difficult step. I say "used to be" because starting more than a decade ago, Apple made it simple for any two interconnected Macintosh computers to communicate with one another. Apple did it by including AppleTalk with each Macintosh. In short, AppleTalk is system software that does the work of letting networked Macs exchange information.

The following pages introduce AppleTalk software and the two main types of Mac networks—LocalTalk and Ethernet. The remainder of this chapter provides the details for setting up a simple network.

Note
The following is not meant to be a comprehensive guide to explaining networking principles, setting up a network, or administrating a network. It is intended to familiarize you with networking and to provide you with the information necessary to get a simple network connected and running in your home or small office. For an excellent tutorial on networking the Mac, refer to Matthew Glidden's online article *Three Macs and a Printer* at `come.to/three.macs`.

LocalTalk Networks

LocalTalk is Apple's name for a system that uses common phone lines to interconnect computers to form a Macintosh-based network. A LocalTalk network works by "packaging" information into a specific format and then transferring that information from one networked Mac to another. The way information is stored is of importance to both the sending and receiving computers, so of course all Macs in a LocalTalk network understand the clearly defined format that LocalTalk uses. It's good that Macs understand LocalTalk, because it means you don't have to! Setting up a LocalTalk network isn't about understanding tricky principles of computer networking—it's only about connecting your Macs together and then entering a little information in a few networking control panels that are already on your computers (Macs come with pre-installed networking software).

As mentioned, LocalTalk cable is simply standard phone line cable. However, since there's no phone jack on the back of a Macintosh, a LocalTalk cable plugs into an adapter, and the adapter in turn plugs into a serial port on the

Mac. Both the printer port and the modem port on a Mac are types of serial ports, so there's never a question of whether a particular Macintosh can be added to a LocalTalk network. That is, until the recent Macs. The iMac was the first Macintosh model without a serial port. Subsequent Macs, such as the iBook, are also without serial port.

How does an iBook, which has no serial port to accept a LocalTalk cable, become a part of a LocalTalk network? It doesn't. Instead, you must turn to the second of the two most popular types of networks that include Macintosh computers: an Ethernet network. Don't worry that you just wasted time reading about LocalTalk networks, though. Through the use of adapters, an Ethernet network is able to support LocalTalk devices. Since many previously released Macintosh computers and printers are LocalTalk devices, there's a chance that your small iBook Ethernet network will include LocalTalk devices.

Note
As you read this chapter, the distinction between LocalTalk and Ethernet will become clearer. You'll also gain a better understanding of how an Ethernet network can support LocalTalk computers and printers, yet still remain an Ethernet network.

Ethernet Networks

Like LocalTalk, Ethernet is a system for "packaging" data in a structured form that is understandable to all computers that make up a network. An Ethernet network is much faster than a LocalTalk network—Ethernet data transfer rates are up to forty times faster than LocalTalk rates. Need I say more in Ethernet's favor? While many older, and most recent, Mac models have included an Ethernet port (see Figure 11-8 for a look at the port and the Ethernet symbol), starting with the iMac Apple has unequivocally said "yes" to Ethernet. Other Macintosh computers that include an Ethernet port also include a serial port (the printer and modem ports of other Mac models are types of serial ports). A prerequisite to including a computer in a LocalTalk network is a serial port—a port the newer Macs (including the iBook) lack. So if you want to create a network centered on your new iBook, you'll need to make it an Ethernet network.

Figure 11-8 An Ethernet port, with the Ethernet symbol above it.

Information traveling from one computer to another via Ethernet cable is always in the same format (and, like a LocalTalk network, the data transfer details are of no importance to us). There are, however, different types of Ethernet cable (unlike LocalTalk, which uses only one type of cable). Some of the different Ethernet cable types include 100Base-T, 10Base-T, 5Base-T, and 10Base-F. There are, of course, reasons for giving these cable types such cryptic names.

The number that prefaces an Ethernet cable type refers to the capacity of the cable (and thus the Ethernet network). A 100Base-T cable is capable of carrying 100 megabits of information per second, while a 10Base-T cable can carry only 10 megabits of information per second. You needn't be concerned with just how much data these capacities translate to. It's enough to realize that a 100Base-T Ethernet network is better than a 10Base-T network because it's faster—the 100Base-T type cable can carry up to ten times the data of the 10Base-T type cable.

Unless your goal is to become a networking guru, the remainder of the cable name is of little importance to you. To satisfy your curiosity, though, I offer the following brief descriptions. The *Base* in cable names such as 100Base-T refers to *baseband*. Suffice it to say that such a cable devotes its complete transmission capacity to the delivery of network information. The *T* in Ethernet cable names, such as 100Base-T and 10Base-T, stands for *twisted-pair*. A twisted-pair cable is made up of two pair of wires, with the pairs, yes, twisted around each other. Creating a cable in this manner maximizes the cable's ability to carry data.

The iBook has a single 10/100Base-T Ethernet port. What this means is that the port can be used with either 10Base-T cable or the higher capacity 100Base-T cable. Given your druthers, of course, you'd always use this port with the better 100Base-T cable. This isn't always possible, though. For instance, you may be adding your iBook to an existing 10Base-T network—a network that consists of older Macs, each of which has only a 10Base-T port. In such a scenario, you could simply use a 10Base-T cable to connect your iBook to the existing 10Base-T network.

The iBook and Networks

The iBook *does* support Ethernet networking via its 10/100Base-T Ethernet port. The iBook does *not* support LocalTalk networking because the iBook doesn't have a serial port to which a LocalTalk connector box can be connected. You can, however, include LocalTalk devices as part of an iBook Ethernet network. Confused? Consider Figure 11-9.

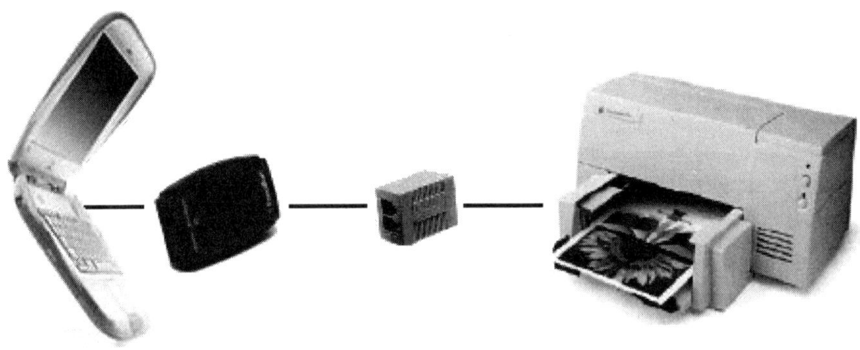

Figure 11-9 A LocalTalk printer as a part of a small Ethernet network.

In Figure 11-9, you see an Apple StyleWriter printer connected to an iBook. The StyleWriter model is one that supports LocalTalk, so a LocalTalk connector box is connected to the printer. Because the iBook doesn't support LocalTalk, a LocalTalk-to-Ethernet adapter such as the Farallon EtherMac iPrint Adapter LT is needed to serve as the link between the LocalTalk printer and the Ethernet iBook. Think of the system in Figure 11-9 as a very simple Ethernet network that happens to include one LocalTalk peripheral. This concept of LocalTalk coexisting with Ethernet in an Ethernet-based network arises again in the *Networking an iBook and a LocalTalk Macintosh* and *Networking an iBook and an Ethernet Macintosh* sections that appear ahead.

The iBook and Networking Software

Physically connecting the devices (such as a couple of Macs and a printer) to one another is the first of two steps in completing an Ethernet network. The second step is to set up the software on each networked Mac. Two factors prevent this *network configuration* from being a daunting task. First, setting up the software is typically a one-time chore—you do it once and then forget about it. Second, there's not much software to deal with, and all of what you will be working with is included as control panels that are included in your Macintosh system software.

Read either or both of the next two sections, *Networking an iBook and a LocalTalk Macintosh* and *Networking an iBook and an Ethernet Macintosh* to learn about connecting the devices that make up your network. Then get some tips on setting up the networking software by reading the last section in this chapter—*Setting Up the Networking Software*.

Networking an iBook and LocalTalk Peripherals

The iBook has an Ethernet port that makes it easy to connect the iBook to another Ethernet-ready peripheral. If you have another Mac, and it also has an Ethernet port, connecting the two is simple. It's also the topic of the next section, *Networking an iBook and Ethernet Peripherals*. If you have another Mac and it doesn't have an Ethernet port (it will lack a port with a marking like the one shown in Figure 11-8), then you should read this section to see how you'll rely on LocalTalk to network your old computer with your new iBook. You should also read this section, along with the following two sections (*Networking an iBook and Ethernet Peripherals* and *Networking an iBook and Both LocalTalk and Ethernet Peripherals*) if you intend to create a network that consists of a mix of Ethernet-ready and LocalTalk-ready devices.

Networking an iBook and Ethernet Peripherals

You use the iBook's Ethernet port to bring the iBook into an Ethernet network. If you're connecting your iBook to a Mac that does have an Ethernet port, then you've come to the correct place. If the network you're creating will include a Macintosh that doesn't have an Ethernet port, then you'll need to read instead this chapter's *Networking an iBook and LocalTalk Peripherals* section. If you plan on creating a network that consists of a mix of Ethernet-ready and LocalTalk-ready devices, read this section, the preceding section (*Networking an iBook and LocalTalk Peripherals*), and the following section (*Networking an iBook and Both LocalTalk and Ethernet Peripherals*).

Networking an iBook and One Ethernet Macintosh

Many Macintosh models other than the iBook come equipped with an Ethernet port. To network such a Macintosh with your iBook, you simply need to connect one end of a standard Ethernet cable to the iBook's Ethernet port and the other end of the cable to the other Mac's Ethernet port. As mentioned in this chapter's About Networking section, Ethernet wiring is available in different capacities. The iBook has a 10/100Base-T Ethernet port, which means the iBook can be a part of either a 10Base-T or a 100Base-T Ethernet network. Many Macintosh computers that came out prior to the iBook have 10Base-T ports, so if you're connecting an iBook directly to a "non-iBook" Ethernet-ready Macintosh, you'll use 10Base-T cable. The reasoning for this? Though 100Base-T is better (because it can carry more data), you need to use the "lowest common denominator." That is, while an iBook with a 10/100Base-T port knows how to communicate with either 10Base-T or 100Base-T devices, a Macintosh with a 10Base-T port only knows how to communicate with 10Base-T devices. So you need to use the Ethernet cable that carries data at a capacity that both Macs recognize.

If you own an iBook and a desktop Mac that has Ethernet (such as an iMac, a G3 Mac, a G4 Mac, or most Mac models made in the last few years), and you want to transfer files between them, then this section is of vital interest to you! The ability to easily transfer files from one computer to another is important. If you have the same type of high capacity removable media drive available for each machine (such as a USB Zip drive), then you can transfer files using those drives. If you don't have a disk-based file transfer solution, then the very simple Ethernet network described here will work just fine. Keep in mind that the network described here isn't a "permanent" one that takes away the portability of your iBook. Instead, your two-Mac network will be set up such that you can simply attach and unattach your iBook from the desktop Mac at any time just by unplugging one cable. When you're finished working on your iBook, set the iBook next to your desktop Mac and plug the one cable into the iBook's Ethernet port. Transfer your new or newly revised files to your desktop Mac by simply dragging and dropping them on the desktop. When you're done (it will only take a minute or two), unplug the cable from the iBook, set your iBook aside, and begin working on the just-copied files on your desktop Mac. And of course this system works the other way too—you can easily copy any files from your desktop Mac to your iBook. Besides taking care of daily file transfers, this system is great for getting those megabytes or gigabytes worth of programs and files from your desktop Mac onto your new iBook's hard drive. Just drag 'em all across the desktop and let the Ethernet connection do the rest.

Making the Connection

If you were to set up an Ethernet network that involved a few Macs, you'd need a piece of hardware called an Ethernet hub. You've been introduced to hubs earlier in this book, and will read more about them later in this chapter. An Ethernet hub acts as a, well, as a hub. An Ethernet hub has several Ethernet ports. You run an Ethernet cable from the Ethernet port of each networked Mac to an Ethernet port on the hub. The Ethernet hub is then the hub of activity, as data transfers from one Mac to the hub and on to another Mac. If you're setting up a simple network that consists of two, and only two, computers, you don't need a hub. Instead, you just need one special Ethernet cable called an Ethernet crossover cable. That crossover part is important. You can't use a "regular" Ethernet cable in our "hubless" network. You get a crossover cable at just about any computer supply store. Some big chain stores that sell computers may not have them. But any computer supply store will. Don't be afraid to appear the novice when you walk in the store. Just walk up to the salesperson, announce that you're connecting two Macs together, and that you need an Ethernet crossover cable. Cables come in different lengths. The length isn't important, as long as it enables the cable to easily reach from your desktop Mac to your iBook. I've got a seven foot cable, but that's because I keep the CPU of my desktop computer on the floor under my desk, and I want adequate cable length so that I can place my iBook on my desk and still have the cable reach under the desk. You might only need a cable a few feet in length. In any case, you'll pay under twenty bucks for the cable.

Note
There are category 3 and category 5 Ethernet cables. Either will work. If both are available, your preference is the category 5. This book doesn't go into too much detail regarding data transfer speeds, but suffice it to say the category of a cable has to do with such speeds. Again, either category of cable will work.

Note
If the store doesn't have a crossover cable, the salesperson may tell you that you can buy a regular Ethernet cable and a little crossover adapter that plugs into one end of that cable. He's telling the truth. This solution is very acceptable, though the combined cost of the regular cable and the adapter will be a few bucks more than the cost of a ready-made crossover cable.

To make the network connection, you simply plug one end of the crossover cable into the Ethernet port of your desktop Mac and the other end of the cable into the Ethernet port of your iBook. I've got a Power Mac 7500 at home. It's a few years old, but it serves me well. Figure 11-10 displays a couple of pictures of the back of my Power Mac 7500, with the emphasis on the Ethernet port. The location of the Ethernet port on your desktop Mac may vary from the location of that port on my 7500, but it should be easy to find. Note that the port looks much like a phone jack (it's a little bigger than a phone jack, though, so don't worry about plugging an Ethernet crossover cable into the modem port of, say, an iMac -- it won't fit). Obviously enough, the picture on the left shows the port without the cable, while the picture on the right shows the port as I plug the cable in.

Now plug the other end of the crossover cable into the Ethernet port on your iBook. That port is just to the right of the modem port on your iBook. Again, the port is a little bigger than the modem port, so there's no chance of you plugging the cable into the wrong port. In Figure 11-11 I'm pointing to the Ethernet port.

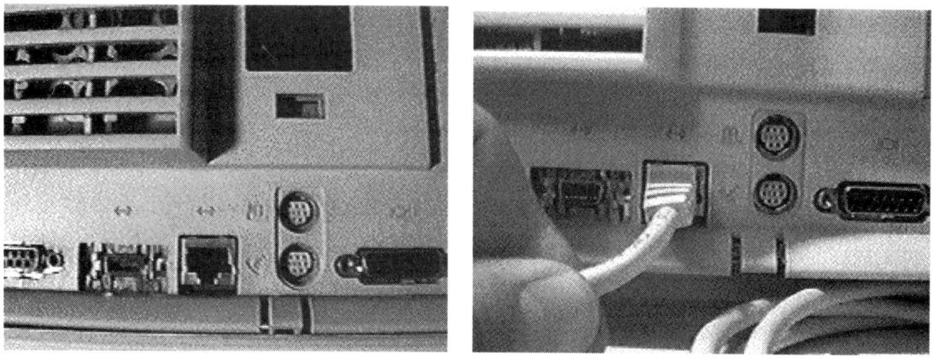

Figure 11-10 The Ethernet port on one Mac model (Power Mac 7500).

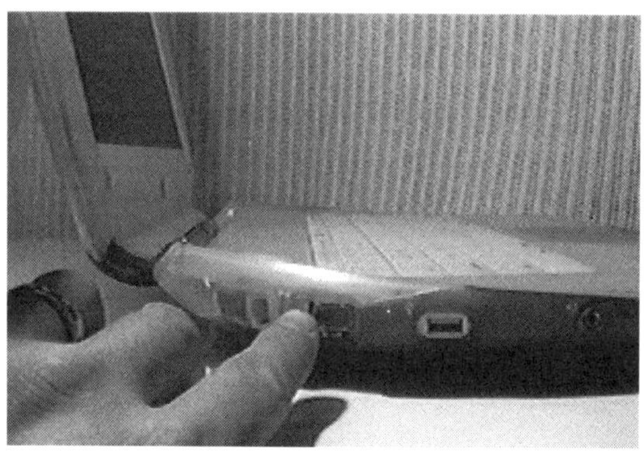

Figure 11-11 The Ethernet port on an iBook.

Note

In Figure 11-10 you may be able to tell that my Power Mac 7500 has two Ethernet ports (there's one just to the left of the port I'm plugging the cable into). Besides the standard Ethernet port, some older Macs also have an AAUI Ethernet port. If your desktop Mac has *only* an AAUI Ethernet port, you need to get something called a 10Base-T transceiver. This is an adapter that plugs into the AAUI Ethernet port. The crossover cable plugs into the transceiver. Most likely you can ignore all this transceiver talk—you only need the $50 transceiver if your Mac has *only* an AAUI Ethernet port. Fortunately, very few Mac models have *only* this type of port.

Figure 11-12 shows my desktop Mac and my iBook connected. For simplicity I've got the other cables detached from my Power Mac, but you get the point—just get that cable connected and you're done with the hardware end of things!

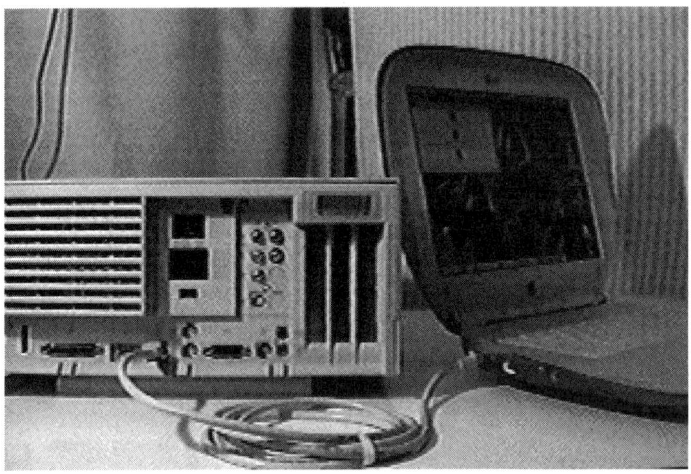

Figure 11-12 A crossover cable connection is made.

With the connection made, you're ready to set up the networking software. This is not a daunting task—and is described thoroughly in this chapter's *Setting Up the Networking Software* section. If you're connected, you can go ahead and skip to that section now.

Note

If you have peripherals attached to your desktop Mac (such as a printer, a Zip drive, and so forth), go ahead and leave those devices connected. Once you've setup the networking software you'll be able to make use of

---

Adding to the Network

It's nice to know that it's so easy to connect two Ethernet-ready Macs together: a single cable does the trick. That solution, though, is only for the simplest scenario—two, and only two, computers. If the transfer of files between your portable iBook and your desktop Mac is the main reason for setting up a network, then the just-described crossover cable technique is perfect. For the situation of networking an iBook to more than one other Ethernet-ready device, you'll need an Ethernet hub.

Just as a USB hub (see Chapter 9 for an introduction to USB hubs) makes it possible to connect several USB devices together, an Ethernet hub makes it possible to connect several Ethernet devices together. Figure 11-13 shows one of several Ethernet hub models—the Farallon Streamline Starlet 10/100 Dual-Speed Hub/8.

Figure 11-13 A typical Ethernet hub(Farallon Streamline Starlet).

To build a network consisting of a number of Ethernet-ready devices, connect one end of a standard Ethernet cable to the Ethernet port of a device and the other end to the hub. Repeat for each device. Figure 11-14 shows a network consisting of an iBook and two other Ethernet-ready Macs, all interconnected using a Farallon Ethernet hub. Note that a hub doesn't have to be used exclusively with computers—it can also be used to create a network that consists of both Ethernet-ready Macs and an Ethernet-ready printer (some Apple LaserWriter printers, for instance, have an Ethernet port).

Figure 11-14 An Ethernet hub in an Ethernet network.

10Base-T Networks

The preceding section discusses the mixing of different Ethernet capacities. Recall that though the iBook's Ethernet port is capable of carrying a capacity of 100 megabits, it can only communicate at a capacity that matches the device it's exchanging data with. If you have a number of 10Base-T devices (the typical capacity of older Ethernet-ready Macs) that you want to hook up to an iBook, then you must use an Ethernet hub that's designed to work with 10Base-T. Farallon makes a number of 10Base-T hubs, with the only difference between the models being the number of ports on the hub. You can get the Farallon Streamline Starlet hub in five, eight, or sixteen port variations.

100Base-T Networks

If your network is to consist of devices that are all capable of transferring data at 100Base-T (such as a network consisting of several iMacs and an iBook), then you'll want to use a hub like Farallon's Fast Starlet hub. For a little more than the cost of a 10Base-T Farallon Streamline Starlet hub, you can buy a 100Base-T Fast Starlet hub. Like its 10Base-T cousin, the 100Base-T Fast Starlet comes in five, eight, or sixteen port flavors.

Dual-Speed Networks

If your network will consist of more than one 100Base-T device (such as two iMacs and an iBook) along with lower 10Base-T devices (such as an older, Ethernet-ready Mac), then your best solution is to use a dual-capacity hub. A high-speed 100Base-T hub won't work because the slower 10Base-T device or devices won't be able to communicate with it. And while the less expensive 10Base-T hub will work, using such a hub will constrain the speed of your network. That's because all data passes through the 10Base-T hub ports, so even when two 100Base-T devices are communicating with one another, the data transfer capability is limited to that of 10Base-T Ethernet. Here the ideal solution is to use a dual-speed hub. Each port on such a hub recognizes both 10Base-T and 100Base-T devices. The hub is thus aware that two 100Base-T devices are attempting to communicate with one another, and can transfer data at that higher capacity. Alternately, the same hub knows when a 10Base-T device is communicating with another device (of either capacity) and knows how to limit the data transfer to the capacity understood by the 10Base-T device. Farallon has an eight-port dual-speed version of its Fast Starlet hub—the Farallon Fast Starlet 10/100 Dual-Speed hub.

Networking an iBook and a LocalTalk Macintosh

Farallon's EtherMac iPrint Adapter LT is an adapter that opens up your iBook's Ethernet network to LocalTalk devices. You saw an example of this adapter's use with a printer in Chapter 10. The LocalTalk device that gets connected to this adapter doesn't have to be a printer, though. As shown in Figure 11-15, the device can just as easily be a Macintosh computer.

To connect a Macintosh that isn't equipped with an Ethernet port to an iBook, just follow these steps:

1. Plug a Farallon PhoneNET Connector box (or some other LocalTalk con nector box) into the serial port (typically the printer port) of the Macintosh that is to be networked with the iBook.

2. Plug a standard Ethernet 10Base-T cable into your iBook Ethernet port and into the EtherMac iPrint Adapter LT.
3. Plug a standard LocalTalk cable into the other end of the EtherMac iPrint Adapter LT and into the LocalTalk connector box that's already connect ed to the older Macintosh (see Step 1).
4. Plug a terminator into the remaining open port on the LocalTalk connec tor box.

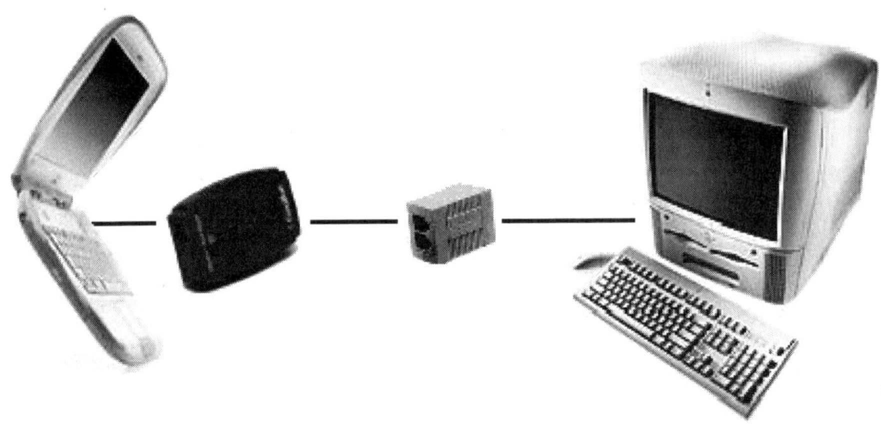

Figure 11-15 A LocalTalk Mac as a part of a small Ethernet network.

Adding to the Network

Networking an iBook and another Mac is a good way to allow the two computers to share files. It's also a good way to let them share a printer or other device (or devices). To add a device to the network created in the previous subsection (*Networking an iBook and a Macintosh*), perform the following steps:

1. Plug a Farallon PhoneNET Connector box (or some other LocalTalk con nector box) into the serial port of the peripheral that is to be networked with the iBook and the other Macintosh.
2. Remove the terminator from the LocalTalk connector box attached to the older Macintosh and plug it into one of the ports of the LocalTalk con nector box which you've just added.
3. Plug a standard LocalTalk cable into the one free port on the newly-added device's LocalTalk connector box and plug the other end into the one free port on the connector box attached to the older Macintosh.

Figure 11-16 shows the use of an iPrint adapter and two PhoneNET connector boxes to form a network with an iBook, an older Power Macintosh, and an Apple StyleWriter printer.

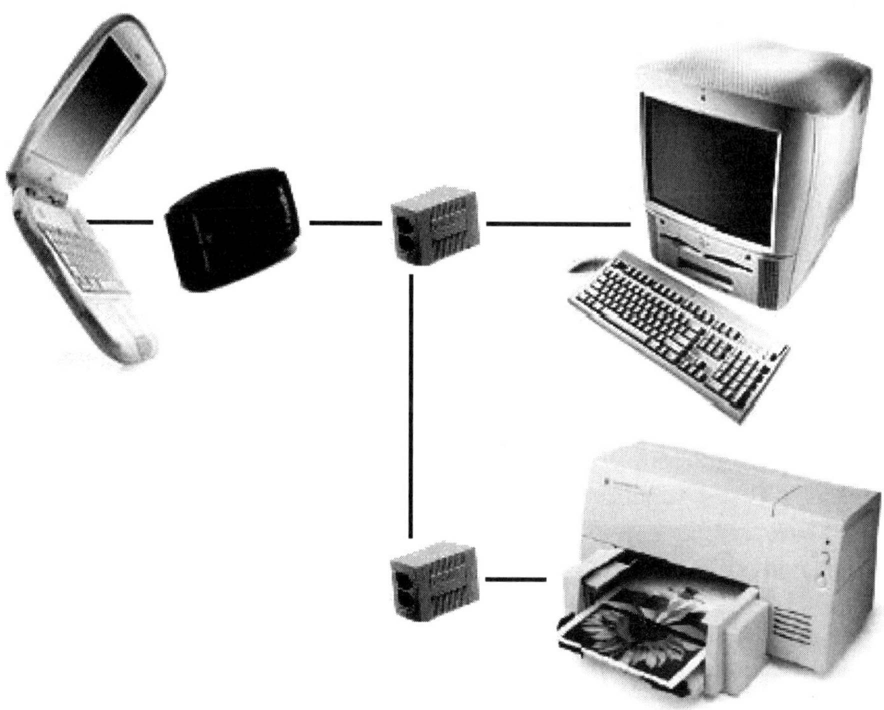

Figure 11-16 Two LocalTalk devices in an Ethernet network.

Note
In Figure 11-16, the order in which the devices are positioned in the network isn't important. That is, the positioning of the printer and the older Macintosh could be switched. What is important is that the last device (which, in Figure 11-16, is the printer) must be terminated. This is done by installing a terminator in the unused port in the LocalTalk connector box connected to that device.

Once the network is physically connected, you need to set up the networking software. Read this chapter's *Setting Up the Networking Software* section to learn how that's accomplished. If your network is set up, feel free to skip ahead to that section now.

Networking an iBook and Both LocalTalk and Ethernet Peripherals

The iBook is Ethernet-ready. Many other Macintosh models are Ethernet-ready. Most Apple printers are LocalTalk-ready. So there's a good chance that someone who wants to create a small network consisting of an iBook, another Mac, and a printer, needs a means of connecting together both Ethernet and LocalTalk devices. There are a couple of ways to accomplish this common task.

Networking an iBook, a LocalTalk Mac, and a Printer

Farallon's EtherMac iPrint Adapter LT has been discussed several times in this chapter. The iPrint adapter is used as an interface, or go-between, that makes it possible to connect an Ethernet-ready iBook with a LocalTalk-ready printer or LocalTalk-ready Macintosh (refer to Figures 11-15 and 11-16). Another Farallon product, the Farallon EtherWave Printer adapter, also allows you to connect a LocalTalk device to an iBook. The EtherWave Printer adapter (see Figure 11-17), though, also includes an additional port that's used to interconnect still another Ethernet device.

Figure 11-17 The Farallon EtherWave Printer adapter.

The EtherWave Printer adapter has a serial-to-Ethernet converter port and two Ethernet ports, so it can be used to interconnect an iBook, another Ethernet-ready Mac, and a LocalTalk printer. Figure 11-18 illustrates this type of arrangement. In this figure, the iBook has one end of a 10Base-T cable connected to its Ethernet port and the other end of the cable connected to one of the Ethernet ports on the EtherWave adapter. The same type of connection hooks the other Ethernet-ready Mac to the adapter. Finally, a standard Macintosh serial cable runs from the LocalTalk printer to the EtherWave adapter's serial-to-Ethernet converter port.

Figure 11-18 An EtherWave Printer adapter in an Ethernet network.

Adding LocalTalk Peripherals to the Network

In a sense, the EtherWave Printer adapter is a three port Ethernet hub, with one of the ports dedicated to a LocalTalk device. A second Farallon adapter, the EtherWave MultiPrinter adapter, looks like—and is used in a manner similar to—the EtherWave Printer adapter. The difference is that with the EtherWave MultiPrinter adapter you can connect up to eight LocalTalk devices to the adapter's one serial-to-Ethernet converter port. This *daisy-chaining* of devices is accomplished through the use of LocalTalk connector boxes like the Farallon PhoneNET (discussed in Chapter 10). Figure 11-19 shows the same network as Figure 11-18, with the addition of a third computer. The newly-added Mac is a LocalTalk-ready computer that lacks an Ethernet port. Plugging a LocalTalk connector box into this Mac's printer port readies the computer to become part of the network. See the Chapter 10 section *Connecting Printers* for introductory material on connecting LocalTalk devices to an iBook. A similar connector box plugs into the printer. Use a standard LocalTalk cable to connect the two connector boxes, then run a standard serial cable to the center port of the EtherWave MultiPrinter adapter. Plugging a terminator into the remaining open LocalTalk port completes the network wiring. In the figure, this port is one of the two ports on the LocalTalk connector box hooked up to the newly added Mac.

Setting Up the Networking Software

Earlier, it was mentioned that the connecting of the components that make up a network is the first of two steps in getting your network up and running. The second step is configuring the network software. Doing this allows each Macintosh in the network to know about the other Mac (or Macs), and it also gives you the opportunity to establish what each Mac is able to "see" on the other Macs. That is, if you are setting up a network with the intention of having others use one of the Macs, you can limit what that person can access on all other Macs in the network.

The following is an overview of how to configure the software for your own small network. The next four subsections, titled *Specifying Network Type*, *Configuring Network Identity*, *Specifying Shared Files*, and *Starting Up the Network*, correspond to the four steps you'll perform for each Macintosh computer that's a part of your network. Sit down at one Macintosh (any Mac that's a part of the network—it doesn't matter in which order you set up the computers), and follow the instructions that appear below. Then move to a different Mac in the network and repeat the same steps.

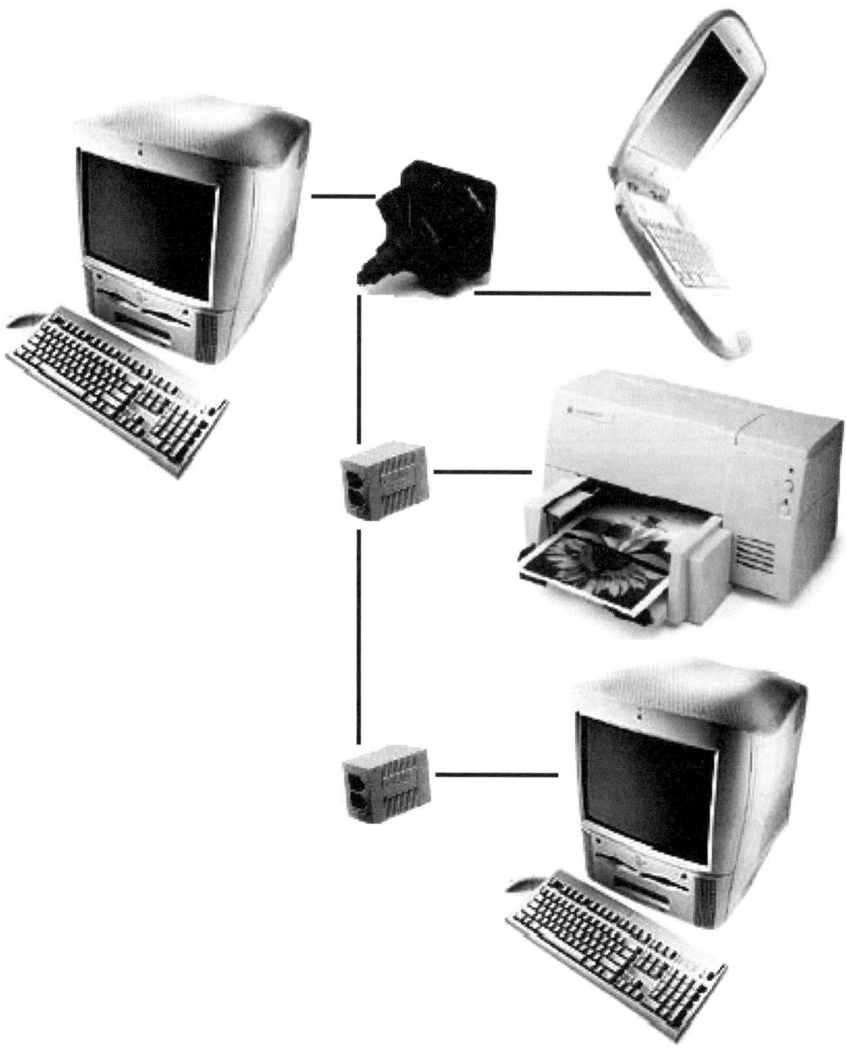

Figure 11-19 An EtherWave MultiPrinter in an Ethernet network.

Specifying Network Type

To begin, open the AppleTalk control panel on one of your Macs. If you have a Mac that doesn't have an AppleTalk control panel, it will instead have a Network control panel. Either will do. When you open the control panel you may see an alert that tells you AppleTalk is currently inactive. If that's the case, go ahead and click the **Yes** button to activate AppleTalk (AppleTalk needs to be turned on in order for a Mac to be networked with another Mac).

In the AppleTalk (or Network) control panel choose **Ethernet** or **Ethernet built-in** from the Connect via pop-up menu. On these pages I'll demonstrate the setting up of a simple networking consisting of just an iBook and a Power Mac 7500 (refer back to this chapter's *Networking an iBook and one Ethernet Macintosh* section for information on the physical connection of this type of network). My Power Mac 7500 running Mac OS 9 says **Ethernet** (left side of Figure 11-20), while my iBook running Mac OS 8.6 says **Ethernet built-in** (right side of Figure 11-20). After making your selections, close the control panels. If presented with an alert that asks if the changes should be saved, go ahead and click the **Save** button to save the new configuration. Repeat this process for each Mac in your network (that is, sit down at each Mac and open the AppleTalk or Network control panel on each).

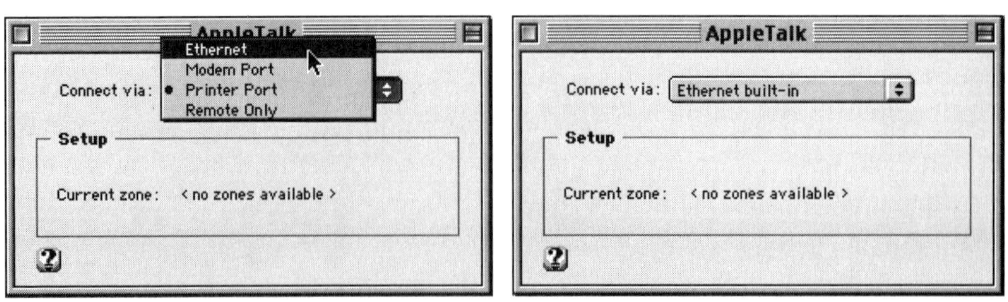

Figure 11-20 Specifying Ethernet in the AppleTalk control panel.

Note
There is no **LocalTalk** item in the **Connect via** pop-up menu. That option is there, indirectly, though—the **Printer port** and **Modem port** items indirectly serve that purpose.

Configuring Network Identity

There may be one, two, or two hundred Macs on your network. There needs to be some means of identifying each so that when information gets passed along the network cabling, the network can see to it that the information ends up at the proper computer. A control panel is your way of giving a Mac a network identity. If your Macintosh is running system software that predates Mac OS 8 (such as any version of Mac OS 7), then you can use the Sharing Setup control panel. If your Mac is running any version of Mac OS 8 or beyond, you should use the newer File Sharing control panel.

After opening a File Sharing control panel you'll notice that your name may automatically appear in the **Owner Name** box. If it doesn't, type it in. Now enter a password. Besides myself, my household consists of a wife and a five year old daughter. Both are smarter than me, yet both have absolutely no interest in computers or in what I do for a living! So I don't need any tricky passwords to keep my work secure. If you too have a disinterested family, then you too can keep things simple. Make your password an easy one, and use the same password for each computer. To give your computer an identity in the network, assign it a name in the **Computer Name** box. The name you choose isn't too important, but select something that makes it readily apparent which computer is involved. On the left side of Figure 11-21 you see that I selected *PM7500* for my Power Mac 7500, while on the right side of that same figure you see I chose *iBook* for my iBook.

Now click the **Start** button in the File Sharing section of the control panel to tell the network that files and folders on this computer are to be shared with the other computer in the network. This, in effect, allows the files on one computer to be visible to the other computer. When you click on a **Start** button, file sharing may be turned on quickly. However, don't be alarmed if the watch cursor appears and you have to wait a bit (even a few minutes) for file sharing to be turned on. Once a control panel reports that file sharing is on, go ahead and close that control panel. Make sure to carry out these steps on each computer in the network.

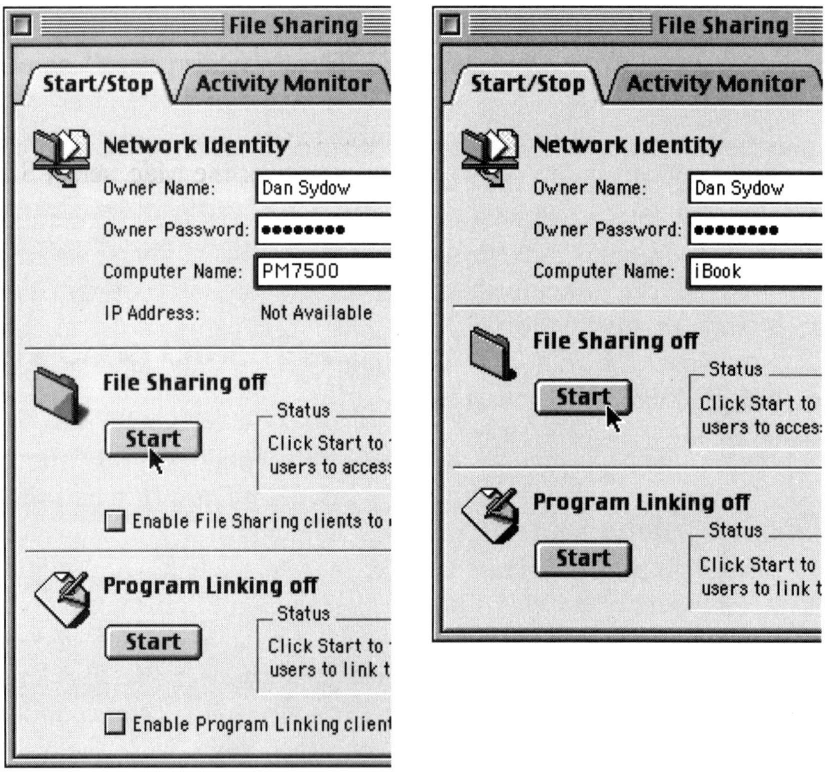

Figure 11-21 The File Sharing control panel on two Macs.

Specifying Shared Files

Each Mac that's a part of a network has the option of sharing none, some, or all of its files with other Macs on the network. Each Mac can independently be more or less "generous" than any other Mac. For instance, if you'll always be working on your iBook, and a child will always be working on a different

Mac on the network, you may want to limit the files that can be viewed on your iBook (so that the child can't inadvertently alter any of your iBook's files). That is, you may want to restrict a child from accessing most of your stuff. At the same time, you may want to give yourself access to most or all of the files on the Mac used by a child. (Just don't tell your daughter or son about all this! She or he already feels life is very unfair!).

On the desktop of one Mac, click the hard drive icon. For instance, if you're currently working on your iBook, you'd click on the Macintosh HD icon (unless you happened to have renamed your hard drive). You're about to report to the network that the contents of this hard drive are to be shared with the other Mac or Macs in the network. Now on the same Mac, select **Sharing** under the **File** menu. As shown in Figure 11-22, this menu item may appear as an item under a **Get Info** item.

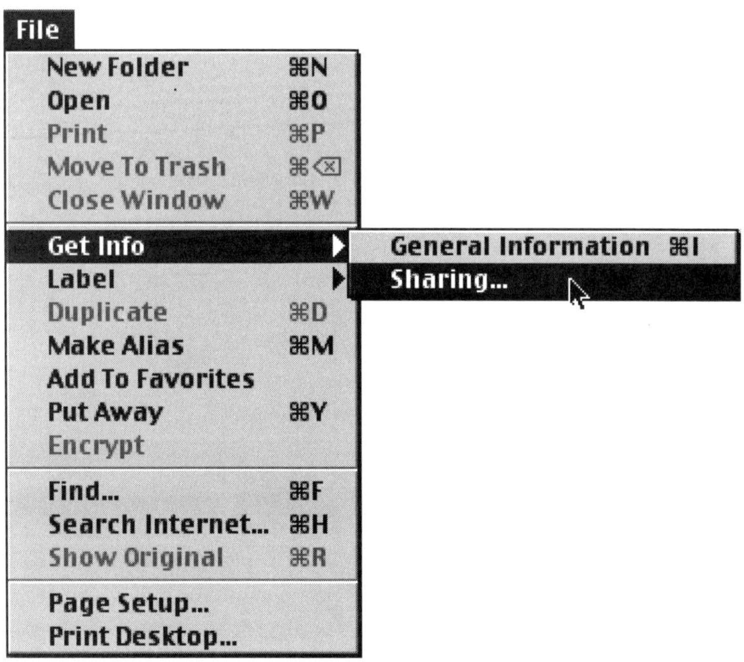

Figure 11-22 Choosing the Sharing menu item.

In the Info window that appears, check the **Share this item and its contents** checkbox. In Figure 11-23 I'm doing that for the hard drive on my iBook. Now close the Info window. If your Mac has more than one hard drive, and you want the other networked Mac or Macs to be able to access items on each drive, repeat the above procedure of clicking on the drive's icon to activate it, choosing **Sharing** from the **File** menu, and checking the checkbox. Now move to the other computer and repeat this procedure (click on the hard drive icon, choose **Sharing** from the **File** menu, and click the checkbox). Close the Info window when finished. Repeat these file sharing steps for each Mac in the network.

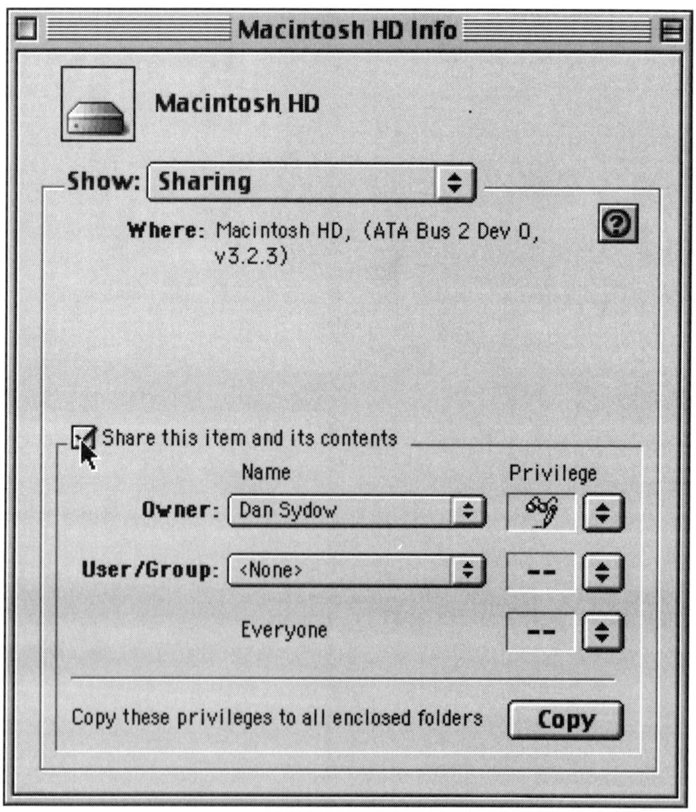

Figure 11-23 Specifying that a drive is to be shared.

Starting Up the Network

Now open the Chooser under the Apple menu on either one of your computers. There will be a few steps here, so focus on one computer, then the other (it doesn't matter which one you work on first). Click the AppleShare icon in the upper-left corner. Then, on the right side of the Chooser, select the computer you want to connect to. If you were setting up a large network, there'd be several computers listed. My example network consists of just two computers, so there's only one computer listed. In Figure 11-24 I show the Chooser on my Power Mac 7500. It's displaying the name of the other computer in the network—the iBook. Note that the computer name matches the name you entered in the File Sharing control panel—so it will differ from what you see in this figure (unless you too gave your iBook the name *iBook* in the File Sharing control panel on the iBook).

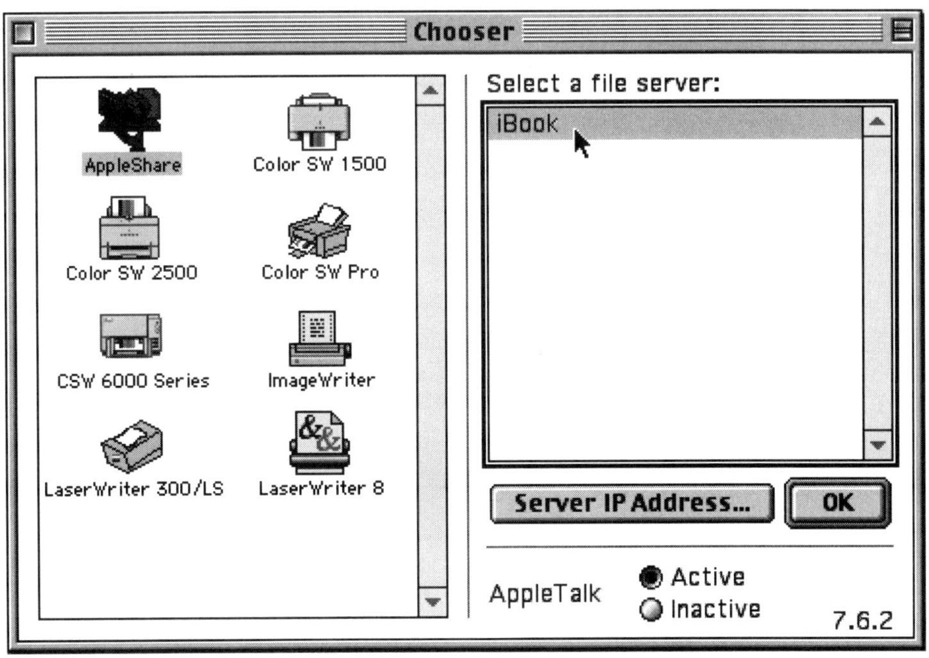

Figure 11-24 Selecting a computer to connect to.

Click the **OK** button in the Chooser. Doing that brings up a dialog box that lets you connect to the selected server (each of the computers in your network acts as a server—each serves files to the other computer or computers in the network). The **Name** box will be filled in for you. Type in the password (use the one you entered in the File Sharing control panel). Figure 11-25 shows the dialog box that appeared when I chose the iBook from the Chooser of my Power Mac 7500.

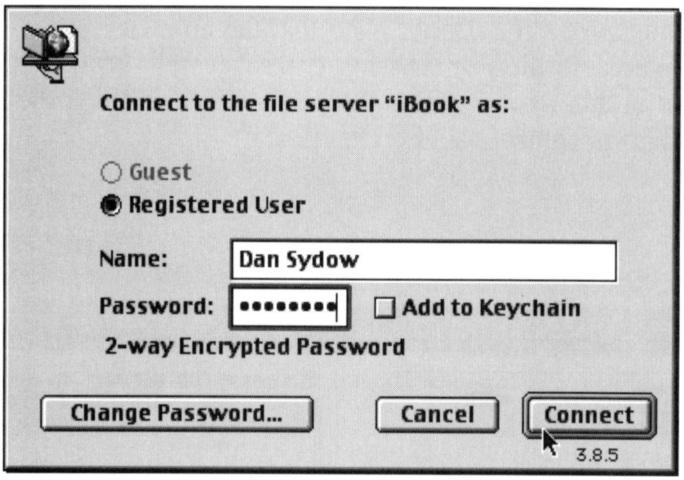

Figure 11-25 Connecting to a computer in the network.

Click the **Connect** button and a dialog box like the one shown in Figure 11-26 appears (don't worry if the dialog box you see doesn't contain a reference to a Keychain). Here you specify which items on the Mac you're connecting to are to be accessible. I'm working on my Power Mac 7500 and connecting to my iBook, so this dialog box lists the items (drives) on the iBook that should be marked as accessible from the Power Mac 7500. You'll probably see just one item listed here—the name of your iBook's hard drive. If you have an additional drive connected to your iBook, or if you have a CD disc in your iBook's CD-ROM drive, though, you'll see other items listed here. Click on the drive name, and also check the checkbox by the name. You needn't be concerned about which radio button is selected, and don't worry if one of them is disabled (dimmed). Click the **OK** button when finished.

Figure 11-26 Selecting the items to use.

Now you find yourself back at the Chooser. Click the Chooser window's close box to dismiss the Chooser. Take a look at the desktop of the computer you've been working on. There you'll notice an icon for the just-selected drive. For instance, in the Chooser of my Power Mac 7500 I chose the iBook, and in the dialog boxes that followed I opted to make the Macintosh HD drive on the iBook accessible to the Power Mac 7500. So now on the Power Mac 7500 desktop I see an icon for the iBook's hard drive. The icon includes a little connector and cable to indicate that this drive exists across the network on a different Mac (see Figure 11-27). At this time I could transfer files from my Power Mac 7500 to the iBook.

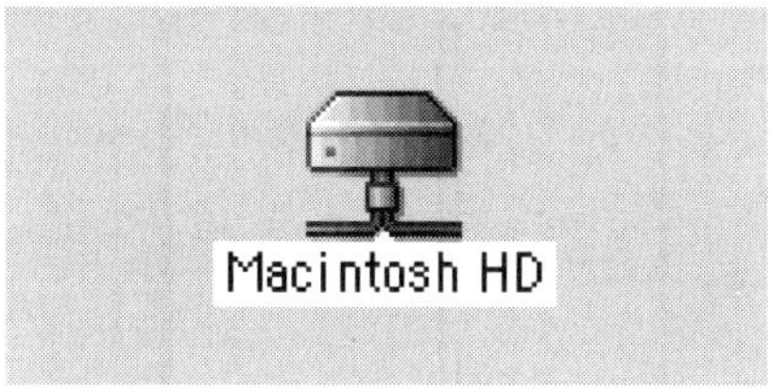

Figure 11-27 The icon for a drive that exists on a networked Mac.

Now repeat all the Chooser steps for the Chooser on the other computer or computers in the network (starting with clicking on the AppleShare icon on the left side of the Chooser). For instance, in my two-Mac network I worked on my desktop Mac first, so I would now move to my iBook and open its Chooser. From that Chooser I'd select AppleShare, then choose the Power Mac 7500 as the server computer. Next I'd choose the drive or drives on the Power Mac 7500 that I want to access from the iBook. Then I would close the Chooser and my network setup would be complete.

Sharing a Printer

If you have a printer connected to your desktop Mac, you can easily share it with your iBook. To do that, select the Chooser from the desktop Macintosh. Click on the icon of the printer that's connected to the desktop Mac, then click on the **Setup** button in the Chooser. For instance, I have an Apple StyleWriter 1500 connected to my Power Mac 7500. Clicking on the Apple SW 1500 icon and then the **Setup** button results in a dialog box like the one shown in Figure 11-28.

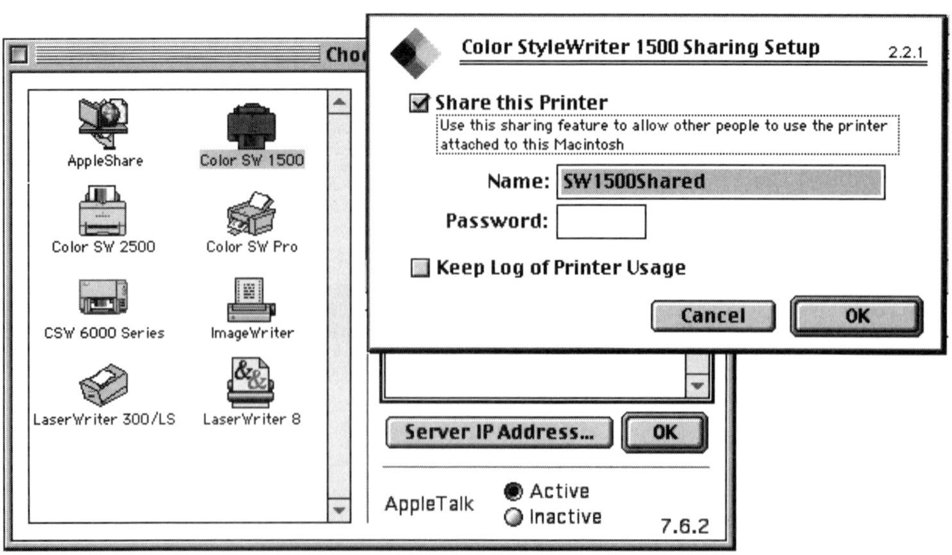

Figure 11-28 Sharing a printer.

Check the **Share this Printer** checkbox, then enter a name for the printer. You can enter a password, but you don't need to. If you aren't concerned with who can access the printer, then skip the password. Click the **OK** button. The name you selected for the printer appears on the right side of the Chooser. Click once on that name to select it. Then close the Chooser. On the networked computer (the iBook in my example), select the Chooser. The shared printer's name will appear on the right side of the Chooser. Click once on the name to select it, then close the Chooser. Now, when you're working on the networked computer (such as the iBook), whenever you choose **Print** from the **File** menu of a program the printer on the desktop computer will be used!

Testing a Network

Everything's set up, so let's see how the network works. Let's assume you're setting up a simple two-Mac network like the one I've been describing. Your desktop Mac and your iBook are connected, and now you want to take your iBook with you when you leave today. From the iBook, choose **Shut Down** from the **File** menu. Because your iBook is a part of a network, you'll be presented with an alert like the one shown in Figure 11-29.

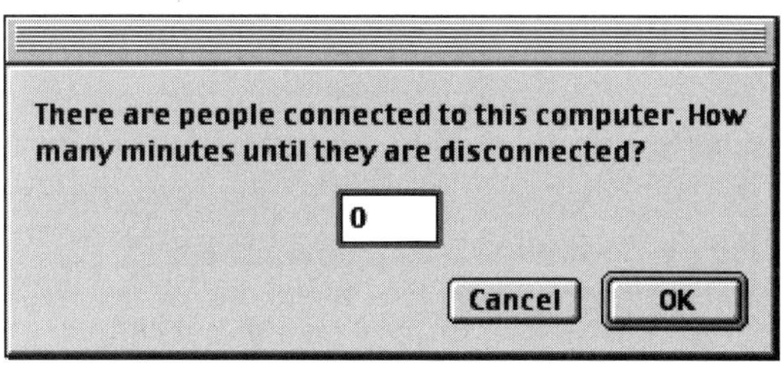

Figure 11-29 Giving connected Macs a warning.

This alert appears on the computer being shut down, and the "people connected to this computer" refers to the desktop Mac. Here you can give those "people" a warning that they're about to lose access to the iBook. Since the "people" in this case are you, you shouldn't need much of a warning! Enter zero (0), then click the **OK** button. After doing that, look over at your desktop Mac. On its screen you'll see an alert like the one pictured in Figure 11-30. It tells you the computer has been disconnected from the iBook.

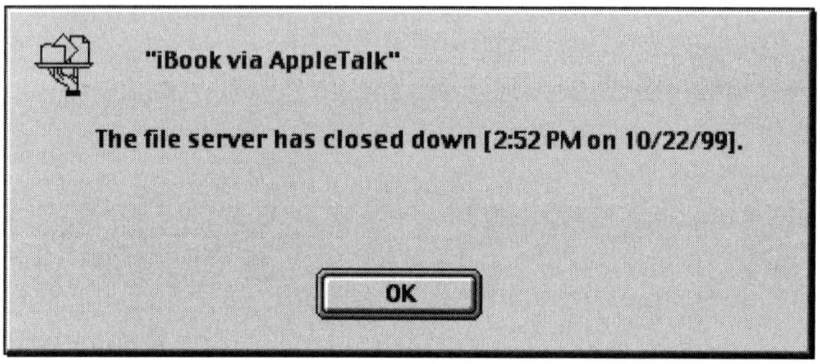

Figure 11-30 The disconnection alert.

Now, disconnect the Ethernet cable from the iBook. Just unplug it. You can (and for convenience, probably should) leave the other end of the cable plugged into your desktop Mac. Take your iBook and go. Do some work. Have some fun. When you're done, you may want to reconnect to the network so that you can transfer your work to the desktop Mac. To do that, make sure your iBook is off, then plug the free end of the crossover cable into your iBook. Start up your desktop Mac, if it isn't running already. When it's up and running, start up your iBook by pressing the power on button. When the iBook has started up, it will bring up a dialog box like the one shown in Figure 11-31 (again, don't be alarmed if the dialog box doesn't mention a Keychain). This dialog box asks you if you want to connect to the network. Enter your password, click the **Connect** button, and voila, the iBook is now networked to the desktop Mac.

There's one more step you may need to take. You might have to get your desktop Mac to recognize the iBook. To do that, choose **Network Browser** from the desktop Mac's **Apple** menu (it's under the **Appl**e menu, but it's not in the control panel folder). In the Network window that appears, click on the arrow by the AppleTalk. (Don't worry if no AppleTalk name is shown—there may be just the iBook name). That displays a list of servers to connect to. As shown in Figure 11-32, in my setup the desktop Mac is only connected to the iBook, so that's the only name listed.

Figure 11-31 Reconnecting to the network.

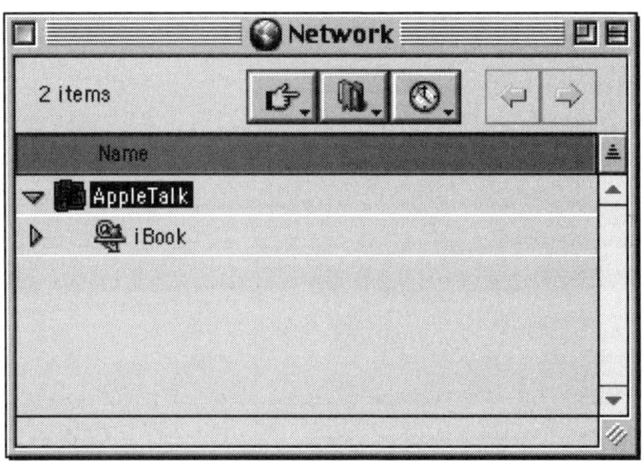

Figure 11-32 Selecting a Mac to connect to.

Double-click on the iBook name and you'll face the "Connect to the file server" dialog box. Enter the iBook's password and click the **Connect** button. You'll then see a new window (see Figure 11-33) that lets you choose which item on the iBook is accessible. Double-click on the hard drive name and the connection is made.

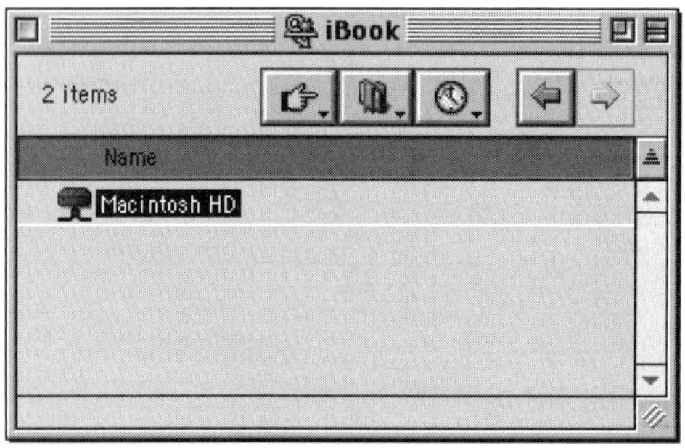

Figure 11-33 Selecting a drive to access.

Now the desktop Mac recognizes the iBook as a part of the network. At this point you're free to transfer files back and forth between computers! You can transfer the files you just worked on from your iBook to your desktop Mac, or copy other files from the desktop Mac to the iBook, or even transfer folders full of megabytes of files. I just remembered that on my Power Mac 7500 I have a very large folder of files I use for my personal Web site, and I'd like to keep a backup copy of the entire folder on my iBook. To do that I simply find the folder on my Power Mac 7500 desktop and drag the folder to the iBook's hard drive icon that is also on the Power Mac 7500 desktop. As shown in Figure 11-34, the copying then begins.

I can double-click on the Macintosh HD icon on the Power Mac 7500 desktop to view the contents of the iBook's hard drive from my Power Mac 7500. I can also verify that the folder was copied by moving to my iBook and looking at the contents of that computer's hard drive. Sure enough, the *My Web Stuff* folder is there.

To get the hang of connecting, fool around with unplugging and replugging in your iBook. I recommend that you connect with the iBook off and then power on that machine, but you could plug the crossover cable into the iBook while it's still running. If you do that note that then you'll need to run the Network Browser utility from the desktop Mac (as discussed) and from the iBook (there's a Network Browser under the iBook's Apple menu too).

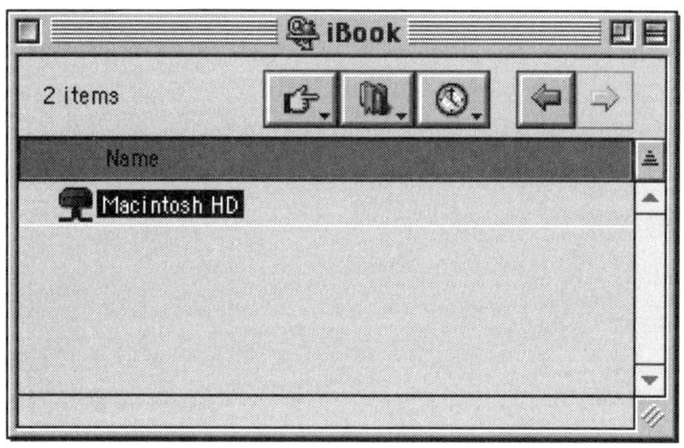

Figure 11-34 Copying a folder from one Mac to another.

Using the Apple Connectivity Web Site

Now that you know a little bit about networking, the information on Apple's Connectivity Web site will be more understandable. This site was mentioned in the Printers section of Chapter 10. This site is helpful for determining how to connect an Apple printer to an iBook, and it's also helpful in getting some tips on networking the iBook to other Macintosh computers. You may have found all the networking information you need in this chapter, but if you want a little extra information specific to the type of computer you're attempting to network to your iBook, go to Apple's Connectivity Web site at `support.info.apple.com/support/imac/connectivity/connectivity.taf`. From there you can click on the **Choose a Computer or Printer** popup menu to reveal a list of choices. In this menu are a number of computer types, such as Power Macintosh, PowerBook, and so forth. Selecting the category of the

Mac you're interested in networking has the effect of changing the title of the popup menu. It also adds a new popup menu to the right of the original one. From this second pop-up you can choose the particular computer model you're interested in networking. Choosing a model of computer brings up information about connecting that model to an iBook (or an iMac).

12

Troubleshooting and Maintaining Your iBook

Right out of the box, your iBook is one cool machine—and you want to keep it that way! You want your computer, and the installed software, to run without a hitch. To make sure that's the case, read this chapter. Here you'll find a variety of maintenance tips and techniques, as well as pointers on where to turn for still more help.

After using your iBook for a while, you may find that it fits your needs perfectly. If you're like most computer users, though, you'll probably get an itch to add a little something to your already special machine. This chapter discusses how to upgrade and improve your iBook to tailor it to your needs.

Solving Software Problems

The software on your computer's hard drive can be loosely divided into two categories: system software and application software. If your iBook's system software isn't functioning properly, there's a good chance that you won't even get a chance to run any of your application software—so you'll most assuredly want to have your system in tip-top shape. With your system working, everything else should be running smoothly. However, independently of how the system software is doing, an individual application (program) can become errant and not run properly. To top it all off, a computer virus could come along and wreak havoc with all of your software! Even though this all sounds somewhat dreadful, try not to become too alarmed—few users experience many of these problems. And even if you should be so unlucky as to encounter a seemingly severe problem, there's a good chance that there's a fix available.

Eliminating Frequent Crashes

A computer program, including the system software, is a collection of instructions that are sent to the computer's processor for . . ., well, processing. That's how software works—the central processing unit, or CPU, handles one instruction after another. Fortunately for computer users, only the processor needs to understand anything about the instructions that make up a program. Unfortunately For computer users, occasionally the processor doesn't understand the instructions either! When that happens, the problematic program quits unexpectedly, or the computer may even *crash* (also called *freezing*, or *hanging*). In most cases, such a problem involves one piece of information that somehow got misread. Rerunning the program that failed, or at worst restarting the computer, generally alleviates the problem. Sometimes, though, the problem occurs again and again. The same program may quit each time you try to run it, or a number of programs may cause the computer to freeze at unpredictable times. When crashes are a recurring problem, one of two situations exists: Either data on your iBook's hard drive is corrupt, or there is a conflict between two or more system extensions.

Repairing Damaged Software

In the case of corrupt software, your best bet is to run utility software whose purpose is to analyze your iBook's hard drive for programs (including system software programs) that are damaged. Symantec's Norton Utilities (`www.symantec.com/nu/index.html`) is a program that includes a number of tools for recovering lost data (such as Unerase to retrieve files you've inadvertently trashed), improving hard disk performance, and repairing damaged hard drives. If your iBook frequently crashes, it may be worth the price of this CD-ROM (about $80) just for the Norton Disk Doctor feature of Norton Utilities. In Figure 12-1 you see the Disk Doctor in action as it surveys an iBook's hard drive.

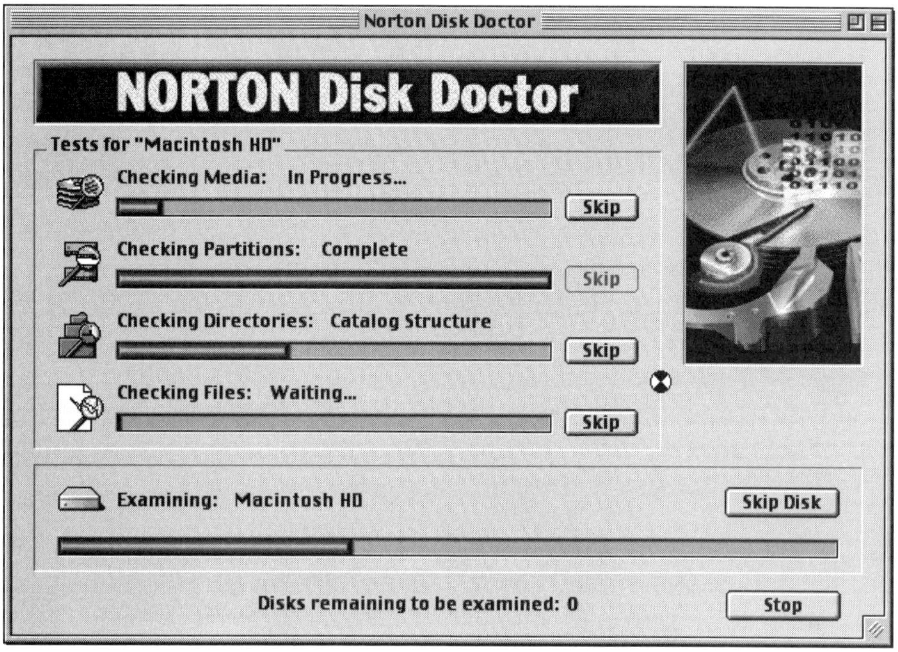

Figure 12-1 The Norton Disk Doctor examining a hard drive.

Norton Disk Doctor examines a hard drive for files that don't have the proper format, and then reports back to you with the results. Once you give the go-ahead, Disk Doctor attempts to make the repair or repairs to the damaged files—usually with good results.

Note

Apple includes a disk repair utility named Disk First Aid on your iBook's hard drive. If you suspect your iBook has disk problems you can run Disk First Aid and, if there *are* problems, this utility *may* repair them. Disk First Aid solves some disk-related problems, but it isn't meant to be a full-featured disk repair program. If you don't own a program such as Norton Utilities, go ahead and give Disk First Aid a try—but don't expect it to solve all disk-related problems.

Catching Conflicts

A system extension is a small program that extends, or enhances, the features of the Macintosh operating system software. Hearing of the existence of software that acts as an extension of the system software raises the question as to why Apple didn't just build the extension software directly into the operating system. There are a few good reasons for this "aftermarket" type of software, the most notable being that extensions allow a user to add features to a Mac without reinstalling a new version of the entire operating system. For instance, if Apple improves QuickTime, the movie-playing system software used by many programs, it can make the new version of QuickTime available to anyone who already has a Macintosh. The user who obtains the new version of QuickTime simply places the QuickTime extension in the Extensions folder of his iBook's System Folder, restarts the computer, and from then on the computer makes use of the new, improved QuickTime software.

Apple doesn't create all extensions—other developers of Mac software also create them. When you install a new program on your iBook's hard drive, the installer may add a new extension, too. The more software you add, the more the contents of your Extensions folder grows. With all this add-on system software running in conjunction with the "main" system software (the Mac operating system), the potential for an *extension conflict* increases. Simplistically, an extension conflict occurs when two extensions, or one extension and the main system software, aren't compatible. In such an instance, the conflict needs to be resolved in order to get the computer back into a fully functioning mode.

Resolving a conflict extension first involves determining which extension is in conflict with another extension, or with the system software. Because your computer has dozens of extensions, making this determination can be difficult. The Extension Manager (choose **Extension Manager** from the **Control Panels** submenu under the **Apple** menu) can be used to help out here. The Extension Manager allows you to create different sets of extensions that are to be loaded, or made use of, each time you start up your iBook. If you turn off some extensions, restart your iBook, and the problem of crashing disappears, you know that one of the extensions in the turned-off set is the culprit. Of course, your work isn't done yet—you still need to determine exactly which one of the extensions in the set is causing the problem.

Carrying out the series of steps involved in resolving conflict catching can be tedious. You can see the list of steps involved by following these steps:

1. Choose **Mac Help** from the desktop's **Help** menu.
2. Click on **Preventing and solving problems** on the left side of the Mac OS Help window
3. Click on **If your computer frequently crashes, freezes, or won't start up** on the right side of the window.
4. Click on **Resolve system extension conflicts**.

One of the best ways to speed up and partly automate the process of finding extension conflicts is to use software such as Casady and Greene's Conflict Catcher (`www.casadyg.com/products/listing.html`). A program such as Conflict Catcher finds conflicts through a process of elimination. That's how you'd find conflicts on your own, too, but Conflict Catcher does the work of choosing and keeping track of extension sets, and also includes a few tests you couldn't perform on your own. For instance, if the conflict occurs as your iBook starts up, Conflict Catcher is able to perform the elimination process automatically without intervention or input from you.

Restoring the Original iBook Software

If the problems you're having with your iBook get really bad, then your system software may be just too damaged to be of any use. That sounds really bad, but all is not lost!

Starting the iBook From Different System Software

One particularly vexing problem a computer user faces is what to do when his or her computer crashes each time it starts up. It's an unlikely scenario, but it can happen if certain system software files somehow become *corrupt*, or damaged. How do you attempt to figure out what's wrong, or begin to replace corrupt files, if the computer won't even start up? If the problem involves an extension conflict, then conflict-seeking software such as Conflict Catcher (see the Catching Conflicts section in this chapter) may help. If the problem instead involves corrupt data on the computer's hard drive, then data repair software such as Norton Utilities (see the *Repairing Damaged Software* section in this chapter) might work.

If neither of these solutions works (or if you don't have programs like the ones just mentioned), you'll need to bypass the system software on your iBook's hard drive and instead start up the computer with *different* system software. Rather than have the iBook run the system software that's on its hard drive, you'll start the iBook from a CD-ROM that has system software on it. Typically, a CD includes only a program and some files that that program requires—it doesn't have system software on it. So Apple has included with the iBook a couple of CDs that do have system software. Such a CD is referred to as a *bootable* CD because you can boot, or start, your computer from it.

To start your iBook from a bootable CD, begin by placing the CD in the iBook's CD-ROM drive. Press and hold down the letter *C* key (for *C*D, as in "start from CD") and then press the iBook's Power On button. Keep the letter C key pressed down until you see the Welcome to Mac OS window. This window doesn't take long to appear, and it names the version of the operating system (such as Mac OS 8.6 or Mac OS 9). Starting the iBook with the letter C key pressed forces the iBook to use the system software on the CD-ROM rather than on its hard drive. With the iBook started from the CD-ROM, you should have access to the files on the iBook's hard drive (its icon should appear on the desktop, along with the icon for the CD-ROM used to start the computer).

Using the iBook Restoration CD-ROMs

Your iBook comes with a pair of CD-ROMs that are bootable. The iBook Software Install CD and the iBook Restore CD can both be used to start up your iBook. The CD you use depends on the severity of your problems. In short, the iBook Software Install CD is used to reinstall the iBook system software and/or some of the applications that came on your iBook, while the iBook Restore CD is used to reinstall *all* of the software (including the system software) on your iBook.

iBook Software Install CD To reinstall just the system software, use this CD-ROM's Mac OS Installer application. You'll traverse a few windows that let you select the drive to install the software on (some people add an additional drive to their iBook), read some notes and an agreement, and then select what part (or all) of the system software you want to install (see Figure 12-2). If you want to reinstall the entire system, click the **Reinstall** button. If you want to add just some components, instead click the **Add/Remove** button. If you click the Add/Remove button, you'll see a window that lets you choose just what it is you want to reinstall (see Figure 12-3).

Note that this iBook Software Install CD also includes backup copies of several of the applications that came preinstalled on your iBook.

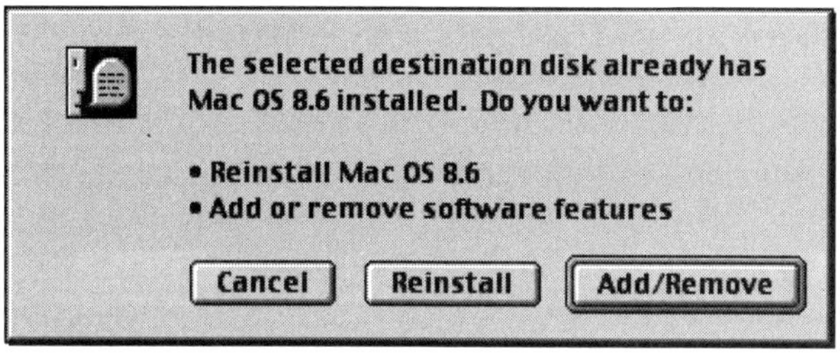

Figure 12-2 Choose to install all, or some, of the system.

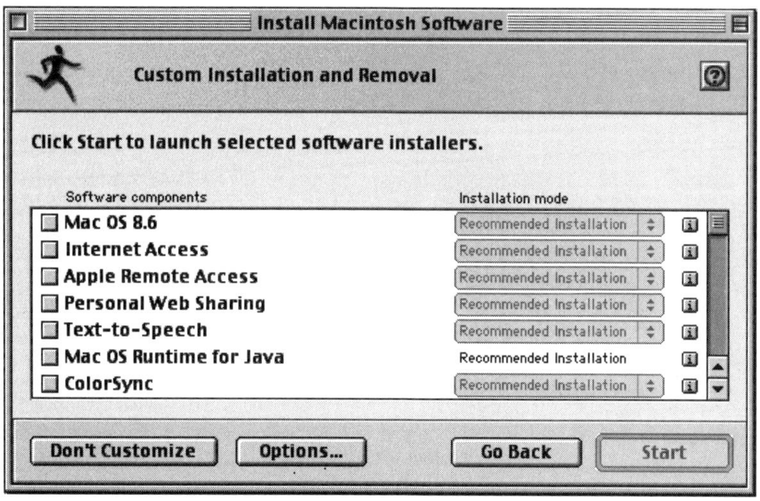

Figure 12-3 Choosing the parts of the system to install.

iBook Restore CD To restore your iBook's hard drive to the state it was in when it rolled off the factory assembly line, use this CD-ROM. The iBook Restore CD includes an *image* of the hard drive contents so that you can return your iBook to its original state. When you run the Apple Software Restore program from this CD-ROM, you'll get the opportunity to preserve any or all of your files or programs during the restore operation (refer to Figure 12-4). It's important to understand the distinction between the three restoration options that the restore program offers:

Restore, saving original items This is the safest option. Before the original software is restored, the restore program saves all the existing contents of your hard drive in a folder named *Original items*. After you've performed the restore, and are comfortable that everything works as expected, you can move the whole *Original items* folder, or just some of its contents, to the Trash.

Restore in Place This option is similar to the *Restore, saving original items* option in that non-system files will be preserved. They won't, however, be placed in a new *Original items* folder—they'll be left in place on the hard drive. *Restore in Place* is also similar to *Restore, saving original items* in that both options place new versions of all system software on your hard drive. *Restore in Place* differs from the *Restore, saving original items* in that the original system files aren't saved. All the system software that is restored will overwrite, or replace, the existing software (in the *Restore, saving original items* option, all original files—including system files—are saved in an *Original items* folder).

Erase "Macintosh HD" before restoring This option is not for the timid! Before replacing the system software, the restore program erases everything on your hard drive—including all your applications and personal files. It then restores the contents of the hard drive to its original state. Typically you would have to be experiencing severe, constant problems with your iBook before you'd use this approach. And, if you are in fact prepared to erase and then restore your hard drive's contents, you had best make sure that you copy all your own files to removable media first (such as to a Zip disc).

Before you use any of the restoration options, you need to start your iBook from a drive other than the one that's to be restored (notice the note at the bottom of the window in Figure 12-4—it won't let me restore the software because I ran the Apple Software Restore program after I started my iBook from its internal hard drive). The easiest means to accomplishing that is to place the iBook Restore CD in your iBook, choose Restart from the Special menu, and then press and hold down the letter *C* key as the iBook restarts. That forces the computer to use the system software from the iBook Restore CD (for information on starting from a CD, see the *Starting the iBook From Different System Software* section earlier in this chapter).

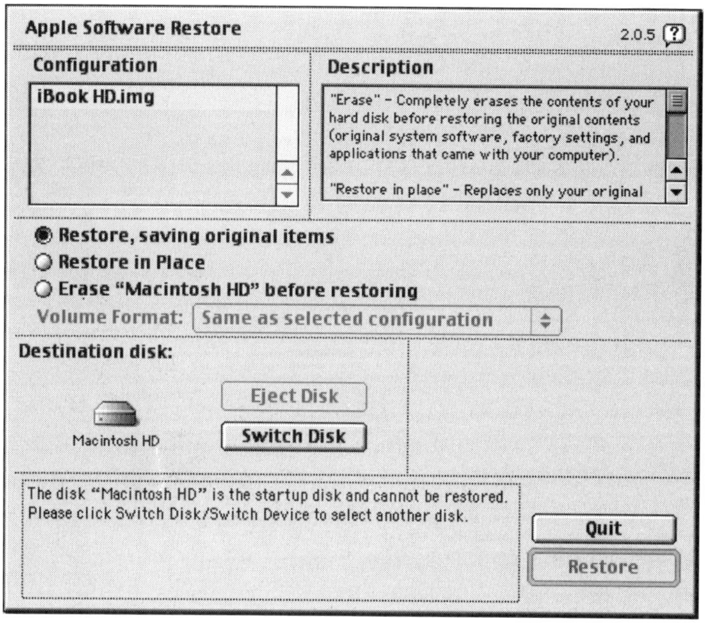

Figure 12-4 The Apple Software Restore program in action.

Helping Out the System

There are a couple of simple tricks you can perform to help out the iBook should the computer start crashing frequently. Best of all, initiating each requires nothing more than a restart and the press of the proper keys (the correct keyboard *key combination*).

Rebuilding the Desktop

Your iBook's hard drive holds an "invisible" (not displayed by an icon on the desktop) database file that the computer uses to keep track of information about all the folders and files on the hard drive. This database file (referred to as the Desktop file) is automatically updated as you create and delete new folders and files, but the updating process isn't perfect. To make sure this database file is updated properly, Apple suggests that you occasionally *rebuild the desktop*. This scary-sounding procedure is simple, foolproof, and is very unlikely to harm the data on your hard drive.

Tip

Every program has its own icon, and files created by each program typically have an icon that makes it easy to visually associate that file with its creator program. This file-icon pairing is kept track of in the desktop file. If you notice that a number of your programs don't seem to have the proper icon (they'll most likely have the "generic" application icon), then rebuilding the desktop may remedy this problem.

To rebuild the desktop, restart your iBook (choose **Restart** from the **Special** menu), and then press and hold down the Command and Option keys. Keep holding these two keys down until a window with the message *Are you sure you want to rebuild the desktop file on the disk "Macintosh HD?"* appears. Click the **OK** button and the iBook does the rebuilding. This will take just a little while, and when the process is complete the desktop appears, without any noticeable changes, on your iBook monitor.

Tip

Apple says once a month or so is a good schedule for rebuilding the desktop. But we aren't talking about a critical timeframe here. Some people rebuild the desktop more often, while some people (like those who never heard of the procedure) never rebuild the desktop. It's a good idea to perform this task occasionally, but don't become alarmed if you haven't ever done it, or if you want to do it on a regular basis but forget to do so.

Zapping the PRAM

An iBook drive, such as the built-in hard drive, can keep track of itself. For instance, the previous section discussed the invisible file that holds information about the files and folders on the startup drive. Some iBook information, though, is *systemwide*. That is, regardless of which drive your computer starts from (if you have more than one drive, then using the Startup Disk control panel your computer can be set to start up from either drive), you'll want the volume of the iBook speakers to be the same. For this purpose your iBook has a very small amount of memory reserved for *parameter RAM* (also referred to as *PRAM*, and pronounced *pee-ram*). This memory keeps track of your preferences for system parameters that aren't related to the startup drive, such as the just-mentioned speaker volume.

A battery powers the PRAM, so the values held in PRAM are preserved when the computer is turned off. The parameter memory very infrequently may become corrupt, which may then be the cause of some iBook problems (such as unexplained crashes). You can *zap*, or *reset*, the PRAM to the information that was stored there initially (to the PRAM original, or factory, settings). To zap the PRAM, restart your iBook and immediately press and hold down the Option, Command, and letter P and letter R keys (Option-Command-P-R). The iBook will shut down, and then you'll hear the startup chime as always. Keep the keys pressed down, and a second or two later you'll heard the same startup sound again. When you do, go ahead and release the keys. Don't worry if you inadvertently keep the keys held down too long and the chime plays a third time. In such a case you've simply zapped the PRAM a second time (which isn't a good or a bad thing).

Important
Don't just zap the PRAM as a maintenance procedure—wait until there are unexplained and frequent crashes before trying this trick. While zapping the PRAM can't harm your iBook, the act does reset (read "erase") any changes you've made to your general iBook settings. Such settings include the speaker volume, your choice of startup drive, and so forth. After zapping the PRAM, you'll need to open the General Controls, Keyboard, Trackpad, and Startup Disk control panels and readjust the various settings to match the options you prefer.

Troubleshooting Software

Hopefully, the tips and techniques listed on the previous pages will eliminate any iBook crashing problems you might encounter. If they don't, you may need to turn to the Mac technical support team at Apple or to the dealer from which you purchased your iBook. In that case, you'll want to provide the technical support personal with information about your particular iBook. Rather than attempting to ascertain all the critical technical details yourself, you'll do best to rely on a software utility that came installed on your iBook—the Apple System Profiler.

The Apple System Profiler, or ASP, is a program that automatically collects and displays technical information about the computer on which the ASP program is housed. For instance, when the Apple System Profiler runs, it examines the computer to see which version of the Mac OS is installed, how much RAM is in the computer, and the type and size of the hard drive (or drives) connected to the computer.

The Apple System Profiler is accessible by choosing **Apple System Profiler** from the **Apple** menu. When ASP starts, a window like the one in Figure 12-5 appears. Clicking on each of the tabs at the top of the window displays a different set of items in the window. In Figure 12-5, I've clicked on the Control Panels tab to display information about the control panels installed on my iBook.

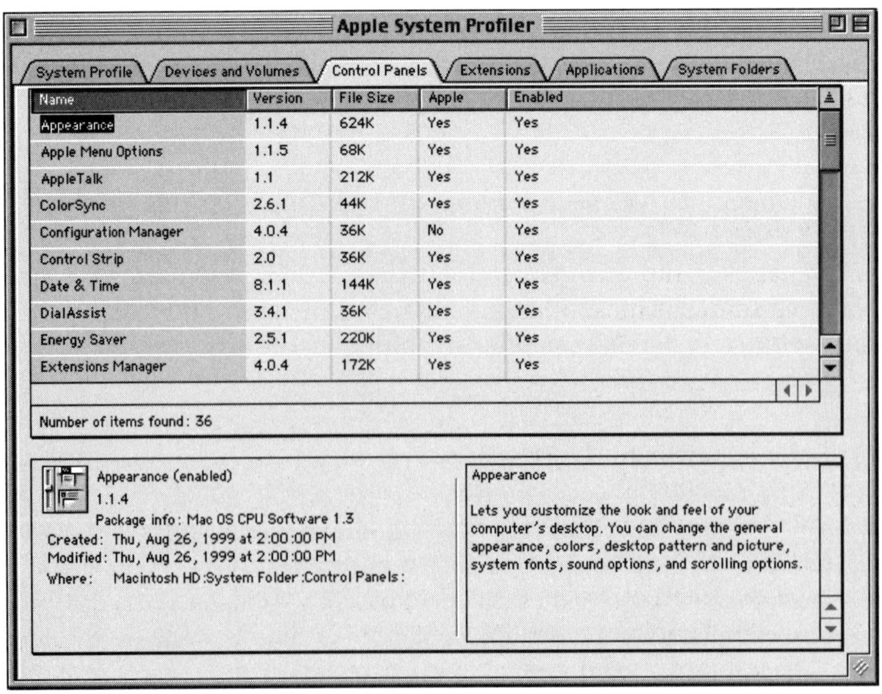

Figure 12-5 The Apple System Profiler window.

Clicking on the various tabs allows you to find out all manner of technical details about your iBook. To save some or all of this information to a report, choose **New Report** from the **File** menu. The report appears in a new window. To save the report to a file, choose **Save** from the **File** menu.

Just what exactly does all the information in the report mean? Fortunately, you don't have to know—the report is intended to be interpreted by Mac technical support persons. Apple Computer provides ninety days of technical telephone support, and Apple technical support personal may ask you to generate an Apple System Profiler report as part of their process of assisting you.

Detecting and Preventing Viruses

A computer virus is a small computer program that reproduces itself so that it can make its way into numerous computer systems. Once a virus makes it to a computer, it carries out some action. The nature of the action depends entirely on the nature of the programmer or programmers who created the virus program. Some viruses are relatively harmless, perhaps doing little more than displaying an annoying message to let you know that your system was just violated without your knowledge. Other viruses are far more malicious, doing actual damage by destroying the system software or data files on the infected computer.

Preventing Viruses

A virus doesn't grow on your computer—it has to come from an outside source. That source is most often the Internet. When you download a program from the Web to your iBook, you're trusting that the program exists for some valid purpose. Most programmers post programs to the Internet to make money, share software utilities that they initially wrote for their own use, or simply to be benevolent. A very few programmers, though, develop and post programs with the intent of causing grief to computer users. The overwhelming majority of programs that are available to download from the Internet are safe, but a few aren't. The best way to avoid viruses is to never download programs from the Internet. Since downloading software may be one of the primary reasons you connect to the Internet, this solution probably isn't feasible. So the next best means of stopping a virus from infecting your iBook is to use caution by following certain safe practices.

Don't download files attached to e-mail If you connect to the Internet, it won't be long before you receive unsolicited e-mail. Most such mail will be *spam*—messages that are sent en masse to thousands of Internet users. Typically, spam messages entice you send money for information on a variety of schemes to make money. Another type of unsolicited e-mail is a far less common kind—it exists to act as a carrier of a virus. An e-mail message alone *can't* infect your computer with a virus. An e-mail message that includes an attached file *can*. To introduce a virus on your computer, a person could include the virus program as an attachment to an e-mail message and send it to you. If you elect to download the attached file, your computer would then be subject to the virus. If you receive e-mail with an attachment, and you don't know the sender, *don't download the attachment*. Instead, delete the e-mail message.

Note
The simple act of attaching a file or program to an e-mail message isn't enough to generate a virus. If you attach a normal (non-viral) program to an e-mail message and send it to a friend, that program can't become infected as it travels the Internet. Only a virus program, or an already infected program attached to an e-mail message, can cause harm to the recipient's computer.

Download files from safe sites Get your software from large Web sites that exist for the purpose of supplying Web surfers with programs. Such sites usually check programs for viruses before making the programs available to the public. This type of site may even display a statement noting that its files have been checked.

Make others aware of viruses If your iBook is shared with family or friends, make sure that each person who has access to the computer is aware of, and knows how to avoid obtaining, viruses.

Keep anti-virus software on your computer Read the next section to learn about anti-virus software and how it acts to combat viruses.

Commercial Anti-virus Products

If your computer is demonstrating strange behavior, such as frequently crashing, a virus may be involved. More than likely, though, the cause of the problem is corrupt data. Read this chapter's *Restoring the Original iBook Software* section to learn more about data corruption. After you've ruled out "natural causes" for your iBook woes, consider the possibility that a virus may have infected your computer. To verify this, and to destroy the virus if it is indeed present, turn to a commercial anti-virus program. The leading commercial anti-viral utilities are Norton AntiVirus (formerly Symantec AntiVirus for Macintosh, or SAM) and Dr. Solomon's Virex.

Norton AntiVirus (NAV) This Symantec (`www.symantec.com`) utility provides fast, automatic virus protection. NAV scans, detects, and removes viruses from Internet downloads, email attachments, disks, shared files, and networks. In the case of infected system files, NAV allows you to restart your iBook directly from the NAV CD-ROM and then repair the damaged files.

Virex From Dr. Solomon (`www.drsolomon.com/products/virex`), this utility offers automatic scanning and repairing of files obtained from a host of sources, including Internet downloads, e-mail, disks, and servers. Virex includes a control panel that's used to provide continuous virus protection by detecting viruses immediately upon arriving on your iBook, and then by quickly removing them before they infect your computer.

Note

The freeware Macintosh anti-virus software Disinfectant is available for download from several shareware and freeware Internet sites, but the program's author recommends that you *not* use it. This has nothing to do with any lack of program quality. For almost a decade Disinfectant has been very popular and has served the Mac community well. However, the program hasn't been updated in a while, and won't see any future upgrades. Thus, it is unable to detect any of the newer viruses.

Finding Solutions For iBook Problems

To this point, this chapter has focused on techniques you can use to overcome iBook software problems. Those that have been discussed (most notably, hard drive data corruption) are the most common problems an iBook user may encounter. But due to the myriad combinations of software that can go on your iBook's drive and hardware that can connect to the iBook ports, there are a host of other difficulties you could face. Fortunately, most iBook problems you encounter are easy to solve—if you know where to turn to for help.

Using Online Help

As is expected of a large software and hardware company, Apple supports the iBook via its own iBook Web site. But as you'll see here, you can also find help from other sources on the Web.

Online System Software Updates

When Apple becomes aware of a problem with the Macintosh system software, they make the necessary corrections. Staying abreast of the latest version of the Mac OS is simple, free, and one of the best ways to keep iBook software-related problems to a minimum.

After making a number of changes to the iBook's system software, Apple releases the result as a system software update. To make use of such an update you don't have to scrap your existing Mac OS. Instead, you simply download the update and run the included installer. The installer program knows what files to add or to update in order to improve your current iBook system. To see if there's an update for the version of the Macintosh system your iBook is running, go to `www.apple.com/support/ibook`—the home of Apple's iBook Support Web site. Click on the Update popup menu to see a listing of the latest updates to iBook-specific software (as of this writing, there are no updates—but there may be by the time you read this). If one of the items in the Update menu is Apple SW Updates, you can choose that item to search for updates. Choosing Apple SW Updates takes you to an Apple search page that lets you search for a variety of updates—enter *ibook* in the keywords box on this page, then click the **Search** button.

You'll want to bookmark Apple's iBook Support Web site in your browser and stop in occasionally—there are bound to be occasional updates for your iBook (not to mention that this site offers a wealth of iBook information aside from software updates).

Solving Common iBook Problems

Occasionally a problem that an iBook user (or a user of any computer, for that matter) encounters is odd in nature. For unusual problems, your best bet to finding a solution may be the iBook Tech Exchange Discussion (see the next section, *Online Tech Exchange Discussion*). For other problems—problems common to a multitude of iBook users—visit Apple's iBook Solving Problems Web page. Go to the main iBook support page at `www.apple.com/support/ibook`, then click on the Solving Problems circle. At the Solving Problems site you'll find links to pages that offer solutions to several common problems. The links, and the problems, will change as bugs are uncovered, then fixed. As of this writing the site links to cures for ailments involving the:

- Computer startup
- Powering of the iBook
- Trackpad and keyboard
- Operation of the iBook
- Modem and Internet

Tip

As you *personally* stumble across problems and solutions, you can be a help to the iBook community by informing people of the error and its solution (by, for instance, posting to the Tech Exchange Discussion Forum, described next).

Online Tech Exchange Discussion Forum

If you're having trouble with your iBook, there's a good chance that you're not the only one. To see what other iBook owners are saying about the situation, visit the iBook Tech Exchange Discussion Form. To get there, go to the main iBook support page at `www.apple.com/support/ibook`, then click on the Tech Exchange circle. That takes you to a list of iBook topics (see Figure 12-6). Click on the arrow to the left of a topic, and you'll then see a list of questions asked by users. Each list entry (refer to Figure 12-7) is a link to the text of the question. Questions are answered by anyone (including other iBook users and Apple technical staff) willing to devote a few minutes to assisting fellow iBook users.

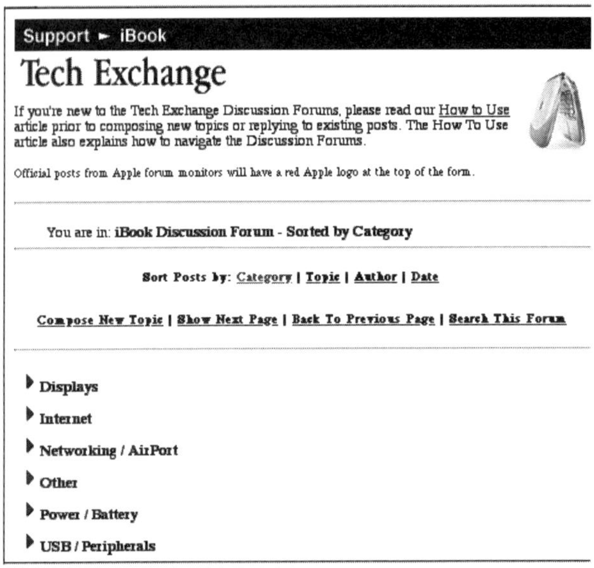

Figure 12-6 iBook Tech Exchange topics.

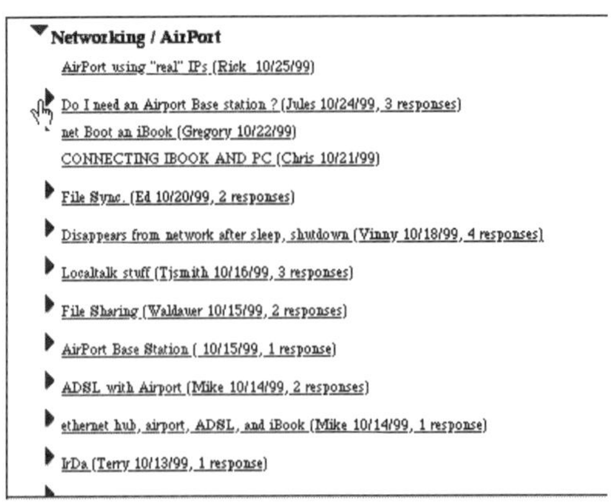

Figure 12-7 Discussions in one topic area of the iBook Tech Exchange.

Figure 12-7 provides a look at the Tech Exchange interface. In this figure, you can see a number of questions pertaining to AirPort.. Many questions have responses. If you have a particular problem in mind, see if someone else has already asked the same question. If so, click on that question title to view the entire question. In Figure 12-7 I'm clicking on a question regarding whether an AirPort base station is needed. That took me to the text of the question, as shown in Figure 12-8. Following the text of the question are links to the various responses people have made. Check each response to see if your question has been answered. Using this method you may not even need to send in your own query. If you can't find a discussion along the lines of your problem, then you'll need to submit a question and hope that someone responds (check back frequently to find out).Figure 12-8 A question posted to the iBook Tech Exchange.

Using the Tech Exchange is intuitive, but if you do have questions about how to read posted information or how to post your own questions, make sure to visit the *Apple's Tech Exchange and How To Use Web* page at `discuss.info.apple.com/commondocs.nsf/doc/1000`. Note that there's a How To Use link to this page at the top of the main page of the Tech Exchange.

Tip

Tech Exchange Discussion Forums exist for Apple products other than the iBook. To choose a different forum, go to the Tech Exchange home page at `support.info.apple.com/te/te.taf`. Here you'll click on the main topic of interest (such as iMac, Mac OS 9, AppleWorks, and so forth). Doing that takes you to a support page for that one product. At that site you'll find a Tech Exchange circle to click on to move to a Tech Exchange forum that's specific to that one product..

The MacFixIt Web Site

For years, Ted Landau, the author of the Mac troubleshooting bible *Sad Macs, Bombs, and Other Disasters*, has maintained the MacFixIt: Troubleshooting Solutions for the Macintosh Web site at `www.macfixit.com`. With the arrival of the iBook, Ted has linked a very useful iBook-specific area to the

MacFixIt site. To visit the iBook area, click on the link titled The iBook and Airport located near the bottom of the MacFixIt main page. Some of the content of the iBook and AirPort area is static, such as the overview of the iBook. But much of the content changes. As new problems—and solutions to those problems—are discovered, descriptions are posted here.

Fortunately, Mac users encounter fewer problems then users of some other computers. But *all* computer systems are susceptible to a variety of problems. To keep up on the solutions to iBook and Macintosh operating system problems, occasionally stop in at MacFixIt.

The About.com Mac Hardware Page

About.com at `www.about.com` is a Web site that provides good collections of links to Web pages related to hundreds of different topics. The About.com Focus on Mac Hardware page holds links to a variety of Mac topics, including AirPort, iBook news, and USB information. Definitely a site you'll want to check out—even if you don't have a problem with your iBook!

Extending the Warranty

Your iBook comes with a one-year limited warranty that covers parts and labor. To put that warranty into effect, make sure to register your new iBook computer. You can do that by sending in the registration card that came in the iBook box, or by visiting Apple's product registration Web site at www.applereg.com.

The standard iBook warranty is for one year, and is a carry-in plan—should your computer need repairs, you must carry it into a local Apple Authorized Service Provider. You can find out the location of the Apple Authorized Service Provider nearest you by calling Apple at 1-800-538-9696, or by visiting the Apple Service Provider Web site at `www.buy.apple.com`.

If you want to extend your iBook's warranty beyond one year, consider the AppleCare Protection Plan. This comprehensive plan provides three (3) years of service and support, and includes telephone support (for both software and hardware problems), Apple-certified repairs (including parts and labor), Internet support, and a software diagnostic and repair CD-ROM (TechTools Delux from Micromat). The plan cost is $229.

For more information on Apple's service options, visit the AppleCare page at `support.info.apple.com/support/applecare_products/overview.shtml`.

Upgrading Your iBook

Out of the box, your iBook may be just what you need—and all you need. Then again . . . when it comes to technology, very few people are ever satisfied for long. If you want to get a little more *out of* your iBook, read this section to see how to put a little more *into* it.

Adding Memory

As mentioned in the *Internal Components* section of Chapter 1, the iBook includes two types of memory. DRAM (Dynamic Random Access Memory) is memory that's used to hold running programs. The second type of memory, VRAM (Video Random Access Memory), is a more specialized memory that the iBook uses to keep track of what's to be displayed on the monitor.

When you're asked how much memory your iBook has, it's the DRAM the questioner is usually referring to. It's the DRAM that's also the most commonly upgraded memory in most computers, and for the iBook, it is the only memory you can upgrade. The more DRAM in your iBook, the more programs you can run concurrently, and the faster your iBook performs.

Note
At the risk of confusing the issue, I feel compelled to mention the following. On the iBook, DRAM is also referred to as SDRAM, with the *S* standing for *Synchronous*. Video memory may be referred to as either VRAM or as SGRAM, with the *SG* standing for *Synchronous Graphic*. So DRAM and SDRAM both refer to the memory that holds your running programs, while VRAM and SGRAM both refer to the memory that's used to display video.

As discussed in Chapter 1, the iBook uses DRAM chips for main memory. The first iBooks shipped with a non-removable 32 MB chip installed (subsequent models may come with more DRAM installed), and one empty slot that can accept a single memory chip. As of this writing there are 32 MB, 64 MB, and 128 MB chips available for the iBook. You'll need 1.25 inch 144-pin 15 ns SDRAM SO-DIMM memory in one of these sizes. Because the memory is a type of RAM, you may hear memory referred to as simply RAM rather than DRAM. And because the memory chip itself is installed on a small card, you'll hear RAM referred to as a *RAM expansion card*. Figure 12-9 shows what such a card looks like. Fortunately, all you need to say when ordering more memory is that you have an iBook—the sales staff at any Macintosh mail order firm (like the ones mentioned in Chapter 4) will know what you need.

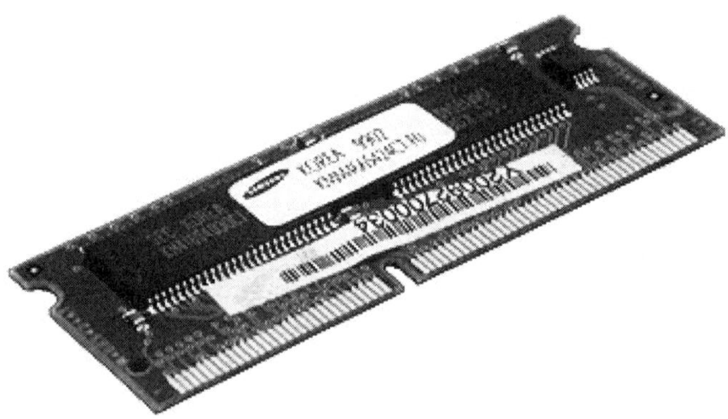

Figure 12-9 A DRAM card for the iBook.

The very small user manual that shipped with your iBook includes instructions for adding additional memory to your computer. Look over those simple instructions. In short, here's what you do:

1. Remove the battery
2. Remove the keyboard
3. Remove the AirPort card if present
4. Remove the metal RAM shield

5. Insert the RAM card into the RAM slot and press down to lock it in

6. Replace what you had removed (the RAM shield, AirPort card (if neces sary), keyboard, battery)

If you want more specific instructions, you can't beat the ones provided in Mac Help. From your iBook desktop, choose **Mac Help** from the **Help** menu (Mac Help is discussed in Chapter 3). In the window that opens, enter the words *memory* and *install* and then click the **Search** button. Among the found items will be one named Installing additional memory. Click on that link to display RAM installation instructions. As shown in Figure 12-10, it's easy to print these instructions. Clicking on the Print these instructions for me results in the printing of not only the displayed page, but also the several pages of instructions that the main page links to. As shown in Figure 12-11, these instructions include detailed figures.

Important
You *could* perform the installation without the aid of Mac Help. But you really should read through Mac Help first. Better still, print out all the instructions. Your iBook will be turned off when you start the memory installation, so Mac Help won't be available once you get under way.

The Mac Help instructions are quite informative, but I'll still provide you with a few figures of my own. The next few figures don't illustrate every step involved in the RAM installation, but they do give you a good look inside the iBook.

Removing the keyboard is as easy as sliding two plastic tabs away from the display and then lifting the keyboard. Figure 12-12 shows the two tabs—one is on the left top of the keyboard, next to the F1 function key, while the other is on the right top of the keyboard, next to the F9 function key.

Place a finger (or, more likely, a fingernail) on each tab and slide the tabs towards you. Then lift up the keyboard and flip it over so it's upside down. Because you can't move the keyboard too far from the iBook (it's attached to the computer by a cable), you'll want to just set it upside down on the iBook—as I'm doing in Figure 12-13. This figure also highlights the two screws that need to be removed in order to lift the RAM shield.

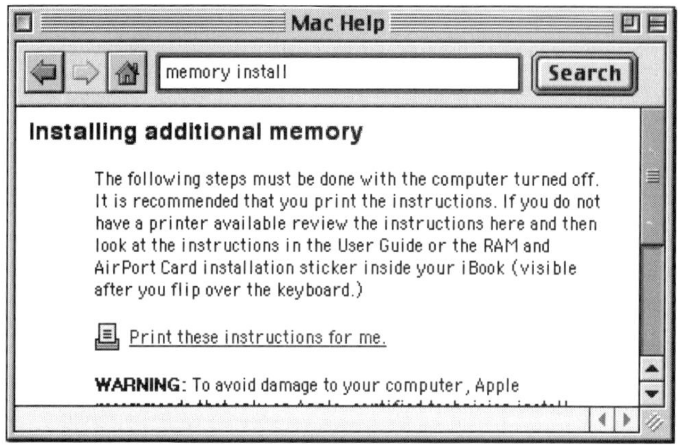

Figure 12-10 Mac Help's RAM installation instructions.

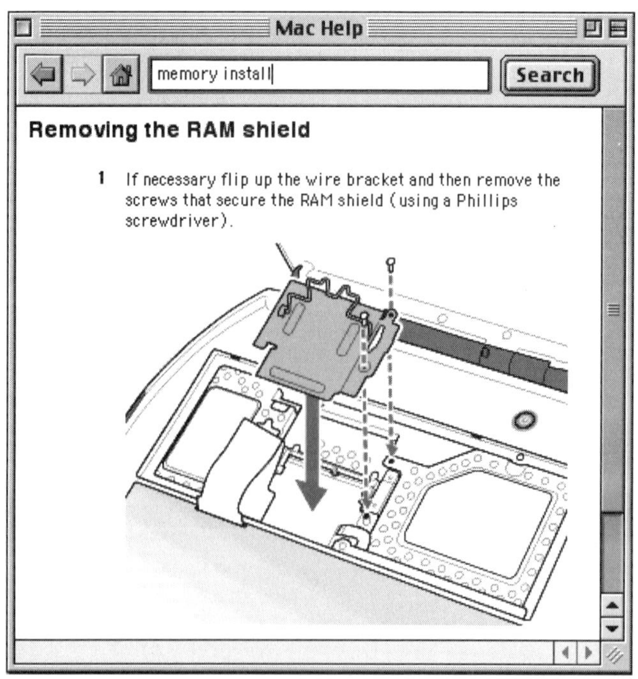

Figure 12-11 Mac Help includes illustrations.

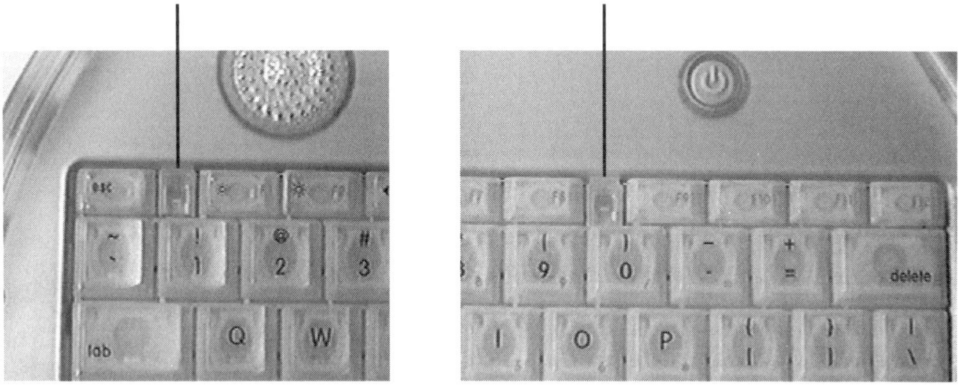

Figure 12-12 The keyboard release tabs.

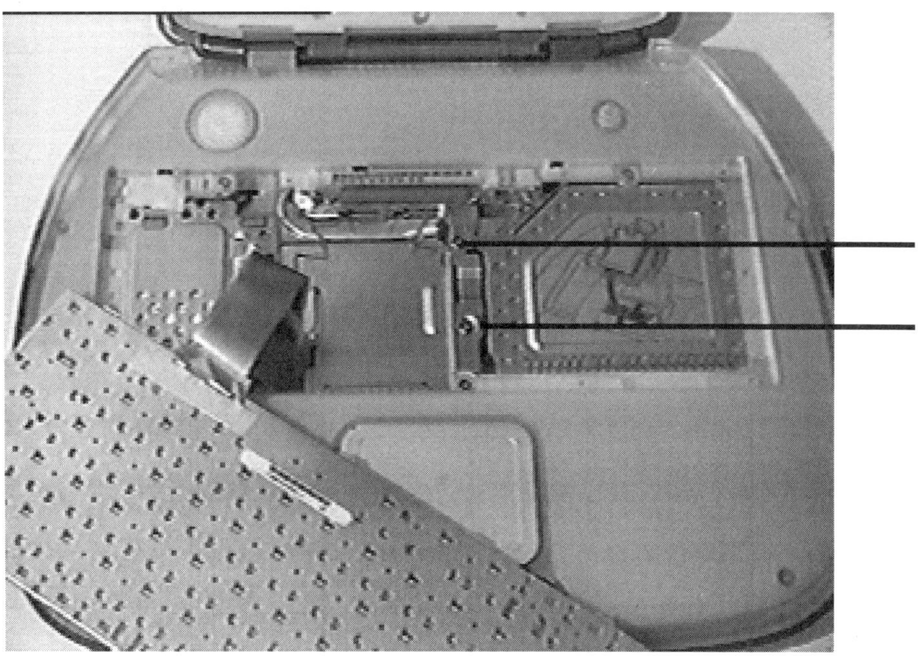

Figure 12-13 Moving the keyboard.

In Figure 12-13 you see that Apple has thoughtfully included an instructive illustration right inside the iBook. Figure 12-14 zooms in a bit to reveal that this illustration shows where the memory card and the AirPort card fit.

To reveal the RAM slot, remove the two screws that hold a metal RAM shield in place—Figure 12-13 points out where the screws are located. Then lift the RAM shield out of the computer. Now you can slide the RAM card towards the back of the computer, in to the RAM slot. Then press the RAM card down to lock it into place. The illustration present inside the iBook (see Figure 12-14) shows you exactly where this slot is located.

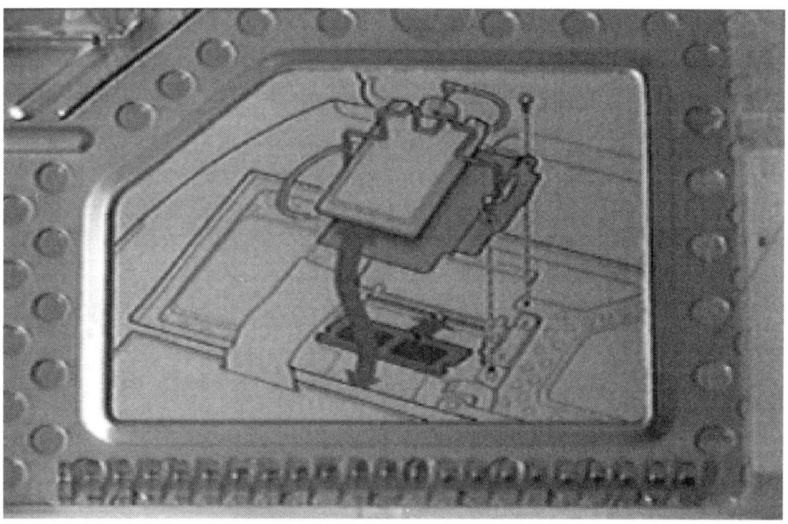

Figure 12-14 Installation instructions.

Adding an AirPort Card

For a wireless connection to the Internet, you'll need the optional AirPort card and AirPort Base Station (refer to Chapter 11 for more information on AirPort). The small user manual that came with your iBook includes brief instructions on how to install an AirPort card into your iBook. In summary, you'll follow these steps:

1. Remove the battery
2. Remove the keyboard
3. Attach the already-present antenna to the AirPort card
4. Slide the AirPort card into the AirPort slot that exists under the trackpad
5. Secure the card under the wire bracket
6. Replace the keyboard and battery

The Mac Help feature (choose **Mac Help** from the **Help** menu) offers few details on this installation process. However, this help feature offers very detailed information on RAM installation, and much of that information pertains to AirPort card installation. Refer back to this chapter's Adding Memory section, and to Figures 12-10 and 12-11. Follow that sections advice of printing the entire Mac Help memory installation instructions. Doing that will provide you with the steps—with figures included—necessary to remove and replace the iBook battery, remove and replace the keyboard. While the information is presented in the context of performing a memory upgrade, those same acts are a part of the AirPort card installation as well.

The Mac Help memory upgrade information also includes illustrations that show where the AirPort card seats in the iBook. Look back at Figures 12-12 and 12-13 to see how the keyboard comes out. Now look at Figure 12-15 to see where the AirPort card gets inserted. After connecting the antenna to the AirPort card, slide that card into its slot. Note that Figure 12-15 was taken while standing behind the iBook.

Adding Peripherals

There is a wealth of peripherals that can easily be connected to your iBook. A printer may be your first need. If it is, refer to Chapter 10 to see how to connect one to your computer. If you want to back up your work, or have a means of transferring files between computers, you might add a high-capacity removable media drive, such as an Imation 120 MB/1.4 MB SuperDisk Drive or an Iomega 100 MB Zip Drive. Again, refer to the chapter that deals with peripherals—Chapter 10. If that other peripheral you want to connect to your iBook just happens to be another Macintosh (including another iBook or an iMac), read Chapter 11 to learn all about networking Macs.

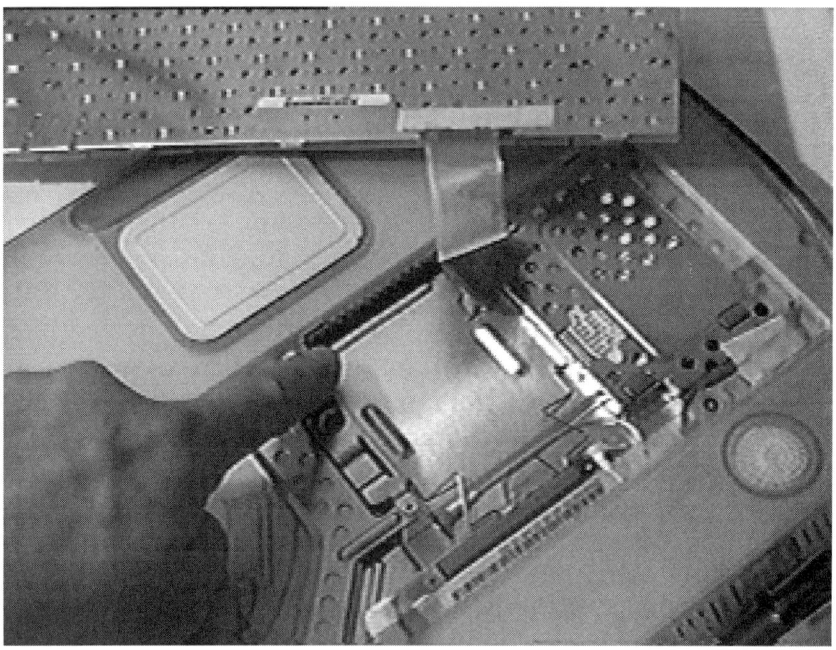

Figure 12-15 The AirPort card connects under the trackpad.

13

Games

The state of gaming on the Macintosh has never been better—thanks in part to the success of the iMac. Companies that in the past were reluctant to produce both a Windows and a Macintosh version of their games are now committing to the Macintosh. And companies that were traditionally supportive of the Mac are increasing the resources they devote to producing top-notch Macintosh games. That's good news for all Mac owners including, of course, iBook owners.

In this chapter you'll see just why the iBook is a good game-playing machine. Here you'll also find out where to go online to get the scoop on new Mac games, download freeware and shareware games, download demos of commercial games, and get help with problems you're having with games you already own. Finally, you'll read about the controllers, such as joysticks and game pads, that work with the USB port on the iBook.

Games and the iBook

Computer games are becoming more and more sophisticated. In particular, the graphics displayed by today's games demand high-quality hardware. Don't worry—the components in the iBook live up to the expectations of modern games.

iBook Game Compatibility

A good computer game displays a lot of graphics and animation, and includes plenty of high-quality sound. A good game requires good hardware to run on: lots of video memory, a fast processor, and 3D graphics acceleration. When a new, cool, game comes out, everyone wants it. But only those with the impressive machines can run it. So to keep home computer sales up, computer manufacturers have worked hard to upgrade performance without driving up prices. Games may, in fact, be the driving force in pushing the performance of home computers.

So how well suited for game playing is the hardware in the iBook? It turns out that for the buck, the iBook is a pretty decent gaming machine.

3D Graphic Acceleration

In order to adequately display 3D graphics, many recent games require that a computer be equipped with graphics acceleration. This acceleration can come in the form of a graphics card that plugs into a slot on the computer (for PCs and most Mac models), or it can be built into the computer itself (as is the case with the iBook). The first iBooks came with an ATI RAGE Mobility graphics controller for built-in 2D/3D graphics acceleration . The ATI RAGE graphics controller is soldered on to the motherboard (the main board that holds the most important chips)..

Video Memory

It wasn't too long ago that when you went to buy a personal computer you only inquired about one type of memory: the main, or RAM, memory that was just described above. As of late, though, computer buyers have had to become aware of a second type of memory: video memory.

Graphic-intense programs such as games require that a lot of memory be dedicated to the display of the game's graphics and animation. Most modern computers come with video memory—a memory that's held on a separate chip (or chips) independent of the computer's main memory. In short, for game playing, the more video memory the better. The original iBook came with a respectable 4 MB of video memory—following versions of the iBook may very well include more video memory.

Processor Speed

How fast a computer can process data is important to games—the display of a moving object requires that the computer constantly makes calculations to determine the placement of the object. How fast a computer can handle such computations is greatly dependent on how fast the computer's central processor runs. The first iBooks shipped with a 300 MHz (megahertz) PowerPC G3 microprocessor. Expect future revisions of the iBook to be equipped with a still faster processor.

Macintosh Games

Your iBook came with the Nanosaur and Bugdom games, but those games certainly won't satisfy your game cravings for long. So which games should you buy? That's a matter of personal taste, of course. But a list of some of the most popular Mac games will certainly be of assistance in your quest for the ideal game.

Myth II

Myth: The Fallen Lords, pulled in a number of awards, including Macworld's Best Game of 1997. Myth II: Soulblighter, from Bungie Software at `www.bungie.com` carries on in the tradition of the original Myth.

Myth II is a real-time 3D strategy game. There are animated windmills, drawbridges, and huge stone library where action (including exploding animals) takes place.

Note

If the term *real-time* isn't familiar to you, here's the scoop. Some games may have time pass in a manner different from how you, the game player, experience it. For instance, you could play one level of a game, move on to the next level, and find that you've moved to a different day, or month, or millennium, in the game. Such a game is *not* a real-time game. A real-time game means that time passes onscreen in the game at the same rate as time passes for you as you play the game. For every second, minute, or hour you play the game, that same amount of time passes for the characters in the game.

Unreal

Hugely popular on the PC, MacSoft www.wizworks.com/macsoft/ now brings Unreal to the Mac. With high-resolution graphics, dynamic lighting, and over a thousand frames of animation, Unreal holds your interest. There are both outdoor and indoor environments, cities, temples, ships at see, and temples to explore. Figure 13-1 shows one screen shot from this 3D action game.

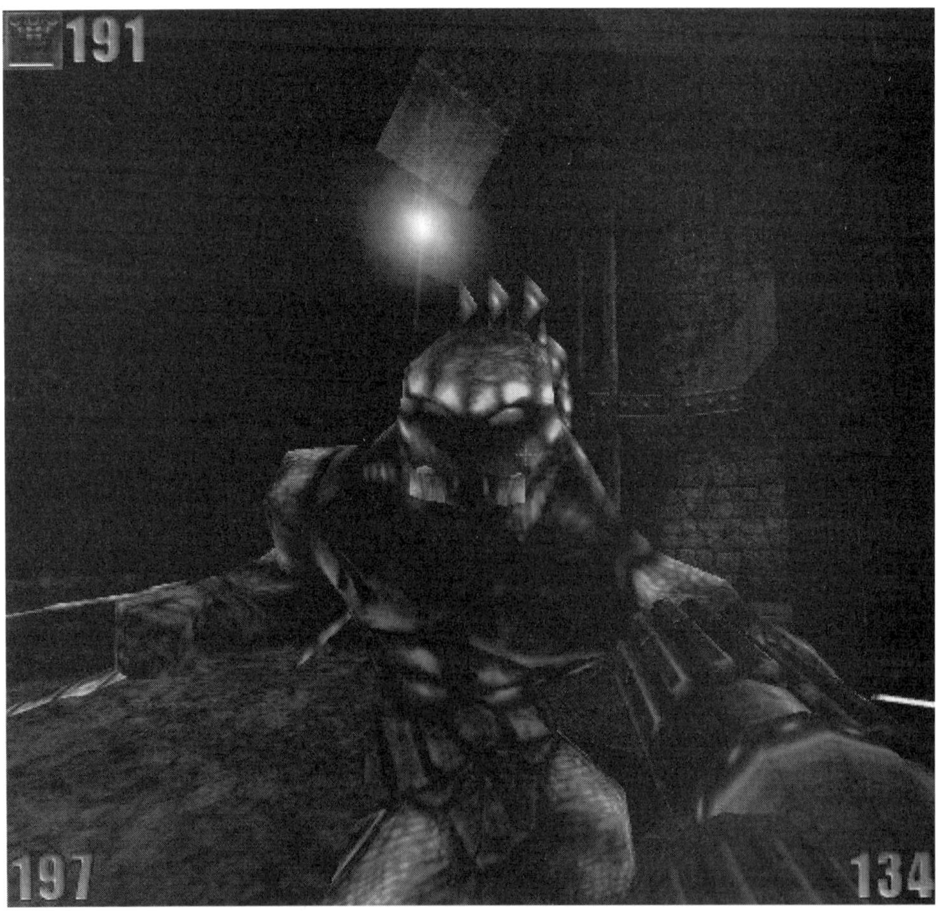

Figure 13-1 A screenshot from the game Unreal.

Duke Nukem 3D

Duke Nukem is another game distributed by MacSoft (`www.wizworks.com/macsoft/`). The popular Duke Nukem game features "39 levels of mayhem" in which Duke takes on the aliens who've landed in Los Angeles. For mature gamers, or use the password-protect feature to limit what younger players see.

Quest for Glory V: Dragon Fire

Sierra Online (`www.sierra.com/products/mac-place/`) has long been a big Mac developer, and Quest for Glory V: Dragon Fire demonstrates this company's commitment to the Macintosh. In this role-playing adventure game you choose a character, select and hone that character's skills, and then work to make that character the hero of the magical land of Silmaria.

Tomb Raider II

Tomb Raider II was created by Core Design and published on the PC by Eidos Interactive. Now Aspyr Media at `www.aspyr.com` brings this award-winning game to the Macintosh. Tomb Raider II is the second chapter (the third chapter, Tomb Raider III is now available on the PC) in the continuing adventures of explorer Lara Croft. Lara's goal is to find the Dagger of Xian, and she'll visit the Great Wall of China and much of the Eastern Hemisphere to find it.

Online Gaming Sites

If you want to download freeware or shareware games, download demos of commercial games, get information on hot new Mac games, or even get information on how to cheat at a game, the Internet is the place to be.

MacGaming.com

MacGaming.com at `www.maccentral.com/games/` is a gaming site hosted by the Mac news site MacCentral. MacGaming.com offers Mac gaming news and a wealth of detailed game reviews. Mac gaming enthusiasts will find the unique Gaming Forum of interest—here you post your own question on any issue pertinent to game playing on the Mac, and at least one other Mac gamer is bound to provide an answer. In Figure 13-2 you see the format of the forum. In the back widow someone has posted a question about USB game pads, and others have answered. Clicking on the question title displays the full question and, as shown in the front window, provides links to responses.

Mac Gamer's Ledge

As shown in Figure 13-3, the Mac Gamer's Ledge at `www.macledge.com` includes Mac gaming news, game reviews, game hints (click the gaming resources link near the bottom of the page), and more.

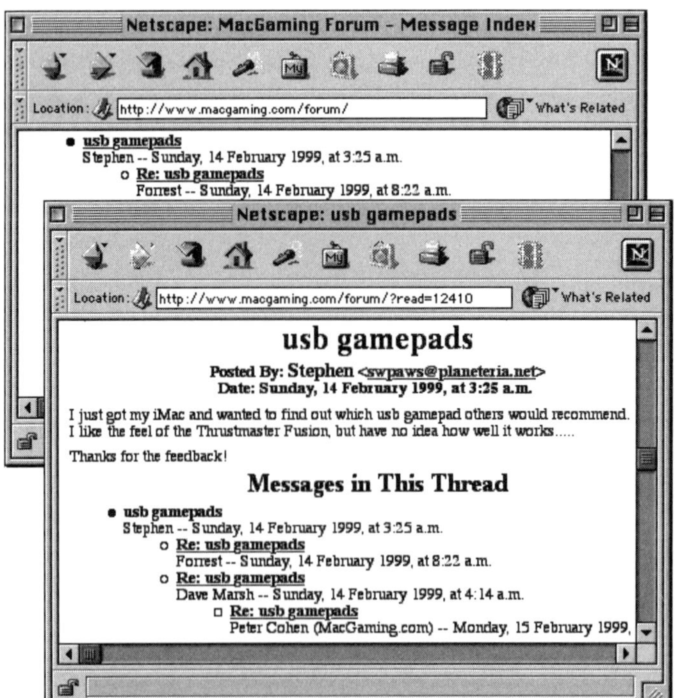

Figure 13-2 The MacGaming.com gaming forum.

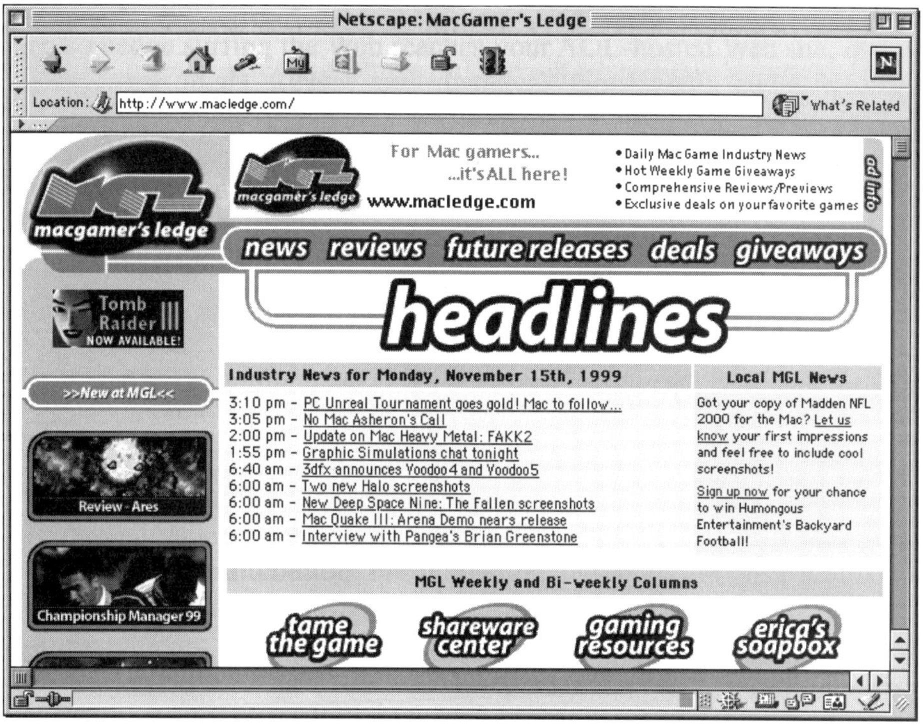

Figure 13-3 The home page of Mac Gamer's Ledge.

The Mac Gamer's Ledge review section is a good one. After clicking on the reviews link near the top of a page, click on a game name to see a very comprehensive review that includes game screen captures, overview, background, synopsis, interface, pluses and minuses, rating, and more.

Mac Game Gate

The Mac Game Gate at `www.macgate.torget.se` has Mac gaming news, game reviews, and a nice page (click the companies link near the top of the main page) that holds links to all the Web sites of the big Mac game companies such as Bungie, Broderbund, and MacSoft.

Ambrosia Software

If you're interested in shareware Mac games, make a stop at Ambrosia Software at www.AmbrosiaSW.com (make sure to include the capitalized letters, as shown here). The dozen or so games in Ambrosia's library are all top-notch action/adventure games that are easily worth their respective shareware fees. And best of all, you get to download any of them (`www.AmbrosiaSW.com/Games.html`) for a free try-before-you-buy test.

Inside Mac Games

There's a free online version of this Macintosh gaming magazine at `www.imgmagazine.com`; a more comprehensive by-subscription CD-ROM version is also available. The online magazine provides news briefs, sneak previews, review, and features. The ten-times-per-year CD-ROM version offers the same goodies, but packages it all in a magazine-like interactive interface that lets the reader play slide shows, QuickTime movies, interviews, and demos. Each CD-ROM is loaded with the latest shareware games and demos of commercial games. The CD-ROM version of Inside Mac Games can be ordered from the Inside Mac Games Web site.

Games Domain

Games Domain at `www.gamesdomain.com` is for everyone—both Mac and PC games are covered here. The main page (shown in Figure 13-4) includes current gaming events and links to several areas of the Games Domain site.

One of the most useful areas of Games Domain may be the one called Downloads. Here you find a list of hundreds of freeware and shareware Mac games—all available for downloading. Begin by clicking the Downloads link located near the top, left of the main page (see Figure 13-4). The Downloads page that is displayed allows you to choose the platform you're interested in—scroll down a bit until you see "DOWNLOADS", then click the mac link. Next, click on the category of game you're interested in to see a list of games that fall into that category. For instance, clicking on the Arcade link displays a list of dozens of games such as MacBrickout. Now click on a game name to see a description of that one game. Along with the description you'll find one or more online locations from which you can download the game—just click on one of the location links to start the download. Once you've downloaded a game, go ahead and give it a try!

Another interesting area of the Games Domain is the Games Arena. Click the Online Games button at the top of the main page (Figure 13-4) to move to `www.gamesdomain.com/GamesArena/index.html`. As shown in Figure 13-5, here you can select to enter the multiplayer game domain or the single-player game arena. Just click on the title of a game to get ready to play that game.

Once a game is selected, its opening screen appears in your browser window. There's no game file to download—you're playing right over the Internet. Figure 13-6 shows the contents of my browser window as I quickly lose a game of Outpost (one of the games listed in Figure 13-5).

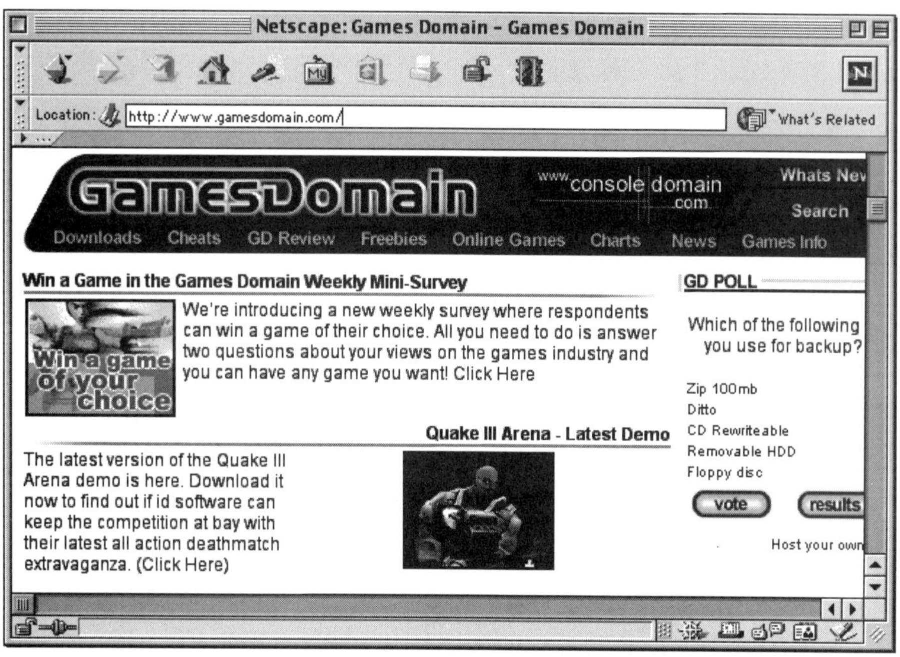

Figure 13-4 The home page of Games Domain.

Figure 13-5 Game Domain Games Arena.

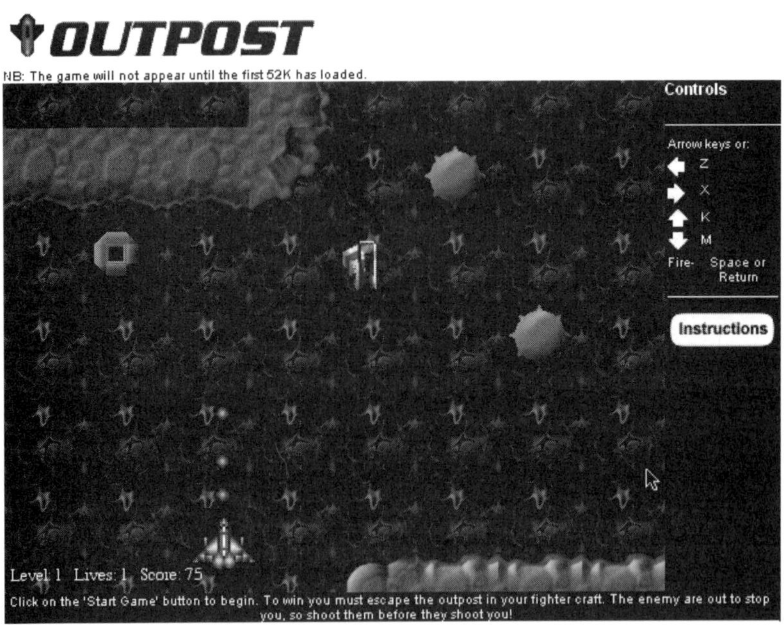

Figure 13-6 Playing Outpost online.

Online games often make use of *Java*. Java is a technology that allows programmers to write applets. An applet is a (usually) fairly small program (including a game) that can be run on a number of different types of computers (including both PCs and Macs). It's also a program that doesn't have to reside on a computer's hard drive in order to run. When a Web browser encounters a Web page that holds an applet, the browser automatically downloads the applet to the computer's memory. From there the browser can run the applet. You don't need to know the details of Java technology or Java programming in order to make use of Java—your Web browser does the work for you. When playing online games, though, a couple of Java-related tips are in order.

In order to get an applet started you may have to click on it. In Figure 13-6 the entire playing area (the "battlefield") is the applet, so a click anywhere on the area is enough to "activate" the game.

If the online game you're playing works fine, then this second tip isn't needed. If you're using Microsoft's Internet Explorer as your Web browser, and things don't seem to be going to smoothly (such as the game isn't responding to keystrokes), then read on. Java is possible because Web browsers have built-in Java virtual machine. A Java virtual machine is fancy name for a miniprogram of sorts that is able to understand Java code. Some browsers include more than one Java virtual machine, though the browser can only use one at a time. If an online game isn't working right, then perhaps your browser can't quite figure out the Java code in the applet that's a part of the game. In such a case, change the Java virtual machine that the browser is using. That's a simple task. In Microsoft's Internet Explorer, choose **Preferences** from the **Edit** menu. then click on Java under the Web Browser category in the scrollable list—as done in Figure 13-7. Now click on the pop-up menu labeled Java virtual machine. In Figure 13-7 I needed to choose the Microsoft Virtual Machine from this menu in order to get my iBook to properly run the Outpost game shown back in Figure 13-6.

The Codebook

No matter how hard you try, you just can't get to the next level. You're frustrated with the adventure game, and you need a little help. Yeah, that's right, you just need a little help. It's not really cheating, is it? Of course it isn't. So don't feel bad when you visit the codebook at `www.codebook.pp.se` to get some tips on how to beat some of the most popular Mac games. As shown in Figure 13-8, the upper-left section of the codebook lists categories: cheats (which tell you exactly what to do to succeed at something), strategy guides (which offer more general tips that help you get through a level of a game), and walkthroughs (which help you get from the start of a game all the way through to the end). Click on a category and in the lower-left section you'll see a list of Mac games for which information is available. Click on a game name and information pertinent to that game appears in the main section. In Figure 13-8 I clicked on Walkthroughs, then Monkey Island 2 in order to get information about how to get from start to finish in the popular game Monkey Island 2.

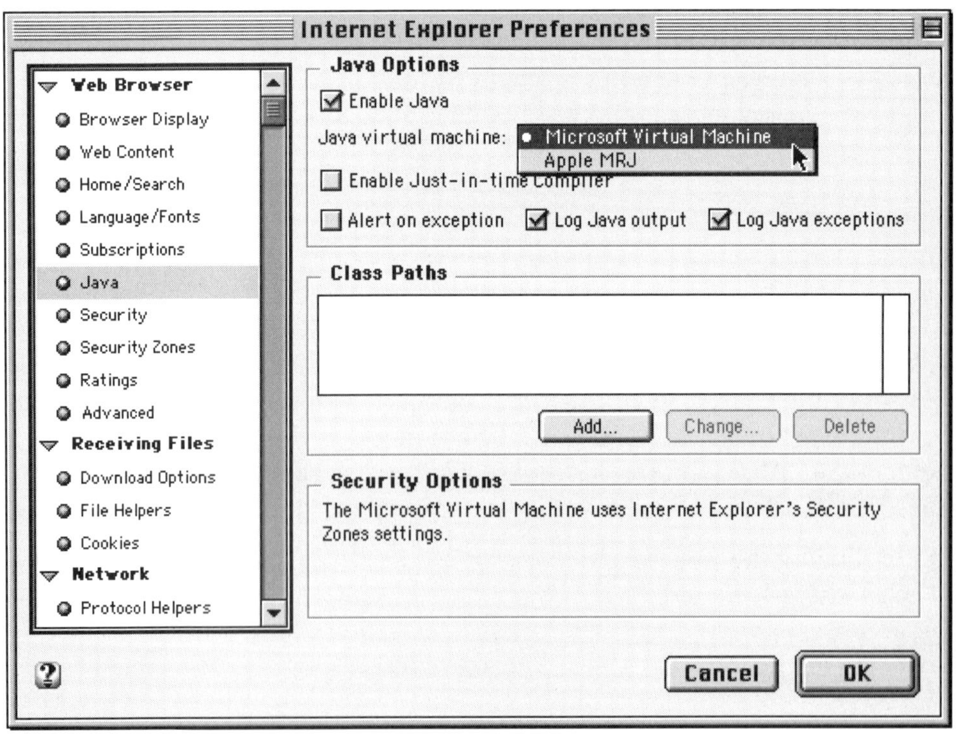

Figure 13-7 Change the Java virtual machine in Internet Explorer.

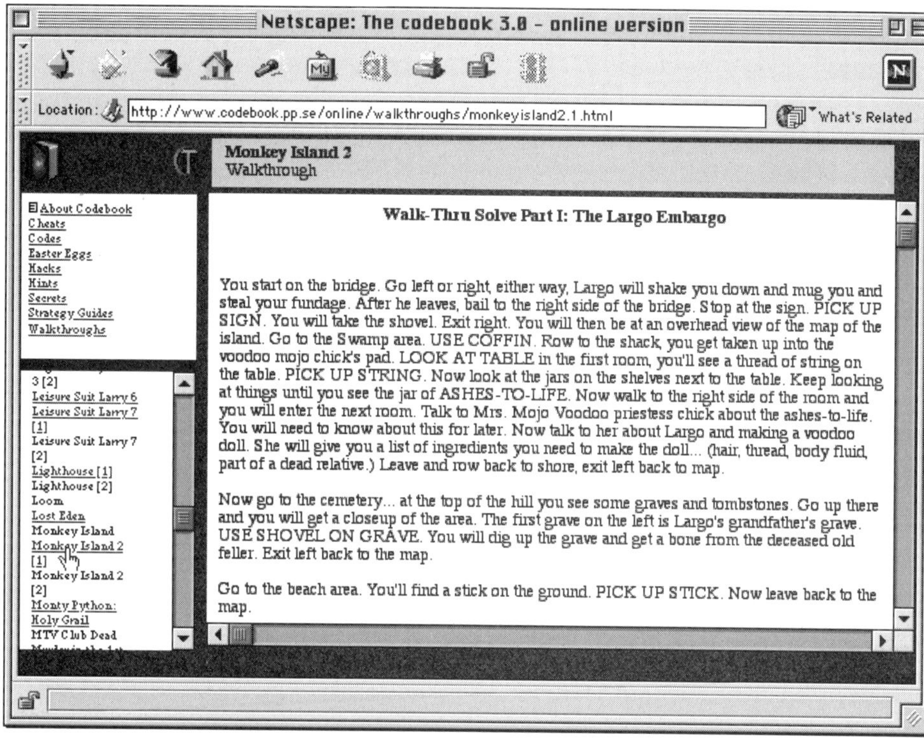

Figure 13-8 Getting help with an adventure game.

Game Controllers

In introducing the iMac, Apple also introduced USB (Universal System Bus) to Mac users—the iMac was the first Macintosh to forego ADB (Apple Desktop Bus) as a device input port in favor of USB. Now new Mac models—including the iBook—use USB as their means of connecting an optional game controller.

Because many PCs already made use of USB at the time Apple switched to USB, there were a lot of USB controllers on the market. To make a USB controller useable on an iBook, a company doesn't have to redesign the controller—it only has to develop a Mac software driver (the small software program that lets the Macintosh system software understand the information transmitted from a device). With over two million potential iMac buyers out there, a lot of companies did do just that—they developed those drivers to bring their controllers to the iMac—and now to the iBook. And that's good news for iBook game players.

Joysticks

A joystick can be used with any game, but its best use is for flight simulators and other games where the user maneuvers about in three-dimensional surroundings.

CH Products Gamestick 3D USB Joystick

The Gamestick 3D USB joystick (shown in Figure 13-9) from CH Products has four buttons and a four-way hat switch. If you're a lefty you'll appreciate that CH Products claims that this joystick's 3D Twisting Action Handle is an ambidextrous handle.

Figure 13-9 CH Products Gamestick 3D USB.

ThrustMaster Top Gun USB Joystick

The Top Gun USB joystick (see Figure 13-10), from ThrustMaster, represents the high end of the controller market. Great for flight simulations and adventure games, this joystick comes with three buttons and a four-way hat switch. The Top Gun joystick has a weighted base and a neoprene grip that's good for long sessions.

Figure 13-10 The Top Gun USB joystick.

Game Pads

For arcade-style games nothing tops a game pad. A game pad, like the controllers that come with game consoles such as the Sega Saturn system, works great for controlling the action in sports, fighting, and other action games.

CH Products USB Gamepad

CH Products makes a number of game pads and joysticks, including the USB joystick mentioned in this chapter's *CH Products Gamestick 3D USB Joystick* section. One of CH Products newest products is the USB Gamepad (see Figure 13-11), which can be bought in black or an iBook-matching teal/opaque.

The USB Gamepad includes ten buttons and an eight-way directional pad. An ergonomic design and an eight-foot cable with a USB connector complete this inexpensive game pad.

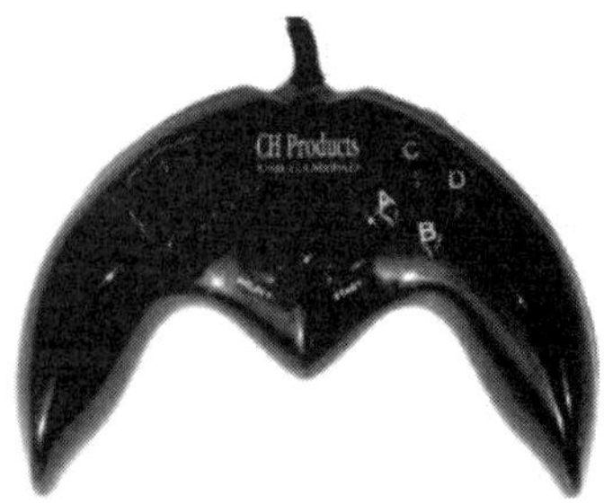

Figure 13-11 The CH Products USB Game Pad.

Gravis GamePad Pro USB Game Pad

Gravis' best-selling game pad is it's digital GamePad Pro USB game pad. Shown in Figure 13-12, this game pad has a thumb-controlled direction pad with a detachable joystick handle, features high precision and instantaneous response, and includes a built-in Y-cable connector to allow for the easy connection of multiple game pads.

Figure 13-12 The GamePad Pro USB game pad.

14

Building Your Own Web Site

You know that visiting Web pages is a great way to get information. But what about *giving* information? If you have something to say, or something to sell, to the world, then you should have your own Web page. People who don't have their own Web presence usually have two concerns that prevent them from becoming a part of the Web: the cost of obtaining a Web site and the technical knowledge required for creating a Web page. Both of these fears are unfounded. First, anyone with Internet access (whether through America Online or an Internet Service Provider) already has a "blank," ready-to-be-filled-in-with-whatever-you-want Web site ready and waiting—no extra charge. Second, filling in this free site with information involves little more than creating a text file that holds a few simple commands. Determining your own Web site's URL, and filling that site with content, are the topics of this chapter.

Your Web Site May Already Exist

As discussed in Chapter 6, an Internet site is one of the many university, business, or government computers that are linked together to form the Internet. Your iBook isn't a part of the Internet—even when you're logged onto the Internet. Instead, you and your computer are just Internet visitors. When you log onto the Internet, you're first connecting to a much larger computer system that is in fact a true part of the Internet. How do you actually become a part of the Internet? That is, how do you host your own Internet site that other

Web surfers can visit? Typically, you lease disk space on one of the server computers of a large business site. America Online has a huge disk capacity set aside just for this purpose for AOL members. Most Internet Service Providers have a large amount of disk space reserved for their members too.

If you're signed up with America Online, you already have server space reserved just for your own Web page—read the next section to learn about it. If you instead access the Internet by way of an Internet Service Provider, then you too may also already have your own private server space—skip the *Your Web Site: For AOL Users* section and go to the *Your Web Site: For ISP Users* section that follows it.

Your Web Site: For AOL Users

America Online (AOL) has over 15 million members—so there's a good chance that you're one of them. If that's the case, then you should be aware of the fact that AOL automatically sets aside 10 MB of disk space on its servers for each and every one of these millions of users. This space is reserved for each member, so it's there for the using.

America Online has a server called *members.aol.com* that is dedicated to America Online members—any AOL member can use it to easily store the file or files that define a Web page. After setting it up, your home page is accessible to everyone browsing the Web. As with visiting any Web site, all a person needs to know is the address (the URL) of your Web page. That is, someone surfing the Web doesn't need to be an AOL user to access your AOL-based Web page.

Since all AOL users have their Web pages on the *members.aol.com* server, all AOL user Web sites include "members.aol.com" in their URL. The file or files that define the contents of a user's Web site are kept on this server in a directory with the same name as the user's screen name (sometimes referred to as the *user name*). The format of the URL of your Web page is as follows:

```
http://members.aol.com/screenname
```

As an example, if your AOL screen name happens to be DanSydow, your Web page has the following URL:

```
http://members.aol.com/DanSydow
```

Your URL isn't case-sensitive, so a user could also enter the following URL into a Web browser and still make it to the same Web page:

```
http://members.aol.com/dansydow
```

If a screen name includes spaces, they're omitted when typing in the URL. So if my screen name was Be Bop 99, then my Web page URL would be:

```
http://members.aol.com/BeBop99
```

If you surf on over to your own AOL-provided Web page you'll see that the page is initially empty. We'll change that in the course of this chapter. After working with AOL's Web tools for even just a few minutes, you'll find that AOL is a great place for a Web novice to set up his or her own page. You don't need any special telephone lines or connections or additional software—you'll do everything by simply logging onto AOL and working within your existing AOL account. And, perhaps best of all, there's no cost to create or maintain your Web page!

Your Web Site: For ISP Users

When you sign up with an Internet Service Provider for Internet connection service, you're often provided with Web site space on one of the ISP's servers. Some ISPs offer a hierarchy of services, such as Basic, Intermediate, and Premium. With such an ISP the lower-level service may not automatically provide you with Web site space. Typically, a service provider will let you upgrade at any time to a higher level (usually for about $10 per month) if you're interested in using the provider's server. To find out about the Web site services provided by your ISP, read over the documentation the ISP provided to you when you signed up, or visit the ISP's Web page.

If you read the previous section, *Your Web Site: For AOL Users*, you know that each AOL member has his or her own Web site with a URL that follows this convention:

```
http://members.aol.com/screenname
```

Like AOL, each ISP has a URL convention for its members—usually based on the name of the ISP's server computer that holds member disk space. So, while a single ISP has a URL format it uses for all its members, each ISP has a different format. In other words, if you're signed up with an Internet Service Provider, and that ISP has server space reserved for you, I can't tell you your URL. To determine your Web site's URL, you need to either consult the documentation your ISP sent you or visit their Web site.

It Can Get Complicated

Gaining Internet access from one ISP does *not* mean you need to also use that same provider to host your Web site. You can sign up with one ISP for Internet access, then sign up with a Web hosting provider for Web hosting services (you might do that if you find a Web hosting provider that is very inexpensive, or offers special services that you need). A Web hosting provider reserves server space for the files that make up your Web site, and they do so in such a way that they can be accessed at a unique URL that you buy. Here's an example. I have an account with a national ISP named IDT `www.idt.net`. When I log on to the Internet I do so through a local phone number that connects me to the IDT server. I subscribe to IDT's inexpensive Basic service, which doesn't include Web hosting. IDT does offer such a package, but I've instead opted to have my Web site hosted by a different provider—Verio at `www.verio.com`. Verio go me a URL that's easy for people to remember—provided you remember my last name. You'll find my Web site at `www.sydow.com`. The files that make up this site are stored on Verio's server.

To further complicate matters I have an America Online account. Because AOL always provides members with Web space, I also automatically have a Web site hosted by America Online. That site is at `members.aol.com/dansydow`. Because Verio offers a better hosting package (more server space to hold my files, a URL of my choice, and so forth), I don't maintain my free AOL Web site.

Once you know your Web site's address, feel free to enter it in your Web browser and visit it. When you get there, however, you'll be a bit disappointed to find that there's little to be found in the way of content. In fact, your Web browser might even report that the Web site couldn't be found. Supplying you with Web site space is your ISP's responsibility. Making use of that space is up to you. How you go about creating a Web page is the topic of the balance of this chapter.

Web Pages and HTML

HTML, short for *HyperText Markup Language*, is the language of the World Wide Web. An HTML document is a text file that holds the commands that specify how a Web page should be laid out. These commands control such things as where text and graphics should appear on a Web page. The commands also specify text characteristics such as size. A Web browser that opens an HTML file is then responsible for properly displaying text and graphics as specified by the HTML commands that are a part of the file.

HTML Files and Web Browsers

A Web browser's primary job is to decipher the HTML commands in a file and properly display the file based on those commands. You're used to using your browser to surf the Web, so you know that your Web browser examines and displays HTML fIles located at various Web sites around the world. But you should also be aware that you can use your Web browser to open and display HTML files that are located on the hard drive of your own iBook. That is, you can use your Web browser even when you aren't connected to the Internet. Why is this feature of note to you? Because it turns out to be a great way to test out your HTML file from your iBook before you ever send it to its eventual final destination—the disk space provided to you by AOL or your ISP.

An HTML file is a text file that holds HTML code and has a file name that ends with *.html* or *.htm*. For instance, if you see a file on your hard drive that has a name such as *index.html*, *myWebPage.html*, or *biography.htm*, it's a pretty safe guess that you've encountered an HTML file. Any such file can be opened right from your hard drive by your Web browser of choice. In all cases, you open an HTML file from the standard Open File window—the window displayed by any Mac program that has an **Open** item in its **File** menu. Use this window to work your way to the HTML file on your hard drive, then double-click the file's name to open it. The browser displays the file's contents in a browser window—just as it would if it came across the file while surfing the Web. To get to the standard Open File dialog box, just follow these simple instructions:

Netscape Navigator Run Navigator, then select **Open File** from the **File** menu. The Open File window appears to allow you to open the HTML file.

Microsoft Internet Explorer Run Internet Explorer, then choose **Open File** from the **File** menu. Open the HTML file from the standard Open File window that appears.

America Online Run America Online, then choose **Open** from the **File** menu. Open the HTML file from the standard Open File window that appears. Selecting an HTML file signals AOL that you may be attempting to access the Internet. If you aren't currently logged on to AOL, you may face an alert that informs you that you need to be signed on. Don't fret—just dismiss the alert. After doing that you'll still be in the America Online program, and the HTML file will open in AOL's Web browser.

You'll be using your Web browser as described above to display your own HTML file. When you're satisfied that your file is working and worthy of viewing by the rest of the world, you'll upload it to your space on the AOL or ISP server—a process discussed later in this chapter. To get a hint of what HTML code looks like (and then to verify that you can open an HTML file from your iBook's hard drive), I'll create a very simple HTML file right now.

The editor you use to create an HTML file is unimportant—provided you save the file as an unformatted text file. That is, if you use a word processor such as Microsoft Word, save the file using the text file option (available as the **Text Only** item in the popup menu at the bottom of the Save As window) rather than as a Microsoft Word document. Since the SimpleText text editor that came with your iBook always saves files in this required text file format, I'd suggest you avoid mistakes by using that program for now. After starting your editor of choice, type the following in the empty window that appears. Type everything exactly as shown, making sure to dot all your t's and cross all your i's (or something like that):

```
<html>
<head>
<title>My Own Home Page</title>
</head>
<body>
<h1>Welcome to My Home Page</h1>
<hr>
I've got an Apple iBook computer.
<p>
</body>
</html>
```

Save the file, giving it a name of *index.html*. You could give the file a different name (provided the name ended with *.htm* or *.html*), but for reasons that become evident later in this chapter, it's best to give it the name *index.html*. Make a mental note of where on your hard drive you're saving the file to so that you'll be able to find it when you open it from your Web browser.

Now, use your Web browser to open the file. When you do that, the contents of the file will be displayed as a Web page—as shown in Figure 14-1. Note that the window has a title, the displayed text appears in different sizes, and that much of the text you typed into the HTML file isn't present in the window. In particular, notice that the pairs of angle brackets and any text that appeared between them (such as `<title>`, `<hr>`, and so forth) aren't displayed in the browser window. Those bracketed items are HTML commands, and are used to tell the browser how to display text.

Figure 14-1 A very minimal Web page.

That's it, you've created a Web page! Of course, simply typing what you were told to type left a few issues unexplained. Chiefly, you'll need to learn how to determine what HTML codes to use and where to use them. That topic is covered next—just after this brief, reassuring message. . . .

Have No Fear of HTML!

If words and phrases such as *computer language*, *code*, and *programming* cause you to break out in hives, they shouldn't. Not when it comes to HTML, anyway. So, stop right now, take a deep breath, and read this short section.

Typically, most of what appears on a Web page is just text. There may be some graphic images and some *hypertext links* (key words, phrases, or graphic images that, when clicked on, take the user to a different page), but the majority of the content of most Web pages is nothing more than text. Consequently, an HTML file also consists mostly of the words that are to appear on a Web page. You may have heard people talk about *HTML code and HTML programming*. Don't let that kind of talk give you the impression that you need programming skills in order to create your own Web page—because you don't! You simply need an understanding of at least a *few* of the many commands that are a part of the HyperText Markup Language.

Figure 14-2 shows a window displaying some of the text in a file created with the text editor program SimpleText. Take a moment to examine the text in that window before continuing on.

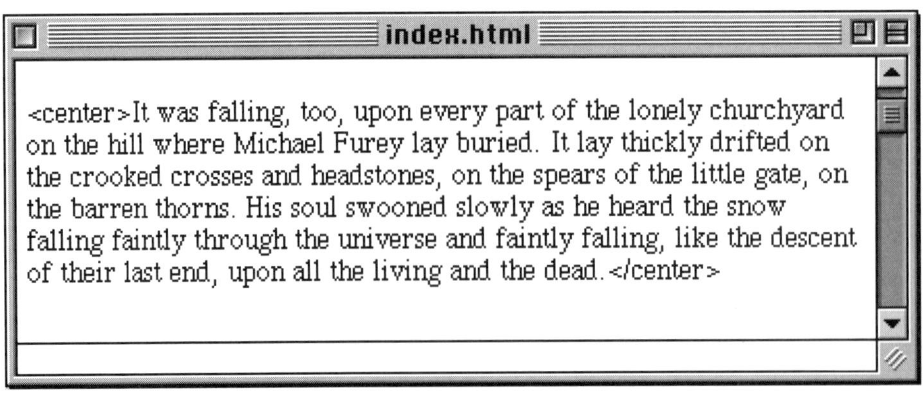

Figure 14-2 A part of an HTML file.

Figure 14-2 shows a part of the contents of an HTML file. Note that there's nothing particularly striking about the contents of the file. With the exception of the somewhat odd-looking `<center>` and `</center>` that precede and follow the rest of the text, there's nothing remarkable about the file's contents. (What *would* be remarkable is if I had been the one to originally pen the words in that file. Instead, they're from the ending of the British author James Joyce's short story "*The Dead*".) If you haven't already guessed it, `<center>` is an HTML command that tells a Web browser to center whatever follows the command. The HTML command `</center>` tells the browser to stop centering. Note the slash in the command. When a starting command (such as `<center>`) is paired with an ending command (such as `</center>`), the ending command is the same as the starting command, but is preceded by a slash. Simple enough. Figure 14-3 shows how a Web browser would display the HTML file shown in Figure 14-2. In this figure, you see that each line of text is centered in the browser window. Resizing the browser window changes the amount of text displayed on each line, but regardless of the text displayed each line will always end up centered in the window.

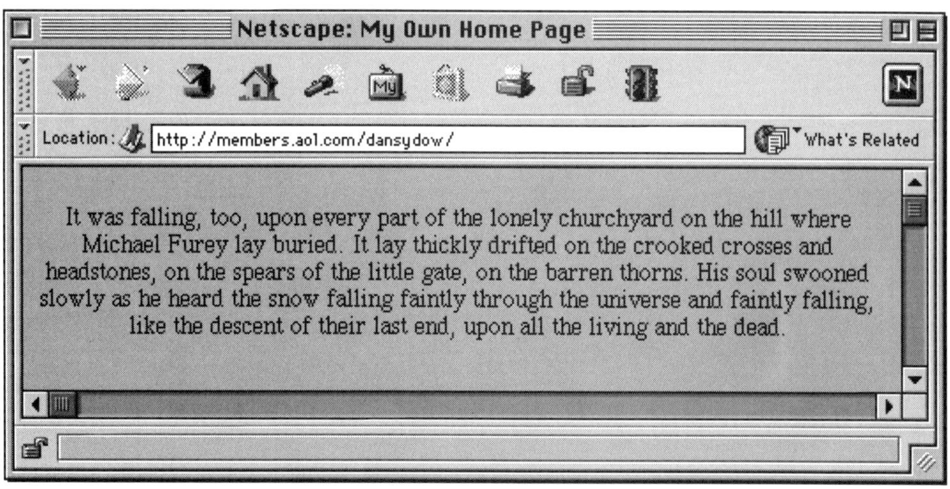

Figure 14-3 A Web page with centered text.

What important point can we glean from this discussion? You should now believe that HTML is nothing to be feared! HTML is your friend! An HTML file looks much like any of the many memos, letters, or reports that you've created with a word processor—with a number of angle brackets and other bric-a-brac thrown in. The main difference between the type of file you normally create and an HTML file is that "bric-a-brac" I just mentioned. What appears as gibberish mixed in with "normal" words are, as you now know, HTML commands.

HTML Authoring Options

So far I've only shown HTML files as created using a text editor program. But there are, in fact, four types of programs available for creating HTML files: text editors, HTML text editors, graphical (WYSIWYG) editors, and HTML converters. Let's take a brief look at each type.

Text Editors

You've already seen an example of this, the most basic HTML-creation tool. An HTML file is a text file, so you can create one with a text editor such as Apple's SimpleText. You can also create an HTML file with a word processor—provided you save the file using the word processors **Text Only** format (typically available as an item in a popup menu in the word processor's Save As window).

HTML Text Editors

Some text editors have been enhanced to make creating HTML files easier. On the Mac, BBEdit, by Bare Bone's Software, is the best known. BBEdit has HTML-friendly features such as the ability to color-code HTML commands so that they stand out in an HTML file, and a spell checker that knows about HTML. Visit `www.barebones.com` for more information.

Graphical (WYSIWYG) Editors

To shield the user from HTML code, some editors have a graphical interface that allows the user to piece together an HTML file, similar to the way a formatted document is produced using a word processor. Of these WYSIWYG (*What You See Is What You Get*) editors, PageMill by Adobe is one of the most popular. As shown in Figure 14-4, PageMill works by letting the user stylize text or add other effects by choosing menu items. When the document is completed, PageMill inserts the appropriate HTML commands and saves the document as an HTML file.

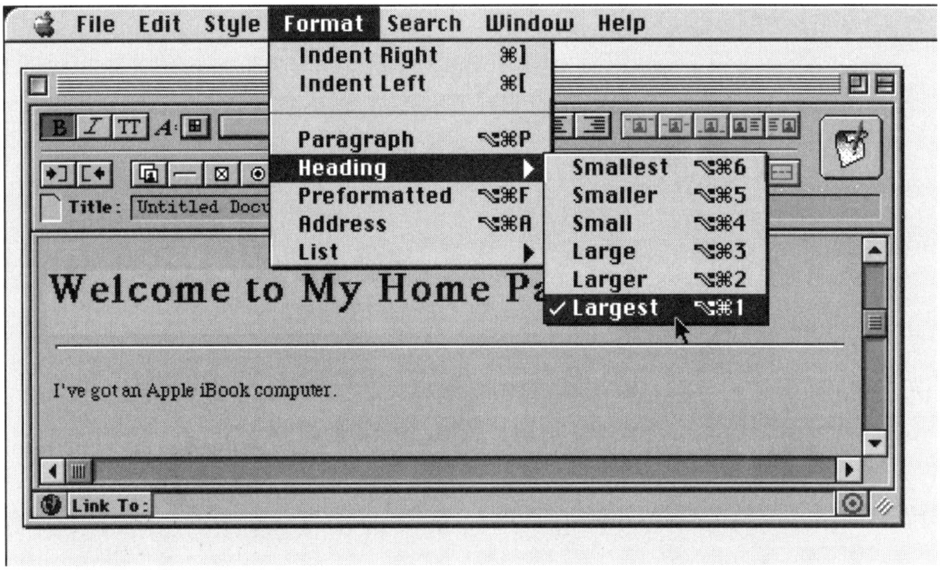

Figure 14-4 Using Adobe PageMill to create an HTML file.

HTML Converters

Some recent versions of word processors include an option that allows one to save a text file as an HTML file. Word 98 Macintosh Edition, for example, includes a **Save as HTML** item in its **File** menu. When you choose that menu item, Word adds HTML commands to your document in an attempt to create an HTML file that, when opened with a Web browser, displays the content as it appeared when viewed in Word. For instance, if you place a phrase in bold in your Word document, then save that document as HTML code, Word will insert an HTML bold command (which, if you're curious, looks like this: <b>) in the appropriate place.

Why Learn HTML?

With tools such as graphical editors and HTML converters available, why bother learning about HTML? As discussed next, there are a couple of compelling reasons.

You Can Do It Better Than They Can

A program that generates HTML files doesn't always produce the same HTML code you would yourself—it looks at what you've typed and takes a "best guess" at the look it thinks you were hoping to produce. Generally, the results are pretty good. But if you want to make subtle—or sometimes not so subtle—changes to the file generated by the program, you'll have a tough time of it if you don't know any HTML.

You Can Learn From the HTML Code of Others

Another reason to learn HTML is so that you can enhance your Web page by mimicking the look of other well-done sites you encounter on the Web. That word *mimicking* sounds suspiciously like we're in the territory of copyright infringement, so a little clarification is in order.

Generally, you can't legally copy the *content* of someone else's Web page and include it on your own site. For instance, without written permission from the creator of an online magazine's Web site, you can't copy an article from that site and display it on your own page. You can, however, determine the HTML code used to generate some interesting effect on someone else's Web site and use similar HTML code on your own Web site. Many sites play background music, run simple animated scenes, or let visitors download files. Looking at the HTML code for a Web page that produces one or more of these tricks is a good (and legitimate) way to include the desired effect on your own page. In fact, your Web browser makes it easy to see what the HTML file of any Web page looks like. To do that, first visit the Web page of interest. Then, save the page as an HTML file by doing one of the following:

Netscape Navigator Select **Save** as from the **File** menu. Choose the **Source** option from the pop-up menu at the bottom of the standard Save File window that appears.

Microsoft Internet Explorer Choose **Save As** from the **File** menu. Select the **HTML Source** option from the pop-up menu located near the bottom of the standard Save File window that appears.

America Online Select **Save As** from the **File** menu. Choose the **HTML Source** item from the pop-up menu found at the bottom of the standard Save File window that appears.

The resulting text file can be opened from a word processor (like Microsoft Word) or a text editor (such as Apple's SimpleText). When it's opened, you can see that the file includes the HTML commands used to generate the original Web page. If you know HTML, you'll most likely be able to find the code that produced the effect you like.

HTML Basics

What I've been calling an HTML command is more formally referred to as a *tag*. A tag designates where different elements start or end on a Web page. Knowing just a few of these tags means that you can tell Web-novices that you know HTML. Becoming familiar with a larger number of these tags, however, is important if you want to convince Web-savvy people that you know HTML. In the remainder of this chapter we'll look at a handful of tags, meaning that you'll be able to convince at least a small number of people that you indeed know the HyperText Markup language!

Tip
The specification that defines the HyperText Markup Language is in the hands of W3C—the World Wide Web Consortium (whose online presence can be found at `www.w3.org`. The complete specification for the most current version of HTML (4.0 as of this writing) can be found at `www.w3.org/TR/REC-html40/`.

HTML Tag Format

An HTML tag is always enclosed by the < and > characters. It's the inclusion of these characters that enable a Web browser to sort out which text is text to display and which text is meant to be a formatting command. You've already seen a number of HTML tags in this chapter, including: `<html>`, `<head>`, `<hr>` and `<h1>`.

Both a start tag and an end tag are necessary to define some page elements. Obviously, a start tag signals the start of an element while the end tag denotes the end of that same element. When a command has both a start tag and an end tag associated with it, then you can assume that the end tag is the same as its corresponding start tag, prefaced by the slash character (/). Here's an example that uses the <b> start tag and </b> end tag to declare that the words "the end" appear in boldface text:

```
Without question, this is <b>the end</b> of the road.
```

As shown in the above line, when a command is to affect whatever follows the tag, the start tag marks the format beginning, while the end tag marks the format ending. Some other elements require only a single tag. An example is a *horizontal rule*. A horizontal rule is a horizontal line that's typically used to separate two parts of a Web page. Figure 14-4 shows a horizontal rule between the two lines of text on the displayed Web page. To create a horizontal rule, you'll use the <hr> tag. There is no complimentary </hr> tag.

Tip

HTML code itself *isn't* case-sensitive. That is, no distinction is made between uppercase and lowercase characters. So it's up to you whether your HTML code appears in uppercase or lowercase. To a Web browser reading an HTML file, it's all the same. For example, both <hr> and <HR> are valid tags and both have the same effect: the generation of a horizontal rule. The examples in this book use lowercase for HTML tags.

HTML Page Format

A Web browser can't open just any file and display it as a properly formatted Web page would be displayed. When a browser opens a file from disk (or loads a file it encounters while connected to the Web), it examines the file for an <html> tag. This tag denotes the start of an HTML file. The browser then attempts to properly format the contents of the file—right up until it encounters an </html> end tag. The large blocked area in Figure 14-5 indicates that the example's entire HTML code is considered an HTML page.

Between the <html> start tag and the </html> end tag should be a head and a body. The file *head* contains the title of the page. This title will appear in the title bar of the browser window that's displaying the HTML file. As expected, the tags <head> and </head> mark the start and end of the head.

The upper block of the two shaded blocks in Figure 14-5 represents the head of the example HTML file.

The *body* defines the content of the Web page. Everything you see on a Web page is considered the page's body. The tags `<body>` and `</body>` mark the start and end of the body. The lower block of the two shaded blocks in Figure 8-5 holds the HTML code that defines the example's body.

```
<html>

<head>
<title>My Own Home Page</title>
</head>

<body>
<h1>Welcome to My Home Page</h1>
<hr>
I've got an Apple iBook computer.
<p>
</body>

</html>
```

Figure 14-5 Some of the most basic HTML tags.

Basic HTML Tags

There are over one hundred tags defined in the HyperText Markup Language—but you only need to know a dozen or so to really get started in Web site-creation.

Document Structure Tags

You're well on your way to knowing the most basic tags. You've already seen the tags that define the overall structure of an HTML document. Those tags consisted of: `<html>`, `</html>`, `<head>`, `</head>`, `<body>`, and `</body>`. Of those tags, the head start and end tags are worthy of additional comment.

Between the `<head>` and `</head>` tags lie the title tags. The head of a Web page contains the page's title. That title comes from the use of the title start tag, `<title>`, and end tag, `</title>`. When a Web browser encounters these tags, it uses the text that lies between this pair of tags as the title of the *window* that holds the page. The example HTML listing presented earlier included this code:

```
<title>My Own Home Page</title>
```

If you've typed the example in and saved it to a text file, open that file now with a Web browser to verify that the browser window has the title *My Own Home Page*. As an exercise, change the text that lies between the title tags (if it's to be your Web page, go ahead and include your own name). Save the file, and then click the load or reload button on your browser to force the browser to use the new contents of the HTML file as it redisplays the page.

Heading Tags

When you write a report for work or school, it often includes bold or underlined headings to separate the paper's topics or themes. You can achieve the same effect in your Web page by using a pair of heading tags. To create the largest, boldest heading, use the first level start and end tags (`<h1>` and `</h1>`) with the text of the heading between them. The next-largest-size heading is accomplished by using the `<h2>` and `</h2>` tags. In all, you can display any of six different sized headings. Figure 14-6 shows what a browser displays when it encounters this bit of HTML code:

```
<h1>Heading, level 1</h1>
<h2>Heading, level 2</h2>
<h3>Heading, level 3</h3>
<h4>Heading, level 4</h4>
<h5>Heading, level 5</h5>
<h6>Heading, level 6</h6>
Text that isn't a heading
```

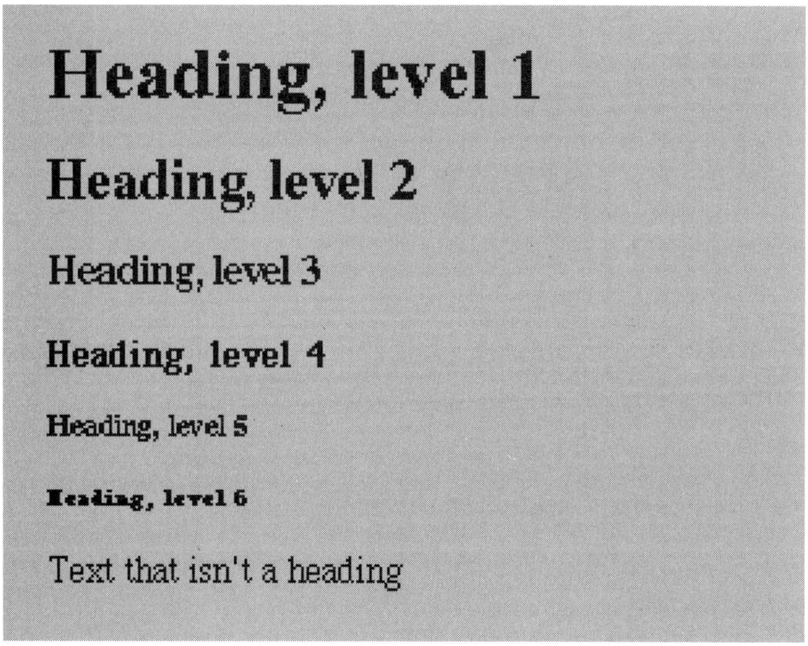

Figure 14-6 The various levels of headings.

Line-ending Tags

Run a text editor such as SimpleText and type in a paragraph of text. Don't press the Return key after each line is entered, just type in the entire paragraph. Then resize the SimpleText window. When you do, the text *word-wraps*. That is, it resizes itself along with the window, as shown in Figure 14-7. If the text you typed becomes a part of an HTML file and is opened by a Web browser, you'll see the same effect when you resize the browser window—the text flows to fit the size of the window.

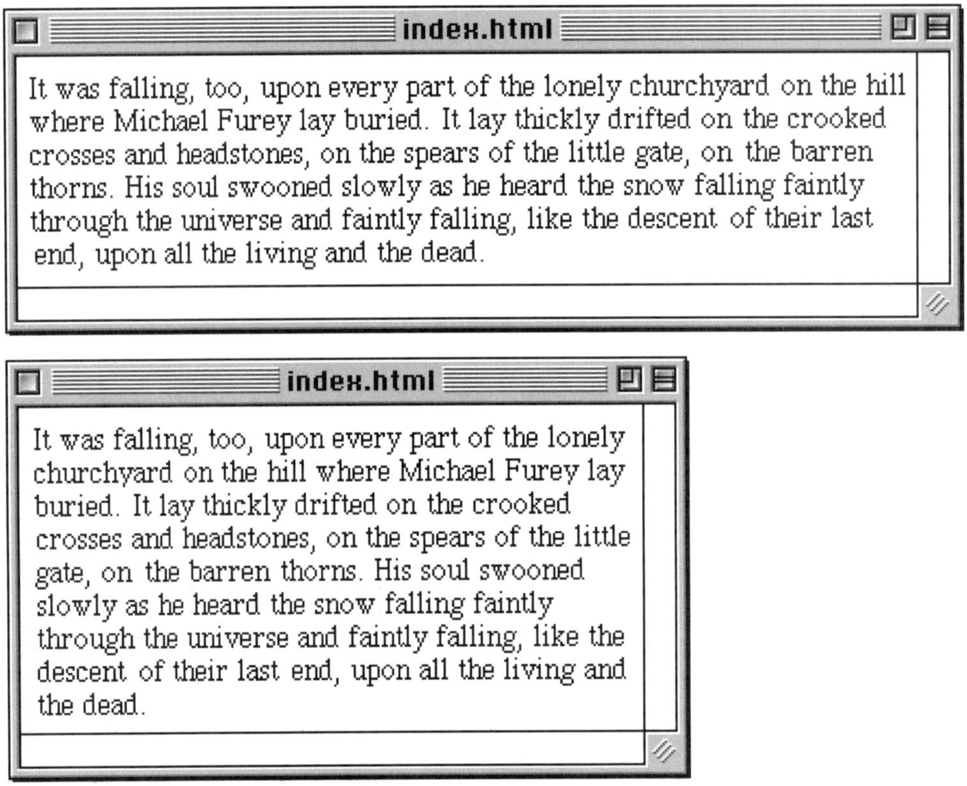

Figure 14-7 Text in a text editor flows with the size of the window.

Word-wrapping is how you'll typically want your Web page text to behave. But there will be instances when you want to force a line of text to end at a particular place—regardless of the size of the browser window displaying the text. To force a break in the displayed text, include a line break tag. When a browser encounters a **
** tag, it begins the next word it encounters on a new line. Consider the following HTML code. Before looking over Figure 14-8, take a guess at how a Web browser would display the words.

```
It was falling, too, upon every part <br>of the
lonely churchyard on the hill where Michael Furey<br>
lay buried. It lay thickly<br> drifted on the
crooked <br>crosses and headstones, on the spears
of the little <br>gate, on the barren thorns.
```

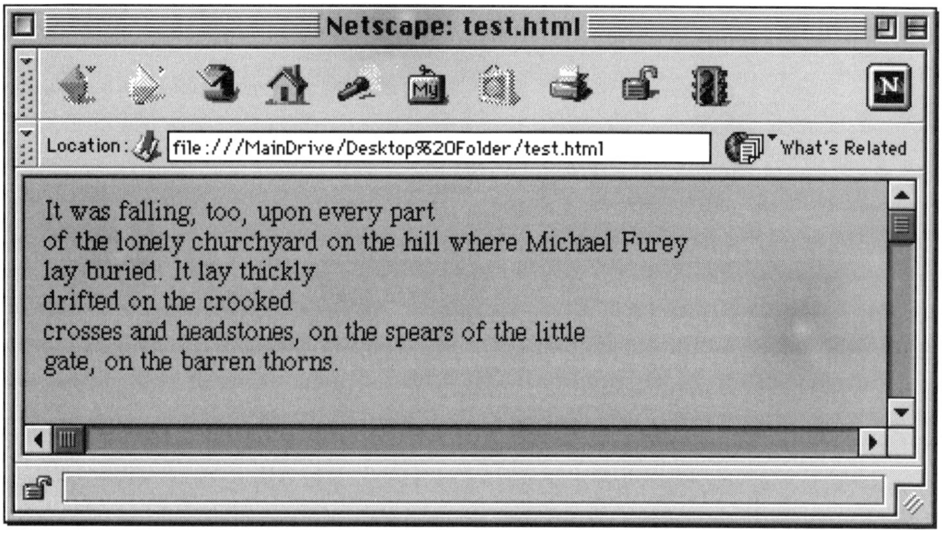

Figure 14-8 The <br> tag forces a line break.

Using a <br> tag forces an end to a line of text and causes the subsequent text to appear on the next line. But it doesn't add any extra space between the two lines. If you want to end one line and begin a new paragraph, you'll use the paragraph tag rather than the break tag. The <p> tag marks the end of one line and the start of another, but it also adds the "white space" that is typically found between paragraphs. Like the <br> tag, the <p> tag has no corresponding end tag.

Divider Tag

Headings are one way to divide a Web page into sections. Another means of visually separating one part of a page from another is by using the horizontal rule tag. The <hr> tag inserts a horizontal divider between sections of a Web page. Jump way back to Figure 14-1 to see an example of what a horizontal rule looks like.

Creating Your Home Page HTML File

Every Web site consists of at least one HTML document—the file that serves as the site's home page. This file holds the tags that define how the home page's text will look and where on the page that text will be placed. As you'll see later in this chapter, this file may also hold tags that specify where graphics should be placed on the page and where hypertext links to other Web pages should appear.

Eventually you may want to design a sophisticated Web site. For now, keep it simple—very simple. There's no need to introduce all sorts of errors—there'll be plenty of opportunities to do that later as you try to improve your Web site! For your first attempt at creating a Web page, you can start with the HTML example code I've been using—you may even already have typed it in and saved it to a text file named *index.html*. If you have, you're all set. If you haven't, at this time you need to create a new, empty text file using a text editor such as SimpleText. Type in the following:

```
<html>
<head>
<title>My Own Home Page</title>
</head>
<body>
<h1>Welcome to My Home Page</h1>
<hr>
I've got an Apple iBook computer.
<p>
</body>
</html>
```

Most Web site hosts (including America Online and many Internet Service Providers) require that an HTML file with the name *index.html* define a site's home page. Make sure your HTML file has that name.

To allow the world to see your home page, you need to upload the *index.html* file to your Web server. If you're an America Online member, read the next section (*Modifying Your Web Site: For AOL Users*) to see how that's done. If you connect via an Internet Service Provider, skip the next section and jump to *Modifying Your Web Site: For ISP Users*. Before moving on, though, you should verify that a Web browser can properly display your HTML file by opening it from your browser of choice. If you don't know how to use a Web browser to open an HTML file from a hard drive, go back to this chapter's *HTML Files and Web Browsers* subsection in the *Web Pages and HTML* section.

Modifying Your Web Site: For AOL Users

America Online has supplied you with server space for your own Web site—now it's up to you to add content to that site.

Uploading A File to AOL

The information that defines your Web page is kept in a file or files stored on an America Online server. When someone surfing the Web enters the URL of your Web page into his or her browser, that browser will locate your *index.html* file on the AOL server and load it.

Moving to My Place

You can load your Web-related file or files from your hard drive to the AOL server from the America Online software. To do that, you'll take advantage of an AOL online area named My Place—a part of AOL set up exclusively for working with Web site files. After logging on to AOL, follow these steps to get to the My Place area.

1. Type *MyPlace* in the Keyword Box in the toolbar and then click the **Go** button to display the My Place window.
2. Click on the My FTP Space picture to open your own workspace window.

The workspace window has the same look for every AOL member. As shown in Figure 14-9, it displays a list of files. The list of files, however, may be different for each member. That's because the workspace is a private area on the AOL server computer that is reserved for, and accessible by, only you. Each AOL member is allotted a 2 MB storage area—the files in this area are the ones displayed in the workspace window.

As Figure 14-9 shows, initially your workspace holds a *README* file and a folder named *private*. The file holds information about My Place, while the folder holds data used by AOL.

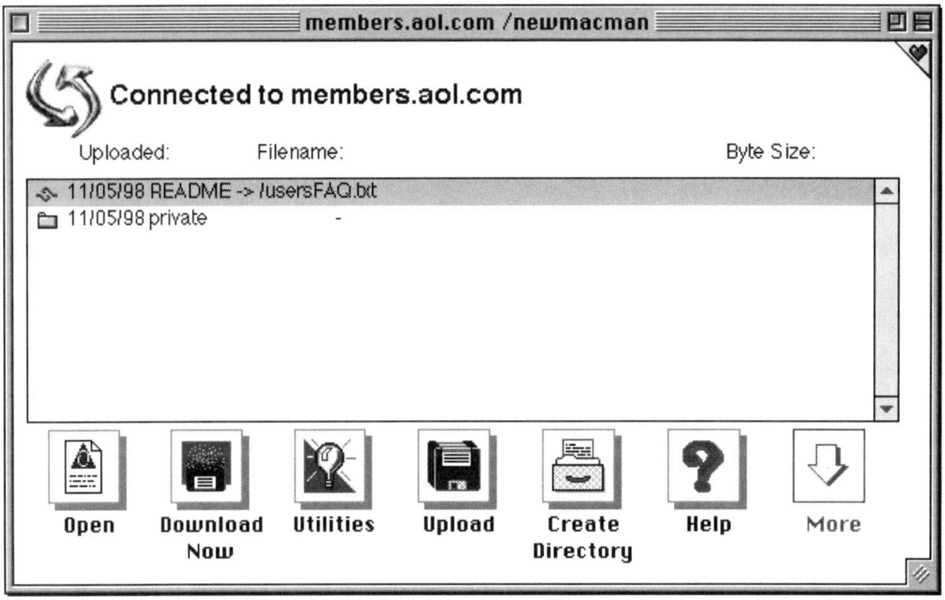

Figure 14-9 The Web workspace window.

Tip

Each AOL member is *really* provided with 10 MB of storage area—most AOL documentation only tells you about two of those ten megabytes. The secret is that *each* screen name has 2 MB reserved for it. America Online allows any one account to create and keep up to five screen names. The 2 MB limit is fine if you aren't including a lot of graphics on your Web site. If you *do* include plenty of images, or several additional Web pages linked to your home page (see this chapter's *Adding Flair to Your Web Site* section for instructions on including graphics and links at your Web site), you'll need more server space to store your files. In such a case you'll create more screen names and store files in more than one workspace. That's a little tricky, and beyond the scope of this book. But keep this trick in mind if AOL ever displays an alert informing you that you've reached your maximum server space.

Uploading a File to My Place

When someone surfing the Web reaches your AOL-hosted Web site, that person's browser loads (opens and displays) the HTML code from your *index.html* file. That means that in order for anyone to properly view your Web page, you need to have a file named *index.html* in your My Place workspace. To upload a file from your iBook hard drive to your AOL My Place workspace, get to the workspace window shown back in Figure 14-9 and then follow these steps:

1. Click on the **Upload** icon to display the file transfer window shown in Figure 14-10.
2. Type the name of the file that is about to be uploaded (*index.html* in this example).
3. Click the **Transfer Mode** radio button that best matches the file type of the file to upload (an HTML file is a text file, so click the **ASCII (text documents)** radio button. For uploading a graphic file, instead click the **Binary (programs and graphics)** button.
4. Click the **Continue** button to display the Upload File window shown in Figure 14-11.
5. Click the **Select File** icon to display the standard Open File window.
6. Find the file to upload and double-click its name to select it and to return to the Upload File window (see Figure 14-11).
7. Click the **Send** icon to upload the file.
8. Click the close box of the file transfer window to return to the My Place workspace window.

After performing the above steps your workspace holds a copy of the file you just uploaded (*index.html* in this example). You're all set—now anyone surfing the Web can visit your site to see your handiwork!

A Quick Test of Your New Web Page

For a simple Web page that doesn't display any graphics, the *index.html* file is all you need. To verify that you successfully have your Web site up and running, launch whichever Web browser you're accustomed to using. If you're still logged on to America Online, you can launch the AOL-supplied Web Browser software now. Type in the URL for your Web page and press the Return key (refer to this chapter's the *Your Web Site: For AOL Users* subsection in the *Your Web Site May Already Exist* section if you don't know your site's URL). Your browser will whisk you off to your very own Web site's home page and the contents of the just-uploaded *index.html* file will be displayed in your Web browser's window.

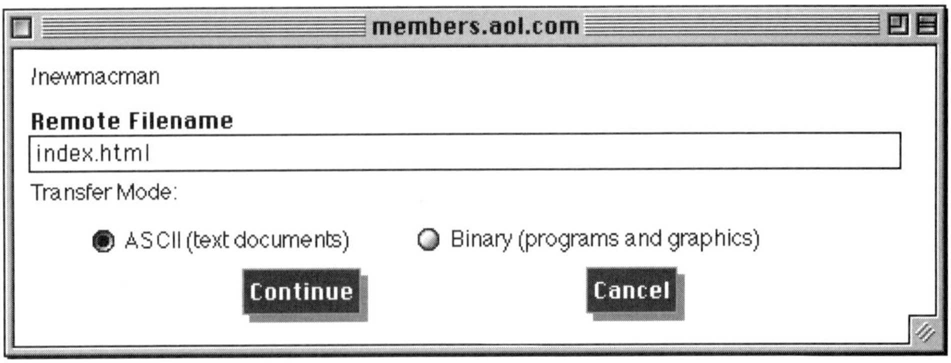

Figure 14-10 Providing AOL with information about the file to upload.

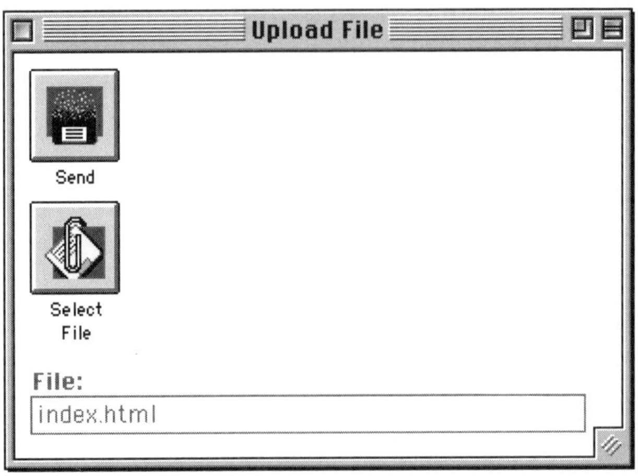

Figure 14-11 Specifying a file to upload to the workspace.

Creating A Better Web Page

After experimenting with this simple example, you'll want to create a more sophisticated Web page. To do that, edit the *index.html* file that is on your hard drive (uploading the *index.html* file to AOL, of course, left the original file on your hard drive). Add more text, and more headings (by placing text between heading start and end tags such as `<h1>` and `</h1>`), and more horizontal rules. Then save your changes.

Tip
Read this chapter's *Adding Flair to Your Web Site* section to see how to *really* improve your Web page by adding graphics and links to other Web pages.

Next, go to your My Place work space on AOL. Replace the existing *index.html* file by simply uploading the new version (the new version then replaces the old). To do that, just follow the steps already provided for uploading a file.

Important
After uploading a file to My Place, you may need to log off of America Online and then log back on if you want to visit your Web site to see the changes. That is, AOL may not recognize the changed or new file until you've logged off and back on once.

Modifying Your Web Site: For ISP Users

If your Internet Service Provider has supplied you with server space for your own Web site, you now need to define the site's look. That's done by creating an HTML file and uploading it to the server space the ISP has reserved just for you. Since the technique for uploading files varies from one ISP to another, I can't provide step-by-step file-uploading instructions as I just did for America Online members. However, I can provide some general uploading tips that apply to a number of ISPs—including EarthLink. Apple has selected EarthLink as the ISP of choice for iBook owners, so I'm making the assumption that many readers have an EarthLink account.

Uploading A File to Your ISP

Your Web page's defining information is kept in a file or files stored on your Internet Service Provider's server computer. When someone surfing the Web enters the URL of your Web page into his or her browser, the browser will locate your *index.html* file on the ISP server and load it.

The primary means of uploading a file from your iBook to an ISP (including EarthLink) is via the Mac shareware program Fetch (available for downloading at `www.dartmouth.edu/pages/softdev/fetch.html`. Here's how you go about getting a file such as *index.html* from your hard drive to your area on an ISP server:

1. Connect to the Internet as you normally do.
2. Run the Fetch application to display a New Connection window, as shown in Figure 14-12.
3. In the **Host** box of the New Connection window type the FTP address to connect to.
4. In the **User ID** box type your username.
5. In the **Password** box type in your password.
6. Click the **OK** button to make the connection and bring up a Connected To window.
7. Click the **Put File** button to bring up a standard Open File window.
8. Move to the folder that holds the file to upload (such as *index.html*) and double-click on the file's name to upload the file.

In Step 3 the Host will be an FTP address that your ISP will have supplied you with. As shown in Figure 14-12, an EarthLink member enters a host name of `ftp-www.earthlink.net`. The User ID and Password mentioned in Steps 4 and 5 will also have been supplied to you by your ISP. For EarthLink subscribers, this information will have been emailed to you at the time you signed up for EarthLink server Web space.

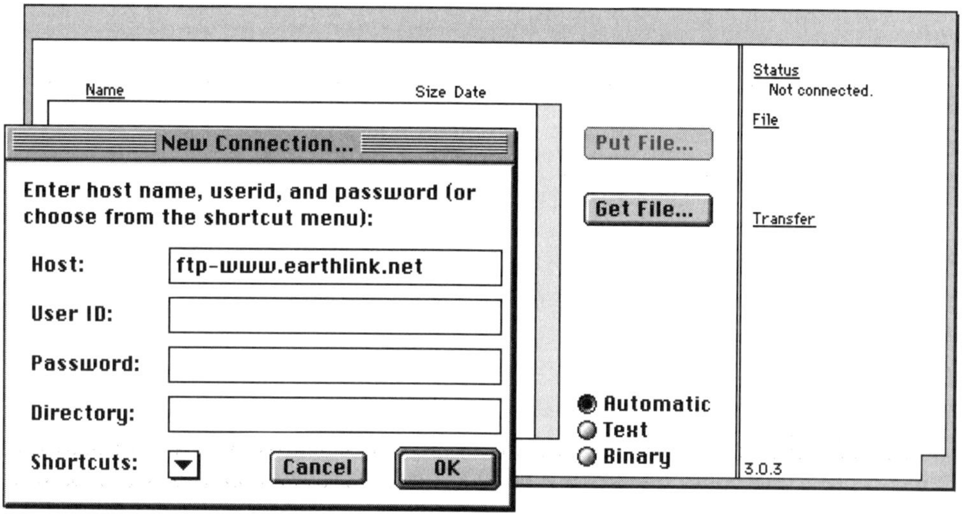

Figure 14-12 Using Fetch to connect to EarthLink.

After performing the above steps, your server space holds a copy of the *index.html* file. You can verify this by looking at the files named in the list in the Fetch window. Now, anyone surfing the Web can visit your site to see what you've created!

A Quick Test of Your New Web Page

The *index.html* file is all that's needed for a simple Web page that doesn't display any graphics. To test your Web site, begin by launching whichever Web browser you make use of. Then type in the URL for your Web page and press the Return key (refer to this chapter's the *Your Web Site: For ISP Users* subsection in the *Your Web Site May Already Exist* section if you don't know your site's URL). Your browser will find your own Web site's home page, and the contents of the just-uploaded *index.html* file will be displayed in your Web browser's window.

Creating A Better Web Page

After succeeding with this simple test, you'll want to move on to more involved Web page design. As a starting point to doing that, edit the *index.html* file that is on your iBook's hard drive (the act of uploading the *index.html* file to your ISP didn't affect the original file on your hard drive). Improve upon the file's content by adding more text, headings, horizontal rules, and anything else you know the hypertext tags for. Now save your changes.

> **Tip**
> Read this chapter's *Adding Flair to Your Web Site* section to see how to *really* improve your Web page by adding graphics and links to other Web pages.

Replace the existing *index.html* file on your ISP server space by simply uploading the new version (the new version then replaces the old). To do that, just follow the steps already provided for uploading a file.

Adding Flair to Your Web Site

The Web pages described in this chapter provide a good grounding in the very basics of writing HTML code and of moving files from your iBook to a remote server. But you've certainly noticed that these Web pages are lacking in excitement. In fact, they're downright boring! That's because they don't take advantage of two of the key features that have made the Web so popular in recent years. Here you will discover how your own Web page can include both graphics and hypertext links to other Web sites.

Adding a Graphic Image

Once a Web surfer reaches your site (whether he intentionally sought it out or stumbled upon it), you want to make sure that person sticks around for a bit. Graphics are an attention-grabbing form of communication and are thus beneficial in achieving this goal. Including an image on a Web page involves these five steps:

1. Obtain or create an appropriate graphic image.
2. Convert the image to a file type recognizable by Web browsers.

3. Include a reference to the image in your HTML file.
4. Upload the graphic file to your server.
5. Upload the new or modified HTML file to your server.

Don't be alarmed that it takes five steps to get a single image on your Web page. As you'll see in the next short sections, each step is short and concise. After you've followed the drill once, repeating the steps will be a breeze.

Obtain or create an appropriate graphic image

If you're artistic, go ahead and fire up your drawing or paint program (such as those that are a part of the AppleWorks software bundled with your iBook) and get creating. If your talents lie in other areas, or the image you have in mind is complex, find an existing image. There are a number of software vendors that sell inexpensive clip art sets. A CD-ROM holding thousands of images can be found for under thirty bucks.

The look of the graphic image is important to you, but the particular type of file that the image is saved to (such as PICT, TIFF, PostScript, and so forth) isn't critical at this point. You'll see why next.

Convert the image to a file type recognizable by Web browsers

A Web browser such as Netscape Navigator or Microsoft Internet Explorer displays the contents of a Web page in a window on your iBook. The contents of the Web page can be text or graphics. If the Web page includes graphics, however, each graphic image must be saved in a file of a type the Web browser recognizes. The most widely supported file types are the GIF format and the JPEG format.

GIF, or *Graphics Interchange Format*, is the graphics file format most widely supported. Black and white, grayscale, and color images can be stored in GIF files. The advantage of GIF is that files of this type become automatically compressed. That's good news for Web surfers because when a person reaches a Web site that includes a graphic image, that person's Web browser must download the image before displaying it. A smaller size (in bytes, not image dimensions) means a quicker download and a shorter wait to view the Web page. The disadvantage of GIF is that it can display a maximum of 256 colors or grays. For photographic-quality images, this may not be sufficient. For such graphics consider using images stored in JPEG files.

JPEG, or *Joint Photographic Experts Group* (and pronounced jay-peg) is the graphics format best used for displaying photographic images. While JPEG images can be compressed greatly, such compression may greatly diminish the image's quality. So a JPEG file is generally larger (in bytes) than a GIF file holding the same image.

Once you have an image, you need to save it to a file of a type that is recognizable by Web browsers. That means that if the file isn't already in either the GIF or JPEG formats, you'll want to open it from a graphics program and resave it in such a format. Most graphics programs recognize only a few file types, so here a graphics conversion program best serves you. Invaluable for this task is the shareware utility GraphicConverter from Lemke Software (available for downloading from `www.lemkesoft.de/`.

To convert a file from one format to another, run GraphicConverter and then carry out the following steps (Figure 14-13 shows GraphicConverter being used to save an iBook image as a GIF file).

1. Choose **Open** from the **File** menu to open the existing graphic file.
2. Select **Trim existing** from the **Edit** menu to remove excess "white space" from around the image.
3. Choose **Save As** from the **File** menu to bring up the Save As window.
4. Type a file name in the **Save Picture As** edit box.
5. Pick the desired format (such as GIF) from the **Format** pop-up menu.
6. Click on the **Save** button to save the new file.

If you start out with an image on the Clipboard rather than stored in a file (perhaps you just copied an image from, say, a clip art collection), replace the first of the preceding steps with this one:

1. Choose **New** from the **File** menu to create a new window into which you can paste your image.

After pasting the image into the new window, continue on with the second step in the previous list.

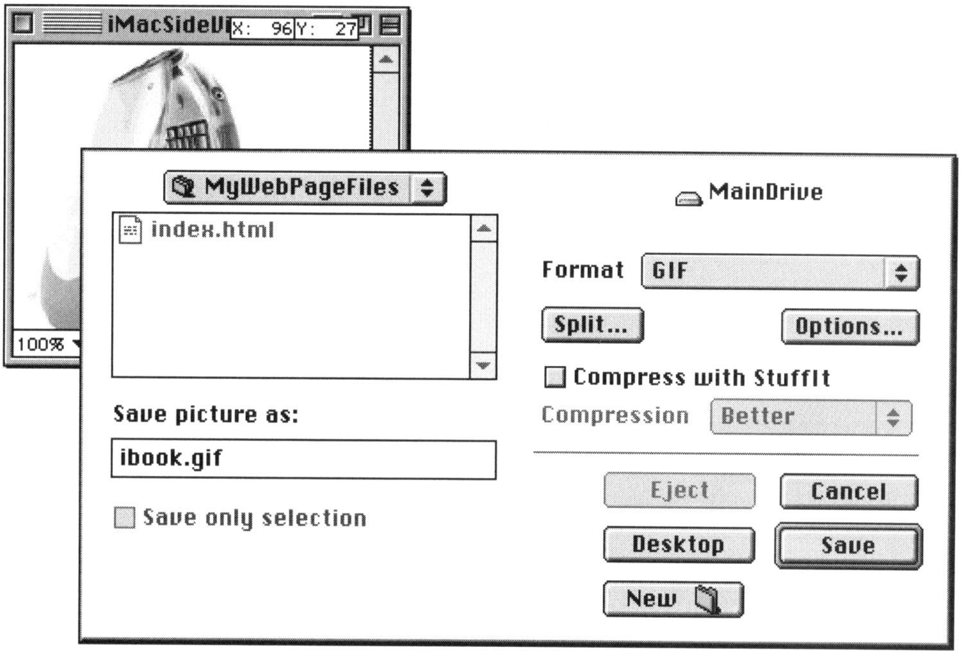

Figure 14-13 Using GraphicConverter to save an image to a GIF file.

Include a reference to the image in your HTML file

To display an image on a Web page, use the `<img>` tag. Use of the *image* tag is slightly more complicated than the use of the other tags you've seen here in that the `<img>` tag makes use of an *attribute*. An attribute allows you to specify additional information within a tag. For the `<img>` tag, that attribute is named `src`. The `src` attribute specifies the *source* of the image: the name of the file that holds the image as well as where that file resides. If the image file is to be stored in the same folder as the HTML file that accesses the image, then simply set the source equal to the name of the image file. As shown in this example, the source file is enclosed in double quotes:

```
<img src = "ibook.gif">
```

Note that there is no end tag associated with the `<img>` tag—you simply use the `<img>` tag with the `src` attribute and you're all set. An image appears on a Web page at the location of the `<img>` tag. Consider this next HTML example. This code should look familiar to you—all I've done is change the words "*I've got an Apple iBook computer*" to "*Here's a look at the Apple iBook computer*" and added an `<img>` tag. Because the `<img>` tag follows the text, you'd expect the iBook image to show up just after the text on the Web page. Figure 14-14 shows this is indeed the case.

```
<html>
<head>
<title>My Own Home Page</title>
</head>
<body>
<h1>Welcome to My Home Page</h1>
<hr>
Here's a look at the Apple iBook computer:
<p>
<img src = "ibook.gif">
</body>
</html>
```

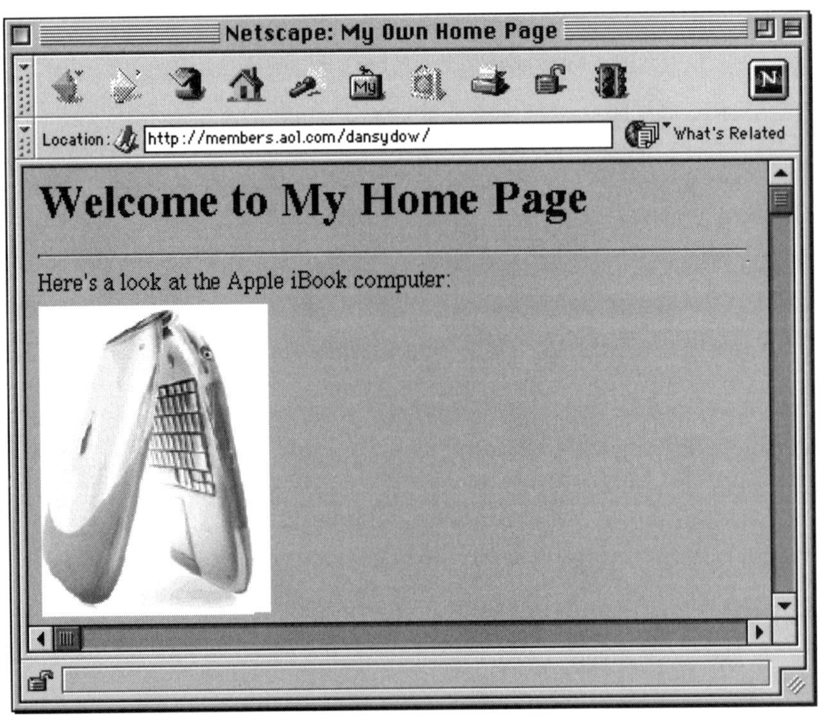

Figure 14-14 A Web page that includes an image tag.

You don't need to upload any files to your server in order to test out the `<img>` tag. First create an HTML file that holds the above code, then open that file from within your Web browser (choose **Open File** from the **File** menu). If you have the image file in the same folder as the HTML file, and if you've given that image file the same name as the `src` attribute in the `<img>` tag, then the graphic will appear on the newly loaded Web page.

Upload the graphic file to your server

The previous paragraph tells you how to test out the `<img>` tag without accessing the Internet. To allow surfers to view your image, though, you need to upload the graphic file to your Web server. When someone visits your Web page, that person's browser downloads your page's images from your Web server—not from your hard drive. Earlier in this chapter, you learned how to upload an HTML file to your Web server—uploading a graphic file is just as easy. Refer back to the *Uploading a File to AOL* section if you're an America Online user or the *Uploading a File to Your ISP* section if you connect to the Internet via an Internet Service Provider.

Important
As described in this chapter, the `<img>` tag specifies that the image file resides in the same Web server folder, or directory, as the HTML file that makes use of the `<img>` tag. So, be sure to upload the graphic file to the same folder as the HTML file.

Upload the New or Modified HTML File to Your Server

Any time you edit your HTML file, you need to re-upload that file to your Web server. Having made changes to the file on your own hard drive doesn't make that new information available to visitors to your Web page. In the case of a change that includes the addition of an `<img>` tag, you need to upload both the altered HTML file *and* the graphic file that the HTML file references (as just mentioned above). Again, refer back to the *Uploading a File to AOL* section if you're Web page is on an America Online server or the *Uploading a File to Your ISP* section if your server is one provided by an Internet Service Provider.

Tip
You've visited Web pages that include family pictures. Now you know how to include such a picture on your own Web page. To get a picture on to your hard drive, you can use the Apple Video Player (listed under the Apple menu) to convert a camcorder video frame to a digital (computer) graphic image. You can also connect a USB scanner to your iBook to convert a picture to a graphic image. Once you have the picture saved to a file on your hard drive, open it in a program like GraphicConverter and save it in GIF format. In your HTML file, include an `<img>` tag that names the GIF file. Then upload the graphic file and modified HTML file to your Web server. Finally, make sure to tell all your friends and relatives to visit your Web site to see the new picture!

Adding a Hypertext Link to Your Web Page

A *hypertext link* is a part of a Web page that, when clicked on, takes the user to a different Web page. The hypertext link is usually a word or a phrase, but, as you'll see ahead, it can also be an image. Hypertext links are what makes the World Wide Web both user-friendly and very powerful. Adding one or more links to your own Web page is an important step in making your site useful to surfers who visit it.

Using Text As a Hypertext Link

To include a word or phrase as a hypertext link at your site, modify your HTML file to include an `<a>` tag. This *anchor* tag associates your own Web page with a different Web page. Like the `<img>` tag (see this chapter's *Adding a Graphic Image* section), the `<a>` tag makes use of an *attribute*—something that allows you to include extra information within a tag. In this case, the attribute is named `href`. This attribute is a *hypertext reference*—it defines the Web page that gets jumped to when the user clicks on the hypertext link.

When I say that the `href` attribute defines the page to jump to, I mean that it names the URL of the Web page that is to be displayed in the user's browser. Consider the URL for Apple's home page, `www.apple.com`. To specify that this page be the destination of a hypertext link, I'd set the `href` attribute to this URL (and enclose it in double quotes, as was done for the `src` attribute of the `<img>` tag back in the *Adding a Graphic Image* section):

```
<a href = "http://www.apple.com">
```

Unlike the `<img>` tag, the `<a>` tag *does* have an end tag associated with it. Unsurprisingly, that tag is the same as the start tag, but preceded by a slash: `</a>`. The end tag doesn't immediately follow the start tag. Instead, there should be some text between the start and end tags. It is this text that the Web browser highlights (displays in a color different from the rest of the Web page's text) and, depending on the browser's settings, underlines.

Carrying on with the Apple home page example, consider that you want your Web page to direct visitors to Apple's site. Also imagine that you want the words "*Visit Apple's home page.*" to appear on your Web page, with the "*Apple's home page*" part of that sentence to be the highlighted text that the user clicks on in order to go to Apple's page. In such a scenario, the complete hypertext link would look like this:

```
Visit <a href = "http://www.apple.com">Apple's home
page.</a>
```

The following HTML listing is a modification of the HTML code you've grown accustomed to seeing. Here an `<a>` tag has been added to create a hypertext link to Apple's home page. After uploading the modified HTML file to the server, a visitor to the site will see a page like the one displayed in Figure 14-15.

```
<html>
<head>
<title>My Own Home Page</title>
</head>
<body>
<h1>Welcome to My Home Page</h1>
<hr>
Visit <a href = "http://www.apple.com">Apple's home
page.</a>
</body>
```

Figure 14-15 A Web page that includes an anchor tag.

Using an Image As a Hypertext Link

You can combine your knowledge of the image tag with your newfound anchor tag skills to turn an image, rather than text, into a hypertext link. You'll recognize an image that serves as a link by the colored border surrounding it.

To create such a link, you'll first need to obtain the appropriate image, save it to a GIF file, and upload it to your server—as described in this chapter's *Adding a Graphic Image* section. Then, when you write the <a> tag in your HTML file, use an image tag in place of the text that precedes the anchor end tag. For instance, this HTML code would make the previously introduced iBook image a hypertext link:

```
Click the iBook to visit Apple's home page <a href =
"http://www.apple.com"><img src= "ibook.gif"></a>
```

To try out the above code, enter it in your HTML file in place of the current anchor code. If you tried out the previous example (the listing from the *Adding a Hypertext Link to Your Web Page* section), then use the above code in place of this code:

```
Visit <a href = "http://www.apple.com">Apple's home
page.</a>
```

After you've uploaded the modified HTML file, a visitor to your site would see a Web page like the one shown in Figure 14-16. While the black and white figure doesn't reflect the fact that the image is outlined by a colored border, comparing the image in Figure 14-16 to that shown in Figure 14-14 (where the image *isn't* used as a hypertext link) demonstrates that the image now indeed does have a border.

Figure 14-16 A Web page that includes an image as a hypertext link.

Web Sites of Interest

A

Who's to say which of the millions of Web sites are the best, or the most interesting? Not me. But I can offer up a list of a number of sites that might be considered "main" sites in their respective categories. You can find any number of additional sites in any area of interest by searching the Web. Refer to Chapter 9 for Web-searching techniques.

Macintosh Programming

Apple Intro to Macintosh Programming Site
`developer.apple.com/macos/intro.html`

MacTech Magazine
`www.mactech.com`

Government Agencies and Offices

Air Force, United States (USAF)
`www.af.mil`

Army
`www.army.gov`

Environmental Protection Agency (EPA)
`www.epa.gov`

Food and Drug Administration (FDA)
`www.fda.gov`

Health and Human Services, Dept. of (HHS)
`www.os.dhhs.gov`

Internal Revenue Service (IRS)
`www.irs.gov`

Justice, Dept. of (DOJ)
`www.usdoj.gov`

Marine Corps (USMC)
`www.usmc.mil`

National Aeronautics/Space Administration (NASA)
`www.nasa.gov`

Navy (USN)
`www.ncts.navy.mil`

United States Postal Service (USPS)
`www.usps.gov`

Veterans Affairs, Dept. of (VA)
`www.va.gov`

White House
`www.whitehouse.gov`

News

MacCentral Online
`www.maccentral.com`

Wall Street Journal (registration, fee)
`www.wsj.com`

Los Angeles Times
`www.latimes.com`

New York Times (registration required)
`www.nytimes.com`

Philadelphia Online
`www.phillynews.com`

USA Today
`www.usatoday.com`

Washington Post
`www.washingtonpost.com`

Computer Games and Gaming

MacGaming
`www.macgaming.com`

MacWorld Gameline
`macworld.zdnet.com/gameline`

Macintosh Magazines Online

MacAddict
`www.macaddict.com`

MacHome
`www.machome.com`

MacToday
`www.mactoday.com`

MacWorld
`www.macworld.com`

Webintosh
`www.webintosh.com`

Sports

ESPN
`ESPN.SportsZone.com`

Major League Baseball (MLB)
`www.majorleaguebaseball.com`

National Basketball Association (NBA)
`www.nba.com`

National Football League (NFL)
`www.nfl.com`

National Hockey League (NHL)
`www.nhl.com`

Sporting News
`www.sportingnews.com`

Recreational

Bicycling
`www.worldbicycle.com`

Hunting/Fishing
`www.fieldandstream.com`

Martial Arts
`pages.prodigy.com/karate`

Running/Jogging
`www.arfa.org`

Health and Medicine

Alternative Medicine
`www.pandamedicine.com`

Exercise
`www.afaa.com`

Medical Education
`www.utmb.edu/meo`

Medical Terminology
`www.geocities.com/Television City/5196`

Women's Interests

Women's Issues, Interests & Items
`www.goddessgear.com`

Internet Backup and File Management

Internet Backup and Daily Information Storage
`www.imagicaldesk.com`

Internet Backup
`www.backjack.com`

Index